LUTHER'S WORKS

LUTHER'S WORKS

VOLUME 1

LECTURES ON GENESIS
Chapters 1-5

Edited by
JAROSLAV PELIKAN

CONCORDIA PUBLISHING HOUSE · SAINT LOUIS

MANUFACTURED IN THE UNITED STATES OF AMERICA

Contents

General Introduction

THE first editions of Luther's collected works appeared in the sixteenth century, and so did the first efforts to make him "speak English." In America serious attempts in these directions were made for the first time in the nineteenth century. The Saint Louis edition of Luther was the first endeavor on American soil to publish a collected edition of his works, and the Henkel Press in Newmarket, Virginia, was the first to publish some of Luther's writings in an English translation. During the first decade of the twentieth century, J. N. Lenker produced translations of Luther's sermons and commentaries in thirteen volumes. A few years later the first of the six volumes in the Philadelphia (or Holman) edition of the *Works of Martin Luther* appeared. Miscellaneous other works were published at one time or another. But a growing recognition of the need for more of Luther's works in English has resulted in this American edition of Luther's works.

The edition is intended primarily for the reader whose knowledge of late medieval Latin and sixteenth-century German is too small to permit him to work with Luther in the original languages. Those who can, will continue to read Luther in his original words as these have been assembled in the monumental Weimar edition (*D. Martin Luthers Werke.* Kritische Gesamtausgabe; Weimar, 1883 ff.). Its texts and helps have formed a basis for this edition, though in certain places we have felt constrained to depart from its readings and findings. We have tried throughout to translate Luther as he thought translating should be done. That is, we have striven for faithfulness on the basis of the best lexicographical materials available. But where literal accuracy and clarity have conflicted, it is clarity that we have preferred, so that sometimes paraphrase seemed more faithful than literal fidelity. We have proceeded in a similar way in the matter of Bible versions, translating Luther's translations. Where this could be done by the use of an existing English version — King James, Douay, or Revised Standard — we have done so. Where it could not, we have supplied our own. To indicate this in each specific instance would have been pedantic; to adopt a uniform procedure would have been artificial — especially in view of Luther's own inconsistency in this regard. In each volume the translator will be responsible primarily for matters of text and language, while the responsibility of the editor will extend principally to the historical and theological matters reflected in the introductions and notes.

Although the edition as planned will include fifty-five volumes, Luther's writings are not being translated in their entirety. Nor should they be. As he was the first to insist, much of what he wrote and said was not that important. Thus the edition is a selection of works that have proved their importance for the faith, life, and history of the Christian Church. The first thirty volumes contain Luther's expositions of various Biblical books, while the remaining volumes include what are usually called his "Reformation writings" and other occasional pieces. The final volume of the set will be an index volume; in addition to an index of quotations, proper names, and topics, and a list of corrections and changes, it will contain a glossary of many of the technical terms that recur in Luther's works and that cannot be defined each time they appear. Obviously Luther cannot be forced into any neat set of rubrics. He can provide his reader with bits of autobiography or with political observations as he expounds a psalm, and he can speak tenderly about the meaning of the faith in the midst of polemics against his opponents. It is the hope of publishers, editors, and translators that through this edition the message of Luther's faith will speak more clearly to the modern church.

J. P.
H. L.

Introduction to Volume 1

ON Monday, May 31, 1535, Luther finished his lectures on Psalm 90. There he had announced that after completing these lectures "I will devote the remaining years of my life to an exposition of the books of Moses" (*Luther's Works*, 13, p. 75) and that "later we shall, if the Lord lengthens my life, interpret Genesis" (ibid., p. 141). It is usually supposed that on Thursday of that week, June 3, Luther began his great *Lectures on Genesis* (Weimar, XLII–XLIV; St. Louis, I–II), which appear in this volume and in those that follow.

Since the usual days for Luther's lectures were Monday and Tuesday, however, it appears more likely that he launched his *Lectures on Genesis* the very next day, Tuesday, June 1, 1535, rather than on June 3, the date usually given (cf. *Luther's Works*, 13, p. 75, note 1). For the next several weeks his lectures proceeded on the basis of his preparatory notes and outlines, which he had worked out up to Gen. 3:14. From the status of Veit Dietrich's notebooks on these lectures it appears that Luther was lecturing on Gen. 3:14 when an outbreak of the plague interrupted his lectures in July of 1535. The University of Wittenberg was transferred to Jena on July 18 as a result of the plague; therefore Luther did not lecture on Monday, July 19, as he had been scheduled to do. It is not clear just when the university returned to Wittenberg or when classes were resumed.

Luther, it seems, did not resume his *Lectures on Genesis* until January 25, 1536, when he picked them up at Gen. 3:15. His references to "hope" in that section of the commentary (cf. p. 191) would seem to fit the mood of the university during and after the plague. From a statement at table, dated October 27–December 4, 1536, it is clear that by the autumn of that year Luther's lectures had progressed to the ninth chapter of Genesis (see *Luther's Works*, 2, Introduction). Thus the material presented in this first volume of the *Lectures on Genesis* came out of Luther's work in the classroom in the middle months of 1535 and the early months of 1536. It is impossible to make the chronology of the lectures any more precise than this. The lectures as we have them are almost totally devoid of contemporary allusions, and some of the allusions we do have are obviously interpolated (cf. p. 288, note 45). Therefore they give us no information about the progress of Luther's lectures. The historical introduction is, therefore, unable to provide very much detail about the time and circumstances of the original composition.

Instead, the historical introduction to these *Lectures on Genesis* must concern itself with a more serious problem than chronology — the authenticity and integrity of the material in the lectures themselves. For as we have it, the work is not a product of Luther's pen or even a transcript of his lectures; it is a transcript that has been reworked and edited. From the instance of other commentaries, where we have both the lecture notes and the printed version, it is evident that the editors of Luther's Biblical commentaries allowed themselves greater liberties in preparing his lectures for publication than the modern conventions of editing and publishing would justify (cf. *Luther's Works*, 13, Introduction, pp. xi—xii). Where we have only the printed version, therefore, we have reason to be on the lookout for marks of redactorial additions and changes.

There are such marks in the *Lectures on Genesis*, as Peter Meinhold, the leading scholar to concern himself with them, has pointed out. Now and again, for example, there are admonitions addressed to the "reader" even though this purports to be a lecture (thus p. 16, note 29). We have already referred to the presence of historical allusions that are clearly anachronistic and are apparently inserted by the editors. A remarkable circumstance is the accuracy with which most classical citations are quoted. Luther had an astonishingly retentive memory, as his Biblical quotations show. He had also read around in the classics and knew some classical works almost by heart. But the citations here in Genesis are almost uniformly accurate; and where a comparison of lecture notes with printed version is possible, it becomes evident that the editors took a chance phrase or allusion from Luther's lectures and amplified it into a full-blown and accurate citation.

Some citations from classical authors do not even have a chance phrase or allusion as their foundation but were inserted by the editors because they seemed to fit. Because of this we are in no position to determine with any degree of finality which of the classical quotations originated with Luther and which did not. The same thing is true of quotations from Christian authors. It is beyond doubt that Luther had read widely in the works of St. Augustine; therefore many, if not most, of the references to Augustine seem to be based on his own reading. Other authors, too, he had studied, as his completely authentic works clearly show. From repeated references we know of his regard for Nicolaus de Lyra, on whom these *Lectures on Genesis* are dependent for the rabbinical learning they display and for at least some of the patristic exegesis they consider. We have used Lyra in an incunabulum of 1492, titled *Postilla fratris Nicolai de lyra de ordine minorum super Genesim Exodum Leuiticum Numeri Deutronomium* [sic] *Josue Judici Regum & Paralyppomenon. Cum additionibus pauli episcopi Burgensis.* (Because Lyra's work is quite rare, we have quoted it at length in some footnotes, to give the English reader a sample of Luther's exegetical sources.) We know, too, that in 1509—10 Luther had lectured on the *Sentences* of Peter Lombard, to which he also makes reference in this commentary. But we cannot be sure how many of the quotations even from these works are actually his own.

The problem of authenticity and integrity becomes most acute, however, not in the question of Luther's erudition but in the question of his actual theological position. And the researches of Peter Meinhold have led him to the conclusion that the theology of the *Lectures on Genesis* has also been adulterated by the editors to conform it to the growing orthodoxy of the second generation of Lutherans. He bases this conclusion on a study of the theology of Veit Dietrich in relation to both Luther and Melanchthon; in several cases he has proved that Dietrich's brand of Melanchthonian theology has been superimposed upon Luther's thought and language, and in other cases he has shown that this is very likely. This has led him to a rather profound skepticism about the reliability of the *Lectures on Genesis* as a source of information about the thought of the old Luther.

Is that skepticism justified? The studies of Prof. Meinhold must certainly cast doubt on those sections of the commentary in which Luther sounds more like Melanchthon than like any Luther we know. One must have some misgivings about passages which present such novel ideas as these: the arguments for the existence of God (p. 25, note 41), rationalistic arguments for the natural immortality of the human soul (p. 45), defenses of astrology (p. 31, note 57), and the like. The line of descent here runs from Melanchthon through his pupils to later Lutheran theologians, but the ancestor of these ideas is apparently not Luther. A reader is, therefore, obliged to keep the facts of this descent in mind when he cites the *Lectures on Genesis* to prove that Luther held a position which is not well authenticated from his other writings. To this extent it must be asserted that Meinhold's skepticism is warranted.

On the other hand, Meinhold's criteria themselves are not beyond suspicion. Taking for granted the emphasis on the young Luther that became canonical for Luther scholars in the past generation, Meinhold makes the early thought of Luther normative for his judgments about the authenticity of many passages in this commentary which are not suspect on other grounds. This procedure makes it impossible to accept Meinhold's conclusions wholesale. Nor does he deny the presence of much material in the lectures that comes directly from Luther. About most sections of the commentary any responsible historian of theology must conclude that if Luther did not really say this, it is difficult to imagine how Veit Dietrich or even Melanchthon himself could have thought it up. Therefore the *Lectures on Genesis* are an indispensable source for our knowledge of Luther's thought, containing as they do his reflections on hundreds of doctrinal, moral, exegetical, and historical questions. The hands are sometimes the hands of the editors, but the voice is nevertheless the voice of Luther (cf. *Luther's Works*, 22, Introduction, p. xi).

J. P.

LECTURES ON GENESIS

Chapters 1–5

Translated by
GEORGE V. SCHICK

CHAPTER ONE

THE first chapter is written in the simplest language; yet it contains matters of the utmost importance and very difficult to understand. It was for this reason, as St. Jerome asserts, that among the Hebrews it was forbidden for anyone under thirty to read the chapter or to expound it for others.[1] They wanted one to have a good knowledge of the entire Scripture before getting to this chapter. Not even with this practice, however, did the Jewish Rabbis achieve anything worthwhile; for in their commentaries men twice thirty and even older prattle most childishly about these extremely important matters.

Until now there has not been anyone in the church either who has explained everything in the chapter with adequate skill. The commentators, with their sundry, different, and countless questions, have so confused everything in the chapter as to make it clear enough that God has reserved His exalted wisdom and the correct understanding of this chapter for Himself alone, although He has left with us this general knowledge that the world had a beginning and that it was created by God out of nothing. This general knowledge is clearly drawn from the text. As to particulars, however, there are differences of opinion about very many things, and countless questions are raised at one point or another.

We know from Moses that the world was not in existence before 6,000 years ago. Of this it is altogether impossible to convince a philosopher, because, according to Aristotle, no first man or last man can be conceded.[2] Although Aristotle leaves unsettled the problem whether the world is eternal, he leans toward the opinion that it *is* eternal.[3] Human reason cannot rise to a higher level than to con-

[1] Such is Jerome's report in his letter to Paulinus, Epistle LIII, *Patrologia, Series Latina,* XXII, 547. The immediate source of the information, however, is probably Nicholas of Lyra in his introduction to Gen. 1 (cf. Introduction, p. xi).

[2] See the quotations from Aristotle assembled in Thomas Aquinas, *Summa theologica,* Part I, Q. 46, Art. 1.

[3] Aristotle speaks of questions "in regard to which we have no argument because they are so vast, and we find it difficult to give our reasons, e. g., the question whether the universe is eternal or no," *Topics,* I, ch. 11.

clude that the world is eternal and that countless men have gone before us and are coming after us; here it is forced to call a halt. But from this very conclusion there follows the most dangerous opinion that the soul is mortal, for philosophy knows no more than one infinite.[4] Indeed, human reason cannot avoid being overwhelmed by the grandeur of this subject matter and coming into conflict with it.

It seems that perhaps in Egypt Plato picked up a few sparks of thought, seemingly from the discourses of the patriarchs and the prophets, and for this reason came closer to the truth.[5] He indeed assumes matter and mind to be eternal but declares that the world had a beginning and was made out of matter.[6] But I shall stop citing the opinions of philosophers, since Lyra enumerates them, although without comment.[7]

Thus among the Hebrews, the Latins, or the Greeks there is no guide whom we could follow with safety in this area. In view of this we likewise shall deserve indulgence if we do the best we can. For apart from the general knowledge that the world had its beginning from nothing there is hardly anything about which there is common agreement among all theologians.

Hilary and Augustine, almost the two greatest lights of the church, hold that the world was created instantaneously and all at the same time, not successively in the course of six days.[8] Moreover, Augustine resorts to extraordinary trifling in his treatment of the six days, which he makes out to be mystical days of knowledge among the angels, not natural ones. Hence debates are customary in schools and churches concerning evening and morning knowledge, subjects brought up by Augustine and scrupulously propounded by Lyra. Whoever wants to gain a knowledge of them, let him get it from Lyra.[9]

---

[4] Cf. Aristotle, *Physics*, III, chs. 4—8.

[5] This is a familiar notion among the church fathers, as, for example, in Clement of Alexandria, *Exhortation to the Heathen*, ch. 6.

[6] Presumably this is an allusion to Plato's *Timaeus;* cf. also p. 47, note 77.

[7] Lyra says: "And so let the reader choose the exposition he wants to hold" (introduction to Gen. 1).

[8] Hilary, *On the Trinity*, XII, ch. 40, *Patrologia, Series Latina*, X, 458, 459; Augustine, *De Genesi ad litteram libri XII*, IV, ch. 33; *Corpus Scriptorum Ecclesiasticorum Latinorum*, XXVIII, Sec. III, Part I, p. 133.

[9] In his introduction to Gen. 1, Nicholas of Lyra states that according to Augustine, "angelic knowledge is twofold: one is a knowledge in general (*in genere*), and this is called evening knowledge. . . . The other is a knowledge in the Word, and this is called morning knowledge."

Although these subjects are debated with keen reasoning, the result is no real contribution. For what need is there of setting up a twofold knowledge? Nor does it serve any useful purpose to make Moses at the outset so mystical and allegorical. His purpose is to teach us, not about allegorical creatures and an allegorical world but about real creatures and a visible world apprehended by the senses. Therefore, as the proverb has it, he calls "a spade a spade," [10] i. e., he employs the terms "day" and "evening" without allegory, just as we customarily do. The evangelist Matthew, in his last chapter, preserves this method of expression when he writes that Christ rose on the evening of the Sabbath which began to dawn into the first day of the week (Matt. 28:1). If, then, we do not understand the nature of the days or have no insight into why God wanted to make use of these intervals of time, let us confess our lack of understanding rather than distort the words, contrary to their context, into a foreign meaning.

Therefore so far as this opinion of Augustine is concerned, we assert that Moses spoke in the literal sense, not allegorically or figuratively, i. e., that the world, with all its creatures, was created within six days, as the words read. If we do not comprehend the reason for this, let us remain pupils and leave the job of teacher to the Holy Spirit. However, these days are distinguished in this way: on the first day the formless mass of heaven and earth was created, to which later on light was added; on the second, the firmament; on the third, the earth, with its fruits, was brought forth out of the water; on the fourth the heavens were adorned by the creation of the sun, moon, and stars; on the fifth, the fishes of the sea and the birds of the air; on the sixth the land animals and man were created. However, I am disregarding the division which some make — into works of creating, of separating, and of adorning — because I do not know whether this tallies well with the facts in every case. Yet if anybody finds pleasure in that sort of thing, let him consult Lyra.[11]

As to Lyra's belief that a knowledge of the philosophers' opinion concerning matter is essential because on it depends the understanding of the six days of activity — I am not sure that Lyra understood what it was that Aristotle called "matter." Unlike Ovid,

[10] This is our rendition of the German-Latin pun *appellat Schapham scapham.*

[11] In his introduction to Gen. 1, Nicholas of Lyra says: "The work of creating (*opus creatoris*) he describes before all days, the work of separating in the first three days, and the work of adorning in the following three days."

Aristotle does not designate the shapeless and crude chaos as matter.[12] Therefore, disregarding these needless opinions, let us turn to Moses as the better teacher. We can follow him with greater safety than the philosophers, who, without benefit of the Word, debate about unknown matters.

THE WORK OF THE FIRST DAY

1. *In the beginning God created the heaven and the earth.*

At this point another necessary and rather difficult question is raised, namely, that Moses mentions the creation of heaven and earth but does not mention the day or the Word by which they were created. Some ponder why Moses did not rather express himself as he did in the other instances where he makes mention of the Word and say: "In the beginning God said: 'Let there be heaven and earth.'"[13] He asserts that heaven and earth were created before God said anything, in spite of the fact that the Decalog (Ex. 20:11) and the entire Scripture bear witness that in six days God made heaven and earth and everything in them. However, I said previously that we are going on this journey without a guide; we shall, therefore, leave others to their opinion and explain what seems right to us.

What Moses calls heaven and earth are not the kind they are now, but the crude and formless masses which they were up to that time. The water was dark; and because it is lighter by nature, it surrounded the still formless earth itself, like an ooze or a dense fog. This primary matter,[14] so to speak, for His later work God, according to the plain words of the Decalog (Ex. 20:11), did not create outside the six days but at the beginning of the first day.

So far as I can see, Moses until now makes no mention of the first day because later on those unordered masses of the crude heaven and earth were given shape, and, as it were, highly perfected and made separate entities. What he later calls the abyss and water — namely, the formless and crude mass of water, not yet arranged in

---

12 Ovid, *Metamorphoses*, I, 6; cf. also p. 4, note 7.

13 Augustine, *De Genesi ad litteram*, I, ch. 3, p. 7.

14 By *prima materia* metaphysicians meant "that elementary constituent in composite substances which appertains in common to them all without distinguishing them from one another," as yet united with no form. By *secunda materia* (see p. 8, note 17) they meant something like what we call "raw material," that which is given *to* an operation, as distinguished from that which is given *by* an operation; thus wood is *secunda materia* to a cabinetmaker, who gives it the form of a bench or cabinet.

an orderly manner and not yet graced with its specific shape — this he designates here as heaven. But if Moses had expressed himself differently and had stated: "In the beginning God said: 'Let there be heaven, etc.,'" there would later on have been no place for the repetition of the word "He said" when these formless waters were illuminated and light was created.

The very simple meaning of what Moses says, therefore, is this: Everything that is, was created by God. Furthermore, at the beginning of the first day were created the crude mass of mire or of earth, and the mists or waters. Into these, within the remaining space of the first day, God introduced light and made day appear, in order to expose to view the crude mass of heaven and earth, rather like an elementary seed, but one suited for producing something.

2. But the earth was empty and void.

A wider significance attaches to the Hebrew words תהו and בהו than can be reproduced in translation. Yet they are used frequently in the Holy Scripture. תהו is employed in the sense of "nothing," so that the earth is a בהו, which so far as it itself is concerned, is empty, where there are no roads, no separate localities, no hills, no valleys, no grass, no herbs, no animals, and no men. Such indeed was the first appearance of the unfinished earth; for since mire was mixed with the water, it was not possible to observe the distinctive marks which are observable now, after it has been finished.

Thus Isaiah, in the chapter where he threatens the earth with desolation, says (34:11): "There will be stretched over it the line תהו and the plummet בהו," i. e., the earth will be laid waste to such an extent that neither human beings nor beasts of burden will remain, and the houses will be laid waste and everything thrown into confusion and disorder. This is how Jerusalem was later laid waste by the Romans, and Rome by the Goths, to such an extent that the traces of the very famous ancient city cannot be pointed out.[15]

You now see the earth standing out above the waters, the heaven adorned with stars, the fields with trees, the cities with houses, etc.; but when all these are removed and thrown together into a shapeless mass — what then results Moses calls תהו and בהו.

But just as the earth was surrounded by darkness or by waters

[15] Like other references to Rome in Luther's lectures and writings (cf. *Luther's Works,* 13, p. 281, note 48), this may be a reminiscence of Luther's trip to Rome in 1510—11.

in which there was darkness, so the heaven, too, was unformed.
It was תהו, not only because it lacked the adornment of the stars,
and בהו, because it was not separated from the earth; but it was also
still without light and was a dark and deep abyss which, either like
a very dense mist or like the already mentioned ooze, surrounded the
earth. For the account of the separation of the waters will follow
later.

So, then, we have this as the first fact: Moses teaches that on the
first day the heaven and the earth were created, but an unformed
heaven, that is, without any separation of the waters, without luminaries, and not yet raised up; likewise an unformed earth, without
animals, rivers, and mountains.

With Lyra's contention that matter is pure potentiality and can
take on form through its own power; likewise, with Augustine's saying
in his *Confessions* — that matter is almost nothing, so close to nothing
that there is no intermediate reality — I disagree entirely.[16] How can
you apply the term "mere nothing" to something that is a genuine
substance of the kind Moses calls heaven and earth? You could not
do so unless you wanted to apply the term "matter" in a contrived
sense to something like wood which is not yet a box or a bench. But
in this sense the philosophers speak of "secondary matter." [17]

Much more noteworthy is what St. Peter says in 2 Peter 3:5-6,
where he is speaking of the wicked: "They deliberately ignore this
fact, that by the Word of God heavens existed long ago, and an earth
formed out of water and by means of water, through which the world
that then existed was deluged with water and perished." Thereby
Peter seems to be referring to the fact that the earth was established
out of water and through water, and afterwards was brought forth
out of the water and, as it were, placed into light, just as it seems
to float on the ocean up to the present time. This, he says, the wicked
know; and therefore, because of their confidence in this state of
affairs, they have no fear of any danger from water, which they know
to be the foundation of the earth. Nevertheless, water destroyed the
earth which it was sustaining and buoying up, just as the earth will
also perish by fire at the end of time. Thus St. Peter seems to refer

16 The Latin sentence reads: *Materiam esse prope nihil, nec posse excogi-
tari intermedium, haec nullo modo probo.* The quotation from Augustine is in
his *Confessions*, XII, ch. 4, 8; its immediate source may be Nicholas of Lyra's
introduction to Gen. 1.

17 Cf. p. 6, note 14.

to the fact that the earth was brought forth in the water and out of the water. Let this be enough on the subject of matter; for I think that if anyone were to argue with greater subtlety, he would not do so with profit.

And darkness was over the face of the abyss.

Water and abyss and heaven are used in this passage for the same thing, namely, for that dark and unformed mass which later on was provided with life and separated by the Word. Now these are functions of the Second Person, that is, of Christ, the Son of God: to adorn and separate the crude mass which was brought forth out of nothing. Furthermore, this may have been the reason why Moses decided not to use the words "He said" in the first instance. Indeed, some mention this as a reason.[18]

And the Spirit of the Lord hovered over the waters.

Some explain that "the Spirit of the Lord" simply means "wind." If something physical is to be understood here under Spirit, I for my part would rather refer it to this phenomenon, that the unformed mass of heaven and earth, which He also called abyss, began to be put into motion, just as it is in motion today. Water never stands still but is always in motion on its surface.

But it is more to my liking that we understand Spirit to mean the Holy Spirit. Wind is a creature which at that time did not yet exist, since so far those masses of heaven and earth lay mixed together. Indeed, it is the great consensus of the church that the mystery of the Trinity is set forth here.[19] The Father creates heaven and earth out of nothing through the Son, whom Moses calls the Word. Over these the Holy Spirit broods. As a hen broods her eggs, keeping them warm in order to hatch her chicks, and, as it were, to bring them to life through heat, so Scripture says that the Holy Spirit brooded, as it were, on the waters to bring to life those substances which were to be quickened and adorned. For it is the office of the Holy Spirit to make alive.[20]

---

[18] Augustine, *De Genesi ad litteram*, I, ch. 4, p. 7.

[19] Augustine, *Confessions*, XIII, ch. 5.

[20] This is a reference to the Nicene Creed: "I believe in the Holy Ghost, the Lord and Giver of Life." In the original the terms "Lord" and "Giver of Life" are both adjectives; a more literal translation would read: "I believe in the Holy Spirit, lordly and life-giving."

So far as I can see, these remarks about the subject under consideration are sufficient for us to set aside other opinions and to establish the following: Out of nothing God created heaven and earth as an unformed mass so that the unformed earth was surrounded by the unformed heaven or mist.

It remains for us to have some discussion also about the words. And here we immediately encounter some who argue in a variety of ways and with subtlety about the phrase "in the beginning." They explain "in the beginning" as "in the Son," on account of the passage in John when Christ gives His reply to the Jews who were asking who He was (John 8:25): "The beginning which I also am saying." Likewise, Ps. 110:3: "With Thee is the beginning in the day of Thy valor." This passage almost all explain as follows: "With Thee is the Son in divine power." [21] But it is well known to those who are acquainted with Greek that in John τὴν ἀϱχήν must be interpreted as an adverb, a figure of speech occasionally met with in Greek. So let those who care to do so, trifle with the expression; I prefer what is simplest and can be understood by those with little education.

So, then, I have the conviction that Moses wanted to indicate the beginning of time. Thus "in the beginning" has the same meaning as if he said: "At that time, when there was no time, or when the world began, it began in this wise, that heaven and earth were first created by God out of nothing in an unformed condition, not beautified as they now are. However, heaven and earth did not lie unimproved this way for a long time, but immediately on the first day the beginning was made to adorn them with light."

The Arians have fancied that the angels and the Son of God were created before the beginning.[22] But let us pass over this blasphemous idea. Let us also disregard another question: What was God doing before the beginning of the world? Was He in a state of rest or not? Augustine relates in his *Confessions* that someone had answered to this effect: "God was making hell ready for those who pried into meddlesome questions," obviously, as Augustine says, to frustrate any injurious effect of the question.[23]

Indeed, the modesty of Augustine pleases me. With perfect frank-

21 See also *Luther's Works*, 22, pp. 7, 8.

22 Cf. *Luther's Works*, 22, pp. 19-26.

23 Augustine, *Confessions*, XI, ch. 12; but Augustine tells the story about someone else.

ness he says that in the case of questions of this kind he hauls in the sails of his acumen, because even if we should engage in endless speculation and debate, these matters nevertheless remain outside our comprehension. And if we do not fully understand even the things which we see and do, how much less shall we grasp those? What will you assume to have been outside time or before time? Or what will you imagine that God was doing before there was any time? Let us, therefore, rid ourselves of such ideas and realize that God was incomprehensible in His essential rest before the creation of the world, but that now, after the creation, He is within, without, and above all creatures; that is, He is still incomprehensible. Nothing else can be said, because our mind cannot grasp what lies outside time.

God also does not manifest Himself except through His works and the Word, because the meaning of these is understood in some measure. Whatever else belongs essentially to the Divinity cannot be grasped and understood, such as being outside time, before the world, etc. Perhaps God appeared to Adam without a covering, but after the fall into sin He appeared in a gentle breeze as though enveloped in a covering. Similarly he was enveloped later on in the tabernacle by the mercy seat and in the desert by a cloud and fire. Moses, therefore, also calls these objects "faces of God," through which God manifested Himself. Cain, too, calls the place at which he had previously sacrificed "the face of God" (Gen. 4:14). This nature of ours has become so misshapen through sin, so depraved and utterly corrupted, that it cannot recognize God or comprehend His nature without a covering. It is for this reason that those coverings are necessary.

It is folly to argue much about God outside and before time, because this is an effort to understand the Godhead without a covering, or the uncovered divine essence. Because this is impossible, God envelops Himself in His works in certain forms, as today He wraps Himself up in Baptism, in absolution, etc. If you should depart from these, you will get into an area where there is no measure, no space, no time, and into the merest nothing, concerning which, according to the philosopher, there can be no knowledge.[24] Therefore we justly pass over this question and are satisfied with the simple explanation of the phrase "in the beginning."

It is more worthwhile to note that Moses does not say: "In the

[24] The phrase "merest nothing" is a translation of *merissimum nihil.*

beginning אֲדֹנָי created heaven and earth" but makes use of a term in the plural number, אֱלֹהִים, a name which Moses and others use to designate the angels as well as judges and magistrates, as in Ps. 82:6: "I have said, 'You are gods.'" Here, however, it is certain that it designates the one true God, by whom all things were created. Why, then, does he make use of the plural number?

The Jews apply their sophistry to Moses in various ways, but to us it is plain that he wants to hint at the Trinity or the plurality of Persons in one single divine nature. Because he is speaking of the work of creation, it follows clearly that he is excluding the angels. There remains, therefore, this contradiction: God is one, and nevertheless that most perfect unity is also the truest plurality. Why else should it be of importance that Moses makes use of the plural number?

Therefore the feeble sophistry of the Jews is unacceptable, that the plural number is made use of for the sake of respect. What room is there here for respect? Especially since our German custom to use the plural number out of respect when we speak of only one person is not common to all languages.

In the second place, even though they loudly claim that this expression is applied also to the angels and men, nevertheless in this passage it is a plural and cannot be understood except of the one true God, because the context deals with the creation. There were many other terms in the singular number of which Moses could have made use if it had not been his definite purpose to indicate to those who are spiritual that in the divine nature, apart from the creation, there is a plurality of Persons. Of course, he does not say in so many words that the Father, the Son, and the Holy Spirit are the one true God; this was to be reserved for the teaching of the Gospel. It was adequate for him to indicate this plurality of Persons by means of the plural term, which later on is applied also to human beings.

Nor should it give us any offense that the same term is later applied to creatures. Why shouldn't God assign us His name, when He assigns us His power and His office? For to forgive sins, to retain sins, to make alive, etc., are works of the Divine Majesty alone; nevertheless, the same works are given to human beings and are done through the Word which human beings teach. As Paul says (Rom. 11:14): "That I might make many to be saved of my flesh." Likewise (1 Cor. 9:22): "I was made everything for all, that all I might save." Therefore just as these works are truly works of God but may also be assigned to men and be performed by men, so the name of God in truth denotes God but may also be applied to human beings.

Arius was unable to deny that Christ existed before the creation of the world, because Christ also says (John 8:58): "Before Abraham was, I am." And it is written in Proverbs (8:27): "Before the heavens were, I am." Therefore he shifted to the position that Christ, or the Word, was created before all things and later on created all things and was the most perfect creature, but that He had not always been in existence. This insane and wicked opinion must be countered with the fact that Moses briefly says "in the beginning" and does not assert that anything else was in existence before the beginning except God, to whom he gives a name in the plural number.

The minds of men arrive at these foolish conclusions when they are determined to do their thinking about such lofty matters without the Word. Yet indeed we lack knowledge about our very selves, as Lucretius says: "It is so far unknown what the nature of the soul is." [25] We feel capable of forming judgments, of assigning numbers, of distinguishing quantities and spiritual creatures (if I may call them so), what is true and what is false; but we are still incapable of giving a definition of the soul. How much less knowledge are we going to have of the nature of God? We do not know how our will is aroused; for it is not aroused qualitatively or quantitively, and yet it is aroused in some way. [26] Much less, then, could we know anything of divine matters.

It is therefore insane to argue about God and the divine nature without the Word or any covering, as all the heretics are accustomed to do. They do their thinking about God with the same sureness with which they argue about a pig or cow. Therefore they also receive a reward worthy of their rashness in that they arrive at so dangerous a view. Whoever desires to be saved and to be safe when he deals with such great matters, let him simply hold to the form, the signs, and the coverings of the Godhead, such as His Word and His works. For in His Word and in His works He shows Himself to us. Those who are in touch with these are made sound, as was the woman with the issue of blood when she touched Christ's garment (Matt. 9:20-22).

[25] Lucretius, *De rerum natura*, I, 113. This is one of the classical quotations which Peter Meinhold regards as interpolations by the editors (cf. Introduction, p. x).

[26] That is, the changes of the human "will" do not correspond to the increase or decrease of quantity, nor to the variation in quality, which we observe in material things.

But those who want to reach God apart from these coverings exert themselves to ascend to heaven without ladders (that is, without the Word). Overwhelmed by His majesty, which they seek to comprehend without a covering, they fall to their destruction. This is what happened to Arius. He thought that there was some intermediate being between the Creator and the creature and that all things were created by that intermediate being. It was inevitable that he should hit upon this idea after he had denied, contrary to Scripture, the plurality of the Persons in the Godhead. Since he argues his position apart from and without the Word of God and relies on his thinking alone, he cannot avoid falling into error.

Similarly, because a monk does not adhere to the Word, he thinks that there is a God sitting in heaven who intends to save anyone wearing a cowl and following a definite rule of life. He is also ascending to heaven without God's disclosure of Himself or without His face leading the way. So also the Jews had their idols and their groves. The fall and destruction of all these is the same; they all run into the same difficulty because, forsaking the Word, they each follow their own thoughts.

Therefore if we want to walk in safety, let us accept what the Word submits for our reflection and what God Himself wants us to know. Let us pass by other things — things not revealed in the Word. What concern is it of mine, and how can I comprehend what God did before the earth was created? These are thoughts concerning the uncovered Godhead; by such thoughts the Jews permit themselves to be led away from this text, so that they do not believe in several Persons, although Moses consistently adheres to the use of the plural noun.

A papal decree condemns the Anthropomorphites for speaking about God as if they were speaking about a human being, and for ascribing to Him eyes, ears, arms, etc.[27] However, the condemnation is unjust. Indeed, how could men speak otherwise of God among men? If it is heresy to think of God in this manner, then a verdict has been rendered concerning the salvation of all children, who think and speak of God in this childlike fashion. But even apart from the children: give me the most learned doctor — how else will he teach and speak about God?

[27] Epiphanius, in his *Panarion,* ch. 70, tells of a sect called "Audians." They were accused of teaching a gross form of anthropomorphism.

And so a wrong was done to good men. Although they believed in the omnipotent God and their Savior, they were found guilty because they said that God has eyes, with which He beholds the poor; that He has ears, with which He hears those who pray, etc. How can this nature of ours understand the spiritual essence of God? Scripture, too, here and there makes use of this very manner of speech. Therefore they were unjustly condemned. Their zeal for simplicity should rather be commended as something supremely necessary in doctrinal matters. When God reveals Himself to us, it is necessary for Him to do so through some such veil or wrapper and to say: "Look! Under this wrapper you will be sure to take hold of Me." When we embrace this wrapper, adoring, praying, and sacrificing to God there, we are said to be praying to God and sacrificing to Him properly.

Thus there is no doubt that our first parents worshiped God early in the morning, when the sun was rising, by marveling at the Creator in the creature or, to express myself more clearly, because they were urged on by the creature. Their descendants continued the custom, but without understanding. Thus this practice turned into idolatry. The sun itself, which is a good creature of God, is not the cause of this development; but the reason lies in the fact that the true doctrine, which Satan cannot endure, gradually became extinct. Thus when Satan led Eve away from the Word, she immediately fell headlong into sin.

But to return to the Anthropomorphites, I think that they should in no wise be condemned, because even the prophets describe God as sitting on a throne. When uneducated persons hear this, they immediately think of a golden throne marvelously adorned, although they know that no such material is found in heaven. Thus Isaiah says that he saw the Lord in a very wide garment (6:1), because God cannot be depicted or viewed in a vision which is absolute or subject to direct perception. Therefore such figures of speech have the approval of the Holy Spirit, and the works of God are set before us so that we can grasp them. Such works are: that He created the heaven and the earth, that He sent His Son, that He speaks through His Son, that He baptizes, that He absolves from sin through the Word. He who does not apprehend these facts will never apprehend God. But I shall stop here, since I have often discussed these facts at great length. Nevertheless, it was necessary at this time to touch upon them on account of Moses, whom the Jews torture so miserably in connection with this passage, from which we prove that there are several Persons in the Godhead. Let us now go on in the text.

3. *And God said: Let there be light, and there was light.*

I have said that in the beginning there was created through the Word that unformed mass of earth and heaven (which he calls waters and likewise abyss), and that this must be assigned to the work of the first day, although this is the first time Moses speaks thus: "God said, 'Let there be light!'" However, this expression is indeed remarkable and unknown to the writers of all other languages, that through His speaking God makes something out of nothing. And so here for the first time Moses mentions the means and the instrument God used in doing His work, namely, the Word.

Furthermore, one must note carefully the difference the Hebrew makes between אָמַר and דָּבָר. We render either word by the verb "say" or "speak," but in Hebrew there is this difference: אָמַר denotes only and strictly the uttered word, but דָּבָר also denotes a thing. Thus when the prophets say: "This is the Word of the Lord," they employ the noun דָּבָר, not אָמַר. Even today the Neo-Arians [28] deceive those who are not familiar with the Hebrew language by making the claim that the word denotes something created and that in this way Christ also is said to be the Word. Over against this wicked and, at the same time, silly distortion the reader [29] is here properly reminded that Moses employs the verb אָמַר, which simply and strictly denotes the uttered word, so that the word is something distinct from him who is speaking and there is a distinction between him who speaks and that which is spoken.

Therefore just as we earlier proved a plurality of Persons from the text, so here there is revealed a distinction of Persons. It says that God is, so to speak, the Speaker who creates; nevertheless, He does not make use of matter, but He makes heaven and earth out of nothing solely by the Word which He utters.

Now compare with this the Gospel of John (1:1): "In the begin-

---

28 We have coined the term "Neo-Arians" to translate *novi Ariani*, which seems to be a reference to the misgivings about the dogma of the Trinity being expressed by some of the radicals in the left wing of the Reformation.

29 Such references to the "reader" further substantiate the supposition that Luther's lectures have undergone revision at the hands of editors (Introduction, pp. x—xii).

ning was the Word." He is in proper agreement with Moses. He says: "Before the creation of the world there was not a single one of the creatures, but God nevertheless had the Word." What is this Word, or what did He do? Listen to Moses. The light, he says, was not yet in existence; but out of its state of being nothing the darkness was turned into that most outstanding creature, light. Through what? Through the Word. Therefore in the beginning and before every creature there is the Word, and it is such a powerful Word that it makes all things out of nothing. From this follows without possibility of contradiction what John expressly adds: "This Word is God and yet is a Person distinct from God the Father, just as a word and he who utters a word are separate entities." Yet this distinction is such that, to use the expression, a most single singleness [30] of essence remains.

These are difficult matters, and it is unsafe to go beyond the limit to which the Holy Spirit leads us. Let us, therefore, come to a halt with the knowledge that when the unformed heaven and the unformed earth, both of them marred by mist and darkness, had come into existence, light also came into existence out of nothing, that is, out of the very darkness. Paul cites this first work of the Creator as an extraordinary work (2 Cor. 4:6): "Who commanded the light to shine out of darkness." "By His command," he says, "He made that light." This, therefore, is sufficient for the confirmation of our faith: that Christ is true God, who is with the Father from eternity, before the world was made, and that through Him, who is the wisdom and the Word of the Father, the Father made everything. But in the passage referred to this point should also be noted: that Paul regards the conversion of the wicked — something which is also brought about by the Word — as a new work of creation.

Here reason commits sacrilegious blunders with its stupid questions. "If," it says, "the Word was always in existence, why didn't God create heaven and earth through this Word at an earlier time?" Likewise: "Because heaven and earth came into existence only when God began to speak, it appears to follow that the Word had its beginning at the same time the creature had its beginning." But these wicked thoughts must be banished. Concerning these matters we cannot establish or think out anything, because outside that beginning of the creation there is nothing except the uncovered divine essence

[30] This is a translation of the clause *ut unissima, ut sic dicam, unitas essentiae maneat.*

and the uncovered God. And so, because He is incomprehensible, that, too, is incomprehensible which was before the world, because it is nothing except God.

It seems to us that He begins to speak because we cannot go beyond the beginning of time. But because John and Moses say that the Word was in the beginning and before all creatures, it necessarily follows that He always was in the Creator and in the uncovered essence of God. Therefore He is true God, but in this manner, that the Father begets and the Son is begotten. This difference Moses brings out when he mentions God, who spoke, and the Word, which was spoken. This was enough for Moses. The clearer unfolding of this mystery properly belongs to the New Testament and to the Son, who is in the bosom of the Father (John 1:18). There we also hear the precise names of the Persons: the Father, the Son, and the Holy Spirit. They are also revealed, but in a most subtle fashion, both in some psalms and in the prophets.[31]

Augustine explains the verb "He said" somewhat differently. This is his interpretation: "He said, that is, from eternity it was so determined in the Word of the Father and was so established with God, because the Son is the reason, the image, and the wisdom of the Father." [32] But the simple and true meaning must be adhered to: God said, that is, through the Word He created and made all things, as the apostle confirms when he says (Heb. 1:2): "Through whom the worlds were created." Likewise (Col. 1:16): "All things were created through Him and for Him." Within these limits our thinking concerning the creation must remain; and we should not go too far afield, because then we shall surely get into darkness and mischief.

When questions are raised concerning the world and its creation, therefore, let us be satisfied with these facts. So far as the matter of the universe is concerned, it was made out of nothing; just as out of nonlight light was made, so out of nothing heaven and earth were made.

As Paul says (Rom. 4:17): "He calls the things which are not that they be." The instrument or means God made use of is His omnipotent Word, which was with God from the beginning and, as St. Paul says, before the establishment of the world (Eph. 1:4). Therefore what Paul says (Col. 1:16): "Through Him all things are made" —

31 For an example of how Luther finds this in the Old Testament see his comments on Ps. 8, Luther's Works, 12, pp. 99—101.

32 Augustine, De Genesi ad litteram, I, ch. 5, pp. 8, 9.

he employs the preposition "in" according to Hebrew usage for "through," for in this sense Hebrew employs the letter ך — and similar passages were drawn from this passage of Moses, who is talking about the spoken Word, by which some command and order is given.

This Word is God; it is the omnipotent Word, uttered in the divine essence. No one heard it spoken except God Himself, that is, God the Father, God the Son, and God the Holy Spirit. And when it was spoken, light was brought into existence, not out of the matter of the Word or from the nature of Him who spoke but out of the darkness itself. Thus the Father spoke inwardly, and outwardly light was made and came into existence immediately. In this manner other creatures, too, were made later. This, I say, is sufficient knowledge for us concerning the manner of the creation.

But here a famous question is raised: "Of what sort, then, was that light by which the unformed mass of heaven and earth was illuminated? Although neither sun nor stars had been created, the text makes it clear that this light was true and physical." This has given rise for some to look for an allegory and to explain "Let there be light" by saying that it is an angelic creature.[33] Likewise, "He separated light from darkness" is said to mean that He separated the good angels from the bad. But this is toying with ill-timed allegories (for Moses is relating history); it is not interpreting Scripture. Moreover, Moses wrote that uneducated men might have clear accounts of the creation. Such preposterous ideas should, therefore, not be propounded here.

Secondly, this, too, is asked: "Did this light move in a circular motion?" I for my part confess that I really do not know. If, however, anyone desires to know what appears to me most likely to be true, I think that this light was in motion in such a way that it brought about a natural day, from its rising to its setting. Although it is difficult to say what sort of light it was, nevertheless I do not agree that we should without reason depart from the rules of language or that we should by force read meanings into words. Moses says plainly that there was light, and he counts this day as the first of the creation.

Therefore I am of the opinion that this was true light and that its motion carried it in a circle, just as sunlight moves in a circle. Nevertheless, it was not such a clear and brilliant light as it was later

[33] This may be a reference to Augustine, *De Genesi ad litteram*, I, ch. 17, pp. 23 ff.

on when it was increased, adorned, and perfected by the light of the sun. Similarly, the Holy Scriptures also bear witness that on the Last Day God will make more brilliant and glorious the present daylight of the sun, as though it were a weak light in comparison with the future glory (Is. 30:26). As, therefore, the present daylight is, so to speak, a crude and coarse mass of light if it is compared with the future light, so that first light was crude when compared with this present light. This is my opinion concerning these two questions. Now Moses continues.

5. And evening and morning became one day.

Here it must be noted that the Jews begin their day in a way different from ours. For them the day began in the evening with the setting of the sun, and it came to an end on the following evening. We begin our day with the rising of the sun. I think that they derive the noun "evening," which is called עֶרֶב by the Hebrews, from עָרַב, which means "to mix," "to confuse." From this designation they get the name עָרֹב, which denotes our dogfly. It is as if you called it a "confused fly"; for in the evening the appearances of objects become indistinct, and after light has gone, things cannot be clearly distinguished.

This is what Moses has now taught us concerning the first day, but we shall see that Moses also retains this expression in the creation of the remaining things: "God said: 'Let there be a firmament,' " etc. This very repetition should be most welcome to us because, as I said above, it provides an important witness for our faith that the Son, in His divine nature, is true God and that in the unity of the Godhead there is a certain plurality of Persons, because one Person is that of the speaker, and another is the Word, or the λόγος.

In this manner the psalm also says (33:6): "By the Word of the Lord the heavens were established." Solomon points to this amazing expression of Moses when he writes that divine wisdom was, as it were, the helper of the creation (Prov. 8:22-27): "Before He made anything in the beginning, I was set up from everlasting. When He prepared the heavens, I was there, when by a sure ordinance and with a circle He enclosed the depths." Here Solomon shows that he understood the doctrine of our religion which was revealed by Moses, but he does it in such a way that the uneducated people heard and read his words and yet did not understand them. If Solomon had not understood this mystery, he could not have spoken thus.

But he drew it all from Moses, as also that question, Prov. 30:5: "What is His name, and what is His Son's name, if you know?"

But I think there were similar writings of other holy men as well, like Enoch or Elijah, in which many testimonies of this kind were prominent. But all this remains hidden even nowadays; although it has been revealed ever so clearly in the New Testament, still it is not accepted by the majority but opposed. This same thing happened much more among the Jewish people, since the holy patriarchs set their testimonies even before the learned in rather mysterious form and did not write them down in very blunt language.

But for us it is a great comfort to know that ever since the beginning of the world there have been such indications that in the Divine Being there is a plurality of Persons and nevertheless a unity of the divine nature and essence. But if there are some who do not believe this or who oppose it, what do we care? Abraham saw three, and he worshiped One (Gen. 18:2). Likewise, the Holy Spirit says in Genesis (19:24): "And the Lord rained fire from the heaven from the Lord." Even if the fanatics [34] do not understand or pay attention to these words, we still know that they are the words, not of a drunken person but of God.

Very many testimonies of this kind are everywhere at hand, and the very excellent Hilary has carefully gathered them.[35] If they are difficult to understand and appear to have too little validity, they appear so to the ungodly and unbelieving. Yet for the godly those matters which are reported and revealed by the divine writings are sure and fully intelligible. They know that one Person is the Person of the speaking God and that another — not in nature but in Person — is the Word, through whom all things were created and are preserved up to the present day, as the author of the letter to the Hebrews says (1:3): "Upholding all things by the Word of His power."

Here attention must also be called to this, that the words "Let there be light" are the words of God, not of Moses; this means that they are realities. For God calls into existence the things which do not exist (Rom. 4:17). He does not speak grammatical words; He speaks true and existent realities. Accordingly, that which among us has the sound of a word is a reality with God. Thus sun, moon, heaven, earth, Peter, Paul, I, you, etc. — we are all words of God,

---

[34] The Latin term *fanatici* is the usual rendition of the German *Schwärmer* (cf. *Luther's Works*, 13, p. 368, note 26).

[35] Hilary, *On the Trinity*, IV, ch. 29, *Patrologia, Series Latina*, X, 118, 119.

in fact only one single syllable or letter by comparison with the entire creation. We, too, speak, but only according to the rules of language; that is, we assign names to objects which have already been created. But the divine rule of language is different, namely: when He says: "Sun, shine," the sun is there at once and shines. Thus the words of God are realities, not bare words.

Here men have differentiated between the uncreated Word and the created word. The created word is brought into being by the uncreated Word. What else is the entire creation than the Word of God uttered by God, or extended to the outside? But the uncreated Word is a divine thought, an inner command which abides in God, the same as God and yet a distinct Person. Thus God reveals Himself to us as the Speaker who has with Him the uncreated Word, through whom He created the world and all things with the greatest ease, namely, by speaking. Accordingly, there is no more effort for God in His creation than there is for us in the mention of it. With thoughts of this kind the good fathers Augustine and Hilary also delighted themselves.[36]

THE WORK OF THE SECOND DAY

6. *God said: Let there be a firmament in the midst of the waters, and let it divide waters from waters.*

Here Moses seems to be forgetting himself, because he does not deal at all with two very important matters, namely, the creation and the fall of the angels, and relates only the state of affairs of physical things, although there is no doubt that the angels were created. But concerning their creation, their battle, and their fall there is nothing at all in Scripture except that Christ says (John 8:44): "He did not abide in the truth," and Moses — below in chapter three — mentions the sad account of the serpent. It is surprising that Moses should remain silent about these weighty matters.

Since men were without definite information, the result was that they invented something, namely, that there were nine choirs of angels and that they fell for nine entire days. They also invented an account of a very great battle and how the good angels withstood the evil ones. This idea, I think, is patterned after the battle of the church; as pious teachers battle the wicked and the fanatics, so they also dream that there was a battle against the wicked angels, who wanted to claim deity for themselves. So it happens that where there are no

[36] Cf. p. 4, note 8.

clear statements on the subject, rash people usually consider themselves free to come up with imaginary ideas.

On the strength of the passage in Isaiah, where Lucifer said (14:13): "I will ascend into heaven; I will exalt my throne above the stars of God," they also give thought to the danger and the fear of the angels, although there the prophet is prophesying concerning the pride of the king of the Babylonians. Bernard thinks that Lucifer had seen God's plan for mankind to be raised higher than the nature of the angels, and that this proud spirit envied mankind this happiness and fell.[37] Let these ideas be worth what they may. I for my part would not compel anybody to agree with such opinions. But this much is certain: the angels fell and the devil was transformed from an angel of light into an angel of darkness. Perhaps there may also have been a conflict between the good and the evil angels.

Because Moses was writing for a people without learning or experience, he wanted to write what was necessary and useful to know. Other, unnecessary information about the nature of the angels and the like he passed over. Therefore we should not be expected to say more about this whole business either, especially since the New Testament, too, deals in a rather limited way with this doctrine; it adds nothing beyond the fact that they have been condemned and are held bound in prison, as it were, until the Day of Judgment (Rev. 20:2, 7). So it is sufficient for us to know that there are good and evil angels and that God created all of them alike, as good. From this it follows necessarily that the evil angels fell and did not stand in the truth. How this came about is unknown; nevertheless, it is likely that they fell as the result of pride, because they despised the Word or the Son of God and wanted to place themselves above Him. More than this I do not have. Let us now return to Moses.

We heard that the work of the first day was this: He made the unformed heaven and earth, both of which He provided with a certain crude and imperfect light. Now the second day's work is that out of this unformed mist which He called heaven God created a beautiful and exquisite heaven, such as it is now, except for its stars and larger luminaries. The Hebrews quite properly derive their noun for "heaven," שָׁמַיִם, from מַיִם, which means water; for the letter שׁ is often used in compounds for a relative, so that שָׁמַיִם denotes something watery or something that has a watery nature. From its color it also appears

---

[37] Bernard of Clairvaux, *Sermones de tempore*, Sermon I, *Patrologia, Series Latina*, CLXXXIII, 36; cf. also *Luther's Works*, 22, p. 103.

that this is correct, and experience shows that the air is by nature moist. The philosophers assert that the atmosphere would be a continually moist mass if there were no sun.[38] It is indeed moist and warm; it is moist as a result of its nature, because the heaven was made from water. And so there is rain, and it has a beneficial moisture. But because sunlight has been added, this moist nature is so kept in bounds that the atmosphere is also warm.

This unformed mass of mist, which was created on the first day out of nothing, God seizes with the Word and gives the command that it should extend itself outward in the manner of a sphere. The Hebrew word רָקִיעַ denotes "something spread out," from the verb רָקַע, which means "to expand" or "to fold out." The heaven was made in this manner, that the unformed mass extended itself outward as the bladder of a pig extends itself outward in circular form when it is inflated — if I may be permitted to make use of a coarse comparison in order to make the process clear.

But as to what Job says, that the heavens were made firm with iron (37:18), this pertains not to the material but to the Word, which makes very strong even that which is very soft by nature. What is softer than water, what is thinner and finer than air? Yet because these very fine and soft substances were created by the Word, they preserve their form and motion most perfectly and firmly. But even if the heaven had been constructed of steel or of an infinitely harder material, it would break and melt because of its swift, long, and continuous motion. The sun, too, would melt one day as a result of its swift motion, even if it consisted of the hardest material. For motion produces great heat; in fact, Aristotle declares that the lead on an arrow melts on account of its swift motion.[39]

These are, therefore, wonders of God, in which the omnipotence of the Word is observed: that although the heaven is softer and more tenuous than water and yet is driven on by the swiftest motion among so great a variety of bodies and motions, no part of it has deteriorated or become weak in the course of so many thousands of years. This is what Job says: that the heavens are cast of bronze, as it were, although by nature they are extremely soft. We know how tenuous the air is in which we live; for it is not only impossible to touch it, but it cannot even be observed. But the heaven is even more tenuous and finer

[38] For a possible source of this information cf. *Luther's Works*, 22, p. 59, note 47.

[39] Aristotle, *De caelo*, II, ch. 7.

by nature than this air. Its blue color is proof, not of its compactness but of its remoteness and tenuousness. If you should compare it with the masses of clouds, the latter are like the smoke of moist wood that is being kindled. It is this tenuousness and yet unchanging permanence that Job notes. The philosophers, too, have the famous statement: "What is wet cannot be limited by its own limit." [40]

Therefore the heaven, which cannot stand firm by means of its bounds (for it is watery), stands firm through the Word of God because we hear these words here: "Let there be a firmament." The more observant among the philosophers drew from this source what is in truth not an insignificant proof: that all things are done and guided, not planlessly but by divine providence, inasmuch as the movements of the masses on high and of the heaven are so definite and unique.[41] Who would say that they are accidental or purely a matter of nature, when the objects fashioned by artisans — such as round or three-cornered or six-cornered columns — are not accidental but the result of a definite plan and skill?

Therefore in truth it is a work of the Divine Majesty that the sun follows its course so exactly and in a most precise manner without deviating a fingerbreadth from the straightest possible line in any part of the heaven. Moreover, it maintains this course in the most tenuous atmosphere without any support by solid masses; but it is borne along like a leaf in the air. However, this comparison is rather unsuited, because the movement of a leaf is irregular and indefinite, while that of the sun is most definite — and in an atmosphere far more tenuous than is the air in which we move and live.

This marvelous expansion of that thick mist Moses calls a firmament in which the sun, together with the remaining planets, has its motion around the earth in that most tenuous matter. What maker gives such solidity to this fluid and unstable material? Nature certainly does not do so; even in easier circumstances it is incapable of this achievement. Therefore this is the work of Him who says to the heaven and to that slippery material: "Be a firmament," who through His Word gives strength to all of them and preserves them through His omnipotence. This Word brings it about that the most tenuous air is harder than any steel and has its own limit, and that, on the

---

[40] The axiom cited here is: *Humidum non terminari termino proprio.*

[41] This is a summary of the "argument from design" for the providence of God, an argument of which Melanchthon thought much more highly than Luther did (cf. Introduction, p. xi).

other hand, steel is softer than water. From such works we should realize what sort of God we have, namely, the almighty God, who made the wondrous heaven from an unformed heaven and did everything according to His will.

I said further that among the Hebrews the firmament got its name from the expanding. Thus in Ps. 104 the comparison with skins and camp tents, taken from military life, cleverly alludes to the word. The expression is: "Stretching out the heaven like a tent curtain" (Ps. 104:2). "For just as a folded-up tent is unfolded and pitched in a field," the psalm says, "so Thou dost spread out and, as it were, unroll by Thy Word the unformed heaven, where Thou dost sit invisibly in the whole of creation, just as in a sphere, within all things and outside all things."

But what is most remarkable is that Moses clearly makes three divisions. He places the firmament in the middle, between the waters. I might readily imagine that the firmament is the uppermost mass of all and that the waters which are in suspension, not over but under the heaven, are the clouds which we observe, so that the waters separated from the waters would be understood as the clouds which are separated from our waters on the earth. But Moses says in plain words that the waters were above and below the firmament. Here I, therefore, take my reason captive and subscribe to the Word even though I do not understand it.

In this connection the question is asked: "Which are those waters, and how are the upper masses separated?" The division the philosophers make is well known.[42] They maintain that there are four elements, and they assign them a place and distinguish them according to their properties. The lowest place they give to the earth, the second to water, the third to air, the last and highest to fire. Some, in addition to these, count the ether as a fifth element. Thereafter are listed the seven spheres or orbits of the planets. There is fair agreement about these among all the philosophers, that there are four spheres of productive and destructible materials, then also eight others of unproductive and indestructible materials.

Aristotle, moreover, teaches this concerning the nature of the heaven: it is not made up of elements but has its own special nature.[43]

---

[42] Luther is reflecting the influence of his university teachers; see the cosmological tables from one of those teachers, Jodocus Trutvetter, *Summa in totam physicen*, reprinted in Otto Scheel, *Martin Luther. Vom Katholizismus zur Reformation*, I (3rd ed.; Tübingen, 1921), 197, 198.

[43] Aristotle, *De caelo*, I, chs. 9 ff.

If it were composed of elements, it would be destructible; for when elements are mixed with one another, they act and react, and destruction is the result. He, therefore, denies the primary qualities to all the masses of the upper regions and declares that they are uncompounded substances endowed with coeternal light and an essential quality which came into existence together with them.

These ideas, to be sure, are not certain; nevertheless, they are useful for teaching because they are the result of plausible reasoning and contain the foundation for the arts.[44] Therefore it would be boorish to pay no attention to them or to regard them with contempt, especially since in some respects they are in agreement with experience. Experience teaches us that by nature fire strives upward; and so lightning and other phenomena of the upper regions of the atmosphere appear fiery. Since these phenomena were noted by experience as elementary facts, men were induced to assign to fire the uppermost place, the next to air, the third to water, and the lowest position to the earth, because it weighs the most.

These concepts have value as first principles. Although someone may maintain that they are not universally true, nevertheless they are true in general and are useful for the proper communication and instruction of the arts. Even though fire can be drawn from flint, this is no reason to deny that the uppermost region has fire in it. Therefore theology has added to the arts this rule, which is not adequately known to the philosophers: that even if by His Word God has established and created all these things, nevertheless He is not bound to those rules in such a way that He cannot alter them according to His will. We see that neither grammar nor the other arts are so bound to rules that they do not have their exceptions. In the same way fairness [45] moderates the law of states. How much more can this happen in the instance of God's actions! Therefore even if we know from experience that those four elements are arranged in that order and have been assigned their positions, nevertheless God can go contrary to this arrangement and can have fire even in the midst of the sea and maintain it there, just as we see it hidden in the flint.

Thus a definite number of spheres has been put down by the mathematicians, not because this must necessarily be so, but because

---

44 The Latin phrase is *principia pulcherrimarum artium*.

45 Aristotle's term ἐπιείκεια was a favorite of Melanchthon's; cf. the Augsburg Confession, Art. XXVI, par. 14, *Die Bekenntnisschriften der evangelisch-lutherischen Kirche* (2nd. ed.; Göttingen, 1952), p. 103, note 4.

no knowledge of these things can be transmitted unless the heavenly bodies are differentiated on account of their unlike motions. Teaching this requires such imagination, if I may use this term. The experts themselves state: "We give examples, not because they are actually true, but because these matters cannot be taught by any other method." [46] It would, therefore, be the height of stupidity to sneer at these ideas, as some do, because they are not so definite that they could not be otherwise. They contribute toward teaching the arts, and this is sufficient.

These, in general, are the teachings of the philosophers. The more recent theologians are in agreement with them and on top of those eight spheres add two more: the crystalline or glacial or watery heaven, and the empyrean.[47]. But the Greeks have treated these subjects far more cleverly and intelligently than our scholars have treated them.[48] Ambrose and Augustine have rather childish ideas. Therefore I commend Jerome, who maintains complete silence on these topics.[49] Some call the crystalline heaven "watery" because they believe that it represents the waters of which Moses is speaking here, and that they were added to the eighth sphere to keep it from going up in flames because of the excessive motion.[50] But these are childish ideas. Rather than give approval to those inept thoughts, I for my part shall confess that I do not understand Moses in this passage.

The tenth heaven they call the empyrean, not because it actually has fire and burns, but from its light, because it is luminous and brilliant. This heaven they make the dwelling place of God and of the blessed, alleging that immediately after its creation it was filled with angels. They assert that Lucifer fell from this heaven. This is approximately what the theologians add to the opinions of the philosophers.

But those among us who were experts in astronomical matters

[46] The pedagogical principles mentioned in this paragraph had been the subject of much thought by Melanchthon.

[47] Cf. p. 26, note 42.

[48] Although the context does not specify, this is evidently a reference to the advanced scholarship of the Christian "Greeks" of the East rather than to the wisdom of classical Greece.

[49] This is taken from Lyra's comments on Gen. 1:6.

[50] Although the text has the plural *conflagrent*, we have translated the word with "it" rather than with "they."

were more generous in the matter of the spheres.[51] They teach twelve spheres and a triple motion of the eighth sphere: a forced motion, a standard motion, and a motion of hesitation. But in no case can these ideas be taught unless each individual motion has its own assigned sphere.

Averroes had other rather silly and rationalistic ideas.[52] He held that the individual spheres were minds or substances with mental capacity. The occasion for this fellow's stupid thinking was that he saw the absolutely sure and unfailing motion of the upper bodies. Therefore he concluded that the spheres were intelligent substances, of which the individual ones kept themselves moving in a definite and continuous manner. These conclusions demonstrate the utmost ignorance of God. Therefore we reject Averroes. The rest of the ideas I have mentioned we approve insofar as they are suited for teaching. For this knowledge of the motions of the upper bodies, whatever it may amount to, is most worthy of praise.

Moses proceeds from the simple and the easily understod, as they say, and mentions three parts: the waters above and below and, in the middle, the firmament. Moreover, in the term "heaven" is included all that the philosophers divide into eight spheres, fire, and air. For on the third day he makes mention of flowing waters for the first time. It is plain that in Holy Scripture the air in which we live is called "heaven" because Scripture speaks of "the birds of the heaven." Likewise, it says that the heaven is shut up when it is not raining; likewise, it says that the heaven rains. All this happens in the air, not in the spheres of the moon or of the other planets. Therefore this division of the spheres is not the teaching of Moses or of Holy Scripture; but it was thought out by learned men for the purpose of teaching, something which we ought to recognize as being of great benefit.

Furthermore, I doubt that the elements may properly be said to be destructible; for I see that they endure. Even though some part undergoes a change, it does not follow that the whole is changed. The changes of the elements affect only a part. Thus the air, in which the birds live and fly about, endures; the earth, on which trees and other plants grow, endures, even though some parts undergo a change.

Although Aristotle makes the Prime Mover the cause of all these,

[51] Cf. p. 24, note 38.

[52] Averroes is the Latinized form for Ibn Rushd (1126—98), the Moslem expositor of Aristotle whose work Thomas Aquinas criticized; we have used the word "rationalistic" to render *nimis rationi consentaneas*.

while Averroes declares that forms which assist from without are the causes of the motions,[53] we follow Moses and declare that all these phenomena occur and are governed simply by the Word of God. He spoke, and it was done. He did not turn over the governing of these bodies to the angels, just as we also are not governed by the angels, although we are guarded by them.

The retrograde motion of the planets is also a work of God, created through His Word.[54] This work belongs to God Himself and is too great to be assigned to the angels. It is God who has separated these bodies in this manner and who governs and preserves them. And the same One who commanded the sun to run, but the firmament to stand, also said to the star Mercury: "Star, move in this fashion." It is the Word that brings it about that the most uncertain motion is the most certain, even though those bodies are carried along in an unsteady heaven, not in some part of it or on some material line. Like a fish in the middle of the ocean or a bird in the open sky, the stars move in their place, but with a most definite and truly miraculous motion. It is also clear that for the same reason the Elbe flows along on its perennial course here in this area and never grows weary.[55] All such works are works of the Word, which Moses here glorifies with the words: "He said."

We Christians must, therefore, be different from the philosophers in the way we think about the causes of these things. And if some are beyond our comprehension (like those before us concerning the waters above the heavens), we must believe them and admit our lack of knowledge rather than either wickedly deny them or presumptuously interpret them in conformity with our understanding. We must pay attention to the expression of Holy Scripture and abide by the words of the Holy Spirit, whom it pleased to distribute His creatures in this way: in the middle was the firmament, which was brought forth out of the unformed heaven and the unformed earth and spread out through the Word; furthermore, above and below the firmament there were waters which were also drawn from this unformed mass. This entirety the Holy Spirit calls "heaven," together with the seven spheres and the whole region of the air, in which the phenomena are produced [56] and in which the birds roam.

53 Aristotle, *Physics*, VII, ch. 1.
54 Aristotle, *De caelo*, II, ch. 2.
55 Wittenberg was, of course, situated on the Elbe.
56 "Phenomena are produced" is a rendering of *fiunt impressiones*.

Therefore we do not deny the commonly accepted statements like: "Everything heavy tends downward, and everything light tends upward" (although we see that even dense vapors are carried upward, but through the drawing force of heat). We say only this: that these things were created in this manner and are being preserved by the Word, yet that on this very day they, too, can be changed by the Word, as all nature will be changed in the end. Likewise, it is contrary to the rule which was quoted that even now there are waters above the heavens or the firmament. Yet the text makes this assertion.

But now to return to the question which was propounded. When the question is raised concerning the nature of those waters, it cannot be denied that, as Moses says, there are waters above the heavens; but I readily confess that I do not know of what sort those waters are. Scripture mentions them nowhere else except in this passage and in the song of the three lads (Dan. 3:60). We cannot establish anything certain concerning all similar matters, such as the heaven in which the angels and God dwell with the blessed; nor can we say anything certain about other things, which will be revealed on the Last Day, when we shall be clothed with a different flesh.

But let me add this for the sake of the less learned: that what we call the horizon often occurs in Scripture under the designation "heaven." Hence the entire firmament is called the heaven of heavens, wherein are included the heavens of all human beings, that is, their horizons. In this way we have here another heaven than those people have who are in France or in Italy. But this contributes nothing to the explanation of this passage. Therefore the majority of the theologians, as we pointed out above, have interpreted these waters to be the icy heaven, which was placed in that area in order to keep the lower spheres moist and, as it were, to keep them cool, so that they may not be consumed by their excessive heat; for their motion exposes them to a great danger of destruction. But whether they are correct in drawing these conclusions I cannot determine. I shall readily confess that I do not know what these waters are. Indeed, the ancient teachers of the church paid little attention to these matters, as we see Augustine disregarding astronomy in its entirety.[57] Even though this science has many superstitious elements, still it should not be

[57] So, for example, Augustine, *Confessions*, IV, ch. 3; the qualified defense of astrology that follows here may well come from the Melanchthonian editors rather than from Luther (cf. Introduction, p. xi). See also p. 45, note 74.

completely disregarded; for as a whole it concerns itself with the observation and contemplation of the divine works, something which is a most worthy concern in a human being. Therefore men of the highest ability have engaged in it and have taken delight in it.

Let these statements be enough concerning the present passage, namely, that on the second day the heaven was separated so that it was in the middle, between the waters.

But here another question arises. Although in connection with the works of all the other days there is added: "And God saw that it was very good," why is it not added also in this passage, when the largest and most beautiful part of the entire creation was created? The answer to this question can be given thus: This closing statement was added at the end of the creation of all things on the sixth day, where Scripture says: "And God saw all things which He had made, and they were very good." There also the heaven is included.

Lyra approves of the opinion of Rabbi Solomon, who says that in the account of the third day this statement appears twice: "And God saw that they were very good." Therefore one of the two statements refers to the work of the second day, which was completed on the third, when the waters under the heaven were separated in a more suitable way.[58]

Others, as a result of considerations unknown to me, philosophize here that the numeral "two" is an ill omen because it is the first number which departs from unity, that God hates this departure and approves harmony, and that for this reason He did not add this notice concerning the second day.[59] Lyra rightly calls this gloss artfully misleading, because every number departs from unity in the same manner.

It is safest in this connection not to be too inquisitive, because these questions are in an area beyond our comprehension. How can we understand the order to which God has given His approval? Reason must become perplexed, because what is order for God we judge to be a confusion of order. Thus because the bright stars are mixed with the less bright, the smaller with the larger, they appear planlessly mingled. Who would say that this is order? Yet there is

---

[58] Lyra says that "the approval which, on other days, is addressed to the work of those days also applies to the completed work" (Gen. 1:8, sec. "v").

[59] As his principal reason for opposing this interpretation Lyra cites the fact "that in the Holy Gospel the number two is called a praiseworthy and mystical number," quoting in substantiation the words of Luke 10:1: "He sent them on ahead of Him, two by two" (Gen. 1:8; sec. "v").

supreme order, established by the wisest mind. In other matters our judgment is similar. There seems to be confusion because our Elbe, and indeed all rivers, reach their mouths in such a roundabout way. Thus the trees seem to be intermingled; so man and woman appear intermingled, and there seems to be no order here. But all these instances prove that God has order and that His interpretation of order is different from ours.

Therefore let us give up pursuing with too great curiosity the question why God adds the statement "And God saw" twice to the third day but omits it on the second day. Nor let us rashly reach a conclusion as to whether the work of the second day was brought to a close on the third day or not. The philosophers have taught the rudiments of the arts, and for this reason they have divided the heaven into its spheres. But we who have agreed that God is the Creator of all things without means, through the word "He said," have a far simpler method of procedure.

THE WORK OF THE THIRD DAY

9. *And God said: Let the waters which are under the heaven be gathered together in one place, and let the dry land appear.*

I said above that we do not understand the order of God's works. If, therefore, He had admitted us to His counsel at this point, we would have advised this order, that He should add this little item to the second day. But He Himself wants to remain the only master of His order and the referee of His world. And so we should not be very inquisitive here. The text plainly says that God commanded the waters to gather under the heaven. He does not say: "Under the firmament," as above: "Let there be a separation of the waters from the waters above and under the firmament." Therefore heaven, in the diction of the Sacred Scriptures, denotes the entire upper structure together with all the air and all the spheres; it derives its Hebrew name from its material, namely, the mingled water previously mentioned, from which it was made by a process of expansion outward, or augmentation. For that first and formless water was not abundant enough but was expanded through the Word. Similarly, Christ, through His blessing in the Gospel (Matt. 14:19), augments a few loaves to make them sufficient for a huge number of human beings.

So, then, what in philosophical terminology we call air with all its spheres here has the name "heaven." But by the term "waters" he means our waters, namely, the seas and the rivers, which also come from that first and formless water and are, as it were, the dregs which remained behind after the heaven had been made from it by the Word. I believe, moreover, that the quality of this water is far below that of the upper waters. These waters of ours are like dregs. Therefore it is stated that they are gathered together, not only in a place but also in a mass, because they are thicker than the waters of the air. For in the air we can breathe, but in water we cannot breathe.

That it says "in one place" collectively must rather be understood in a plural and distributive sense, as if you said: "In individual places or various places." Thus the entire quantity is not gathered in one ocean in one place; but there are many oceans and rivers, some lower and some higher, some larger and some smaller, etc.

And let the dry land appear.

These words must be noted, because above he said that the earth was a תהו and a בהו, that is, unimproved, crude, and formless, surrounded on all sides by water and mixed with water. Therefore here, too, He intimates that the mass of earth was submerged by the waters and was covered by them. Otherwise why would He say: "Let there appear," unless it was surrounded by the abyss and was completely covered by those first mistlike waters? This confirms again what we pointed out several times above: that the world which was created in the beginning was nothing else than crude water and earth, and only on the third day was the earth brought forth and made visible. And just as previously light was brought to the waters, so here the adornment of light is also brought to the earth. To become habitable, it had to be illumined as well as made dry.

He calls the earth dry because the waters had been removed. So we see the ocean seething miraculously, as if it were about to swallow up the entire earth. The sea stands out higher than the land, but it cannot pass over its limits. This statement at the first creation fixes the limits of the earth and establishes a most solid embankment against the sea. Likewise Job (Job 38:10) and the Psalmist (Ps. 104:9) bear witness that although the sea is higher and is not bounded by its own bounds, nevertheless it cannot range beyond what is permitted. In view of the fact that it is the center, the earth ought to be shut in and covered by the sea; but God holds back the sea by His Word and causes that surface to stand out to the extent necessary for habitation and for life.

Thus it happens through divine power that the waters do not pass over us, and until today and until the end of the world God performs for us the well-known miracle which He performed in the Red Sea for the people of Israel. At that time He displayed that might of His in a unique manner by an obvious miracle, in order that He might be worshiped with greater zeal by the small nation. For what is our entire life on this earth but a passage through the Red Sea, where on both sides the sea stood like high walls? Because it is very certain that the sea is far higher than the earth, God, up to the present time, commands the waters to remain in suspense and restrains them by His Word lest they burst upon us as they burst forth in the Deluge. But at times God gives providential signs, and entire islands perish by water, to show that the sea is in His hand and that He can either hold it in check or release it against the ungrateful and the evil.

The philosophers discourse also about the center of the world and the water that flows around it.[60] Indeed, it is remarkable that they have advanced to the point that they agree that the earth is the center of the entire creation. For from this it is deduced that the earth cannot fall, because it is hemmed in on the inside from everywhere by the remaining spheres. The heaven and the rest of the spheres support themselves on the center. Therefore they, too, are permanent. All this is worth knowing. But what the philosophers do not know is that this permanence is entirely the result of the power of the Word of God. Therefore even though the water is higher, still it cannot leave its bounds and cover the earth. Yet we live and breathe just as the Children of Israel did in the midst of the Red Sea.

10. *And God saw that it was good.*

Here Moses adds this favorable comment in spite of the fact that nothing had been done beyond the separating of the waters and the bringing forth of the insignificant bit of earth. Above he did not add this brief statement to a most beautiful part of the works of God. Perhaps this is because God wanted to indicate to us that He was more concerned about our dwelling place than about His own, and thus to arouse our gratitude. We were not to live in the air or in the heaven but on the earth, where we were to support our life with food and drink.

So, then, after He has prepared the roof of this building, namely,

[60] See the tables referred to on p. 26, note 42.

the heaven, and has added light, He now also gets ready a piece of ground and brings forth the earth, fit for the habitation and activity of mankind. That this work is pleasing to Him he says twice on our account. So much does He care about us that He also reassures us concerning the future. He promises that He will continue to be greatly concerned about this structure which He has so carefully erected, and that He will be close at hand and ward off the enemy and most certain death, namely, the water. Thus He makes a superb beginning with the foundations and the roof of this house. Now let us see how He also adorns it.

11. *And God said: Let the earth sprout herbage that is green and produces seed, and fruit trees.*

He has built the first parts of the house. It has a most elegant roof, the heaven, though this is not yet fully adorned. Its foundation is the earth. Its walls on every side are the seas. Now He also makes provision for our sustenance, so that the earth brings forth herbs and trees of all kinds. Here again you see why above he called the earth תהו and בהו, namely, because it was not only dark and mixed with waters but was also without any fruits and barren.

You see also what sort of food He provides for us, namely, herbs and fruits of the trees. Hence I believe that our bodies would have been far more durable if the practice of eating all sorts of food — particularly, however, the consumption of meat — had not been introduced after the Deluge. Even though the earth was cursed after Adam's sin and later on, at the time of the Deluge, had also become very corrupt, nevertheless a diet of herbs rather than of meat would be far finer today. Indeed, it is clear that at the beginning of the world herbs served as food and were created for this use, that they might be food for man.

So, then, the fact that the earth brings forth grain, trees, and all sorts of herbs is the work of its kind. Now indeed everything is produced from seed of its kind. But the first creation without seed was brought about simply as a result of the power of the Word. However, the fact that seeds now grow is also a work of creation full of wonderment. It is a unique property that a seed corn which falls on the ground comes up in due time and brings fruit according to its kind. A sure proof that the creation is not fortuitous but the exclusive work of divine foresight is the fact that similar plants are brought forth from similar plants in uninterrupted sequence. Thus from wheat is produced nothing but wheat, from barley nothing but barley, and from rye nothing but rye. Perpetually the same inherent character, the process of development, and the nature of the individual kinds are preserved unimpaired.

Philosophy does not know the cause of these phenomena and ascribes them to nature. But we know that nature was so created through the Word that the seeds and the kinds of plants are preserved. Thus not only the waters in the heaven were increased; but also the first seeds were increased, and they preserve their kind exactly.

Here the question is raised about the time of the year when the world was created, whether in spring or in fall.[61] Although opinions vary, each group has its conjectures. Those who favor fall support their opinion with the argument that the trees produced fruit, for Adam and Eve ate the fruits of trees. In proof of their view they further submit that God's works are finished. Others favor springtime, because then the year is most delightful; and this is, at it were, the time of the infancy or childhood of the world. Hence the poet also writes that spring was the beginning of the nascent world.[62]

But neither side has adequate reasons; for the text supports either of the two views, stating both that the earth sprouted (which surely is not a matter of fall but of spring) and that at that time fruits were available. Therefore we declare that it was a miracle of the first world that suddenly all these plants came into existence in such a way that the earth sprouted and the trees bloomed, and suddenly also fruits followed. This miracle came to an end at that time. For those kinds, as they were created at that time, are now reproduced through seeds. Therefore it is fallacious to argue from the natural working to the supernatural. It must be granted that in the first work of creation the Creator speeded up the functions of spring and fall so far as the herbs and the fruits of the trees were concerned.

Furthermore, this is the reason which induced Hilary and others to maintain that the world came into existence suddenly in a finished

---

[61] Lyra cites two groups of rabbinical exegetes on this question: basing its interpretation on the sprouting referred to in the text, one group ("Rabbi Joshua and his followers") maintains that the world was created in March and cites Ex. 12:2 in support of this interpretation; starting from the fruits referred to in the text, the second group ("Rabbi Eliezer and his followers") prefers September as the month of creation and cites Deut. 32:4 in support of this interpretation (Gen. 1:11, sec. "d").

[62] This is another of the classical quotations which Peter Meinhold ascribes to the editors of the lectures rather than to Luther (cf. Introduction, p. x).

state and that God did not make use of the space of six natural days
for His work of creation.[63] The text compels us to admit that the
trees, together with their fruits, were standing there on the day Adam
was created. Even though this may have been achieved more quickly
than is customary today (for among us almost half a year is necessary),
nevertheless the text makes use not only of a verb denoting "to bear
fruit" but also of a verb meaning "to sprout."

So far as the question propounded above is concerned, it is very
likely that it was spring when the world took its beginning. This is
also how the Jews begin their year; they make the springtime their
first month, when the earth is opened, as it were, and everything
bursts forth.

Here it is also asked when the fruitless or sterile trees were created,
likewise the sterile herbs. Although I have no conclusive answer,
I shall nevertheless give my opinion. I think that in the beginning all
trees were good and productive and that the beasts of the field,
together with Adam, had a common table, as it were, and lived on
rye, wheat, and other higher products of nature. There was also the
greatest abundance of all creatures.

But only after Adam's sin was it said to the earth that it should
produce thorns and thistles (Gen. 3:18). There is no doubt, therefore, that it is also a punishment for sin that we have so many trees
and herbs which have no use as food. Hence it happened, that some,
because of the blessing and overflowing supply of the first creation,
declared Paradise to be the entire earth. But the expulsion from
Paradise they declared to consist in this, that Adam was placed out
of this happy world among thorns, where often, even after much toil,
nothing worthwhile is produced. But a discussion of this matter will
follow below. So far as the question before us is concerned, I for my
person readily lean to the opinion that in the beginning all trees were
fruit-bearing.

The inquisitiveness of our people is vain.[64] At this point they even
discuss the reason why God provided the earth with fruit on the third
day, before he had equipped the heaven with stars. According to
them, this belongs rather to the work of the sixth day. As the heaven
began to be expanded before the earth was brought forth, so also it

63 See p. 4, note 8.

64 The text reads *odiosa*, "worthy of hate"; but with the Erlangen edition
we have conjectured the reading *otiosa*.

would be more consistent that the heaven be equipped earlier than the earth; thus the equipping of the earth belongs rather to the sixth day. Moreover, Lyra makes the subtle distinction that this was not an adornment but a characteristic.[65] I am undecided whether or not this is satisfactory. To me, as I said before, it seems more in place that the order of these events should not be viewed on the basis of our own judgment. Furthermore, was not the heaven adorned with light, which was created on the first day, something which was surely the most beautiful adornment of the entire creation?

Therefore I prefer that we reflect on the divine solicitude and benevolence toward us, because He provided such an attractive dwelling place for the future human being before the human being was created. Thus afterwards, when man is created, he finds a ready and equipped home into which he is brought by God and commanded to enjoy all the riches of so splendid a home. On the third day He provides kitchen and provisions. On the fourth, sun and moon are given to man for attendance and service. On the fifth the rule over the fish and the birds is turned over to him. On the sixth the rule over all the beasts is turned over to him, so that he might enjoy all this wealth free, in proportion to his need. And all this generosity is intended to make man recognize the goodness of God and live in the fear of God. This care and solicitude of God for us, even before we were created, may rightly and profitably be considered here; the rest of the ideas are without profit and even uncertain.

There is a similar beneficence of God toward us in His spiritual gifts. Before we were brought to faith, Christ, our Redeemer, is above in the Father's house; He prepares mansions so that when we arrive, we may find a heaven furnished with every kind of joy (John 14:2). Adam, therefore, when he was not yet created, was far less able to concern himself with his future welfare than we are; for he was not yet in existence. We, however, hear these promises given us by the Word of God. Therefore let us look upon the first state of this world as a type and figure of the future world; and so let us learn the kindness of God, who makes us rich and gives us wealth before we are able to concern ourselves with ourselves. It is far better to meditate and wonder at this concern, care, generosity, and benevolence of God, both in this life and in the one to come, than it is to speculate about why God began to equip the earth on the third day.

[65] Lyra on Gen. 1:14, sec. "f."

Let this be enough about the work of the third day, on which a home was made ready for man. Now follow the other days, on which we are also appointed masters of all creatures.

THE WORK OF THE FOURTH DAY

14. *And God said: Let there be luminaries in the heaven, and let them divide the day and the night.*

This is the work of the fourth day, on which those most beautiful creatures were created by the Word, namely, the sun and moon, together with all the rest of the stars. They were created not only so far as their substance and their masses are concerned but also so far as their blessing, that is, their function, power, and effects, are concerned.

You heard above that light was created on the first day. Until the fourth day this light took the place of the sun, of the moon, and of the rest of the stars; then, on the fourth day, the very originators and rulers of day and night were created.

Here, then, it is asked concerning this first light whether it disappeared again after the sun and the moon were created or remained with the sun.[66] Here there is a great variety of ideas and opinions. I for my part indeed simply believe that the procedure of all the works of God is the same. Thus on the first day the crude heaven and the crude earth were created and then perfected and made elegant, so that the heaven might be expanded and be adorned with light and that the earth, after it was brought forth from the waters, might be clad with trees and herbs. So I believe that the incipient and, as it were, crude light of the first day was perfected by the addition of new creatures: the sun, the moon, the stars, etc.

Others maintain that this first light continues to exist until now but is dimmed by the brightness of the sun, just as the moon and the stars in daytime are made dim by the sun. Both may be true, namely, that the first light remained and yet was the seed, as it were, of the sun and of the moon.

But Moses makes a difference and calls the sun and the moon the larger lights. The fact that the astronomers debate about the size of these bodies really has nothing to do with this passage. But this has something to do with the passage, that we observe that Scripture so designates these bodies, not on the basis of the magnitude of their masses but on the basis of the magnitude of their light. After all,

[66] See the comments of Lyra on Gen. 1:14.

even if you should make a comparison between the sun and the stars and put all the stars into one mass, the result will be a much larger mass indeed than that of the sun; but the stars will in no wise be equal to the light of the sun. By way of contrast, if the sun were cut apart into the smallest possible sections, those small parts would still far exceed the stars in brightness. For these bodies were so created with a difference, as we see from Paul's statement, that another is the brightness of the sun, another that of the moon, another that of the stars among themselves (1 Cor. 15:41). This difference exists not by reason of the bodies but by reason of the creation, that the work of creation may be the more miraculous. It is indeed something most worthy of wonderment that the rays of the sun are scattered over so great a length and width with such great speed, likewise with such great power to keep warm and to heat the bodies put under it.

The astronomers also assert that the stars are lighted, as it were, by the sun that they may shine.[67] They also say that the moon derives its light from the sun. This is really well proved at an eclipse of the moon, when the earth, intervening in a direct line between the sun and the moon, does not permit the light of the sun to pass to the moon. I do not deny or condemn these claims, but I declare it is by divine might that such power has been given to the sun that through its own light it also lights up the moon and the stars; likewise, that the moon and the stars were so created that they are receptive to the light which is sent out by the sun.

Augustine, in the beginning of what he says about Ps. 12, quotes two opinions about the moon; and from those discussions he seeks to derive an allegory dealing with the church, although he himself puts nothing down as sure.[68] But I am giving no consideration to these ideas, for the astronomers are the experts from whom it is most convenient to get what may be discussed about these subjects. For me it is enough that in those bodies, which are so elegant and necessary for our life, we recognize both the goodness of God and His power, that He created such important objects and preserves them to the present day for our use. These are views which are proper to our profession; that is, they are theological, and they have power to instill confidence in our hearts.

[67] Cf. *Luther's Works,* 22, p. 59, note 47.

[68] Augustine, *Enarratio in Psalmum X, Patrologia, Series Latina,* XXXVI, 131—133.

As for the views which are presented concerning the nature of these creatures — although very many are propounded with the likelihood of probability and are learned with profit — I am nevertheless aware that human reason is far too inadequate to be able to gain a perfect knowledge of these matters. For this reason the greatest minds, overwhelmed by the grandeur of these creatures, were unable to reach any other conclusion than that they are eternal and, as it were, some sort of deities. But whereas the philosophers assert that a star is a denser part of its orb, we assert with much greater certainty that it is a light created by God through His Word. Indeed, it is more likely that the bodies of the stars, like that of the sun, are round, and that they are fastened to the firmament like globes of fire, to shed light at night, each according to its endowment and its creation.

And let them be signs and times and days and years.

Moses' additional statement, "to divide day and night," refers to the distinction of the natural and the artificial day, which is also customary among the astronomers. For above he said: "Evening and morning became one day." There he is speaking of the natural day, which consists of twenty-four hours, during which the *primum mobile* revolves from east to west.[69] When God says here: "That they divide the day and the night," He is speaking of the artificial day, during which the sun is above the horizon.

Therefore this is the first function of the sun and of the moon, to be like kings and overseers of night and day. The stars are not called in for this task. But when the sun rises, it brings on the day even without the rest of the stars which are rising at that time. So the moon, too, without the stars, is the sovereign of the night and brings about night. This is the way it has been divinely created. Night and day alternate for the purpose of refreshing our bodies by rest. The sun shines that work may be done, but the moon has a dimmer light and so is more suited for sleep than for work.

What is the meaning of the words "that they may be for signs"? Lyra interprets the signs as those of rain and storms — something to which I do not greatly object, although I, too, doubt that these can be indicated in advance with the certainty with which Vergil and others write.[70] The Gospel declares the red dawn to be a sign of

[69] See p. 30, note 53.

[70] Lyra on Gen. 1:14, sec. "h"; Vergil, *Aeneid*, III, 516.

rain, and, in contrast, a clear evening to be a sign of clear weather (Matt. 16:2-3). Therefore so far as the claim is concerned that the rising of the Pleiades indicates rain and the like, I neither voice my utter disapproval nor express my direct agreement, because I see that these claims are not reliable in every instance.

I take the very simple sense of this passage to be that He is speaking, not of such rather insignificant signs but of more outstanding signs, such as the eclipses and the great conjunctions. Therefore the sign is the same as something unbelievable, something momentous or miraculous, by which God indicates to the world either His wrath or some misfortune. If this appears to be a rather crude interpretation, let us remember that Moses was writing for an unlearned people.

Here belong also the phenomena and effects which occur in the air, when stars appear to fall, when halos,[71] rainbows, and events similar to these occur in the air, etc. Moses calls "heaven" that entire watery mass in which the stars and the planets are borne along, likewise the uppermost region of the air. But that scheme of the spheres was thought out by later people for the purpose of teaching. Scripture knows nothing about them and simply says that the moon, the sun, and the stars were placed, not in individual spheres but in the firmament of the heaven (below and above which heaven are the waters), to be signs of future events, as we know from experience that eclipses, great conjunctions, and some other phenomena in the air are.

The expression "for times," לְמוֹעֲדִים, must also be noted. For מוֹעֵד denotes a fixed, definite, and certain time. Hence the noun is commonly used in the Bible for the Tabernacle of the Covenant, because here definite solemnities were observed in a precise place, at a precise time, and with precise rites. In this manner Moses states that the sun and the moon are for times, not only because the times are governed and noticeably changed by the sun (the way we see that the lower masses are subject to change either by the drawing near or by the receding of the sun; for in the winter, in the summer, in the fall, and in the spring there is a different kind of air, under the influence of which our bodies also change) but also because in our civil life we make use of other variations and signs of the times derived from the motion of those bodies. Thus at a certain time of the year houses are rented out, day laborers are hired, interests are collected, etc. All these are services which the sun and the moon render us, so that we divide

71 Seneca, *Quaestiones naturales*, I, 2, 1.

the times according to the tasks and other conveniences. Thus we count weeks, months, statute labor, as they call it, etc.

The following "and for days" denotes the natural day, when the sun revolves around the earth. That we count days and years is a benefit stemming from the creation and the divine direction. From this also comes the time which the philosophers call the numbering of motion.[72] This would be impossible if the upper bodies were not kept in motion in this fashion by a definite law but stood still in the same place. Where there is no number, there is no time either. Thus someone overcome by sleep does not know how long he is sleeping, because the ability to count has ceased.

We recall our early childhood to some extent; but we do not remember nursing at our mothers' breasts, although we did have life at that time. The reason is that we lacked the ability to count. This is also why beasts have no knowledge of time, just as infants have no knowledge of it either. Therefore counting indicates that man is an extraordinary creature of God. We see Augustine gladly extolling this endowment of our nature and proving the immortality of our souls from it, since man alone counts time and has an understanding of it.[73]

Here some raise a question concerning the future life: Will this service of the heavenly bodies come to an end? However, that future life will be without time; for the godly will have an eternal day; the wicked will have everlasting night and darkness. The sun brings about the day not only through its brightness and light but through its motion, by which it moves from the east to the west, while after twenty-four hours it rises again and thus brings about another day. Accordingly, the astronomers also count three useful qualities of the sun: its influence, its motion, and its light. Its influence I am not going to discuss in greater detail. It is enough for me to know that these bodies were created for our use, to serve us as signs either of wrath or of favor, and for times, that we may mark definite distinctions of time, etc. Because these facts are revealed by the sacred Scriptures, they are certain. Although the rest of the ideas have the support of experience, they are not so sure, because experience can be deceiving.

But here some are wont to ask questions concerning the predictions of the astrologers, which they base on, and prove from, this passage.

[72] Aristotle, *De caelo*, I, ch. 9.

[73] This may be a reference to the profound discussion of time and related questions in Augustine, *Confessions*, XI, chs. 11—31.

If someone should uphold them with less insistence, I for my part have no great objection. Geniuses must be allowed their pastime! Therefore if you put aside all superstition, it does not offend me greatly if anyone exercises his ingenuity in toying with those predictions.[74]

So far as this matter is concerned, however, I shall never be convinced that astrology should be numbered among the sciences. And I shall adhere to this opinion because astrology is entirely without proof. The appeal to experience has no effect on me. All the astrological experiences are purely individual cases. The experts have taken note of and recorded only those instances which did not fail; but they took no note of the rest of the attempts, where they were wrong and the results which they predicted as certain did not follow. Aristotle says that one swallow does not make a spring,[75] and so I do not believe that from such partial observations a science can be established. Hunters have a similar saying: A hunt may be carried on every day, but the hunt is not successful every day. The very same thing may be said of the astrologers and their predictions, because very often what they predict fails to come true.

Even if there were something sure about these predictions, what stupidity it is to be much concerned about the future! For granted that the future can be known through the astrological predictions — if they are bad, ignorance of them is certainly better in many respects than knowledge of them, as Cicero also declares.[76] An abiding fear of God and prayer are preferable to the fear of future events. But more of this elsewhere.

Therefore I think that the astrological predictions find no adequate support in this passage; for they are signs based on reason, so to speak; that is, they are gathered by reason. But it is more fitting, if we understand Moses concerning the signs which God shows, that men in general should either be warned or frightened by them.

Let these remarks about the fourth day suffice. But here the immortality of the soul begins to unfold and reveal itself to us, inasmuch as no creature apart from man can either understand the motion of the heaven or measure the heavenly bodies. A pig, a cow, and a dog are unable to measure the water they drink;

[74] Cf. Weimar, *Tischreden*, I, Nos. 855—858.

[75] Aristotle, *Nicomachean Ethics*, I, ch. 7.

[76] Cicero discusses astrology in his *De divinatione*, II, 88—99.

but man measures the heaven and all the heavenly bodies. And so here there gleams a spark of eternal life, in that the human being busies himself by nature with this knowledge of nature. This concern indicates that men were not created to live permanently in this lowest part of the universe but to take possession of heaven, because in this life they admire, and busy themselves with, the study of, and the concern about, heavenly things.

If this were not the case, what would have been the advantage of this knowledge, or why would it have been necessary to give it to man, whose very posture and physique strongly indicate that he belongs to the heavenly things despite his wretched and humble origin? The first human being was made from a clod by God. Then the human race began to be propagated from the male and female semen, from which the embryo is gradually formed in the womb, limb by limb; and it grows, until at last, through birth, man is brought out into the light of day. Thereafter begins the life of sensation, and soon that of action and motion.

When the body has gained strength, and mind and reason are fully developed in a sound body — only then does there come a gleam of the life of the intellect, which does not exist in other earthly creatures. With the support of the mathematical disciplines — which no one can deny were divinely revealed — the human being, in his mind, soars high above the earth; and leaving behind those things that are on the earth, he concerns himself with heavenly things and explores them. Cows, pigs, and other beasts do not do this; it is man alone who does it. Therefore man is a creature created to inhabit the celestial regions and to live an eternal life when, after a while, he has left the earth. For this is the meaning of the fact that he can not only speak and form judgments (things which belong to dialectics and rhetoric) but also learns all the sciences thoroughly.

Now, therefore, from this fourth day our glory begins to be revealed: that God gives thought to making a creature which may understand the motion of the bodies created on the fourth day and may take delight in that knowledge as part of his nature. All these facts should stir us to an expression of thanks. By citizenship we belong to that homeland which we now look at, admire, and understand, yet like strangers and exiles; but after this life we shall look at these things more closely and understand them perfectly.

So far, then, we have been hearing of lifeless and insensible creatures. Nevertheless, some of the philosophers have spoken about the stars and the heavenly bodies as if these were endowed with life and reason. I think that this happened because of the motion, which is so logical and stable, unlike anything else among the other physical substances. Therefore they said that they were made up of mass and intellect, and yet that their mass is not like that of an element. In his *Timaeus* Plato discourses in this manner.[77]

But this opinion must be entirely rejected, and our intellect must adjust itself to the Word of God and to Holy Scripture, which plainly teaches that God created all these things in order to prepare a house and an inn, as it were, for the future man, and that He governs and preserves these creatures by the power of His Word, by which He also created them. Finally, then, after everything that belongs to the essence of a house is ready, man is brought, as it were, into his possession that we may learn that the divine providence for us is greater than all our own anxiety and care. Other ideas, which are advanced without the support of Scripture, must be rejected.

Here I have considered it necessary to repeat the principle I mentioned several times above, namely, that one must accustom oneself to the Holy Spirit's way of expression. With the other sciences, too, no one is successful unless he has first duly learned their technical language. Thus lawyers have their terminology, which is unfamiliar to physicians and philosophers. On the other hand, these also have their own sort of language, which is unfamiliar to the other professions. Now no science should stand in the way of another science, but each should continue to have its own mode of procedure and its own terms.

Thus we see that the Holy Spirit also has His own language and way of expression, namely, that God, by speaking, created all things and worked through the Word, and that all His works are some words of God, created by the uncreated Word. Therefore just as a philosopher employs his own terms, so the Holy Spirit, too, employs His. An astronomer, therefore, does right when he uses the terms "spheres," "apsides," and "epicycles"; they belong to his profession and enable him to teach others with greater ease.[78] By way of contrast, the Holy Spirit and Holy Scripture know nothing about those designations and

[77] See also p. 4, note 6.

[78] This sounds like a reflection of what Immanuel Kant calls "the conflict of the faculties," when specialists in one area lampooned the jargon of specialists in another; we know from contemporary reports that this went on at Wittenberg too.

call the entire area above us "heaven." Nor should an astronomer find fault with this; let each of the two speak in his own terminology.

So also the word "time" must be understood in this passage. "Time" does not have the same meaning for the Hebrew and the philosopher; but for the Hebrew the word "time" denotes theologically fixed festivals, likewise intervals of days which make up a year. For this reason it is translated almost everywhere with the noun "feast" or "festival," except when the text deals with the tabernacle. I consider this warning to be in place before we proceed, and I believe that this maxim is useful: Every science should make use of its own terminology, and one should not for this reason condemn the other or ridicule it; but one should rather be of use to the other, and they should put their achievements at one another's disposal. This is what craftsmen do to maintain the whole city which, as Aristotle says, cannot be composed of a physician and another physician but of a physician and a farmer.[79]

THE WORK OF THE FIFTH DAY

20. *God also said: Let the waters bring forth creeping thing of living soul, and winged being that flies.*

We see that Moses consistently adheres to his method of expression in the verb "to say." So far, then, he has told about the higher creatures and about the heaven, with its entire host of planets and the rest of the stars, which God brought forth from the water by His Word. Then He added light, the way we see this air bright through its inherent light.

Now he adds something about new creatures brought forth from the waters, namely, the birds and the fish. He combines these two kinds because of their similar nature. As the fish swims in water, so the bird flies in the air; and although they have different flesh, they have the same beginning. Here the text is clear, that after the birds had been brought forth from the water, they took to the air in which they live. Moreover, Moses continues to use his method of expression in that he calls "heaven" all that is above.

In the first place, it is amazing that although birds and fish were created from the same matter, nevertheless, just as a bird cannot live in water, so fish cannot survive if they are in the air. Physicians correctly declare that the flesh of birds is more healthful than that

---

[79] Aristotle, *Nicomachean Ethics*, V, ch. 5.

of fish (although birds, too, are of a watery nature), because they live in the thinner air, of which the waters in which the fish come into being and live are the thicker lees, as it were; on the other hand, philosophers put no faith in this. But for us the trustworthiness of Holy Scripture is greater, and it declares that each of the two beings had the same beginning.

So this also belongs to the grandeur of this book which in such various ways reveals to us the power of God through which He created all things by a method surpassing all reason and understanding. Who could conceive of the possibility of bringing forth from the water a being which clearly could not continue to exist in water? But God speaks a mere Word, and immediately the birds are brought forth from the water. If the Word is spoken, all things are possible, so that out of the water are made either fish or birds. Therefore any bird whatever and any fish whatever are nothing but nouns in the divine rule of language; through this rule of language those things that are impossible become very easy, while those that are clearly opposite become very much alike, and vice versa.

These things are written down and must be carefully learned that we may learn to be filled with wonderment at the power of the Divine Majesty and from those wonderful deeds build up our faith. Nothing — even raising the dead — is comparable to the wonderful work of producing a bird out of water. We do not wonder at these things, because through our daily association with them we have lost our wonderment. But if anyone believes them and regards them more attentively, he is compelled to wonder at them, and his wonderment gradually strengthens his faith. Since God is able to bring forth from the water the heaven and the stars, the size of which either equals or surpasses that of the earth; likewise, since He is able out of a droplet of water to create sun and moon, could He not also defend my body against enemies and Satan or, after it has been placed in the grave, revive it for a new life? Therefore we must take note of God's power that we may be completely without doubt about the things which God promises in His Word. Here full assurance is given concerning all His promises; nothing is either so difficult or so impossible that He could not bring it about by His Word. The heaven, the earth, the sea, and whatever is in them prove that this is true.

Here we must deal also with what the holy fathers, and Augustine in particular, have noted, namely, that Moses employs these three words — "God said," "He made," "He saw" — as if in this manner he wanted to point to the three Persons of the Divine Majesty.[80] By the term "He said" the Father is denoted. He begets the Word in eternity and in time establishes this world through that Word. Therefore they have attributed the verb "made" to the Person of the Son. The Son has in Himself not only the image of the Divine Majesty but also the image of all created things. Therefore He bestows existence on things. Just as the objects are spoken by the Father, so all things have their existence through the Son and the Word of the Father. To these, however, is joined the Third Person, the Holy Spirit, who "sees" the created things and approves them.

The statements which beautifully and suitably assign these verbs were made for the purpose of understanding the doctrine of the Trinity more clearly. The sole reason why these helps were piously thought out by the holy fathers was this, to make somewhat comprehensible a matter which in itself is beyond comprehension. Therefore I do not find fault with those thoughts, since they are in accordance with the faith and are suitable and useful for strengthening and teaching our faith.

St. Hilary makes this distinction by means of other attributes: Eternity is in the Father; the form, in the image; the use, in the gift.[81] He says that the Holy Spirit is a gift in the use because He grants the use of the things that they may not perish, and governs the things and preserves them. Likewise, they say: "The Father is the mind; the Son, the intellect; the Holy Spirit, the will." [82] They do not mean that the Father is without intellect or that the Son is without will; but they are attributes, that is, statements which separately are assigned not to individual Persons but to several. Nor do they wish to say that the Father is without wisdom, but they speak thus because we picture these matters to ourselves this way in order to remember and explain the doctrine of the Trinity.

Therefore when the text says: "And God saw that it was very good," it refers to the preservation itself, because the creature could not continue in existence unless the Holy Spirit delighted in it and preserved the work through this delight of God in His work. God did not create things with the idea of abandoning them after they had been created, but He loves them and expresses His approval of

---

80 Augustine, *De Genesi ad litteram,* II, ch. 6, p. 40.

81 This seems to be quoted via Augustine, *On the Trinity,* VI, ch. 10.

82 Augustine, *On the Trinity,* X, chs. 11, 12.

them. Therefore He is together with them. He sets in motion, He moves, and He preserves each according to its own manner. I thought that this should be mentioned in brief words. It is worthwhile to learn these pious thoughts of those who have preceded us on the same course we are running now.

What Jerome translates as "creeping thing of living soul" [83] is נֶפֶשׁ for the Hebrews and denotes a soul or something living. But Moses designates the fish by this name. Concerning the birds it is known that they are like amphibia, inasmuch as they live on land and in the air.

21. *And God created great sea animals.*

The question can be raised here why he mentions only the sea monsters by name. Similarly the Scripture rarely makes mention of any but the larger fish. Familiar are the leviathan and the dragons in Job and in other passages of Scripture.[84] But it is certain that this is the name given to whales, dolphins, and other larger fish, some of which have something similar to wings, like the dolphin, which is like a king of the ocean, although he does not surpass others in size. For that matter, neither the eagle, king of birds, nor the lion, king of the quadrupeds, surpasses others in size.

I believe the reason for this is that we should know that such ·large bodies are the works of God, lest we be frightened by their size and believe that they are apparitions. Then it is easy to conclude that since such large bodies were created by God, the smaller fish (such as herring, trout, carp, and others) were also created by God. Let him who wishes read chapter forty-one of Job. There it is clearly noted how the Holy Spirit, through that poet, praises the amazing monster leviathan, whose strength and courage is such that it takes no notice even of arrows. Descriptions of this kind open our eyes and buoy up our faith that we may more readily believe that God can preserve us too, even though we are far smaller beings.

Here questions are raised also about the mice and the dormice, whence they originate and how. Indeed, we have learned from experience that not even ships which are continually floating on the sea are safe from mice. Likewise, no house can be so thoroughly cleaned that no mice are produced in it. We can also inquire about

[83] Jerome's rendition is: *Reptile animae viventis.*

[84] The reference is to Job 41:1; Ps. 74:14; Ps. 104:26; Is. 27:1 and to passages like Job 30:29 and Ps. 44:19.

the manner in which flies come into existence. Likewise, where the birds go in fall.

But so far as mice are concerned, Aristotle states that certain animals are produced by their like, others by their unlike.[85] Thus mice belong to the kind produced by their unlike, because mice originate not from mice alone but also from decay, which is used up and gradually turns into a mouse.

If you should ask by what power such a generation takes place, Aristotle has the answer that the decayed moisture is kept warm by the heat of the sun and that in this way a living being is produced, just as we see dung beetles being brought into existence from horse manure. I doubt that this is a satisfactory explanation. The sun warms; but it would bring nothing into being unless God said by His divine power: "Let a mouse come out of the decay." Therefore the mouse, too, is a divine creature and, in my judgment, of a watery nature and, as it were, a land bird; otherwise it would have the form of a monster, and its kind would not be preserved. But for its kind it has a very beautiful form — such pretty feet and such delicate hair that it is clear that it was created by the Word of God with a definite plan in view. Therefore here, too, we admire God's creation and workmanship. The same thing may be said about flies.

About birds I surely have no knowledge. It is not likely that they go to regions lying more toward the south, inasmuch as from experience it has been learned that the swallows lie dead in the waters throughout the winter and return to life at springtime. This is truly a weighty proof of our resurrection. Therefore I think that birds are preserved either in trees or in waters. These works of the Divine Majesty are plainly miraculous. So we see them, and yet we do not understand them. But I think that even if someday a species should perish (but I doubt that this can happen), it would nevertheless be replaced by God.

Thus there belong to the creation of the fifth day all the creeping, gliding, and flying beings, and such as move by any other method, either in the air or in the water.

21. 22. *And God saw that it was good, and He blessed them.*

Why didn't God use the word "bless" also in connection with the inanimate bodies? There He merely said that they pleased Him, but He did not bless them. However, when we get to the generation

---

[85] This appears to be a reference to Aristotle, *Historia animalium*, VI, ch. 37.

of living bodies, then He initiates a new method of growth and increase. As we see, the sun and the stars do not beget similar bodies from themselves, while the herbs and trees have this blessing that they may grow and produce fruit. But it is in no wise similar to this present blessing of the living bodies.

By the word "blessing," therefore, Moses separates the bodies which were created earlier from the living bodies created on the fifth day, because here there is a new method of procreation. For from a living body are produced separate offspring, which also live. This certainly does not happen in the case of trees or in the case of herbs; unless these are sown again, they do not bear fruit, and seed is not directly produced from seed but from the plant. But here there is procreation from a living body into a living body. This, therefore, is a new work, that a living body grows and multiplies out of its own body. What the pear tree produces is not a pear tree but a pear. But here what the bird produces is a bird, and what a fish produces is a fish. Truly miraculous and great in number is the increase of each of the two species, and boundless their fertility; especially is this so in the case of the marine and aquatic creatures.

What, then, is the reason for this remarkable procreation? The hen lays an egg; this she keeps warm while a living body comes into being in the egg, which the mother later on hatches. The philosophers advance the reason that these events take place through the working of the sun and her belly. I grant this. But the theologians say, far more reliably, that these events take place through the working of the Word, because it is said here: "He blessed them and said: 'Increase and multiply.'" This Word is present in the very body of the hen and in all living creatures; the heat with which the hen keeps her eggs warm is the result of the divine Word, because if it were without the Word, the heat would be useless and without effect.

Therefore because of this miraculous creation God adds the blessing of fruitful bodies. Here one can observe what the blessing really is, namely, the increase. As for ourselves, when we bless, we do nothing else than express our good wishes; what we wish, we are unable to bestow. But God's blessing announces an increase and is effective immediately. Likewise, in contrast, His curse, involves a decrease. This, too, is effective.

Here, then, Moses' terminology must again be noted. What he calls a blessing the philosophers call fertility, that is to say, a state in which sound and living bodies are brought forth by sound and living bodies. Nothing like this happens among the trees; no tree produces anything similar to itself, but it produces seed, etc. This is a great miracle; but, like the rest, so this one has also become commonplace through experience.

Here someone asks about harmful worms or vermin, such as toads, flies, butterflies, among which there is an amazing fertility. It happens as a rule that the more harmful one is, the greater its fertility is. But this question must be postponed until the third chapter.[86] I believe that at this time those troublesome and harmful creatures were not yet in existence but were brought into being later on out of the cursed earth as a punishment for sin, to afflict us and to compel us to call upon God. But this will be dealt with elsewhere.

So now we have the living creatures that were created on the fifth day. We see that the Word of this day is effective until now because fish are brought into existence directly out of the water. Ponds and lakes generate fish, since we see that carps have been brought forth in ponds in which there were none before. The tall story is told that fish caught by birds had dropped their seed into ponds and lakes while they were being carried along in the air and that this then grew in the waters. To me this does not seem likely. But the sole and true reason is that here the water is commanded to bring forth fish. This Word is still effective and brings about these results.

THE SIXTH DAY

24. *And God said: Let the earth bring forth living soul according to its kind.*

We now have the heaven with its hosts, the sun, the moon, the stars; likewise, the sea with the fish and the birds. As the fish swim in the water, so birds swim, as it were, in the air. To the earth were also added the adornments of fruits, trees, herbs, etc. Even before man is brought into this quasi home, the land animals are added, the beasts of burden and the reptiles, after which man is created. He is not made to fly with the birds or to swim with the fish; but he shares with the rest of the living things the common characteristic, so far as this side is concerned, that he spends his life on land. The use of ships, whereby the human being endeavors to imitate the fish and the birds, is an invention. Indeed, a ship does both: it sails in the air,

[86] Cf. p. 204.

and it swims in the water. But here we are speaking of natural situations, not of invented ones.

The Hebrews make a distinction in their terms. They call בְּהֵמָה what we call beasts of burden; likewise, the smaller beasts of the forest, such as deer, roes, hares, and whatever others there may be, which use the same food with us and support themselves by means of herbs and the fruits of the trees. חַיְתוֹ־אֶרֶץ (which is correctly translated by "beasts of earth"), however, they say are the flesh-eating animals, such as wolves, lions, and bears. I do not know whether this is an unvarying distinction; to me indeed it does not seem to be consistently carried through.[87] However, this much is sure: that here Moses wants to include all the land animals, whether they live on flesh or on herbs. The mother of all these, he says, is the earth, which brought them forth out of itself through the Word, just as the sea brought forth fish.

But we heard above that God said to the water: "Let the water be set in motion," so that by this motion the sea might be filled with fish and the air with birds, and that only later on was the ability to procreate added. Here, in connection with the land animals, He employs a different word and says: "Let the earth bring forth." He does not say: "Let it be moved"; for the earth is a body which is at rest. For the same reason He also said on the fourth day: "Let the earth bring forth herbs"; for He wants it to send forth animals and herbs without motion.

Even though Scripture makes no definite statement as to whether these animals were formed from a clod, as man was, or burst forth suddenly, nevertheless, because Moses describes the formation of man solemnly and with a special purpose in mind, I hold that the land animals had an origin like that of the fish, which were suddenly brought into being in the sea. The reason why he does not add the blessing here is obvious. Below he includes these together with man, and now it was sufficient to say: "God saw that it was very good." Now let us proceed to the last and most beautiful work of God, the creation of man.

26. *Let Us make a man according to Our image and likeness.*

Here again Moses employs a new expression. He does not say: "Let the sea be set in motion," "Let the earth bring forth herbs,"

---

[87] In Deut. 28:26 and Is. 18:6, for example, בְּהֵמָה is used for carnivorous beasts.

or "Let it bring forth." He says: "Let Us make." Therefore he includes an obvious deliberation and plan; he did nothing similar in the case of the earlier creatures. There, without any deliberation and counsel, He said: "Let the sea be put in motion," "Let the earth produce," etc. But here, when He wants to create man, God summons Himself to a council and announces some sort of deliberation.

Therefore, in the first place, there is indicated here an outstanding difference between man and all the other creatures. The beasts greatly resemble man. They dwell together; they are fed together; they eat together; they receive their nourishment from the same materials; they sleep and rest among us. Therefore if you take into account their way of life, their food, and their support, the similarity is great.

But here Moses points out an outstanding difference between these living beings and man when he says that man was created by the special plan and providence of God. This indicates that man is a creature far superior to the rest of the living beings that live a physical life, especially since as yet his nature had not become depraved. Epicurus holds the opinion that man was created solely to eat and drink. But this is equivalent to making no difference between man and the rest of the beasts, which also have their desires and follow them. Here the text definitely sets man apart when it says that in a special deliberation God gave consideration to the creation of man, and not only that but also to making him in the image of God. This image is something far different from the concern of the belly, namely, food and drink, things for which the beasts also have understanding and appreciation.

Moses, therefore, indicates to those who are spiritually minded that we were created for a better life in the future than this physical life would have been, even if our nature had remained unimpaired. Therefore the scholars put it well: "Even if Adam had not fallen through his sin, still, after the appointed number of saints had been attained, God would have translated them from this animal life to the spiritual life." [88] Adam was not to live without food, drink, and procreation. But at a predetermined time, after the number of saints had become full, these physical activities would have come to an end; and Adam, together with his descendants, would have been translated to the eternal and spiritual life. Nevertheless, these activities of physical life — like eating, drinking, procreating, etc. — would have

[88] Cf. Peter Lombard, *Sententiarum libri quatuor*, II, Dist. XX, *Patrologia, Series Latina*, CXCII, 692—694.

been a service pleasing to God; we could also have rendered this service to God without the defect of the lust which is there now after sin, without any sin, and without the fear of death. This would have surely been a pleasant and delightful life, a life about which we may indeed think but which we may not attain in this life. But this we have, that we believe in a spiritual life after this life and a destination for this life in Paradise, which was devised and ordained by God, and that we confidently look for it through the merit of Christ.

Attention should, therefore, be given to the text before us, in which the Holy Spirit dignifies the nature of man in such a glorious manner and distinguishes it from all other creatures. His physical or animal life was, indeed, to be similar to that of the beasts. Just as the beasts have need of food, drink, and rest to refresh their bodies, so Adam, even in his innocence, would make use of them. But what is added — that man was created for his physical life in such a way that he was nevertheless made according to the image and likeness of God — this is an indication of another and better life than the physical.

Thus Adam had a twofold life: a physical one and an immortal one, though this was not yet clearly revealed, but only in hope. Meanwhile he would have eaten, he would have drunk, he would have labored, he would have procreated, etc. In brief words I want to call attention to these facts concerning the difference which God makes through His counsel, by which He sets us apart from the rest of the animals with whom He lets us live. Below we shall deal again with these matters at greater length.

In the second place, the word "Let Us make" is aimed at making sure the mystery of our faith, by which we believe that from eternity there is one God and that there are three separate Persons in one Godhead: the Father, the Son, and the Holy Spirit. The Jews indeed try in various ways to get around this passage, but they advance nothing sound against it. This passage bothers them to death, to use an expression of Occam, who applies it to irksome and difficult problems which he cannot solve.[89]

The Jews, then, say that God is speaking thus with the angels, likewise with the earth and with other creatures.[90] But I for my part ask: Why did He not also do this previously? In the second place:

---

[89] William of Occam (ca. 1300—ca. 1349) was a critic of Thomistic scholasticism who influenced Luther's thought.

[90] Lyra quotes this exegesis from a "Rabbi Eben Ezra" (Gen. 1:26).

What concern is the creation of man to the angels? In the third place: He does not mention the angels but simply says: "We." Therefore He is speaking of makers and creators. This certainly cannot be said of the angels.

In the fourth place, this is also sure: that it cannot be said in any way that we were created according to the image of the angels. In the fifth place, here both appear: "Let Us make" and "He made," in the plural and in the singular; thereby Moses clearly and forcibly shows us that within and in the very Godhead and the Creating Essence there is one inseparable and eternal plurality. This not even the gates of hell (Matt. 16:18) can take from us.

Next, when the Jews say that God is speaking with the earth concerning the earth, this is also worthless. For the earth is not our maker. Moreover, why didn't He rather speak to the sun, since Aristotle says: "Man and the sun bring man into existence." [91] But this does not fit either, because we were not made according to the image of the earth; but we were made according to the image of those Makers who say "Let Us make." These Makers are three separate Persons in one divine essence. Of these three Persons we are the image, as we shall hear later.

It is utterly ridiculous when the Jews say that God is following the custom of princes, who, to indicate respect, speak of themselves in the plural number. The Holy Spirit is not imitating this court mannerism (to give it this name); nor does Holy Scripture sanction this manner of speech. Consequently, this is a sure indication of the Trinity, that in one divine essence there are three Persons: the Father, the Son, and the Holy Spirit. Not even so far as Their activity is concerned, therefore, is God separated, because all three Persons here co-operate and say: "Let Us make." The Father does not make one man and the Son another, nor the Son one man and the Holy Spirit another; but the Father, the Son, and the Holy Spirit, one and the same God, is the Author and Creator of the same work.

Nor is it possible in this manner to divide God subjectively,[92] for the Father is not known except in the Son and through the Holy Spirit. Therefore as there is one God objectively, so also subjectively; nevertheless, within Himself, so far as His substance or essence is

[91] Apparently a reference to Aristotle, *De generatione et corruptione*, II, ch. 10.

[92] Because of a shift in the antithesis of subject and object that took place during the seventeenth and eighteenth centuries, the term *obiective* used here must be translated with "subjectively" rather than with "objectively."

concerned, He is Father, Son, and Holy Spirit, three distinct Persons in one Godhead.

These evidences should be precious to us and welcome. Even though both Jews and Turks laugh at us because we are convinced that there is one God and that there are three Persons, nevertheless, unless they are brazen enough to deny the authority of Scripture, they are compelled by this passage and also by those quoted above to adopt our conviction. They may scoff at these ideas, as the Jews zealously do; but meanwhile there remains in their hearts that little sting: "Why should He say 'Let Us make'?" Likewise: "Why should Moses employ the plural noun אֱלֹהִים?" These thoughts they cannot shut out from their minds, even though they can make the attempt and raise questions of various kinds. If it were a matter of intelligence to scoff at such evidences, you don't think, do you, that we lack the ability to do the same thing? But among us the authority of Scripture is too great, especially since the New Testament points this out even more clearly. The Son, who is in the bosom of the Father (John 1:18), teaches us the same fact much more clearly; and not to believe Him is the utmost blasphemy and eternal death. Therefore away with those utterly blinded corrupters of the divine doctrines until the time of their judgment!

But, you say, these evidences are too dark to prove so important an article of faith. I answer: At that time these statements had to be made so darkly by divine counsel, or at least because all things were reserved for that future Lord for whose arrival was reserved the restitution of all things (Acts 3:21), of all knowledge, and of all revelations. Therefore what had previously been taught through enigmas, as it were, Christ made clear and commanded to be preached in plain language. And yet the holy patriarchs had this knowledge through the Holy Spirit, although not with such clarity as now, when we hear mentioned in the New Testament the Father, the Son, and the Holy Spirit. When Christ came, those seals had to be broken; and what had been communicated in dark words previously, solely out of respect for the future Teacher, had to be preached plainly. If the Holy Spirit had not postponed this clear knowledge to the time of the New Testament, the Arians would have existed long before the birth of Christ. And so in the last days the Holy Spirit wanted to confront the devil with this sun of knowledge, to put a bandage over his eyes, to make him envy men even more for this clear knowledge, and so to torture him still more.

In the third place, there is stirred up here, as it were, a sea of questions: What is that image of God according to which Moses says that man was made? Augustine has much to say in his explanation of this passage, particularly in his book *On the Trinity*.[93] Moreover, the remaining doctors in general follow Augustine, who keeps Aristotle's classification: that the image of God is the powers of the soul — memory, the mind or intellect, and will.[94] These three, they say, comprise the image of God which is in all men. Just as in the divine relationships, they say, the Word is begotten from the substance of the Father and the Holy Spirit is the delight of the Father, so, in the case of man, from the memory comes forth the word of the heart, which is the mind. When this has been brought forth, the will brings out that which it sees as mind and is delighted by it.

Moreover, they say that the similitude lies in the gifts of grace.[95] Just as a similitude is a certain perfection of an image, so, they say, our nature is perfected through grace. And so the similitude of God consists in this, that the memory is provided with hope, the intellect with faith, and the will with love. In this way, they say, man is created according to the image of God; that is, he has a mind, a memory, and a will. Likewise, man is created according to the similitude of God; that is, the intellect is enlightened by faith, the memory is made confident through hope and steadfastness, and the will is adorned with love.

In the third place, they also make other divisions, namely, that the memory is the image of the power of God, the mind of His wisdom, and the will of His justice, etc. In this manner Augustine chiefly, and others after him, have exerted themselves to think out different kinds of trinities in man; for they believed that in this way the image of God could more easily be beheld. Although these not unattractive speculations point conclusively to keen and leisurely minds, they contribute very little toward the correct explanation of the image of God.

Therefore although I do not condemn or find fault with that effort and those thoughts by which everything is brought into relationship with the Trinity, I am not at all sure that they are very useful, espe-

[93] Augustine, *On the Trinity*, IX—XI.

[94] See p. 50, note 82.

[95] This distinction between "image" and "similitude," which are parallels in the Hebrew text, goes back at least to Irenaeus, *Against Heresies*, V, ch. 6, par. 1.

cially when they are subsequently spun out further; for there is also added a discussion concerning free will, which has its origin in that image. This is what they maintain: God is free; therefore since man is created according to the image of God, he also has a free memory, mind, and will. In this way many statements are carelessly made, statements that are either not properly expressed or later on are understood in a wicked way. Thus this was the origin of the dangerous opinion that in governing men God permits them to act under their own impulse. From this assertion came many inconvenient ideas. It is similar to the quotation: "God, who created you without you, will not save you without you." [96] From here the conclusion was drawn that free will co-operated as the preceding and efficient cause of salvation.[97] No different is the assertion of Dionysius, though more dangerous than the former, when he says that although the demons and the human beings fell, nevertheless their natural endowments, such as the mind, memory, will, etc., remained unimpaired.[98] But if this is true, it follows that by the powers of his nature man can bring about his own salvation.

These very dangerous opinions of the fathers were discussed in all the churches and schools, but I really do not see what the fathers intended to achieve by them. Therefore my advice is to read them with discretion. They often speak as the result of an emotion and of a particular mood which we do not have and cannot have, since we do not have similar situations. And so the inexperienced appropriate everything without discrimination, in the sense they give to it and not in the one the fathers had. But I pass over these things and return to the subject.

I am afraid that since the loss of this image through sin we cannot understand it to any extent. Memory, will, and mind we have indeed; but they are most depraved and most seriously weakened, yes, to put it more clearly, they are utterly leprous and unclean. If these powers are the image of God, it will also follow that Satan was created according to the image of God, since he surely has these natural endowments, such as memory and a very superior intellect and a most determined will, to a far higher degree than we have them.

[96] This is an Augustinian aphorism.

[97] The efficient cause is "that from which the change or the resting from change first begins," Aristotle, *Metaphysics*, V, ch. 2.

[98] Cf. *Luther's Works*, 13, p. 110, note 55.

Therefore the image of God is something far different, namely, a unique work of God. If some assert nevertheless that these powers are that image, let them admit that they are, as it were, leprous and unclean. Similarly, we still call a leprous human being a human being even though in his leprous flesh everything is almost dead and without sensation, except that he is rather violently excited to lust.

Therefore the image of God, according to which Adam was created, was something far more distinguished and excellent, since obviously no leprosy of sin adhered either to his reason or to his will. Both his inner and his outer sensations were all of the purest kind. His intellect was the clearest, his memory was the best, and his will was the most straightforward — all in the most beautiful tranquillity of mind, without any fear of death and without any anxiety. To these inner qualities came also those most beautiful and superb qualities of body and of all the limbs, qualities in which he surpassed all the remaining living creatures. I am fully convinced that before Adam's sin his eyes were so sharp and clear that they surpassed those of the lynx and eagle.[99] He was stronger than the lions and the bears, whose strength is very great; and he handled them the way we handle puppies. Both the loveliness and the quality of the fruits he used as food were also far superior to what they are now.

But after the Fall death crept like leprosy into all our perceptive powers, so that with our intellect we cannot even understand that image. Adam would not have known his Eve except in the most unembarrassed attitude toward God, with a will obedient to God, and without any evil thought. Now, after sin, we all know how great passion is in the flesh, which is not only passionate in its desire but also in its disgust after it has acquired what it wanted. Thus in both instances we see neither reason nor will unimpaired, but passion greater than that of cattle. Is this not a serious and pernicious leprosy, of which Adam was free before sin? Moreover, he had greater strength and keener senses than the rest of the living beings. To what extent is man today surpassed by the boars in their sense of hearing, by the eagles in their sense of sight, and by the lion in his strength? Therefore no one can picture in his thoughts how much better nature was then than it is now.

Therefore my understanding of the image of God is this: that Adam had it in his being and that he not only knew God and believed that

---

[99] Cf. *Luther's Works*, 12, p. 119, note 8.

He was good, but that he also lived in a life that was wholly godly; that is, he was without the fear of death or of any other danger, and was content with God's favor. In this form it reveals itself in the instance of Eve, who speaks with the serpent without any fear, as we do with a lamb or a dog. For this reason, too, if they should transgress His command, God announces the punishment: "On whatever day you eat from this tree, you will die by death," as though He said: "Adam and Eve, now you are living without fear; death you have not experienced, nor have you seen it. This is My image, by which you are living, just as God lives. But if you sin, you will lose this image, and you will die."

So we see now what great dangers and how many varieties of death and chances of death this wretched nature is compelled to meet with and to endure in addition to the execrable lust and other sinful passions and inordinate emotions that arise in the hearts of all. We are never secure in God; apprehension and terror cause us concern even in sleep. These and similar evils are the image of the devil, who stamped them on us. But Adam lived in supreme bliss and in freedom from fear; he was not afraid of fire, of water, or of the other discomforts with which this life is beset and of which we are inordinately afraid.

And so let those who wish to do so minimize original sin; it surely appears both from the sins it produces and from the punishments it incurs that it is by far the greatest sin. Consider lust alone. Is it not most monstrous both in its passion and in its disgust? Moreover, what shall we say about hatred against God and about blasphemy? These are the outstanding moral failings which truly demonstrate that the image of God was lost.

Therefore when we speak about that image, we are speaking about something unknown. Not only have we had no experience of it, but we continually experience the opposite; and so we hear nothing except bare words. In Adam there was an enlightened reason, a true knowledge of God, and a most sincere desire to love God and his neighbor, so that Adam embraced Eve and at once acknowledged her to be his own flesh. Added to these were other lesser but exceedingly important gifts — if you draw a comparison with our weakness — namely, a perfect knowledge of the nature of the animals, the herbs, the fruits, the trees, and the remaining creatures.

If all these qualities are combined, do they not make up and produce the sort of man in whom you would think that the image of God is reflected, especially when you add the rule over the creatures? Just as Adam and Eve acknowledged God as their Lord, so later on they themselves ruled over the other creatures in the air, in the water, and on the earth. Who could adequately describe this glory in words? I believe that Adam could command a lion with a single word, just as we give a command to a trained dog. And he was free to cultivate the soil to produce what he wished. Our later discussions will show that thorns and thistles were not in existence at that time.[100] Similarly, I also believe that in those days the beasts were not as fierce as they are now.

But this condition is the fault of original sin, and from it all the remaining creatures derive their shortcomings. I hold that before sin the sun was brighter, the water purer, the trees more fruitful, and the fields more fertile. But through sin and that awful fall not only our flesh is disfigured by the leprosy of sin, but everything we use in this life has become corrupt, as we shall point out more clearly below.

But now the Gospel has brought about the restoration of that image. Intellect and will indeed have remained, but both very much impaired. And so the Gospel brings it about that we are formed once more according to that familiar and indeed better image, because we are born again into eternal life or rather into the hope of eternal life by faith, that we may live in God and with God and be one with Him, as Christ says (John 17:21).

And indeed, we are reborn not only for life but also for righteousness, because faith acquires Christ's merit and knows that through Christ's death we have been set free. From this source our other righteousness has its origin, namely, that newness of life through which we are zealous to obey God as we are taught by the Word and aided by the Holy Spirit. But this righteousness has merely its beginning in this life, and it cannot attain perfection in this flesh. Nevertheless, it pleases God, not as though it were a perfect righteousness or a payment for sin but because it comes from the heart and depends on its trust in the mercy of God through Christ. Moreover, this also is brought about by the Gospel, that the Holy Spirit is given to us, who offers resistance in us to unbelief, envy, and other vices that we may earnestly strive to glorify the name of the Lord and His Word, etc.

[100] See p. 204.

In this manner this image of the new creature begins to be restored by the Gospel in this life, but it will not be finished in this life. But when it is finished in the kingdom of the Father, then the will will be truly free and good, the mind truly enlightened, and the memory persistent. Then it will also happen that all the other creatures will be under our rule to a greater degree than they were in Adam's Paradise.

Until this is accomplished in us, we cannot have an adequate knowledge of what that image of God was which was lost through sin in Paradise. But what we are stating faith and the Word teach, which, as if from a distance, point out the glory of the divine image. Just as in the beginning the heaven and the earth were unfinished masses, so to speak, before the light had been added, so the godly have within themselves that unfinished image which God will on the Last Day bring to perfection in those who have believed His Word.

Therefore that image of God was something most excellent, in which were included eternal life, everlasting freedom from fear, and everything that is good. However, through sin this image was so obscured and corrupted that we cannot grasp it even with our intellect. Although we utter the words, who is there who could understand what it means to be in a life free from fear, without terrors and dangers, and to be wise, upright, good, and free from all disasters, spiritual as well as physical? However, greater than these was the fact that Adam was fitted for eternal life. He was so created that as long as he lived in this physical life, he would till the ground, not as if he were doing an irksome task and exhausting his body by toil but with supreme pleasure, not as a pastime but in obedience to God and submission to His will.

After this physical life was to come a spiritual life, in which he would neither make use of physical food nor do the other things which are customary in this life but would live an angelic and spiritual life. As the future life is pictured to us in Holy Scripture, we shall not drink, eat, or carry on any other physical functions. Therefore St. Paul says (1 Cor. 15:45): "The first man was made a living soul"; that is, he lived an animal life, which needs food, drink, sleep, etc. But "the second man will be renewed into the life-giving spirit"; that is, he will be a spiritual man when he reverts to the image of God. He will be similar to God in life, righteousness, holiness, wisdom, etc. Now follows:

Let him have dominion over the fish of the sea, etc.

Here the rule is assigned to the most beautiful creature, who knows God and is the image of God, in whom the similitude of the divine nature shines forth through his enlightened reason, through his justice and his wisdom. Adam and Eve become the rulers of the earth, the sea, and the air. But this dominion is given to them not only by way of advice but also by express command. Here we should first carefully ponder the exclusiveness in this: no beast is told to exercise dominion; but without ceremony all the animals and even the earth, with everything brought forth by the earth, are put under the rule of Adam, whom God by an express verbal command placed over the entire animal creation. Adam and Eve heard the words with their ears when God said: "Have dominion." Therefore the naked human being — without weapons and walls, even without any clothing, solely in his bare flesh — was given the rule over all birds, wild beasts, and fish.

Even this small part of the divine image we have lost, so much so that we do not even have insight into that fullness of joy and bliss which Adam derived from his contemplation of all the animal creatures. All our faculties today are leprous, indeed dull and utterly dead. Who can conceive of that part, as it were, of the divine nature, that Adam and Eve had insight into all the dispositions of all animals, into their characters and all their powers? What kind of a reign would it have been if they had not had this knowledge? Among the saints there is evident in this life some knowledge of God. Its source is the Word and the Holy Spirit. But the knowledge of nature — that we should know all the qualities of trees and herbs, and the dispositions of all the beasts — is utterly beyond repair in this life.

If, then, we are looking for an outstanding philosopher, let us not overlook our first parents while they were still free from sin. They had a most perfect-knowledge of God, for how would they not know Him whose similitude they had and felt within themselves? Furthermore, they also had the most dependable knowledge of the stars and of the whole of astronomy.

Eve had these mental gifts in the same degree as Adam, as Eve's utterance shows when she answered the serpent concerning the tree in the middle of Paradise. There it becomes clear enough that she knew to what end she had been created and pointed to the source from which she had this knowledge; for she said (Gen. 3:3): "The

Lord said." Thus she not only heard this from Adam, but her very nature was pure and full of the knowledge of God to such a degree that by herself she knew the Word of God and understood it.

Of this knowledge we have feeble and almost completely obliterated remnants. The other animals, however, completely lack this knowledge. They do not know their Creator, their origin, and their end; they do not know out of what and why they were created. Therefore they certainly lack that similitude of God. For this reason the psalm also urges (Ps. 32:9): "Do not become like the horse and the mule."

Thus even if this image has been almost completely lost, there is still a great difference between the human being and the rest of the animals. Before the coming of sin the difference was far greater and more evident, when Adam and Eve knew God and all the creatures and, as it were, were completely engulfed by the goodness and justice of God. As a result, there was between them a singular union of hearts and wills. No other beautiful sight in the whole world appeared lovelier and more attractive to Adam than his own Eve. But now, as the heathen say, a wife is a necessary evil.[101] Why they call her an evil can be perceived readily enough; but they do not know the cause of evil, namely, Satan, who has so vitiated and corrupted this creation.

What we achieve in life, however, is brought about, not by the dominion which Adam had but through industry and skill. Thus we see the birds and the fish caught by cunning and deceit; and by skill the beasts are tamed. Those animals which are most domesticated, such as geese and hens, nevertheless are wild so far as they themselves and their nature are concerned. Therefore even now, by the kindness of God, this leprous body has some appearance of the dominion over the other creatures. But it is extremely small and far inferior to that first dominion, when there was no need of skill or cunning, when the creature simply obeyed the divine voice because Adam and Eve were commanded to have dominion over them.

Therefore we retain the name and word "dominion" as a bare title, but the substance itself has been almost entirely lost. Yet it is a good thing to know these facts and to ponder them, so that we may have a longing for that coming Day when that which we lost in Paradise through sin will be restored to us. We are waiting for that life for which Adam also should have waited. And we duly marvel at this

101 See p. 70, note 110.

and thank God for it, that although we are so disfigured by sin, so dull, ignorant, and dead, as it were, nevertheless, through the merit of Christ, we wait for the same glory of the spiritual life for which Adam would have waited if he had remained in his physical life, which was endowed with the image of God.

27. *And God created man according to His image, according to the image of God He created him.*

Here Moses does not employ the word "similitude," but only "image." Perhaps he wanted to avoid an ambiguity of speech and for this reason repeated the noun "image." I see no other reason for the repetition unless we should understand it for the sake of emphasis as an indication of the Creator's rejoicing and exulting over the most beautiful work He had made, so that Moses intends to indicate that God was not so delighted at the other creatures as at man, whom He had created according to His own similitude. The rest of the animals are designated as footprints of God; but man alone is God's image, as appears in the *Sentences*.[102] In the remaining creatures God is recognized as by His footprints; but in the human being, especially in Adam, He is truly recognized, because in him there is such wisdom, justice, and knowledge of all things that he may rightly be called a world in miniature.[103] He has an understanding of heaven, earth, and the entire creation. And so it gives God pleasure that He made so beautiful a creature.

But without a doubt, just as at that time God rejoiced in the counsel and work by which man was created, so today, too, He takes pleasure in restoring this work of His through His Son and our Deliverer, Christ. It is useful to ponder these facts, namely, that God is most kindly inclined toward us and takes delight in His thought and plan of restoring all who have believed in Christ to spiritual life through the resurrection of the dead.

Male and female He created them.

In order not to give the impression that He was excluding the woman from all the glory of the future life, Moses includes each of the two sexes; for the woman appears to be a somewhat different

[102] Peter Lombard, *Sententiae,* II, Dist. XVI, pp. 683—685, is a discussion of the image of God in man.

[103] This is the familiar Renaissance idea of man as a μιϰϱόϰοσμος.

being from the man, having different members and a much weaker nature. Although Eve was a most extraordinary creature — similar to Adam so far as the image of God is concerned, that is, in justice, wisdom, and happiness — she was nevertheless a woman. For as the sun is more excellent than the moon (although the moon, too, is a very excellent body), so the woman, although she was a most beautiful work of God, nevertheless was not the equal of the male in glory and prestige.

However, here Moses puts the two sexes together and says that God created male and female in order to indicate that Eve, too, was made by God as a partaker of the divine image and of the divine similitude, likewise of the rule over everything. Thus even today the woman is the partaker of the future life, just as Peter says that they are joint heirs of the same grace (1 Peter 3:7). In the household the wife is a partner in the management and has a common interest in the children and the property, and yet there is a great difference between the sexes. The male is like the sun in heaven, the female like the moon, the animals like the stars, over which sun and moon have dominion. In the first place, therefore, let us note from this passage that it was written that this sex may not be excluded from any glory of the human creature, although it is inferior to the male sex. About marriage we shall have something to say below.[104]

In the second place, there is here an argument against Hilary and others, who maintained that God created everything at the same time.[105] Here our opinion is supported: that the six days were truly six natural days, because here Moses says that Adam and Eve were created on the sixth day. One may not use sophistries with reference to this text. But concerning the order of creation of man he will state in the following chapter that Eve was made sometime after Adam, not like Adam, from a clod of earth, but from his rib, which God took out of the side of Adam as he slept. These are all works of time, that is, works that require time. They were not performed in one moment; neither were these acts: that God brings to Adam every animal and that there was not found one like him, etc. These are acts requiring time, and they were performed on the sixth day. Here Moses touches on them briefly by anticipation. Later on he will explain them at greater length.

[104] See p. 117.
[105] Cf. p. 4, note 8.

Many scholars also believe that Adam sinned on the sixth day, and they celebrate the sixth day for its twofold fame, namely, that just as Adam sinned on the sixth day, so Christ also suffered on the sixth day.[106] Let them see themselves whether this is true. What Moses clearly states is that man was created on the sixth day and that a wife was given to him. But to me, as I shall point out below,[107] it seems more likely that Adam sinned on the seventh day, that is, on the Sabbath, just as even now Satan disturbs the Sabbath of the church when the Word is being taught; but not even this can be clearly proved from Moses. Thus on each side there are reasons against reasons, as Emperor Maximilian used to say.[108] Therefore I leave these matters undecided and within anyone's discretion.

Lyra also relates a Jewish tale, of which Plato, too, makes mention somewhere, that in the beginning man was created bisexual and later on, by divine power, was, as it were, split or cut apart, as the form of the back and of the spine seems to prove.[109] Others have expanded these ideas with more obscene details. But the second chapter refutes these babblers. For if this is true, how can it be sure that God took one of the ribs of Adam and out of it built the woman? These are Talmudic tales, and yet they had to be mentioned so that we might see the malice of the devil, who suggests such absurd ideas to human beings.

This tale fits Aristotle's designation of woman as a "maimed man"; others declare that she is a monster.[110] But let them themselves be monsters and sons of monsters — these men who make malicious statements and ridicule a creature of God in which God Himself took delight as in a most excellent work, moreover, one which we see created by a special counsel of God. These pagan ideas show that reason cannot establish anything sure about God and the works of God but only thinks up reasons against reasons and teaches nothing in a perfect and sound manner.

28. *And He blessed.*

This he did not say about the animals; therefore he includes them here.

---

106 Cf. p. 81.

107 See p. 144.

108 On Maximilian see Luther's comments, *Luther's Works*, 13, pp. 214, 215.

109 Lyra on Gen. 1:27, sec. "e."

110 Apparently this is a reference to Aristotle, *De generatione animalium,* I, ch. 20.

Be fruitful.

This is a command of God added for the creature. But, good God, what has been lost for us here through sin! How blessed was that state of man in which the begetting of offspring was linked with the highest respect and wisdom, indeed with the knowledge of God! Now the flesh is so overwhelmed by the leprosy of lust that in the act of procreation the body becomes downright brutish and cannot beget in the knowledge of God.

Thus the power of procreation remained in the human race, but very much debased and even completely overwhelmed by the leprosy of lust, so that procreation is only slightly more moderate than that of the brutes. Added to this are the perils of pregnancy and of birth, the difficulty of feeding the offspring, and other endless evils, all of which point out to us the enormity of original sin. Therefore the blessing, which remains till now in nature, is, as it were, a cursed and debased blessing if you compare it with that first one; nevertheless, God established it and preserves it. So let us gratefully acknowledge this "marred blessing." And let us keep in mind that the unavoidable leprosy of the flesh, which is nothing but disobedience and loathsomeness attached to bodies and minds, is the punishment of sin. Moreover, let us wait in hope for the death of this flesh that we may be set free from these loathsome conditions and may be restored even beyond the point of that first creation of Adam.

And have dominion over the fish of the sea.

We are so overcome by our ignorance of God and the creatures that we cannot establish with certainty what use would have been made of the cattle, the fish, and the other animals in the first creation and state of perfection. We see now that we eat flesh, vegetables, etc. If they were not used in this manner, we would not know why they were created; for we neither see nor have any other use for these creatures. But Adam would not have used the creatures as we do today, except for food, which he would have derived from other, far more excellent fruits. For he under whose power everything had been placed did not lack clothing or money. Nor would there have been any greed among his descendants; but, apart from food, they would have made use of the creatures only for the admiration of God and for a holy joy which is unknown to us in this corrupt state of nature.

By contrast, today and always the whole creation is hardly sufficient to feed and support the human race. Therefore what this dominion consisted of we cannot even imagine.

29. *And God said: Behold, I have given you every herb bearing seed.*

Here you see how solicitous God is for the man He has created. First He created the earth like a house in which he should live. Then He arranged the other things He regarded as necessary for life. Finally He gave the gift of procreation to the man He had created. Now He also provides his food that nothing may be lacking for leading his life in the easiest possible manner. Moreover, I believe that if Adam had remained in the state of innocence, his children would have run immediately after birth to the enjoyment of those delights which the initial creation afforded. But it is vain to mention these things; they cannot be acquired by thought, and they are irrecoverable in this life.

And all the trees.

Moses seems to be making a difference between the seeds and the green herbage, perhaps because the latter were to serve for the use of the beasts, the former for that of man. I have no doubt that the seeds we use for food today were far more excellent then than they are now. Moreover, Adam would not have eaten the various kinds of meat, as the less delightful food, in preference to the delightful fruits of the earth, whereas for us nothing is more delicious than meat. From the use of these fruits there would not have resulted that leprous obesity, but physical beauty and health and a sound state of the humors.[111]

But now people do not content themselves with meats, with vegetables, or with grain; and rather often, because of unsuitable food, we face dangers of health. I am saying nothing about those increasingly widespread sins of overindulgence in food and drink which are worse than brutish. The curse which followed because of sin is apparent. It is also likely that only then were the accursed and pernicious insects produced out of the earth, which was cursed because of man's sin.

But here comes the question of how the granting to Adam of the enjoyment of all the trees of the field harmonizes with the later

111 The medieval medical term used here is *sana humorum temperatura.*

assignment to him of a single portion of the earth for tilling, the portion called Paradise. It is also asked whether the whole earth is called Paradise, etc. But we shall put off these matters to the second chapter.[112]

31. *And God saw all things that He had made, and they were very good. And evening and morning became the sixth day.*

After God has finished His works, He speaks after the custom of one who has become tired, as if He wanted to say: "Behold, I have prepared all things in the best way. The heaven I have prepared as a roof; the earth is the flooring; the animals — with all the appointments of the earth, the sea, and the air — are the possession and wealth; seeds, roots, and herbs are the food. Moreover, he himself, the lord of these, man, has been created. He is to have knowledge of God; and with the utmost freedom from fear, with justice and wisdom, he is to make use of the creatures as he wishes, according to his will. Nothing is lacking. All things have been created in greatest abundance for physical life. Therefore I shall keep a Sabbath."

All these good things have, for the most part, been lost through sin; and we, who have kept hardly a shadow of that realm, are today like a corpse of that first human being. Or shall we not say that he has lost everything who became mortal after being immortal, a sinner after being righteous, a condemned man after being welcome and well-pleasing? For now man is mortal and a sinner. But if these thoughts do not move us to hope and longing for the coming Day and the future life, nothing could move us. Let this suffice as an exposition of the first chapter. In the next Moses will give information about the work of the sixth day, how man was created.

112 See p. 88.

CHAPTER TWO

1. *And the heavens and the earth were finished, and all the host of them.*

O UR text has "and all their adornment," but in the Hebrew it is "their army" or "their host," צְבָאָם. The prophets have retained this manner of speech. Therefore they call the stars and the planets the host of the heavens. Thus it is stated in Jer. 19:13 that the Jews worshiped "the entire heavenly host," that is, the sun, the moon, and the other stars; and in Zeph. 1:5: "I shall destroy those who worship on the roofs the host of the heaven." And Stephen, in Acts 7:42, said: "They served the host of the heaven."

Expressions of this kind the prophets borrowed from Moses, who uses military terminology in this passage and calls the stars and the luminaries of heaven the army or host of heaven; but men, beasts, and trees he calls the host of the earth. Perhaps he does this in view of later usage, because later on God calls Himself the God of the armies or of the hosts, that is, not only of the angels or of the spirits but of the entire creation, which carries on warfare for Him and serves Him. After Satan had been cast away by God on account of his sin, he was filled with such hatred of God and of man that, if he were able, he would in one moment rob the sea of its fish, the air of its birds, the earth of its fruits of every kind, and would destroy everything. But God created all these creatures to be in active military service, to fight for us continually against the devil, as well as against men, and to serve us and be of use to us.

2. *And on the seventh day God completed His work which He had made, and He rested on the seventh day from all His work that He had made.*

Here a question arises. Moses says that the Lord rested on the seventh day from the work which He had done, that is, that He ceased to work on the seventh day. On the other hand, Christ says in John 5:17: "My Father works until now, and I work." Moreover, what

Heb. 3:18 and 4:3 state concerning the rest pertains to this passage: "If they shall enter," not indeed into the Land of Promise but "into My rest."

We simply answer in this way: The solution is given by the text itself when it says: "The heaven and the earth were finished." The Sabbath, or the Sabbath rest, denotes that God ceased in such a way that He did not create another heaven and another earth. It does not denote that God gave up preserving and governing the heaven and the earth which had already been created. For in the preceding chapter Moses very plainly informs us about the manner of the creation when he says that God had created all things through the Word: "Let the sea bring forth fish; the earth, herbs, beasts," etc.; likewise: "Grow, fill the earth and the sea." These words are in force until today, and for this reason we see increase without end. Therefore if the world were in existence for an infinite number of years, the effectiveness of these words would not pass away; but there would be continuous increase through the power of that Word or, to express myself so, of the original endowment.[1]

Thus the solution is easy. God rested from His work, that is, He was satisfied with the heaven and earth which had then been created by the Word; He did not create a new heaven, a new earth, new stars, new trees. And yet God works till now — if indeed He has not abandoned the world which was once established but governs and preserves it through the effectiveness of His Word. He has, therefore, ceased to establish; but He has not ceased to govern. In Adam the human race had its beginning; in the earth the animal race, to use this expression, had its beginning through the Word; and in the sea that of the fish and of the birds had its beginning. But in Adam and in the first little beasts[2] or animals they did not reach their end. Until today there abides the Word which was pronounced over the human race: "Grow and multiply"; there abides the Word: "Let the sea bring forth fish and birds of the heaven." Almighty, therefore, is the power and effectiveness of the Word which thus preserves and governs the entire creation.

Thus Moses has clearly established that the Word was in the beginning. But because all things grow, multiply, and are preserved and governed until now in the same manner as from the beginning of

---

[1] An allusion to the medieval practice of establishing a prebend from which a canon or other ecclesiastic was supported; cf. *Luther's Works*, 21, p. 182, note 28.

[2] The original is *bestiolis seu animalibus*.

the world, it obviously follows that the Word still continues in force
and is not dead. Therefore Moses' statement, "God rested from His
work," is not to be understood of that course of events which involves
their preservation and government but simply of the beginning,
namely, that God had ceased creating classes, as they say in common
speech, and new species or new creatures.

If you look at my person, I am something new, because sixty years
ago I was nothing. Such is the judgment of the world. But God's
judgment is different; for in God's sight I was begotten and multiplied
immediately when the world began, because this Word, "and God
said: 'Let Us make man,'" created me too. Whatever God wanted
to create, that He created then when He spoke. Not everything has
come into view at once. Similarly, an arrow or a ball which is shot
from a cannon (for it has greater speed) is sent to its target in
a single moment, as it were, and nevertheless it is shot through a definite space; so God, through His Word, extends His activity from the
beginning of the world to its end. For with God there is nothing
that is earlier or later, swifter or slower; but in His eyes all things
are present things. For He is simply outside the scope of time.

Therefore these words, "God said: 'Let there be, grow, multiply,'"
established the creatures as they are now and as they will be to the
end of the world. But He ceased creating new ones. He did not
create a new earth or a new heaven; but as He wanted the sun and
the moon to course, so they still course. Just as at that time He
filled the sea with fish, the heaven with flying things, and the earth
with cattle, so these are complete, remain up to the present time,
and are preserved. It is as Christ says (John 5:17): "My Father is
working still, and I work." The Word which He spoke in the beginning is still in existence, as Ps. 33:9 says: "He spoke, and it came
into being."

But here another objection is voiced, namely: "How can it be
true that God has created nothing new, when it is certain that the
rainbow, or iris, was created at the time of Noah (Gen. 9:13)? Likewise, after Adam's fall the Lord threatens that the earth will produce
thorns and thistles (Gen. 3:18), which it would not have produced
if Adam had not sinned. Likewise, it is stated about the serpent that
it would have to creep face down on the ground (Gen. 3:14), although
without a doubt, in the state in which it was originally created, it
walked upright, just as deer and peacocks do today. This is surely
a new state of affairs, brought about by a new Word. Moreover, if

Adam had not fallen into sin, wolves, lions, and bears would not have acquired their well-known savage disposition. Absolutely nothing in the entire creation would have been either troublesome or harmful for man. For the text states plainly: 'Everything that was created by God was good.' And yet, how troublesome they are! How many great afflictions of disease affect our body! I am passing over the fleas, the flies, and the spiders. And how great the dangers are from the other fierce and poisonous animals! But even if not one of these things is pertinent, surely this is something supremely new, that a virgin gives birth to the Son of God. Therefore God did not stop on the seventh day. He works not only by preserving His creation but also by changing and renewing His creation. Nor is it true, as was stated above, that God has refrained from creating new classes."

My answer is: Here Moses is speaking about the uncorrupted creation; if, therefore, man had maintained himself in the state of innocence in which he was created, no thorns or thistles or diseases would have come into existence, and beasts would not have become ferocious. This appears clearly enough from the fact that Eve speaks to a serpent with as little fear as we have when we speak to a charming little bird or a fawning puppy. Nor do I have any doubt that the serpent was a most beautiful creature singularly endowed with a reputation for greater cleverness than the remaining beasts, just as little foxes, weasels, etc., have a reputation for cleverness.

Since Adam was still holy and innocent, all the living beings dwelt with him with the greatest delight, ready for every kind of service. If he had remained so, there would have been no fear of the Flood; and, in consequence, iris, or the rainbow, would not have come into existence. But because of sin God changed many things. And on the Last Day there will be a far greater change and a renewal of the entire creature, which, as Paul says (Rom. 8:20), is now subjected to futility because of sin.

Therefore when Moses states that the Lord rested, he is speaking about the original state of the world. Because there was no sin, nothing new was created in it. There were neither thorns nor thistles, neither serpents nor toads; and if there were any, they were neither venomous nor vicious. Thus he is speaking about the creation of the world in its perfection. At that time the world was pure and innocent because man was pure and innocent. Now, when man is different on account of sin, the world, too, has begun to be different; that is, the fall of man was followed by the depravation and the curse of the creation. "Cursed is the earth," said God to Adam (Gen. 3:17-18), "on your account; thorns and thistles it will bring forth for you." On account of the sin of one single cursed Cain the earth is cursed so that even if it is tilled, it will not yield its best products. Later on there comes the Flood because of the sin of the whole world, and the entire human race is destroyed. A few righteous people were preserved, however, lest the promise concerning Christ should not be fulfilled. But inasmuch as it appears that the earth was disfigured by sin, therefore I for one believe that the light of the sun also was more brilliant and beautiful when it was created, before man's sin.

In the theological schools the saying is current: "Distinguish the times, and you will bring the Scriptures into harmony."[3] Therefore what we say about the world after that wretched depravity which came in through sin must be far different from what we say about the original pure and unimpaired world. Let us consider an example that is before our eyes. Those who have seen the Promised Land in our time declare that it in no way resembles the favorable description which appears in Holy Scripture. Therefore when Count Stolberg had explored it with special care, he stated that he preferred his own lands in Germany.[4] On account of sin, on account of the wickedness and vileness of men, the land was made unfruitful, as Ps. 107:34 says. So Sodom, too, was a sort of Paradise before it was destroyed by fire from heaven (Gen. 13:20).

Thus a curse generally follows sin, but the curse changes things so that the best becomes the worst. Therefore Moses is speaking about the perfection of the creatures as it was before sin. If man had not sinned, all the beasts would have remained obedient until finally God would have transferred man from Paradise, or from the earth; but after sin all things underwent a change for the worse.

In this way the solution proposed above stands: that in six days God finished His work, that is, that He ceased establishing classes; and whatever He wanted to make He made then. He did not say

[3] Luther discusses the necessity of this exegetical skill at greater length in his comments on Gen. 33:17 (Weimar, XLIV, 133).

[4] Count Henry the Elder of Stolberg had been in the Holy Land in 1461; Count Henry the Younger, in 1493, on a pilgrimage with Frederick the Wise. In his *Table Talk* Luther quotes the elder count as saying: "Is this the Promised Land? I would rather have the Golden Meadow!" — a section of Thuringia (Weimar, *Tischreden*, I, No. 1223).

again: "Let there be a new earth, a new sea," etc. As to the fact that the Virgin Mary gave birth to the Son of God, it is clear that the reason also for this charitable act was the misfortune into which we fell through sin. God performed this marvelous and extraordinary work in such a way that He first revealed through His Word that He would do it in the future. Similarly, God indicated through His Word that other miracles would also take place in the future.

This, then, is the first disquisition concerning the statement that God finished the heaven and the earth and that He made nothing new. Now, that we may learn, this, too, should be explained: What is the Sabbath or the rest of God? Likewise, in what manner did God sanctify the Sabbath, as the text says?

3. *And God blessed the seventh day and sanctified it, because on it He had rested from all His work which God created, so that He made it.*

In Matt. 12 Christ says that the Sabbath was made for man, not man for the Sabbath.[5] But Moses says nothing here about man; he does not say in so many words that the Sabbath was commanded to man; he says that God blessed the Sabbath and that He sanctified it for Himself. Moreover, He did not do this to any other creature. He did not sanctify for Himself the heaven, the earth, or any other creature; but the seventh day He did sanctify for Himself. This has the special purpose of making us understand that the seventh day in particular should be devoted to divine worship. For "holy" is that which has been set aside for God and has been removed from all secular uses. Hence to sanctify means to set aside for sacred purposes, or for the worship of God. In this manner Moses rather frequently employs the expression, also of sacred vessels.[6]

It follows, therefore, from this passage that if Adam had remained in the state of innocence, he nevertheless would have held the seventh day sacred. That is, on this day he would have given his descendants instructions about the will and worship of God; he would have praised God; he would have given thanks; he would have sacrificed, etc. On the other days he would have tilled his fields and tended his cattle. Indeed, even after the Fall he kept this seventh day sacred; that is, on this day he instructed his family, of which the sacrifices

[5] This passage is not from Matt. 12, as the text has it, but from Mark 2:27.

[6] Apparently a reference to the usage in passages like Ex. 40:9.

of his sons Cain and Abel give the proof. Therefore from the beginning of the world the Sabbath was intended for the worship of God.

Unspoiled human nature would have proclaimed the glory and the kindnesses of God in this way: on the Sabbath day men would have conversed about the immeasurable goodness of the Creator; they would have sacrificed; they would have prayed, etc. For this is the meaning of the verb "to sanctify."

Moreover, this also implies the immortality of the human race, as the Letter to the Hebrews (3:11) learnedly expounds concerning God's rest on the basis of Ps. 95:11: "They shall not enter into My rest." For God's rest is eternal. Adam would have lived for a definite time in Paradise, according to God's pleasure; then he would have been carried off to that rest of God which God, through the sanctifying of the Sabbath, wished not only to symbolize for men but also to grant to them. Thus the physical life would have been blissful and holy, spiritual and eternal. Now we wretched men have lost that bliss of our physical life through sin, and while we live we are in the midst of death.[7] And yet, because the Sabbath command remains for the church, it denotes that spiritual life is to be restored to us through Christ. And so the prophets have carefully searched those passages in which Moses intimates the resurrection of the flesh and life immortal.

Then it is also shown here that man was especially created for the knowledge and worship of God; for the Sabbath was not ordained for sheep and cows but for men, that in them the knowledge of God might be developed and might increase. Therefore although man lost his knowledge of God, nevertheless God wanted this command about sanctifying the Sabbath to remain in force. On the seventh day He wanted men to busy themselves both with His Word and with the other forms of worship established by Him, so that we might give first thought to the fact that this nature was created chiefly for acknowledging and glorifying God.

Moreover, this is also written that we might preserve in our minds a sure hope of the future and eternal life. All the things God wants done on the Sabbath are clear signs of another life after this life. Why is it necessary for God to speak with us through His Word if we are not to live in a future and eternal life? If we are not to hope for a future life, why do we not live like people with whom God does

7 See also *Luther's Works*, 13, p. 83, note 16.

not speak and who do not know God? But because the Divine Majesty speaks to man alone and man alone knows and apprehends God, it necessarily follows that there is another life after this life; to attain it we need the Word and the knowledge of God. For this temporal and present life is a physical life, such as all the beasts live that do not know God and the Word.

This is what the Sabbath, or the rest of God, means, on which God speaks with us through His Word and we, in turn, speak with Him through prayer and faith. The beasts, such as dogs, horses, sheep, and cows, indeed also learn to hear and understand the voice of man; they are also kept by man and fed. But our state is better. We hear God, know His will, and are called into a sure hope of immortality. This is the testimony of the clear promises concerning eternal life which God has revealed to us through His Word after giving those dark indications, like this one concerning the rest of God and the sanctifying of the Sabbath. And yet this one dealing with the Sabbath is rather clear. Suppose that there is no life after this life; does it not follow that we have no need of God or of His Word? What we need or do in this life we can have even without the Word. The beasts graze, live, and grow fat, although they do not have the Word of God or hear it. What need is there of the Word to get food and drink that has already been created?

Therefore that God gives His Word, that He commands us to occupy ourselves with the Word, that He issues orders for sanctifying the Sabbath and for His worship — all this clearly proves that there remains a life after this life and that man was created not for this physical life only, like the other animals, but for eternal life, just as God, who has ordered and ordained these practices, is eternal.

But here another question arises, on which we touched above, namely, about the time of Adam's fall. When did he fall, on the seventh day or on another? Although nothing certain can be proposed, still I can readily imagine that he fell on the seventh day. On the sixth day he was created; Eve likewise was created toward evening or near the end of the sixth day, while Adam was sleeping. Early in the morning of the seventh day, which had been sanctified by the Lord, God speaks with Adam, gives him directions concerning His worship, and forbids him to eat the fruit of the tree of the knowledge of good and evil. This is the real purpose of the seventh day: that the Word of God be preached and heard. Henceforth both in the Scripture and in common usage the practice remained that the morning time was set aside for prayer and preaching, as Ps. 5:3 says: "In the morning I shall stand before Thee, and I shall see."

Thus early on the seventh day Adam appears to have heard the Lord charge him with the management of household and world affairs, and at the same time forbid him to eat the fruit. Satan was intolerant of this most magnificent creation and arrangement. He also envied man such great bliss, that an overflowing supply of everything was at hand for him on the earth and that after so blissful a physical life he had the sure hope of eternal life, which Satan himself had lost. And so, perhaps about noon, after God's conversation, he also converses with Eve. So it is wont to be to this day. Where the Word of God is, there Satan also makes it his business to spread falsehood and false teaching; for it grieves him that through the Word we, like Adam in Paradise, become citizens of heaven. And so he successfully incites Eve to sin. Moreover, the text states plainly that when the heat of the day had ended, the Lord came and condemned Adam, together with all his descendants, to death. I am easily convinced that all these events took place on the very Sabbath — and that one not complete! — on which Adam lived in Paradise and enjoyed its fruits.

And so through sin man lost this bliss. But Adam would not have spent his life in Paradise in idleness if he had remained in the state of innocence. On the Sabbath day he would have taught his children; through public preaching he would have bestowed honor on God with the praises which He deserved; and through reflection on the works of God he would have incited himself and others to expressions of thanks. On the other days he would have worked, either tilling his field or hunting. But this would have been far different from the way it is done now. For to us work is something burdensome; but for Adam it would have been a supreme joy, more welcome than any leisure. Therefore just as the other misfortunes of this life remind us of sin and of the wrath of God, so work, too, and the well-known hardship of providing sustenance should remind us of sin and rouse us to repentance.

Now Moses proceeds with a clearer description of man, after first repeating what he had said in the first chapter. Although these statements appear to be unnecessary, nevertheless the repetition is not altogether unnecessary, because he wishes to continue his account in a connected manner.

4. *These are the generations of the heavens and the earth, when they were created, on the day when the Lord God made the earth and the heaven, 5. before there came forth any shrub on the earth, or any herb sprouted on the field.*

"On the day" is to be understood in the sense of indefinite time, as if he were saying: "At that time the condition of all things was most delightful. But now I must say something else." There is no need, however, to search superstitiously for the reason why Moses wanted to make use of this rustic style of speech concerning shrubs and herbs.[8] For he is at the point of relating more details about the state of man.

5. *For God had not rained upon the earth, nor was there a man to till the earth, 6. but a mist rose from the earth, which moistened the whole surface of the earth.*

Not yet, says he, was there rain to water the earth; but a sort of steam or dew rose up, which made the earth fruitful, so that later on it could make things sprout more readily. But these things belong properly to the third day.

7. *And so the Lord God formed man from dust of the ground, and He breathed into his face a breath of life; and man became a living soul.*

Here Moses returns to the work of the sixth day and points out whence the cultivator of the earth came, namely, that God formed him from a clod, as a potter forms a pot out of clay with his hands. For this reason he did not say above, as in the case of the other creatures: "Let the earth bring forth man," but: "Let Us make a man," in order to point out the superiority of the human race and to disclose the unique counsel of God, of which He availed Himself when He created man, although after this man increased and multiplied in the same manner as the other beasts. For the semen congeals in the womb and is given form in an identical manner. Here there is no difference between a pregnant cow and a woman with child. But Moses shows that in their first state there was a very great difference, inasmuch as man was created by a unique counsel and wisdom and shaped by the finger of God.

[8] It is not clear whether Luther is taking issue here with specific exegetes or with a general medieval attitude.

This difference between the origin of man and that of cattle also points to the immortality of the soul, of which we have previously spoken. Although all the remaining works of God are perfect objects of wonder and are very sublime, this nevertheless proves conclusively that man is the most outstanding creature: when God creates him, He takes counsel and employs a new procedure. He does not leave it to the earth to produce him, like the animals and the trees. But He Himself shapes him according to His image as if he were God's partner and one who would enjoy God's rest. And so Adam is a dead and inactive clod before he is formed by the Lord. God takes that clod and forms from it a most beautiful creature which has a share in immortality.

If Aristotle heard this, he would burst into laughter and conclude that although this is not an unlovely yarn, it is nevertheless a most absurd one — that, so far as the first origin is concerned, man had been a clod but was formed by divine wisdom and so created that he was fit for immortality. Although some of the philosophers, like Socrates and others, maintain the immortality of the soul, they were ridiculed by the rest of the philosophers and all but scorned. But isn't it folly for human reason to be so offended, since it sees that even now the procreation of man is full of wonder? Does it not seem contrary to reason that man, who is to live forever, is born, as it were, from one single droplet of semen in the loins of the father? This is even more absurd than when Moses says that man was formed from a clod by the fingers of God. But reason shows in this way that it knows practically nothing about God, who, merely by a thought, makes out of a clod, not the semen of a human being but the human being itself, and, as Moses states later, makes the woman out of the rib of the man. Such was the origin of man.

But once the male and the female are so created, man is then procreated out of their blood through the divine blessing. Although this procreation is something man has in common with the brutes, it detracts nothing from that glory of our origin, namely, that we are vessels of God, formed by God Himself, and that He Himself is our Potter, but we His clay, as Is. 64:8 says. And this holds good not only for our origin but throughout our whole life; until our death and in the grave we remain the clay of this Potter.

Moreover, this helps us to learn something about the properties of free will, a subject with which our opponents concern themselves so extensively. In a certain way we indeed have a free will in those things that are beneath us. By the divine commission we have been appointed lords of the fish of the sea, of the birds of the heavens, and of the beasts of the field. These we kill when it pleases us; we enjoy the foods and other useful products they supply. But in those matters that pertain to God and are above us no human being has a free will; he is indeed like clay in the hand of the potter, in a state of merely passive potentiality, not active potentiality.[9] For there we do not choose, we do not do anything; but we are chosen, we are equipped, we are born again, we accept, as Isaiah says (64:8): "Thou art the Potter; we, Thy clay."

But here comes a new question. For as Moses, in a new expression, says here concerning man: "God formed man from the clay of the earth" but above did not speak in these terms about the other living beings, so here, too, he says something unusual about man, namely, that God breathed a breath into his face. This is something that Moses did not say about the other animals, although in all the animals, just as in man, there is breath in the nostrils. And so it is asked why Moses should have wanted to express himself in this way. In the second place, this, too, is asked (although it deals with the same matter): "Since throughout the entire Scripture all animals are called living souls, why should it be stated in this passage concerning man alone that he was made a living soul?" He did indeed say before (Gen. 1:24): "Let the earth bring forth living souls, each one according to its kind." But here he makes a great change and says: "Man was made a living soul."

These facts no doubt induced the patriarchs, the holy fathers, and the prophets to examine passages of this kind rather closely, because this unusual manner of speech indicates that Moses wanted to point out something outstanding. If you consider the animal life about which Moses is speaking here, there is no difference between man and the donkey. Animal life has need of food and drink; it has need of sleep and rest; their bodies are fed in like manner by food and drink, and they grow; and through hunger they become faint and perish. The stomach receives the food, and when the food has been digested, passes it on to the liver, which produces blood, by which all the limbs are given fresh strength. In this regard there is no difference between man and beast. And yet Moses gives distinction

[9] By "passive potentiality" is apparently meant the idea that the only possibility a man has lies in what can be done *to* him rather than in anything that can be done *by* him.

to the life of man in this manner that he says about him alone that he was made a living soul — not simply like the other animals but an eminently living soul, because he was created after the image of God. In the state of innocence no doubt this image was reflected in a unique way in the face of Adam and Eve. Similarly, even after sin the Gentiles concluded from the carriage of man, from the fact that he alone walks upright and raises his eyes to heaven that he is a rather outstanding creature among all the rest of the creatures.

Paul's thoughts go back to this when he quotes the following words in 1 Cor. 15:45: "It is written: The first human being, Adam, was made a living soul; but the last Adam, a quickening spirit." "Living soul" he calls the physical life, which consists of eating, drinking, begetting, growing, all of which are also present in the brutes. But by antithesis he says that the last Adam was made a quickening spirit, that is, such a life as has no need for those animal requirements of life. Paul also teaches that even if Adam had not sinned, he would still have lived a physical life in need of food, drink, rest. He would have grown, procreated, etc., until he would have been translated by God to the spiritual life in which he would have lived without any animal qualities, if I may use this expression, namely, from within, from God alone, not from without, as he had previously, on herbs and fruits. This would have been in such a manner that he would still have flesh and bones and would not be a mere spirit like the angels.

Therefore I answer the question as follows: Through the mouth of Moses God wanted, also in this passage, to point to the hope of a future and eternal life, which Adam, had he remained in the state of innocence, would have had as his possession after this animal life. It is as if Moses said: Man was made a living soul, not simply in the same way the animals live, but as one which God would later bring to life even without the animal life. This hope of immortality through Christ we also have, although on account of sin we are subject to death and all sorts of misfortunes. Adam's would have been a better state. On earth he would have lived delightfully and with the utmost enjoyment; then without any inconvenience he would have been transported from the animal life into the spiritual. We are not brought out of this animal life to the spiritual except through death and after countless dangers and crosses.

In this manner we, together with the holy prophets, should look at Moses carefully and note why with a special design he says of man what he otherwise said of the rest of the living things. This is intended to strengthen in us our faith and hope of immortality, that, although according to his animal life man is similar to the remaining living brutes, he has the hope of immortality, which the remaining living things do not have; for he carries in himself the image and similitude of God, which the remaining living beings do not carry in themselves.

And here by a very beautiful allegory, or rather by an anagoge,[10] Moses wanted to intimate dimly that God was to become incarnate. The statement that though man is created according to the similitude of God, he does not differ from cattle in his animal life is clearly contradictory, or, as they call it in the schools, "a contradiction in the predicate." [11] Nevertheless, because he was created in the image of the invisible God, this statement is a dim intimation, as we shall hear, that God was to reveal Himself to the world in the man Christ. These seeds, as it were, of very important facts the prophets have carefully gathered from Moses and considered.

8. *And the Lord God planted a garden in Eden towards the east, in which He placed the man whom He had formed.*

Here a sea of questions concerning Paradise arises. In the first place, the word itself is either Hebrew or Aramaic or Persian (for I do not think it is Greek, although Suidas looks in vain for a Greek origin.[12] It denotes a garden. This, Moses states, was planted בְּעֵדֶן, in Eden; for this is the name of a place and is not an appellative, as our version has it, which translates "the Paradise of delight." [13] Eden indeed denotes pleasure or delight, and from it is no doubt derived the Greek word ἡδονή. But the prefixed preposition adequately shows

---

[10] The difference between these two modes of medieval exegesis and their relationship to the other two is well summarized in a Latin verse, which has been translated thus:

> The letter shows us what God and our fathers did;
> The allegory shows us where our faith is hid;
> The moral meaning gives us rules of daily life;
> The anagoge shows us where we end our strife.

[11] The technical term from logic employed here is *oppositum in adiecto.*

[12] *Suidae Lexicon,* ed. by Ada Adler, IV (Leipzig, 1935), p. 32.

[13] This translation is reflected in the rendition of the Douay Version: "And the Lord God had planted a paradise of pleasure from the beginning." See also p. 97, note 25.

that here Eden is to be taken as a proper noun of place, just as the same conclusion is indicated by the statement concerning the boundary of the place, namely, that it was located toward the east. "From the beginning," which our translation has, is also a poor rendering.[14] The word is מִקֶּדֶם, which does not strictly denote "from the beginning" but "from before," that is, as we say, "toward the east." It is an adverb of place, and it describes the location of Paradise, not the time.

At this point people discuss where Paradise is located.[15] The interpreters torture themselves in amazing ways. Some favor the idea that it is located within the two tropics under the equinoctial point. Others think that a more temperate climate was necessary, since the place was so fertile. Why waste words? The opinions are numberless.

My answer is briefly this: It is an idle question about something no longer in existence. Moses is writing the history of the time before sin and the Deluge, but we are compelled to speak of conditions as they are after sin and after the Deluge. And so I believe that this place was called Eden either by Adam or at the time of Adam because of its fertility and the great charm which Adam beheld in it. And the name of the lost place persisted among his descendants, just as the names of Rome, Athens, and Carthage, are still in existence today, although hardly any traces of those great states are apparent. For time and the curse which sins deserve destroy everything. Thus when the world was obliterated by the Deluge, together with its people and cattle, this famous garden was also obliterated and became lost. Therefore it is vain for Origen and others to carry on senseless discussions. Moreover, the text also states that it was guarded by an angel lest anyone enter it. Therefore even if that garden had not perished as a result of the ensuing curse, the way to it is absolutely closed to human beings; that is, its location cannot be found. This is also a possible answer, although my first opinion, involving the Deluge, seems more probable to me.

But what answer shall we give in regard to the passage in the New Testament (Luke 23:43): "Today you will be with Me in Paradise"? Also regarding 2 Cor. 12:4: "I was snatched up into Paradise"? Indeed, I myself, do not hesitate to assert that Christ and the thief

[14] This information is derived from Lyra's exposition of Gen. 2:8.

[15] Evidently this is a criticism of the exegesis of Origen and others, known to Luther through Lyra.

did not enter any physical place. In Paul's case the matter is clear
when he says that he did not know whether he was in the body or
outside the body. Therefore I am of the opinion that in each of the
two instances Paradise designates the state in which Adam was in
Paradise, abounding in peace, in freedom from fear, and in all gifts
which exist where there is no sin. It is as if Christ said: "Today you
will be with Me in Paradise, free from sin and safe from death (except
that the Last Day must be awaited, when all this will be laid open
to view), just as Adam in Paradise was free from sin, death, and
every curse, yet lived in the hope of a future and eternal spiritual
life." Thus it is an allegorical Paradise, as it were, just as Scripture
also gives the name "Abraham's bosom" (Luke 16:22), not to Abraham's mantle but, in an allegorical sense, to that life which is in the
souls who have departed in the faith. They have peace, and they are
at rest; and in that quiet state they await the future life and glory.

Hence my answer is that Moses is now engaged in a historical
account and says that toward the east there was a certain place in
which there was a most delightful garden. As I said above, the word
מִקֶּדֶם properly designates a place, not a time, as our text has it. Hence
it was customary to call the east wind קָדִים, a dry and cold wind
which parches the fields. In that region of the world was Paradise,
or the garden, in which there were no linden trees, no oaks, no holly
trees, or whatever other fruitless trees there are; but there were fine
fruit trees of every variety, such trees as we today count among the
better, which yield cinnamon, cloves, etc. Although the rest of the
earth was also gorgeous (for thorns and thistles were not yet in existence), nevertheless this place had its own superior magnificence.
Thus Eden was a choice garden in comparison with the magnificence
of the whole earth, which itself also was a Paradise compared with
its present wretched state.

Into this garden, which the Lord Himself had planted with such
special care, He placed man. All this, I say, is historical. Therefore
we ask in vain today where or what that garden was. Some insist
that the rivers of which Moses speaks later on were in Syria, Mesopo-
tamia, Damascus, Egypt, in the center of which, as it were, Jerusalem
is located. Since it was designed for man with his descendants, we
would be mistaken to think of a narrow garden a few miles in cir-
cumference. It was a more excellent and better part of the earth.
And I judge that this garden remained until the time of the Deluge;

but before the Deluge it was guarded by God, as Moses says, by a watch of angels, so that the place was known to the descendants of Adam but inaccessible until later on it was disintegrated and obliterated by the Flood. Such is my opinion, and this is how I answer all questions inquisitive people raise about something that does not exist after sin and the Deluge.

The distance between the rivers troubles Origen, for he has in mind a garden area of the size they are among us.[16] Therefore he turns to allegory. Paradise he takes to be heaven; the trees he takes to be angels; the rivers he takes to be wisdom. Such twaddle is unworthy of theologians, though for a mirthful poet they might perhaps be appropriate. Origen does not take into consideration that Moses is writing a history and, what is more, one that deals with matters long since past.

Our adversaries today maintain the foolish position that the image and similitude of God remain even in a wicked person.[17] To me their statement would appear to be far more correct if they said that the image of God in man disappeared after sin in the same way the original world and Paradise disappeared. For man was righteous from the beginning; the world was most beautiful from the beginning; Eden was truly a garden of delight and joy. After sin all these things were marred to the extent that all creatures and the things which were good at first later on became harmful on account of sin. Even the sun and the moon appear as though they had put on sackcloth. Moreover, later on there was added the greater curse through the Flood, which utterly ruined Paradise and the entire human race. If today rivers overflow with such great damage to men,[18] cattle, and fields, what would be the result of a worldwide flood? Thus when we must discuss Paradise now, after the Flood, let us speak of it as a historical Paradise which once was and no longer exists. We are compelled to discuss man's state of innocence in a similar way. We can recall with a sigh that it has been lost; we cannot recover it in this life.

Moreover, just as Moses above makes various differences between the brutes and man, who shares with the brutes their origin from the ground, so in this passage he sets man apart by the particular place

[16] See, for example, Origen's *Homilies on Genesis, Werke,* VI (Leipzig, 1920), 20—22.

[17] Cf. p. 60, note 95.

[18] See *Luther's Works,* 13, p. 353, note 4.

and abode which the Lord planted for man and, as it were, constructed with greater sumptuousness and with more careful application than all the rest of the earth. Moses is most intent on having it clearly understood that man is a far nobler and better creature than the others. The brute animals have the earth on which they may feed; for man the Lord Himself provides a more excellent dwelling place, to the tilling and adorning of which he would joyfully apply himself and in which he would have his livelihood, separate from the beasts which he nevertheless had in subjection under his rule. Therefore the ideas of Origen and Jerome, together with those of other allegorists, are silly.[19] Because they no longer find Paradise on earth, they think some other meaning must be looked for. But saying that Paradise existed is different from saying that Paradise exists. As he is wont to do in his accounts, Moses records only this, that Paradise once existed. Thus there once existed such a dominion over all the beasts that Adam could call a lion and give him an order according to his wish; today this state of affairs does not exist. Those things have passed away, but it is recorded by Moses that once they did exist.

Some also ponder the question in what spot of the earth God created man.[20] There are those who maintain with great zeal that he was created in the area of Damascus, because they have heard that the soil of Damascus was reddish and also fertile. But I am passing over this kind of really foolish and superfluous questions. For us it is enough to know that on the sixth day, after the other animals had been created, man was created from the earth and placed in the Garden of Eden. What need is there to know where he was created? He was created outside of Paradise; for the text states that he was brought or placed into Paradise before the creation of Eve, who, as Moses here points out, was created in Paradise. To know this is enough. Let us now pass on to what follows.

9. *For the Lord God had brought forth from the ground every tree that was beautiful to behold and delightful to eat.*

These statements properly belong to the description of Paradise. Although the entire earth was so created that it produced fruit trees, herbs, and seeds, nevertheless the place called Eden had its own

---

[19] Jerome, *Liber Hebraicarum quaestionum in Genesin, Patrologia, Series Latina,* XXIII, 988—989.

[20] This question is discussed by Lyra in his commentary on Gen. 2:8.

special culture. To illustrate we may borrow a sort of parallel from
the state of affairs among us. Forests and fields produce their own
trees; but when we set aside a place for special cultivation, the garden
fruits are always given preference over those of the forests. Thus
Paradise was created with its unique culture, and, more than the rest
of the earth, it was provided with trees which were both delightful
to behold and pleasant to use. And so when he says in the first chapter (Gen. 1:29): "I have given you every herb and tree," this means
the food that was necessary. But Paradise also gave pleasure by
supplying finer, better, and more delightful foods than the trees produced on the rest of the earth, foods which the brutes, too, used to eat.

*Also the tree of life was in the midst of Paradise, and the tree of
the knowledge of good and evil.*

Moses describes Paradise in such a way that he makes of God
a gardener who, after planting his garden with great care according
to his design, chooses one or more trees which he tends and loves
more than the rest. One of these was the tree of life, created that man,
by eating of it, might be preserved in full bodily vigor, free from
diseases and free from weariness.

Here again man is set apart from the brutes, not only in regard
to place but also in regard to the advantage of a longer life and one
which always remains in the same condition. The bodies of the remaining living things increase in size and are stronger in their youth,
but in their old age they become feeble and die. The situation of man
would have been different. He would have eaten; he would have
drunk; and the conversion of food in his body would have taken place,
but not in such a disgusting manner as now. Moreover, this tree of
life would have preserved perpetual youth. Man would never have
experienced the inconveniences of old age; his forehead would never
have developed wrinkles; and his feet, his hands, and any other part
of his body would not have become weaker or more inactive. Thanks
to this fruit, man's powers for procreation and for all tasks would
have remained unimpaired until finally he would have been translated from the physical life to the spiritual. Therefore the remaining
trees would have supplied delightful and most excellent food, but this
one would have been like a medicine by which his life and his powers
were forever maintained at their utmost vigor.

Here again a question is proposed: How did a physical food or
a fruit have the power to preserve a body in this way that in the

course of time it did not become more inactive or sickly? But the answer is easy (Ps. 33:9): "He spoke, and it was done." For if God can make bread out of a stone, why couldn't He also preserve our powers by means of a fruit? Even after sin we see what great virtues are inherent even in the smallest herbs and seeds.

But let us take a look at our own bodies. Where did we get the ability to use natural heat in digesting the bread we have eaten and in converting it into blood, which later on gives strength to the whole body and makes it grow? Bring on all your hearths with their fire, and yet you will not cause blood to be produced out of bread, something which the mild heat in our bodies can perform. Let us, therefore, not be surprised that this tree was the tree of life, since the Lord wanted it so, planted it, and made it. Adam had a physical and nimble body which procreated, ate, and worked. These activities might be assumed to bring on deterioration or at least some change, through which finally man would naturally have become weak. But against this natural course of events God provided a remedy in the tree of life, so that without any decrease of his powers man could lead a long and healthy life in a state of perpetual youth.

These, then, are all historical facts. This is something to which I carefully call attention, lest the unwary reader be led astray by the authority of the fathers, who give up the idea that this is history and look for allegories. For this reason I like Lyra and rank him among the best, because throughout he carefully adheres to, and concerns himself with, the historical account.[21] Nevertheless, he allows himself to be swayed by the authority of the fathers and occasionally, because of their example, turns away from the real meaning to silly allegories.

But even more remarkable is what is stated about the tree of the knowledge of good and evil. Here it is asked "What sort of a tree was it? Why does it have this name, and what would have happened if this tree had not been in Paradise?" Augustine and those who follow him state correctly that it was so named from the event which lay in the future.[22] Adam was so created that if anything troublesome to his nature had happened, he would have a protection against it in the tree of life, which preserved his powers and perfect health at all times. And so, completely surrounded as he was by the goodness of

---

[21] In his exegesis of "The Last Words of David" from 2 Sam. 23, Luther praises Lyra for his knowledge of Hebrew and his able refutation of rabbinical interpreters (Weimar, LIV, 30).

[22] Augustine, *De Genesi ad litteram*, VIII, 15—16, pp. 253—257.

the Creator, if he had remained in the state of innocence, he would have acknowledged God as his Creator and would have governed the beasts according to His will without any inconvenience, in fact, with extreme joy. For all things were such that they could not harm man but could delight him in the highest degree.

And so when Adam had been created in such a way that he was, as it were, intoxicated with rejoicing toward God and was delighted also with all the other creatures, there is now created a new tree for the distinguishing of good and evil, so that Adam might have a definite way to express his worship and reverence toward God. After everything had been entrusted to him to make use of it according to his will, whether he wished to do so for necessity or for pleasure, God finally demands from Adam that at this tree of the knowledge of good and evil he demonstrate his reverence and obedience toward God and that he maintain this practice, as it were, of worshiping God by not eating anything from it.

Thus the statements which Moses has so far made deal with natural science or with economics or with politics or with jurisprudence or with medicine. But this is a matter of theology that here this statement about the tree is put before Adam in order that he may also have some outward physical way of indicating his worship of God and of demonstrating his obedience by an outward work. In a similar way the Sabbath, of which we spoke above, has to do chiefly with demonstrating inner and spiritual worship, with faith, love, prayer, etc.

But alas! Despite its fine purpose this method of showing outward obedience brought about a most wretched result. Similarly, we see even today that the holy and excellent Word is an offense to the wicked. Christ instituted Baptism to be a washing of regeneration (Titus 3:5). But haven't the sects stirred up a great offense on account of it? Has not the entire doctrine concerning Baptism been wretchedly corrupted? And yet what is more necessary to us than the institution of this very rite? In the same way it was necessary that man, as a physical being, also have a physical or external form of worship by means of which he might be trained according to his body in obedience to God.

Thus this text truly pertains to the church or theology. After God has given man the administration of government and of the home, has set him up as king of the creatures, and has added the tree of life as a safeguard for preserving this physical life, He now builds him, as it were, a temple that he may worship Him and thank the God who has so kindly bestowed all these things on him. Today in our churches we have an altar for the administration of the Eucharist, and we have platforms or pulpits for teaching the people. These objects were built not only to meet a need but also to create a solemn atmosphere. But this tree of the knowledge of good and evil was Adam's church, altar, and pulpit. Here he was to yield to God the obedience he owed, give recognition to the Word and will of God, give thanks to God, and call upon God for aid against temptation.

Our reason indeed becomes provoked at the creation of this tree, since because of it we sinned and fell into the wrath of God and into death. But why does it not become provoked in the same way because the Law was given by God and later on the Gospel was revealed by the Son of God? Have not endless offenses of errors and heresies followed as a result of this? Therefore let us learn that some external form of worship and a definite work of obedience were necessary for man, who was created to have all the other living creatures under his control, to know his Creator, and to thank Him. If, therefore, Adam had not fallen, this tree would have been like a common temple and basilica to which people would have streamed. Similarly, later on, after our nature had become depraved, a definite place was set aside for divine worship: the temple at Jerusalem. Now, after this tree has become the occasion of so awful a fall, it is correctly called by Moses the tree of the knowledge of good and evil on account of the unfortunate and wretched outcome.

Moreover, someone may ask here whether there was only one tree or several, and whether, in the fashion of Scripture, the singular is used for the plural, just as we speak collectively and say pear and apple when we have in mind the species and not the individual fruits. To me it does not appear at all preposterous that we understand the tree of life as a definite area in the midst of Paradise, a sort of grove in which there stood several trees of the species called arborvitae. It is also possible that the tree of the knowledge of good and evil is designated collectively as a wood or a grove, because it was somewhat like a chapel in which there were many trees of the same variety, namely, the trees of the knowledge of good and evil, from which the Lord forbade Adam to eat anything, or he would surely die. This tree was not deadly by nature; it was deadly because it was stated to be so by the Word of God. This Word assigns to all creatures their function and also preserves all creatures that they may not degenerate but that the distinct species may be preserved in endless propagation.

Thus it was brought about by the Word that the rock in the desert provided a most abundant supply of water (Num. 20:11) and that the bronze serpent healed those who looked at it (Num. 21:9). In this manner this one tree — or that particular kind of several trees in the midst of Paradise — killed Adam for not obeying the Word of God, not indeed because of its nature but because it had been so laid down by the Word of God. In this way we should also interpret the tree of life, from which God commanded Adam to eat as often as he desired to restore his powers; it was through the potency of the Word that the tree brought this about.

To our reason it appears very ludicrous for one fruit to be so injurious that the entire human race, in an almost infinite series, perished and died an eternal death. But the fruit did not have this power. Adam did indeed put his teeth into the fruit, but actually he put his teeth into a sting. This God had forbidden; this was disobedience to God. This is the true cause of the evil, namely, that Adam sins against God, disregards His order, and obeys Satan. The tree of the knowledge of good and evil was a good tree; it produced very fine fruit. But because the prohibition is added and man is disobedient, it becomes more injurious than any poison.

Similarly, because the Word of God inviolably declares (Ex. 20:15): "You shall not steal," anyone who appropriates the property of another is committing a sin. When the Jews in Egypt were commanded to seek to get money from their neighbors and to take it away with them (Ex. 3:22), this was not a sin; for they were exculpated by the command of God, to whom obedience is due in every situation. When a suitor loves a girl, desires her for his wife, and marries her, he does not commit adultery, even though the Law forbids desire;[23] for matrimony was divinely instituted and commanded for those who cannot live a chaste life without it. The situation with respect to these trees is clearly the same. The tree of life makes alive through the potency of the Word of Him who gives the promise and ordains it so; the tree of the knowledge of good and evil kills through the potency of the Word of Him who issues the prohibition.

[23] Cf. *Luther's Works,* 21, p. 89, note 35.

But it has its name "of the knowledge of good and evil," as Augustine says,[24] since after Adam had sinned because of it, he saw and felt not only what good he had lost but also into what great misery he had been hurled through his disobedience. So, then, the tree was good in itself; likewise, the command which had been added was good. Thus it was for Adam a tree of divine worship on which to show God his obedience by an outward work. But because of the sin which follows, it becomes a tree of curse. Now in a sort of digression Moses describes the garden at greater length.

10. *And a river came out from Eden to water the garden, and from there it is divided into four heads.*

Our translator is again in error when he makes an appellative out of the proper noun Eden.[25] Likewise, Origen and his followers also have to be faulted here for fabricating allegories. For it just happened that Eden had a large river by which the garden was watered. This river, which came from the east, divided into four parts, so that every part of the garden was watered. We must think of a very wide area of land, because this garden had been created to be the exclusive and perpetual dwelling place for Adam and all his descendants, of whom there would be a very great number.

11. *The name of the one was Pison; that is the one which flows around all the land of Havilah, where gold originates, 12. and the gold of that land is very good, and there is found bdellium and the onyx stone.*

This is one of the greatest causes of offense in Moses. For anything that lies before the eyes cannot be denied. Now this description applies properly to India, which he calls Havilah, where there is the Pison or the Ganges. Regarding the other three rivers, the Gihon, the Hiddekel, and the Prath — that is, the Nile, the Tigris, and the Euphrates — it is known also that their sources are very far apart. And so the question is: Since it is established that these rivers, the best-known to the entire world, are very far removed from one another, how can it be true when Moses says that they flow from one single source, that is, that they rush forth in the Garden of Eden

[24] See p. 93, note 22.

[25] The translation which Luther is criticizing here is reflected in the Douay rendition of this verse: "And a river went out of the place of pleasure to water paradise."

toward the east? For although the source of the Nile is unknown, there are certain evidences that it has its source in the south.[26] But the Ganges, the Tigris, and the Euphrates flow from the north and thus have their source in the opposite direction.

Moses, therefore, is most obviously contradicting reason. This has given many the opportunity to imagine that Eden was the entire earth. Even if this were not obviously wrong, it still would not safeguard Moses' statement that the source of these rivers is the same. Moreover, though it is likely that if Adam had remained in the state of innocence, God would have extended the garden after his descendants had increased, even this does not mean that Eden was the whole earth. For the text expressly distinguishes the Garden of Eden from the rest of the earth. What shall we say, then, about this passage of Moses? Because it opposes reason and experience, it has been a very abundant source of offense, giving Origen and others an opportunity for amazing twaddle. Some interpreters disregard this cause of offense and, as it were, walk through this sea with dry feet. But this attitude, too, should be far removed from an interpreter.[27]

Hence my opinion, which I also pointed out above, is, first, that Paradise was closed to man by sin, and, secondly, that it was utterly destroyed and annihilated by the Flood, so that no trace of it is visible any longer. For, as I also said above, I am fully of the opinion that after Adam's fall Paradise remained in existence and was known to his descendants, but was inaccessible because of the angel who kept watch over the garden with his flaming sword, as the text states. But the Flood laid everything waste, just as it is written that all the fountains and abysses were torn open (Gen. 7:11). Who, then, would doubt that these sources, too, were rent and thrown into confusion? And so, just as there are mountains after the flood where previously there were fields in a lovely plain, so undoubtedly there are now springs where there were none before, and vice versa. For the entire surface of the earth was changed. I have no doubt that there are remains of the Flood, because where there are now mines, there are commonly found pieces of petrified wood.[28] In the stones themselves there appear various forms of fish and other animals. Thus I believe

26 The location of the headwaters of the Nile was a mystery to the ancient world, not solved until the nineteenth century.

27 See p. 90, note 16.

28 This may reflect Luther's recollections from his boyhood as a miner's son.

that before the Flood the Mediterranean Sea was not surrounded by land, but that the channel in which it now has its place was produced for it by the Flood. Likewise, the area of the Red Sea without a doubt was formerly a fertile plain and, as is likely, some part of this garden. So also the remaining gulfs, the Persian, the Arabian, etc., consist of remnants of the Flood.

Therefore one must not imagine that the source of these rivers is the same today as it was at that time; but the situation is the same as in the case of the earth, which now exists and brings forth trees, herbs, etc. If you compare these with the uncorrupted creation, they are like wretched remnants of that wealth which the earth had when it was created. Thus these rivers remain like ruins, but, to be sure, not in the same place; much less do they come from the same sources. How much was lost of our bodies through sin? Therefore after its corruption one must speak about all of nature as about a new face of things, which nature put on first because of sin, then because of the universal Flood.

Moreover, God's practice has always been this: Whenever He punishes sin, He also curses the earth. Therefore in Zephaniah (1:3) He threatens that He will gather up the fish of the sea and the birds of the heaven. Similarly, in our age many streams have fewer fish than they had within the memory of our ancestors. The birds are less abundant, etc. A similar statement appears in Is. 13:19-22 about Babylon also. For when people are carried away, the beasts of the field also depart, and nothing remains except monsters and harmful wild beasts. Similarly, the land of Canaan, once most fertile, is now said to be full of barrenness, as Ps. 107:34 threatens. If this happens in the instance of particular punishments, what shall we imagine was effected by that universal punishment?

Therefore let no one be vexed or offended when he hears Moses state that the four rivers, which today are very far apart and have different sources, originate from the same source. We must not suppose that the appearance of the world is the same today as it was before sin. Since Origen held this supposition, he resorted to most silly allegories.

The Nile indeed exists to this day, also the Ganges; but, as Vergil says about Troy after its destruction: "And the field where Troy once was." [29] If anyone had seen the Nile and the other rivers in their first

29 Vergil, *Aeneid*, III, 11.

state and beauty, he would have seen far different ones. Now not only is their source not the same, or their state, but not even their course is the same. In the same way also all the other creatures have become misshapen and corrupted. For this reason St. Peter says in Acts 3:21: "The heaven must receive Christ until the time of the restitution of all things." He indicates, as Paul also says (Rom. 8:20), that the entire creation has been subjected to vanity and that we hope for the restitution of all things, not only of man but of the heaven, the earth, the sun, the moon, etc.

And so my answer regarding this passage is that the Nile, the Ganges, and the rest of the rivers are still in existence, but not such as they were. Not only were their sources thrown into disorder, but they themselves have been changed. Thus man still has feet, eyes, and ears the way each part was created in Paradise; but after sin these very members have been most wretchedly corrupted and misshapen. Before sin Adam had the clearest eyes, the most delicate and delightful odor, and a body very well suited and obedient for procreation. But how our limbs today lack that vigor! The situation with these rivers is the same if you consider their first beginning and that of the entire creation.

And so we now wait for the restoration of all things, not only of the soul but also of the body, because on that Day we shall have a better and statelier one than the one in Paradise was. For we shall not be placed into a physical life, which by its nature is subject to change, but into a spiritual life, into which Adam, too, would have been translated if he had lived without sin. To this hope we are led by Christ, who has restored our freedom from guilt through the remission of sins and who makes our state better than the state of Adam was in Paradise.

The verb קָבַב, which Moses employs here, has a wide meaning; for it denotes "to go around," as, for instance, watchmen walk around in the city. And so the Pison or Ganges is still the same so far as the name is concerned; but if you consider its attractiveness, its productiveness, its good qualities, and its course, there is almost nothing left of this noble river.

The land Havilah is India, located in the Orient. Scripture extols it for its wealth both in this passage and elsewhere.[30] The jewels and the gold of India have always been regarded as the best. But I sur-

---

[30] Perhaps this is an allusion to Esther 1:1-7.

mise from Moses' statements that in the designation Havilah there is included what we today call Arabia Felix [31] and other adjacent areas.

What he says about bdellium and the onyx I understand in the sense of the species for the genus. We still see India abounding not only in these jewels but also in others: emeralds, rubies, sapphires, turquoises, and diamonds — I am, to be sure, retaining the popular designations. Here I again refer you to what I stated previously. Now if such vast wealth has been granted to this land by God in the present, how much more blessed and wealthy shall we believe that it was before sin? For all that we have today hardly deserves to be termed a remnant.

13. *The name of the second river is Gihon; that is the one which flows around all of the land of Ethiopia.* 14. *The name of the third river is Hiddekel, but the fourth river is the Prath itself.*

The remaining three rivers Moses mentions merely by name. The Gihon is the Nile. Since it flows through Egypt, Moses includes Egypt in the name Cush or Ethiopia. The Hiddekel is the Tigris, the swiftest river of all. The fourth, he says, is the Prath itself; that is, it is close to us.[32]

Thus in this passage we have a description of Paradise with its rivers. But Paradise is now completely lost. Nothing more remains of it except these four corrupted and, as it were, leprous rivers, made so first by the sin of man and then by the Flood.

Now Moses proceeds to explain how, before Eve was created, the Law was given to Adam that he might have an outward form of worship by which to show his obedience and gratitude toward God.

15. *And so the Lord God took man and placed him in the Garden of Eden to work it and to guard it.*

After God had equipped the entire world in various ways, He also made ready the Garden of Eden, which He intended to be the dwelling place and royal headquarters of man, to whom He had assigned the rule over all the beasts. Now He places man into that garden as into a castle and temple. Of course, Adam was at liberty

[31] The geographers of Luther's day divided the Arabian peninsula into three parts: the northwest part was Arabia Petrae, the northern part was Arabia Deserta, and the main part of the peninsula was Arabia Felix, "Fertile Arabia."

[32] The etymology is still debated, but the relationship of this name to Euphrates is clear.

to leave it, stroll about on the rest of the earth — which itself was
most fertile and delightful — and amuse himself with the animals
as often as he wished.

Moreover, God assigns to Adam a twofold duty, namely, to work
or cultivate this garden and, furthermore, to watch and guard it.
Some traces of this assignment remain in the wretched remnants we
possess. Today, too, these two things must be done together; that is,
the land is not only tilled, but what has been tilled is also guarded.
But in endless ways each of the two activities has been disfigured.
Not only the cultivation but also the protection is attended by all sorts
of inconveniences and troubles. The reason for this situation will be
adequately shown below in chapter three. There we shall see that
the working of the ground has been interfered with and made utterly
disagreeable by thorns, thistles, the sweat of the face, and endless
vexation. For, to say nothing about providing food, how much difficulty, work, and inconvenience is involved in bringing up a child!

If, then, Adam had remained in the state of innocence, he would
have tilled the earth and planted little plots of aromatic herbs, not
only without inconvenience but, as it were, in play and with the
greatest delight. The children that were born would not have needed
their mother's milk for so long a time. Perhaps they would have
stood on their feet immediately, as we see in the case of chicks, and
would have sought their food without any effort on the part of their
parents. You can see how much trouble there is at the beginning of
life nowadays.

But if you should wish to discuss the matter of food, it is obvious
that not only do the animals have it in common with us, but human
beings deprive other human beings of it and steal it by fraud. For
this reason there must be walls, hedges, and other defenses; and yet
only with difficulty can you keep unharmed what you have raised with
much toil. Thus we still have the activity left; but it is far different
from what it was, not only because it is fraught with the utmost
inconvenience, but also because the earth seems to yield unwillingly
and sparsely what it would have yielded to Adam with the greatest
good will and in utmost abundance, whether he had made his sowing
within the garden or outside it on the rest of the earth. There would
have been no danger from thieves and murderers; everything would
have been safe.

Thus when we look at the thorns and thistles, at the sweat of the
face, etc., we see here, too, what a great evil original sin is. For just

as through sin man fell in his spirit, so also in his body he fell into
punishment. Work, which in the state of innocence would have been
play and joy, is a punishment. Even now in this wretched state of
nature we observe that for someone who has a delightful garden
sowing, planting, or digging are not a hardship but are done with zeal
and a certain pleasure. How much more perfect this would have
been in that garden in the state of innocence!

But it is appropriate here also to point out that man was created
not for leisure but for work, even in the state of innocence. Therefore
the idle sort of life, such as that of monks and nuns, deserves to
be condemned.

Moreover, just as we stated that work or activity would have been
without any inconvenience, so also defense or protection would have
been most pleasant, whereas now it is fraught with much danger.
By one single word, even by a nod, Adam would have put bears
and lions to flight. Indeed, we have protection today, but it is obviously awful. It requires swords, spears, cannons, walls, redoubts, and
trenches; and yet we can scarcely be safe with our families. And so
there are only faint and almost extinct traces of the activities involved
both in working and in guarding.

Others explain this passage by saying that God was to do the
working and protecting.[33] But the text speaks solely of human working and guarding. Similarly, it states below (Gen. 4:2) that Cain was
a husbandman; and in Job and Ecclesiastes the kings are called tillers
of the earth,[34] not only because of the work they perform but also
because of the protection they give. But, as I said, working and
guarding are sad and difficult words. At that time they represented
a pastime and man's greatest delight.

16. *And He commanded him, saying: Eat from every tree of Paradise,*
    17. *but from the tree of the knowledge of good and evil do not eat.*

Here we have the establishment of the church before there was
any government of the home and of the state; for Eve was not yet
created. Moreover, the church is established without walls and
without any pomp, in a very spacious and very delightful place. After
the church has been established, the household government is also
set up, when Eve is added to Adam as his companion. Thus the

[33] Augustine, *De Genesi ad litteram,* VIII, 10, p. 247.

[34] The passages referred to here are Eccl. 5:9 and possibly Job 3:14.

temple is earlier than the home, and it is also better this way. Moreover, there was no government of the state before sin, for there was no need of it. Civil government is a remedy required by our corrupted nature. It is necessary that lust be held in check by the bonds of the laws and by penalties. For this reason you may correctly call civil government the rule of sin, just as Paul calls Moses also the minister of death and of sin (Rom. 8:2). This is the one and foremost function of government, to hold sin in check, as Paul says (Rom. 13:4): "Government bears the sword for the punishment of the wicked." Therefore if men had not become evil through sin, there would have been no need of civil government; but Adam, together with his descendants, would have lived in utmost serenity and would have achieved more by moving one finger than all the swords, instruments of torture, and axes can achieve now. At that time there would have been no robber, murderer, thief, envier, and liar. What need, therefore, would there have been of laws and of civil government, which is like a cauterizing iron and an awful remedy by which harmful limbs are cut off that the rest may be preserved?

Therefore after the establishment of the church the government of the home is also assigned to Adam in Paradise. But the church was established first because God wants to show by this sign, as it were, that man was created for another purpose than the rest of the living beings. Because the church is established by the Word of God, it is certain that man was created for an immortal and spiritual life, to which he would have been carried off or translated without death after living in Eden and on the rest of the earth without inconvenience as long as he wished. There would not have been in him that detestable lust which is now in men, but there would have been the innocent and pure love of sex toward sex. Procreation would have taken place without any depravity, as an act of obedience. Mothers would have given birth without pain. Infants would not have been brought up in such a wretched manner and with such great toil.

But who can describe in words the glory of the innocence we have lost? There still remains in nature the longing of the male for the female, likewise the fruit of procreation; but these are combined with the awful hideousness of lust and the frightful pain of birth. Shame, ignominy, and embarrassment arise even among married people when they wish to enjoy their legitimate intercourse. So universal is the most oppressive evil of original sin! The creation indeed is good, and the blessing is good; but through sin they are so corrupted that married people cannot make use of them without shame. All these things would not have existed in Adam's state of innocence; but just as married people eat and drink together without shame, so there would have been a transcendent decency, not shame and embarrassment, in procreation and birth. But I return to Moses.

In this passage the church is established, as I said, before there was a home government. Here the Lord is preaching to Adam and setting the Word before him. Although the Word is short, it is nevertheless worth our spending a little time on it. For if Adam had remained in innocence, this preaching would have been like a Bible for him and for all of us; and we would have had no need for paper, ink, pens, and that endless multitude of books which we require today, although we do not attain a thousandth part of that wisdom which Adam had in Paradise. This brief sermon would have brought to its conclusion the whole study of wisdom. It would have shown us, as if written on a tablet, the goodness of God, who had created this nature without those familiar inconveniences which followed later on because of sin.

This sermon was delivered on the sixth day; and if, as the text indicates, Adam alone heard it, he later on informed Eve of it. If they had not fallen into sin, Adam would have transmitted this single command later on to all his descendants. From it would have come the best theologians, the most learned lawyers, and the most expert physicians. Today there is an infinite number of books for instructing theologians, lawyers, and physicians; but whatever we learn with the help of books hardly deserves to be called dregs in comparison with that wisdom which Adam drew from this single Word. So corrupt has everything become through original sin.

So, then, this tree of the knowledge of good and evil, or the place where trees of this kind were planted in large number, would have been the church at which Adam, together with his descendants, would have gathered on the Sabbath day. And after refreshing themselves from the tree of life he would have praised God and lauded Him for the dominion over all the creatures on the earth which had been given to mankind. Psalms 148 and 149 suggest a kind of liturgy for such thanksgiving, where the sun, the moon, the stars, the fish, and the dragons are commanded to praise the Lord. Yet every one of us could have composed a better and more perfect psalm than any of these if we had been begotten by Adam in innocence. Adam would have extolled the greatest gift, namely, that he, together with his descendants, was created according to the likeness of God. He would have admonished his descendants to live a holy and sinless life, to work faithfully in the garden, to watch it carefully, and to beware with the greatest care of the tree of the knowledge of good and evil. This outward place, ceremonial, word, and worship man would have had; and later on he would have returned to his working and guarding until a predetermined time had been fulfilled, when he would have been translated to heaven with the utmost pleasure.

But we are speaking of these good things as of a lost treasure, and we properly long with sighing for the day on which everything will be restored. Nevertheless, it is useful to recall both the good things which we lost and the evils which we endure and in which we live most wretchedly, so that we may be incited to that longing for the redemption of our bodies of which the apostle speaks in Rom. 8:22. For so far as our soul is concerned, we are free through Christ; and this freedom we keep in faith until it is revealed.

But it is useful to note also that God gave Adam Word, worship, and religion in its barest, purest, and simplest form, in which there was nothing laborious, nothing elaborate. For He does not prescribe the slaughter of oxen, the burning of incense, vows, fastings, and other tortures of the body. Only this He wants: that he praise God, that he thank Him, that he rejoice in the Lord, and that he obey Him by not eating from the forbidden tree.

We have the remnants of this worship, since Christ has restored it in some measure amid this weakness of our flesh; for we also praise God and thank Him for every spiritual and bodily blessing. But these are truly nothing but remnants. After this wretched life, however, when we join the choirs of the angels, then we shall offer this worship in a holier and purer form. In the same way it is a remnant of this bliss when through marriage we beware of adultery and avoid it, or when this physical life has not only its hard-won sustenance but also some safeguard and protection against various adversities which would otherwise overwhelm us. These are remnants, but certainly wretched remnants if you compare them with our original condition.

Here you must be warned once more against the false prophets through whose agency Satan tries in various ways to corrupt sound doctrine. I shall relate an instance from my own life, when I was shaken by a fanatic in regard to the elements of this doctrine.[35] The text indeed has the verb "to command," וַיְצַו יְהֹוָה, "and the Lord commanded." But he reasoned thus: For the just no Law has been given; Adam was just; therefore for the just Adam no Law was given. From this he later deduced that this was not a Law but only an exhortation. Moreover, because there is no lie where there is no Law, he was gradually brought to the point where he denied original sin. And over this logical conclusion he celebrated great triumphs, as though he were someone who had found a treasure hitherto unknown to the entire world. But it is profitable to be aware of the great exertions of Satan that we may learn to oppose them wisely.

Both statements are Paul's: that no Law has been given to the just (1 Tim. 1:9); and that where there is no Law, there is also no transgression (Rom. 4:15). But it is the part of a good dialectician to take note of the tricks and devices of the devil which his slaves, the abominable sophists, also use as their own. Indeed, they support themselves with Scripture, because they would look laughable if they tried to force only their own dreams on men; but they do not quote Scripture in its entirety. They always snatch up what appears to favor them; but what is against them they either cleverly conceal or corrupt with their cunning glosses.

Thus when Satan heard that Christ, in His great hunger, was supporting Himself by His reliance on the mercy of God, he tried to delude Him into a forbidden reliance, that is, into tempting God (Matt. 4:5-8). He made use of a statement of the psalm which suited his purpose (Ps. 91:11-12): "He commanded His angels concerning you that they should carry you on their hands and you do not strike your foot on a stone." But what was contrary to Satan's purpose — namely, that this custody of the angels would be "on our ways," or while we are engaged in our calling — this he cunningly concealed. For in this lies the solution of the entire argument, namely, that the angels are our guardians, but on our ways. This solution Christ points out learnedly when He, in turn, quotes the commandment: "You shall not tempt the Lord your God." He points out that it is man's way not to fly in the air (for that is the way of the flying creatures) but to use the steps which had been constructed from the roof of the temple in order that the descent might be easy and without danger. Therefore when we are engaged in our calling and in the performance

[35] Cf. *Luther's Works,* 22, p. 39, note 36

of our duty, by a command either from God or from men who have the legitimate right to call upon us, then let us believe that we shall not lack the protection of the angels.

This is a useful rule whenever one must carry on a discussion with fanatics. For the unwary are deceived when cunning men, according to their habit, switch from the parts to the whole, make use of the fallacy of composition and division, or fail to cite passages in their entirety.[36]

The same thing happens in the instance of this argument when the reasoning runs as follows: No Law has been given for the just; Adam was just; therefore no Law has been given to him, but only a sort of exhortation. In this situation anyone who is not wise and on his guard is caught, contrary to his expectations, in the awful conclusion that eating from the fruit was not even a sin, inasmuch as there was no Law. For it is true that where there is no Law, there is no transgression (Rom. 4:15).

I am sure that even in our time some have been fooled by this very reasoning. They speak about original sin as if it were not guilt but only a punishment. Thus Erasmus also declares somewhere in so many words that original sin is a punishment imposed on our first parents, a punishment which we, as their descendants, are also forced to bear because of someone else's guilt, without any fault on our part, just as a son born of a harlot is forced to bear the disgrace, not through his own fault but through his mother's.[37] For what sin has a person committed who was not yet in existence? These ideas are full of comfort for reason, but they are actually full of wickedness and blasphemy.

What, then, is the error in this syllogism? Obviously, this common one, that the text is not quoted in its entirety but is truncated in an utterly dishonest manner. For the complete text reads (1 Tim. 1:9-10): "The Law has not been given for the just person, but for murderers, adulterers, etc." From this there follows nothing else than that Paul is speaking about that Law which was given after sin, and not about this Law which the Lord gave when Adam was still guiltless and righteous. For the righteous, he says, no Law was given; therefore it follows undeniably that the Law was given to wicked and sinful nature.

[36] Aristotle, *Sophistici Elenchi*, ch. 4.
[37] See also p. 269, note 32.

Is it not a monstrous crime to jumble passages this way when so much is at issue? After sin Adam is not the person he was before sin in the state of innocence; and yet those people make no distinction between the Law given before sin and that given after sin. What Paul says about the Law which came in after sin they deceitfully and blasphemously apply to the Law which was given in Paradise. If sin had not been in existence, then that Law which forbids sin would also not have been in existence, just as I stated above that in the perfect creation there was no need of civil government or of laws, which are like branding irons, or of what Paul calls a schoolmaster (Gal. 3:24). A boy needs a schoolmaster and a switch because he is bad. Similarly, because a prince has disobedient citizens, he must have police and executioners. Paul is speaking strictly of a Law for which there was need after nature had become corrupted by sin.

But I also stated above why Adam had need of this command concerning the tree of the knowledge of good and evil, namely, that there should be an outward form of worship and an outward work of obedience toward God. The angel Gabriel, too, is without sin, a very pure and guiltless creature. And yet he accepts from God the command to instruct Daniel about very important matters (Dan. 8:16) and to announce to Mary that she will be the mother of Christ, who had been promised to the fathers (Luke 1:26). These are in truth commands which were addressed to a guiltless being. Likewise, Adam is here commanded by the Lord before sin to refrain from eating of the tree of the knowledge of good and evil. He would have obeyed this command readily and with the greatest joy if it had not been for Satan's deceit. But Paul is speaking of another Law; for he clearly states that he is speaking about the Law which was not given to the just but to the unjust. Who, then, is either so ignorant or so deranged as to conclude from this that no Law was given to Adam when he hears it stated that Adam was righteous? For nothing else follows from this than that the Law given to the unrighteous is not the same Law that was given to righteous Adam. Moreover, when a Law is given to righteous Adam, it follows that this is a different Law from the one which later was given to the unrighteous.

And so there is in this reasoning the fallacy of composition and division, because a truncated Scripture text is introduced. There is also the fallacy of equivocation.[38] The first consists in this, that the

[38] See p. 108, note 36.

Law before sin is one thing and the Law after sin is something else; the second consists in this, that "righteous" does not have the same meaning after sin and before sin. It is useful to take note of these procedures, and the arts [39] should be applied in this way for use in important discussions. They were not thought out for those leisurely debates in schools but in order that very important matters might be clarified by means of them. By this reasoning Satan is making a great effort to deny original sin. And yet this is in truth the same as denying the suffering and resurrection of Christ. Therefore Paul's statement should in no wise prevent us from declaring with Moses that a Law was given to righteous Adam not to eat from the tree of the knowledge of good and evil, just as commands are given to the angels. Because he transgressed this command, he sinned and later on reproduced sinners.

For on whatever day you will eat from it you will die.

This threat, which was so clearly added, also proves that a Law was given to Adam. Moreover, it shows too that Adam was created in the state of innocence, or was righteous. There was not yet any sin, because God did not create sin. Therefore if Adam had obeyed this command, he would never have died; for death came through sin. Thus the remaining trees of Paradise were all created for the purpose of helping man and maintaining his physical life sound and unimpaired.

For us today it is amazing that there could be a physical life without death and without all the incidentals of death, such as diseases, smallpox, stinking accumulations of fluids in the body, etc. In the state of innocence no part of the body was filthy. There was no stench in excrement, nor were there other execrable things. Everything was most beautiful, without any offense to the organs of sense; and yet there was physical life. Adam ate, he masticated, he digested; and if he had remained as he was, he would have done the other things physical life demands until at last he would have been translated to the spiritual and eternal life.

This, too, we have lost through sin, because now the present life is separated from the future life by that awful intermediate event, death. In the state of innocence that intermediate event would have been a most delightful one; by it Adam would have been translated

---

[39] By "arts" here logic and dialectic seem to be meant.

to the spiritual life or, as Christ calls it in the Gospel, to the angelic life (Matt. 22:30), in which physical activities come to an end. For in the resurrection of the dead we shall not eat, drink, or marry. This present physical state would have come to an end, and the spiritual life would have followed, just as we also believe that it will follow, thanks to Christ. Adam would have been divested of the glory which befitted a child and invested with heavenly glory; he would have been divested of his lower activities, which nevertheless would have been pure and not burdensome, as they are now after the Fall. And from the innocence of a child, so to speak, he would have been translated into the virile innocence which the angels have and which we, too, shall have in the future life.

I call it the innocence of a child because Adam was, so to speak, in a middle position and yet could be deceived by Satan and fall into disaster, as he did. The danger of such a fall will not exist in that perfect innocence which will be found in the future and spiritual life. This is the meaning of the threat of punishment: "On whatever day you will eat of this tree, you will die." It is as if God were saying: "You can indeed remain in the life for which I have created you. And yet you will not be immortal in the same way as the angels. Your life is, as it were, placed in the middle: you can remain in it and afterwards be carried to an immortality that cannot be lost; contrariwise, if you do not obey, you will become a victim of death and lose your immortality."

Therefore there is a great difference between the spiritual state of the angels and the innocence of Adam. The angels, as they are now, cannot fall; but Adam could fall. He was in a state in which he could become immortal (for he was without any sin) and be translated from his glory befitting a child to the deathless life in which there would be no further opportunity of sinning. From that innocence of a child he could also plunge into a curse, sin, and death. And so it happened. Adam was immortal because the trees created for him had the power to maintain his life unimpaired. But this immortality had not been made so sure for him that it was impossible for him to fall into mortality.

It is not our business to determine or to investigate too inquisitively why God wanted to create man in this middle condition, or why man was so created that all people are brought into being from one through procreation. The angels were not created in this condition; for they neither beget nor reproduce. They live a spiritual life. What is worthy of wonderment is God's plan in creating man, that although He had created him for physical life and bodily activity, He nevertheless added intellectual power, which is also in the angels, with the result that man is a living being compounded of the natures of the brute and of the angels.[40]

Furthermore, since in passing we touched on the nature of the angels, it must not be concealed that there was a certain likeness between the state of the human being and that of the angels, a fact which the fathers mention in their writings. But this likeness must not be applied to procreation, which has no place in a spiritual being, but only to incompleteness. For just as I said that to man there had, as it were, been assigned a middle position, so also the angels, as soon as they were created, were not so firmly established in their nature that they were incapable of sinning.[41] For this reason Christ says in John 8:44 that the devil did not abide in the truth. Hence the holy fathers have fancied that there arose a battle or a rebellion among the angels, some favoring the side of a very beautiful angel who, because of certain natural endowments, exalted himself over all.[42] These are likely ideas, and they fit in with Christ's statement that the devil did not abide in the truth, and with the statement in Jude's letter (Jude 6) that the evil angels left their habitation and became apostates.

Moreover, in support of this opinion they also made use of Is. 14:16. But so far as Isaiah is concerned, it is certain that he is speaking of the king of Babylon, who wanted to sit on God's throne, that is, rule over the holy people and the temple. Therefore whether there was any disharmony — or, as seems more likely to me, whether some proud angels, displeased by the meekness of the Son of God, wanted to place themselves above Him [43] — it is certain that the angels were in a state of innocence that could undergo a change. However, after the evil angels had been judged and condemned, the good were

40 Cf. *Luther's Works*, 13, p. 125, note 79.

41 See p. 113, note 44.

42 Cf. *Luther's Works*, 22, p. 103.

43 Luther had developed this exegetical insight in his lecture on Is. 14:12 of 1525—30 (Weimar, XXXI-2, 99—100).

confirmed so that they are no longer capable of sinning.[44] For they all became elect, while the evil angels were cast away.

But if the dragon or the evil angels had remained in their innocence, they, too, would have been confirmed later on so that they could not fall. The fathers put it this way: The angels were created in righteousness and later on were also confirmed in it; but according to Christ's saying, those who fell did not stand in the truth. However, we should not believe that they were few in number. Christ states in the Gospel that Satan has a kingdom (Luke 11:18) and that just as among brigands there is one who governs everything with his authority and counsel, so also the evil angels have their prince, Beelzebub, who was the leader of that rebellion.

But here a question arises about which the books of all the sophists make foolish statements and yet clear up nothing, namely: "What is original righteousness?" [45] Some make it a quality; others make it something else. If we follow Moses, we should take original righteousness to mean that man was righteous, truthful, and upright not only in body but especially in soul, that he knew God, that he obeyed God with the utmost joy, and that he understood the works of God even without prompting. A clear example of this state of affairs is this: When Adam was sleeping very soundly and God formed Eve out of his rib, Adam recognized the work of God immediately upon awaking, and said (Gen. 2:23): "This is bone of my bone." Is this not a superb intellect which at the first glance understands and recognizes the work of God?

It is part of this original righteousness that Adam loved God and His works with an outstanding and very pure attachment; that he lived among the creatures of God in peace, without fear of death, and without any fear of sickness; and that he had a very obedient body, without evil inclinations and the hideous lust which we now experience. In this way a very beautiful and very accurate picture of original righteousness can be inferred from the deprivation which we now feel in our own nature.

[44] Christian theologians had long discussed the question whether the good angels could fall as the evil angels had, and as a speculative inference from passages like Matt. 18:10 had developed the idea that after the fall of the evil angels the remaining angels had been "confirmed" in their virtue so that they could not fall. Cf. Peter Lombard, *Sententiae,* II, Dist. V, col. 661—662.

[45] For a representative discussion, see Thomas Aquinas, *Summa theologica,* I, Q. 95.

When the sophists speak of original sin, they are speaking only of wretched and hideous lust or concupiscence.[46] But original sin really means that human nature has completely fallen; that the intellect has become darkened, so that we no longer know God and His will and no longer perceive the works of God; furthermore, that the will is extraordinarily depraved, so that we do not trust the mercy of God and do not fear God but are unconcerned, disregard the Word and will of God, and follow the desire and the impulses of the flesh; likewise, that our conscience is no longer quiet but, when it thinks of God's judgment, despairs and adopts illicit defenses and remedies. These sins have taken such deep root in our being that in this life they cannot be entirely eradicated, and yet the wretched sophists do not mention them even with a word. Thus, as it always is with correlatives, original sin shows what original righteousness is, and vice versa: original sin is the loss of original righteousness, or the deprivation of it, just as blindness is the deprivation of sight.

This involves much more than the monks think when they restrict original righteousness almost exclusively to chastity.[47] But the soul ought to be given consideration first; thereafter also the body, which has been made so hideous by lust. But in the case of the soul the outstanding fact is this: that the knowledge of God has been lost; that we do not everywhere and always give thanks to Him; that we do not delight in His works and deeds; that we do not trust Him; that when He inflicts deserved punishments, we begin to hate God and to blaspheme Him; that when we must deal with our neighbor, we yield to our desires and are robbers, thieves, adulterers, murderers, cruel, inhuman, merciless, etc. The passion of lust is indeed some part of original sin. But greater are the defects of the soul: unbelief, ignorance of God, despair, hate, blasphemy. Of these spiritual disasters Adam, in the state of innocence, had no knowledge.

Moreover there must be added here the punishments for original sin. For the name "original sin" is correctly given to whatever was lost of those conditions which Adam enjoyed while his nature was still unimpaired: that he had a very keen intellect, so that he immediately realized that Eve was his own flesh; that he had an accurate knowledge of all the creatures; that he was righteous and upright;

---

46 See Luther's criticism of monastic exegesis on this score, *Luther's Works*, 13, p. 95, notes 32—33.

47 Cf. the passages referred to in note 46.

that he was endowed with extraordinary perception and an upright yet imperfect will. (For perfection was postponed until the spiritual life after the physical one.) Let this be enough about this text, in which the church was established. Now Moses proceeds:

18. *The Lord God also said: It is not good that man is alone; I shall make him a help which should be before him.*

We have the church established by the Word and a distinct form of worship. There was no need of civil government, since nature was unimpaired and without sin. Now also the household is set up. For God makes a husband of lonely Adam and joins him to a wife, who was needed to bring about the increase of the human race. Just as we pointed out above in connection with the creation of man that Adam was created in accordance with a well-considered counsel, so here, too, we perceive that Eve is being created according to a definite plan. Thus here once more Moses points out that man is a unique creature and that he is suited to be a partaker of divinity and of immortality. For man is a more excellent creature than heaven and earth and everything that is in them.

But Moses wanted to point out in a special way that the other part of humanity, the woman, was created by a unique counsel of God in order to show that this sex, too, is suited for the kind of life which Adam was expecting and that this sex was to be useful for procreation. Hence it follows that if the woman had not been deceived by the serpent and had not sinned, she would have been the equal of Adam in all respects. For the punishment, that she is now subjected to the man, was imposed on her after sin and because of sin, just as the other hardships and dangers were: travail, pain, and countless other vexations. Therefore Eve was not like the woman of today; her state was far better and more excellent, and she was in no respect inferior to Adam, whether you count the qualities of the body or those of the mind.

But here there is a question: "When God says: 'It is not good that man should be alone,' of what good could He be speaking, since Adam was righteous and had no need of a woman as we have, whose flesh is leprous through sin?"

My answer is that God is speaking of the common good or that of the species, not of personal good. The personal good is the fact that Adam had innocence. But he was not yet in possession of the common good which the rest of the living beings who propagated their kind through procreation had. For so far Adam was alone; he still had no partner for that magnificent work of begetting and preserving his kind. Therefore "good" in this passage denotes the increase of the human race. In this way, although Adam was innocent and righteous, he did not yet have that good for which he was created, namely, immortality, into which he would have been translated in due time if he had remained in innocence. Hence the meaning is that Adam as the most beautiful creature is well provided for so far as his own person is concerned but still lacks something, namely, the gift of the increase and the blessing — because he is alone.

Today, after our nature has become corrupted by sin, woman is needed not only to secure increase but also for companionship and for protection. The management of the household must have the ministration of the dear ladies. In addition — and this is lamentable — woman is also necessary as an antidote against sin. And so, in the case of the woman, we must think not only of the managing of the household which she does, but also of the medicine which she is. In this respect Paul says (1 Cor. 7:2): "Because of fornication let each one have his own wife." And the Master of the *Sentences* declares learnedly that matrimony was established in Paradise as a duty, but after sin also as an antidote.[48] Therefore we are compelled to make use of this sex in order to avoid sin. It is almost shameful to say this, but nevertheless it is true. For there are very few who marry solely as a matter of duty.

But the rest of the animals do not have this need. Consequently, for the most part they copulate only once a year and then are satisfied with this as if by their very action they wanted to indicate that they were copulating because of duty. But the conduct of human beings is different. They are compelled to make use of intercourse with their wives in order to avoid sin. As a result, we are begotten and also born in sin, since our parents did not copulate because of duty but also as an antidote or to avoid sin.

And yet, in the presence of this antidote and in so wretched a state, the Lord fulfills His blessing; and people are begotten, though in sin and with sin. This would not have been the case in Paradise. The act of begetting would have been a most sacred one without any passion of lust such as there is now, and children would have been in

48 Peter Lombard, *Sententiae*, IV, Dist. XXVI, col. 908—909.

original righteousness and uprightness. Immediately, without any instruction, they would have known God; they would have praised Him; they would have given thanks to Him, etc. All this has now been lost; and yet it serves a purpose to think of these things that we may gain some idea of the difference between that state in which we now are, that is, original sin, and that one in which Adam was, that is, original righteousness, for which we hope when all things are restored (Acts 3:21).

In connection with the expression "Let Us make" [49] I suggested that Eve was created according to a unique counsel that it might be clear that she has a share in immortality, a life better than that of the remaining animals, which live only their animal life, without hope of eternal life.

What appears in the Latin text as "like unto himself" is in Hebrew "which should be about him." With this expression the text also makes a difference between the human female and the females of all the remaining animals, which are not always about their mates: the woman was so created that she should everywhere and always be about her husband. Thus imperial law also calls the life of married people an inseparable relationship.[50] The female of the brutes has a desire for the male only once in a whole year. But after she has become pregnant, she returns to her home and takes care of herself. For her young born at another time she has no concern, and she does not always live with her mate.

But among men the nature of marriage is different. There the wife so binds herself to a man that she will be about him and will live together with him as one flesh. If Adam had persisted in the state of innocence, this intimate relationship of husband and wife would have been most delightful. The very work of procreation also would have been most sacred and would have been held in esteem. There would not have been that shame stemming from sin which there is now, when parents are compelled to hide in darkness to do this. No less respectability would have attached to cohabitation than there is to sleeping, eating, or drinking with one's wife.

Therefore was this fall not a terrible thing? For truly in all nature there was no activity more excellent and more admirable than procreation. After the proclamation of the name of God it is the most

[49] See p. 69.

[50] Cf. *Luther's Works*, 21, pp. 96 ff.

important activity Adam and Eve in the state of innocence could carry on — as free from sin in doing this as they were in praising God. Although this activity, like the other wretched remnants of the first state, continues in nature until now, how horribly marred it has become! In honor husband and wife are joined in public before the congregation; but when they are alone, they come together with a feeling of the utmost shame. I am not speaking now about the hideousness inherent in our flesh, namely, the bestial desire and lust. All these are clear indications of original sin.

So the woman was a helper for Adam; for he was unable to procreate alone, just as the woman was also unable to procreate alone. Moreover, these are the highest praises of sex, that the male is the father in procreation, but the woman is the mother in procreation and the helper of her husband. When we look back to the state of innocence, procreation, too, was better, more delightful, and more sacred in countless ways.

Today you find many people who do not want to have children. Moreover, this callousness and inhuman attitude, which is worse than barbarous, is met with chiefly among the nobility and princes, who often refrain from marriage for this one single reason, that they might have no offspring. It is even more disgraceful that you find princes who allow themselves to be forced not to marry, for fear that the members of their house would increase beyond a definite limit.[51] Surely such men deserve that their memory be blotted out from the land of the living. Who is there who would not detest these swinish monsters? But these facts, too, serve to emphasize original sin. Otherwise we would marvel at procreation as the greatest work of God, and as a most outstanding gift we would honor it with the praises it deserves.

This is also the source of the aspersions against the female sex, aspersions which ungodly celibacy has augmented. However, it is a great favor that God has preserved woman for us — against our will and wish, as it were — both for procreation and also as a medicine against the sin of fornication. In Paradise woman would have been a help for a duty only. But now she is also, and for the greater part at that, an antidote and a medicine; we can hardly speak of her without a feeling of shame, and surely we cannot make use of her without

51 Perhaps this is a reference to the military orders of the Middle Ages — e. g., the Teutonic Knights — who tried to observe the threefold monastic vow of poverty, chastity, and obedience, though they were often dispensed from the second.

shame. The reason is sin. In Paradise that union would have taken place without any bashfulness, as an activity created and blessed by God. It would have been accompanied by a noble delight, such as there was at that time in eating and drinking. Now, alas, it is so hideous and frightful a pleasure that physicians compare it with epilepsy or falling sickness.[52] Thus an actual disease is linked with the very activity of procreation. We are in the state of sin and of death; therefore we also undergo this punishment, that we cannot make use of woman without the horrible passion of lust and, so to speak, without epilepsy.

Because of sin the same thing has happened to us in the case of spiritual gifts. Even though we have faith and live in faith, nevertheless we cannot avoid doubt and an awareness of death. These punishments of original sin the holy fathers have clearly seen and felt. For this reason Scripture, too, uses the term עֶרְוָה for pudendum or disgrace.

The account which follows is, as it were, a repetition, to make it easier for Moses to turn to the description of the manner in which woman was created. Therefore it must be understood in the sense of a pluperfect.

19. *When the Lord God had formed from the ground all the animals of the earth, He brought them to Adam to see what he would call them.*

It is as if Moses were saying: According to His definite plan, which He had carefully considered in advance, God wanted to create woman; for He saw that all the other animals had a help for procreation, but Adam alone had none. And so God brought all the animals to Adam; and when he had assigned to each of them its name, he found none that was like himself. Here again we are reminded of the superior knowledge and wisdom of Adam, who was created in innocence and righteousness. Without any new enlightenment, solely because of the excellence of his nature, he views all the animals and thus arrives at such a knowledge of their nature that he can give each one a suitable name that harmonizes with its nature. From this enlightenment there also followed, of course, the rule over all the animals, something which is also pointed out here, since they were named in accordance with Adam's will. Therefore by one single word he was able to compel lions, bears, boars, tigers, and whatever

[52] The source for this may be Aristotle, *Problemata*, Book IV.

else there is among the more outstanding animals to carry out whatever suited their nature. This ability, too, we have lost through sin.

Since we do not possess a knowledge even of the natures of the animals, what their abilities and activities are, it is not surprising that we have no knowledge of God. There are in existence various books with descriptions of the natures of plants and animals.[53] But how much time and how much observation were necessary until these could be collected this way through experience! There was a different light in Adam, who, as soon as he viewed an animal, came into possession of a knowledge of its entire nature and abilities, and, moreover, a far better one than we can acquire even when we devote an entire life to research into these things. Just as this knowledge in Adam was an outstanding gift of God, so it also pleased God exceedingly and delighted Him. Therefore He commands him to make use of this knowledge by giving names to all the animals.

20. *For everything that Adam called a living being, that was its name. And Adam called all the animals by their names, and all the birds of the heaven and all the beasts of the land. But for Adam was not found a help that might be about him.*

What an ocean of knowledge and wisdom there was in this one human being! Moreover, although Adam lost much of this knowledge through sin, I nevertheless believe that everything still to be found in the books of all the wise men who have written for the many centuries since scientific pursuits had their first beginning could not equal that wisdom which still remained in Adam later on but gradually became fainter in his descendants and has almost been blotted out.

Moreover, we must again be reminded here that Moses is still dealing with a description of the work of the sixth day. What he had briefly stated in the first chapter: "Let Us make a man," that he wants to develop more fully in this chapter in order to establish the difference between man and the rest of the animals by more than a single proof. And so he devotes the entire second chapter to describing the creation of man. About the male he said that he was made out of the dust, that the breath of life was breathed into his face, and that all the living beings were brought before him. When Adam saw no help among them, the woman was made — his partner in procreation and

53 Perhaps this is a reference to Pliny's *Natural History;* cf. p. 204, note 50.

in the preservation of the species. God did not want his descendants to originate in the same way in which Adam was made out of earth; it was His desire that man should have the power of procreation, such as the other animals had. So far as our physical life is concerned, we drink, we eat, we procreate, and we are born just like the rest of the animals. And yet Moses deals with this matter with the important purpose of distinguishing man from the other living beings, because after his physical life man was to share in the spiritual and eternal life. All this belongs to the work of the sixth day. For because God had said: "Grow and increase," it became necessary to describe how the woman was added to Adam, how she was made and was joined to him.

But this also has a bearing on our firmly holding the conviction that there were really six days on which the Lord created everything, in contrast to the opinion of Augustine and Hilary, who believed that everything was created in a single moment.[54] They, therefore, abandon the historical account, pursuing allegories and fabricating I don't know what speculations. However, I am not saying this to vilify the holy fathers, whose works should be held in high regard, but to establish the truth and to comfort us. They were great men, but nevertheless they were human beings who erred and who were subject to error. So we do not exalt them as do the monks, who worship all their opinions as if they were infallible. To me the great comfort seems to lie rather in this, that they are found to have erred and occasionally to have sinned. For this is my thought: If God forgave them their errors and sins, why should I despair of His pardon? The opposite brings on despair — if you should believe that they did not have the same shortcomings that you have. Moreover, it is certain that between the call of the apostles and that of the fathers there is a great difference. Why, then, should we regard the writings of the fathers as equal to those of the apostles?

So far as the present passage is concerned, how, pray, is it possible that six days were either an hour or a single moment? Neither reason nor a faith which has its support in the Word can agree to this. Therefore let us have the conviction that there were certain intervals of time. Thus Adam was created alone; later on the animals were brought to him, and Adam was put to a test whether he could find or see a partner in that group; finally Eve was created. And because these def-

[54] Cf. p. 4, note 8.

inite words, "From every tree you will eat," struck Adam's ears, this proves that they were all spoken in time at intervals, unless you wish to turn senseless allegories after the manner of Origen. For the subject under discussion here is not God, in whose sight all past and future events are present ones, but Adam, who was in time and lived in time, and with whom there was a difference between the future and the past, just as with any creature. These facts, I thought, would bear brief repetition here. Let us now proceed.

21. *Then the Lord God sent a deep sleep upon Adam, and when he had fallen asleep, He took one of his ribs and closed the place with flesh.*

Here, too, not only faith but also reason and the situation demand that the time of waking be taken as one time and the time of sleeping as another. Both of these activities have their own allotted times. That Adam was created on the sixth day, that the animals were brought to him, that he heard the Lord giving him a command regarding the tree of the knowledge of good and evil, that the Lord sent a sleep upon him — all these facts clearly refer to time and physical life. Therefore it is necessary to understand these days as actual days, contrary to the opinion of the holy fathers. Whenever we see that the opinions of the fathers are not in agreement with Scripture, we respectfully bear with them and acknowledge them as our forefathers; but we do not on their account give up the authority of Scripture. Aristotle's statement in the first book of his *Ethics* is well put and true: "Better it is to defend the truth than to be too much devoted to those who are our friends and relatives." [55] And this is, above all, the proper attitude for a philosopher. For although both, truth and friends, are dear to us, preference must be given to truth.[56] If a pagan maintains that this must be the attitude in secular discourses, how much more must it be our attitude in those which involve the clear witness of Scripture that we dare not give preference to the authority of men over that of Scripture! Human beings can err, but the Word of God is the very wisdom of God and the absolutely infallible truth.

[55] In his *Nicomachean Ethics*, I, ch. 6, Aristotle says: "While both are dear, piety requires us to honor truth above our friends."

[56] The statement of Aristotle quoted in note 55 had become a proverb in the form: "Plato is dear to me, but dearer still is truth."

But so far as this account is concerned, what, I ask you, could sound more like a fairy tale if you were to follow your reason? Would anyone believe this account about the creation of Eve if it were not so clearly told? This is a reversal of the pattern of the entire creation. Whatever is born alive, is born of the male and the female in such a manner that it is brought forth into the world by the female. Here the woman herself is created from the man by a creation no less wonderful than that of Adam, who was made out of a clod of earth into a living soul. This is extravagant fiction and the silliest kind of nonsense if you set aside the authority of Scripture and follow the judgment of reason. Accordingly, Aristotle declares that neither a first nor a last man can be conceded.[57] Reason would compel us, too, to make the same statement if it did not have this text. If you should reach the conclusion that what the unvarying experience of all creation proves is true, namely, that nothing comes into existence alive except from a male and a female, then no first human being can be conceded.

The same thing would also have to be stated about the world, which the philosophers have, therefore, asserted is eternal.[58] But reason with all its force inclines to this conviction even though proofs founded on reason are thought out by which it is demonstrated that the world is not eternal. How can it take its beginning from nothing? Moreover, if you should say that the world had a beginning and there is a time when the world was not in existence, it immediately follows that there was nothing prior to the world. An endless series of other absurdities follows, and these induce philosophers to conclude that the world is eternal. But if you should say that the world is infinite, then immediately another new infinite will also appear, namely, the succession of human beings. But philosophy does not grant the existence of several infinites, and yet it is compelled to grant them because it knows of no beginning of the world and of men. These contradictions and the lack of clarity gave the Epicureans the opportunity to say that the world and man came into existence without any reason and will also perish without any reason, just as cattle perish, which die as though they had never existed. This leads to another conclusion, namely, that God either plainly does not exist or does not concern Himself with human affairs. Into these perplexing mazes

[57] See p. 3, note 2.

[58] See p. 3, note 3.

reason is misled when it is without the Word and follows its own judgment.

However, it is useful to realize how it comes about that our reason or wisdom is unable to make a greater advance in understanding the creation. For what, I ask, does a philosopher know about heaven and the world if he does not even know whence it came and whither it tends? Indeed, what do we know about ourselves? We see that we are human beings. But that we have this man for a father and this woman for a mother — this must be believed; it can in no wise be known. Thus our entire knowledge or wisdom is based solely on the knowledge of the material and formal cause, although in these instances, too, we sometimes talk disgraceful nonsense.[59] The efficient and final cause we obviously cannot point out, especially — and this is a wretched situation — when we must discourse or do some thinking about the world in which we exist and live, likewise about ourselves. Such pitiable and inadequate wisdom!

Aristotle declares: "Man and the sun bring mankind into existence."[60] Well said. But follow this wisdom, and you will arrive at the point where you maintain that man and the sun are eternal and infinite. For you will never find a human being who is either the beginning or the end, just as I cannot find the beginning and the end of my person if I want to gain certain knowledge about this and am not willing to rely on belief. But what sort of wisdom and knowledge is it that knows nothing about the final cause and the efficient cause? So far as our having a knowledge of the form is concerned, a cow likewise knows her abode and (as the German proverb has it) looks at and recognizes her door. This also makes clear how awful was the fall into original sin, through which we have lost this knowledge and have become incapable of seeing either the beginning or the end of ourselves.

Plato, Cicero, and other philosophers who belong to the better sort state in their discussions that man walks with his head erect, while the rest of the beings look at the earth with their heads bent down. To man they attribute reason or the ability to understand; and later they reach the conclusion that man is an extraordinary

---

[59] The material cause is "that from which, as immanent material, a thing comes into being," while the formal cause is "the form or pattern, i. e., the definition of the essence, and the classes which include this . . . and the parts included in the definition." Aristotle, *Metaphysics*, V, 2.

[60] See p. 58, note 91.

animal created for immortality. But how tenuous and almost useless this is! All this is based on a knowledge of man's form. But if you go on to give consideration to his substance, does not reason compel you to declare that this being must again be disintegrated and cannot be immortal?

Therefore let us learn that true wisdom is in Holy Scripture and in the Word of God. This gives information not only about the matter of the entire creation, not only about its form,[61] but also about the efficient and final cause, about the beginning and about the end of all things, about who did the creating and for what purpose He created. Without the knowledge of these two causes our wisdom does not differ much from that of the beasts, which also make use of their eyes and ears but are utterly without knowledge about their beginning and their end.

Therefore this is an outstanding text. The more it seems to conflict with all experience and reason, the more carefully must it be noted and the more surely believed. Here we are taught about the beginning of man that the first man did not come into existence by a process of generation, as reason has deceived Aristotle and the rest of the philosophers into imagining. The reproduction of his descendants takes place through procreation; but the first male was formed and created from a clod of the field, and the first female from the rib of the sleeping man. Here, therefore, we find the beginning which it is impossible to find through Aristotle's philosophy.

After this beginning was made, there then follows the no less wonderful propagation through the union of a male and female, whereby the entire human race is brought into being from a droplet of the human body. In a similar vein Paul, on the basis of this passage, has a clever discourse among the philosophers in Athens (Acts 17:25): "God Himself gives to all ζωὴν καὶ πνοήν, spirit and life everywhere, and from the blood of one man He makes the whole human race that it may dwell on the entire earth, that they may seek God, if perhaps they may feel Him or find Him, although He is not far from each one of us." Here Paul is speaking of the propagation brought about by the first man when he says "from the blood of one man." If, therefore, man is brought into existence from a droplet of blood, as the experience of all men on the entire earth bears witness, surely this is

[61] See p. 124, note 59.

no less miraculous than that the first man was created from a clod, and the female from a rib of the man.

But why does the creation of Adam and Eve seem so unbelievable and miraculous, while man's propagation, which all men know and see, does not seem so miraculous? Undoubtedly because, as Augustine says, miracles become commonplace through their continuous recurrence.[62] Thus we do not marvel at the wonderful light of the sun, because it is a daily phenomenon. We do not marvel at the countless other gifts of creation, for we have become deaf toward what Pythagoras aptly terms this wonderful and most lovely music coming from the harmony of the motions that are in the celestial spheres. But because men continually hear this music, they become deaf to it, just as the people who live at the cataracts of the Nile are not affected by the noise and roar of the water which they hear continually, although it is unbearable to others who are not accustomed to it. Without a doubt he took over this very statement from the teaching of the fathers, but they did not want to be understood as though sound were given off by the motion of the celestial bodies. What they wanted to say was that their nature was most lovely and altogether miraculous, but that we ungrateful and insensible people did not notice it or give due thanks to God for the miraculous establishment and preservation of His creation.

Thus it is a great miracle that a small seed is planted and that out of it grows a very tall oak. But because these are daily occurrences, they have become of little importance, like the very process of our procreation. Surely it is most worthy of wonder that a woman receives semen, that this semen becomes thick and, as Job elegantly said (Job 10:10), is congealed and then is given shape and nourished until the fetus is ready for breathing air. When the fetus has been brought into the world by birth, no new nourishment appears, but a new way and method: from the two breasts, as from a fountain, there flows milk by which the baby is nourished. All these developments afford the fullest occasion for wonderment and are wholly beyond our understanding, but because of their continued recurrence they have come to be regarded as commonplace, and we have verily become deaf to this lovely music of nature.

But if we regarded these wonders in true faith and appraised them for what they actually are, they surely would not be inferior

---

[62] Augustine, *De utilitate credendi*, XVII, 35, is one such discussion.

to what Moses says here: that a rib was taken from the side of Adam as he slept and that Eve was created from it. If it had pleased the Lord to create us by the same method by which Adam was created from the clay, by now this, too, would have ceased to hold the position of a miracle for us; we would marvel more at the method of pro-creation through the semen of a man. This crude doggerel is right, and there was certainly good reason for composing it: "Everything that is rare is appreciated, but what is an everyday occurrence comes to be regarded as commonplace." [63] If the stars did not rise during every single night or in all places, how great a gathering of people there would be for this spectacle! Now not one of us even opens a window because of it.

Therefore our lack of gratitude deserves to be reproved. If we believe that God is the efficient and the final cause, should we not wonder at His works, delight in them, and proclaim them always and everywhere? But how many are there who really do this from the heart? We hear that God took a clod and made a human being; we wonder at this, and because of our wonder we regard it as a fairy tale. But that He now takes a drop from the blood of the father and creates a human being, this we do not wonder at, because it happens every day, while the other thing was done only once; yet each of the two is brought about through the same skill and the same power and by the same Author. For He who formed man from a clod now creates men from the blood of their parents.

Aristotle, therefore, prates in vain that man and the sun bring man into existence. Although the heat of the sun warms our bodies, nevertheless the cause of their coming into existence is something far different, namely, the Word of God, who gives a command to this effect and says to the husband: "Now your blood shall become a male; now it shall become a female." Reason knows nothing about this Word. Therefore it cannot get away from its childish prattle about the causes of such important matters. Thus the physicians, who have followed the philosophers, ascribe procreation to a matching mixture of qualities which are active in predisposed matter.[64] Although reason cannot disprove this (for it sees that dry and cold natures are unsuited for generating, while moist and fairly warm ones are better suited), still they have not arrived at the first cause. The Holy Spirit leads

[63] The verse is: *Omne rarum carum.*
[64] Cf. p. 52, note 85.

us to something higher than nature, higher than qualities and their proper mixture, when He puts before us the Word by which everything is created and preserved.

Therefore that a man is developed from a drop of blood, and not an ox or a donkey, happens through the potency of the Word which was uttered by God. And so, as Christ also teaches in the Lord's Prayer (Matt. 6:9), we call God our Father and our Creator, as the Creed calls Him. When we look at this Cause, then with a chaste and pure heart and with gladness we can speak of those things which otherwise, if this Cause is disregarded, we could not mention without filthiness and indecency.

This discussion also shows how awful the fall into original sin was, since the entire human race knows nothing of its origin. Indeed, we see a man and a woman being joined; we see the woman made pregnant by a droplet of blood; and later, at a definitely fixed time, a baby is brought into the world. These are facts that lie before the eyes of all and are well known; and yet without the reminder and instruction of the Word you have no actual knowledge of the very activity which you are carrying on consciously and with open eyes. The discussions of the philosophers, with which we have already dealt, give sufficient evidence of this. Such horrible blindness and such a pitiful lack of knowledge!

Accordingly, if Adam had persevered in innocence, it would have been unnecessary to instruct his descendants about their origin, just as it was unnecessary to instruct Adam about the creation of his Eve, because the moment he saw her, he himself was aware that she was bone from his bones and flesh from his flesh. That kind of knowledge of themselves and of the remaining creatures would have remained also among the descendants of Adam. All would have become aware at once of the final and efficient cause about which we now have no more knowledge than cattle have.

For the ears of reason, consequently, this is a very beautiful and pleasing fairy tale, which the philosophers enjoyed ridiculing when they heard about it, as some of them did, especially those who had become acquainted with the science and wisdom of the Egyptians.[65] But it is incalculable wisdom for us to know what is taught by this foolish fairy tale, as the world calls it, namely, that the beginning of man's coming into existence was through the Word, inasmuch as

[65] An allusion to Acts 7:22; see also the patristic theory mentioned p. 4, note 5.

God takes a clod and says: "Let Us make a man." Later He likewise takes a rib of Adam and says: "Let Us make a helper for man." Now, after discussing whatever was necessary about the content, let us give consideration to the words.

The Lord God, says Moses, caused a תַּרְדֵּמָה, a "deep sleep," to fall upon Adam. The verb רדם denotes to be overwhelmed by "sleep," like those who fall asleep unawares and nod their heads. There are different kinds of sleep.[66] Some are deep or heavy and are not disturbed by dreams. These are healthful, for they moisten the body well and are useful for digestion; they do not tire the head either. Others are lighter and, as it were, mixed with periods of waking. In the case of these, dreams are more frequent; they also bother the head and are evidence of a less healthy body.

Moses says that Adam was overcome by a deep sleep, so that, as he lay stretched out on the green earth, he drew long breaths, as people do when they are enjoying a good, sweet sleep. This sleep, he says, the Lord caused to fall upon him. Sleep is in truth a divine and most excellent gift which streams down from above like dew and moistens the entire body. While Adam was sleeping this way, the Lord took one of his ribs. The Hebrew word צֵלָע denotes a rib and side. Therefore I hold that the Lord did not take a bare rib, but one covered with flesh, since Adam says below: "This is bone from my bones and flesh from my flesh." Moreover, the Lord does this also through His Word. We should not suppose that, like a surgeon, He did some cutting. He said: "From this bone thus covered with flesh let there be made a woman," and it was done. This gap in the side He later on closed with flesh.

Here a discussion arises among the faultfinders, who come up with some prodigious prattle.[67] They assert that the male has more ribs on one side than on the other. But in this matter the physicians are better informed, because they have a knowledge of anatomy. Lyra has a discussion on whether that rib was superfluous in the body of Adam. If this was the case, he says, it was something

---

[66] See Weimar, Tischreden, I, No. 508.

[67] "This seems inappropriate, for either that rib belonged to the completeness of [Adam's] nature, or it was superfluous. If the first, then his body became imperfect and diminished, which would not be proper for the condition of the first man, who was simply perfect in both soul and body. If the second, then that rib was a freak in Adam, as a sixth finger would be on a hand, which would be inappropriate in a perfect man, as was said before." Lyra on Gen. 2:21, sec. "h."

abnormal; if it was not the case, it follows that Adam was later on minus one rib. But he says that this, too, is abnormal. Finally he comes up with this answer: The rib was superfluous so far as the individual was concerned. Therefore even though it had been removed, Adam's body was complete. Yet Adam's body had need of this rib because of the woman who was to be formed from it.

Our answer to all this is the statement: "God said." This statement puts an end to all such debates. Why is it necessary to discuss where God found the remaining material, God, who is able to do anything by a single word and who creates all things? These questions have their origin in philosophy and in the science of medicine, which discuss the works of God without the Word. Moreover, the result of this procedure is that the glory of Holy Scripture and the majesty of the Creator are lost. Therefore, passing over these discussions, we shall simply adhere to the account as it is presented by Moses: Eve was created from a rib of Adam, and part of his body was again closed with flesh. Just as Adam was made from a clod, so I was made from a droplet of my father's blood. How my mother conceived me, how I was formed in the womb, and how my growth took place — all this I leave to the glory of the Creator. For it is truly unbelievable that a human being comes into existence from a drop of blood; and yet it is true. Therefore if there is that power of bringing a human being into existence from a drop of blood, why not also from a clod? Likewise, why not from a rib?

But the sleep of Adam — so sound that he was not aware of what was being done to him — is a picture, as it were, of the transformation which would have taken place in the state of innocence. The righteous nature would have experienced no death but would have lived in the utmost joy, in obedience to God, and in admiration of the works of God until the time of the change had arrived. Then Adam would have experienced something similar to this sleep which happened to him as something most delightful while he lay among roses and under the loveliest trees. During that sleep he would have been changed and transported into the spiritual life without experiencing any pain, just as he did not realize that his body was being opened and that a rib, with flesh, was being taken out. Now this corrupt nature suffers death. In the case of the godly a sweet sleep follows this disintegration of the body until we awake in a new and eternal life. Moreover, here Adam is impelled by admiration and says: "This is bone from my bones," and yet he had been so overcome by sweet sleep that he did not realize that it had been taken out of him. So on that Day we shall say: "Behold, into what great glory this body, consumed by worms, has suddenly risen!"

We have talked enough about the creation of Eve. Although it sounds like a fairy tale to reason, it is the most certain truth. It is revealed in the Word of God, which alone, as I said, imparts true information about the two main causes, the effective and the final; knowledge of these, if available, is considered to be of the greatest importance also in matters pertaining to nature. What advantage is there in knowing how beautiful a creature man is if you are unaware of his purpose, namely, that he was created to worship God and to live eternally with God? Aristotle says something worthwhile when he declares that the goal of man is happiness, which consists in a virtuous life.[68] But in view of the weakness of our nature who can reach this goal? Even those who are the most fortunate encounter discomforts of various kinds, which both misfortune and the ill will and meanness of men bring on. For such happiness peace of mind is necessary. But who can always preserve this amid the great changes of fortune? It is vain, therefore, to point out this goal which no one reaches.

The main goal, then, to which Scripture points is that man is created according to the likeness of God; in eternity, therefore, he is to live with God, and while he is here on earth, he is to preach God, thank Him, and patiently obey His Word. In this life we lay hold of this goal in ever so weak a manner; but in the future life we shall attain it fully. This the philosophers do not know. Therefore the world with its greatest wisdom is most ignorant when it does not take advantage of Holy Scripture or of theology. Human beings know neither their beginning nor their end when they are without the Word. I say nothing about the remaining creatures.

22. *And the Lord God built the rib which He had taken from Adam into a woman, and He brought her to Adam.*

Here Moses uses a new and unheard-of expression, not the verb "form" and "create," as above, but "build." This induced all the interpreters to suspect that there is some underlying mystery here. Lyra, in common with his Rabbi Solomon, believes that the reference is to the novel form of the woman's body.[69] As the shape of buildings is

---

[68] Aristotle, *Nicomachean Ethics*, I, ch. 4.
[69] Lyra on Gen. 2:21, sec. "i."

wider in the lower part but narrower in the upper, so, he says, the
bodies of women are thicker in their lower part but more drawn
together in the upper, while men have broader shoulders and larger
chests. But these are nonessential features of the body. Moreover,
Scripture says of the entire body that it is a building,[70] just as Christ
(Matt. 12:44) calls the body a person's house.

Others look for an allegory and say that the woman is called
a building because of an analogy to the church. For as there are
various parts in a house — walls, joists or beams, a roof, etc. — so in
the church, which is analogous to the body because of the diversity
of members, there are different kinds of services and offices. I for my
part am not annoyed by what is appropriately applied to Christ and
the church. But because these explanations are altogether allegorical,
the historical and strict meaning of this passage must be sought and
adhered to. A woman, especially a married one, is called a building,
not for the sake of allegory but historically. Scripture employs this
method of speech everywhere. Thus Rachel said to Jacob (Gen. 30:3):
"Take the maid that I may be built by her." Scripture states the same
thing of Sara (Gen. 16:2). And in Exodus it is said of the midwives
(Ex. 1:21): "The Lord built them houses"; that is, through the blessing of a family He repaid the kindnesses which they showed to Israel
contrary to the king's command. Likewise, in the account about
David, when he wanted to build a house for the Lord, he receives the
answer (2 Sam. 7:11): "You shall know that the Lord will build you
a house."

Thus this expression is common in Scripture, that the wife is
called a household building because she bears and brings up the
offspring. The form which this building would have had in Paradise
we have lost through sin so completely that we cannot even conceive
of it in our thinking. But, as I said above, this present life of ours
possesses some small and pitiable remnants of its culture and safe-
guards as well as of its dominion over the beasts. Sheep, oxen, geese,
and hens we govern, although boars, bears, and lions pay no attention
to our rule. Similarly, some faint image of this building remains; for
he who marries a wife has her as a nest and home where he stays at
a certain place, just as birds do with their young in their little nest.
Those who, like the impure papists, live as celibates do not have
such a home.

---

[70] This seems to be a reference to passages like 1 Cor. 3:16-17.

This living-together of husband and wife — that they occupy the same home, that they take care of the household, that together they produce and bring up children — is a kind of faint image and a remnant, as it were, of that blessed living-together because of which Moses calls the woman a building. If Adam had continued in his innocence, his descendants would have married and wandered away from their father Adam to some little garden of their own. There they would have lived with their wives, and together they would have tilled the soil and brought up their children. There would have been no need for imposing buildings of hewn stone or for kitchens or for cellars, as we have now. Just as birds live in their little nests, so they would have dwelt here and there in God's work and calling. And the wife would have been the main reason for the husbands' dwelling in fixed habitations. Now in this disaster of sin, when we must have houses because of the severity of the climate, we cannot even conjure up a picture of this bliss; and yet these pitiable remains are excellent gifts of God, and it is truly wicked to use them ungratefully.

We all realize how much of the dominion which man received in Paradise was lost after our defilement by sin. And yet what a great blessing it still is that this dominion was turned over to man and not to the devil! For how could we withstand our invisible enemy if he had not only the determination to inflict harm but also the power to do so? In one hour, in one moment, we would all be annihilated if Satan stirred up merely the wild beasts against us. Thus even if the dominion has been almost entirely lost, it is still a very great blessing that some remnants of it are in existence to this day.

Similarly, there are also some remnants in the instance of procreation, although in the state of innocence women would not only have given birth without pain, but their fertility would also have been far greater. Procreation is now hindered by a thousand diseases, and it happens either that unborn children do not survive the period of gestation or that at times marriages are altogether barren. These are flaws and punishments resulting from Adam's awful fall and from original sin. In the same way the wife is still the house of the husband, to which he goes, with whom he dwells, and with whom he joins in the effort and work of supporting the family. In this sense it will be stated below (Gen. 2:24): "Man will cling to his wife, and he will forsake his father and mother."

But in addition to the countless other troubles which it has because of sin, this living-together is marred to an astonishing degree by wicked persons. There are not only men who think it is clever to find fault with the opposite sex and to have nothing to do with marriage but also men who, after they have married, desert their wives and refuse to support their children. Through their baseness and wickedness these people lay waste God's building, and they are really abominable monsters of nature. Let us, therefore, obey the Word of God and recognize our wives as a building of God. Not only is the house built through them by procreation and other services that are necessary in a household; but the husbands themselves are built through them, because wives are, as it were, a nest and a dwelling place where husbands can go to spend their time and dwell with joy.

What Moses adds, "And He brought her to Adam," is a sort of description of betrothal, which is worthy of special note. Adam does not snatch Eve of his own will after she has been created, but he waits for God to bring her to him. So Christ also says (Matt. 19:6): "What God has joined let no man part." For the lawful joining of a man and a woman is a divine ordinance and institution.

Here, therefore, Moses keeps his own particular expression. "He brought," he says. Who? No doubt יְהוָה אֱלֹהִים, that is, the entire Divinity — Father, Son, and Holy Spirit. These say to Adam: "Behold, this is your bride, with whom you shall dwell, with whom you shall beget children." Without a doubt Adam received her with great joy, just as even now in this corrupt nature the mutual love of bridegroom and bride is extraordinary. But then it was without the epileptic and apoplectic lust of present-day marriage; it was a chaste and delightful love, and the very coming-together would also have been most honorable and most sacred. But now sin forces itself in everywhere; it presents itself to the eyes and ears and then also to all the senses.

Therefore it should be particularly noted that this passage is not only directed against all the awful abuses of lust but that it also gives support for marriage in opposition to the wicked invectives with which the papacy has brought shame on marriage. For is it not a great thing that even in the state of innocence God ordained and instituted marriage? But now this institution and command are all the more necessary, since sin has weakened and corrupted the flesh. Therefore this comfort stands invincible against all the doctrines of demons (1 Tim. 4:1), namely, that marriage is a divine kind of life because it was established by God Himself.

What has come into the minds of the tools of Satan and the enemies of Christ? They have denied that there is any chastity in marriage, and they have declared that those most suited for the ministry of a congregation are celibates, because Scripture says (Lev. 11:44): "You shall be pure." Are spouses impure? Is God the author and establisher of impurity when He Himself brings Eve to Adam? Does Adam commit evil when he permits himself to be talked into impurity though he was able to do without marriage in his innocent nature? The papacy has truly paid the deserved penalties for such blasphemies. Not only have they defiled themselves with a crowd of harlots, but they have also connived at other crimes so loathsome that by now they are ready for the punishment visited on Sodom and Gomorrah.

When I was a boy, the wicked and impure practice of celibacy had made marriage so disreputable that I believed I could not even think about the life of married people without sinning. Everybody was fully persuaded that anyone who intended to lead a holy life acceptable to God could not get married but had to live as a celibate and take the vow of celibacy. Thus many who had been husbands became either monks or priests after their wives had died. Therefore it was a work necessary and useful for the church when men saw to it that through the Word of God marriage again came to be respected and that it received the praises it deserved. As a result, by the grace of God now everyone declares that it is something good and holy to live with one's wife in harmony and peace even if one should have a wife who is barren or is troubled by other ills.

I do not deny, of course, that there are some who can live chastely without marriage. Because they have a greater gift than ordinary folk, such people can sail by their own wind. But the chastity which the pope recommends to his monks, nuns, and priests is contaminated and polluted with awful sins. In addition, celibacy has been instituted without the Word of God — nay even, as the account before us bears witness, against the Word of God. What triumphs they would celebrate if they could adduce proof for their celibacy from the Word of God in the same way we bring proof that marriage is divinely instituted! How much more vigorously they would then force everyone into their celibacy! As it is, they have only this single true commendation for celibacy, namely, that it is a human tradition or, to speak with Paul, a doctrine of demons (1 Tim. 4:1).

23. *And Adam said: This, then, is bone from my bones and flesh from my flesh. She will be called Woman because she has been taken from man.*

The statement which will follow a little later, "Therefore a man will forsake father and mother," is quoted by Christ as if it had been said by God Himself and not by Adam (Matt. 19:5). But there is no difficulty here; for, because Adam was pure and holy, his utterance is rightly declared to be a divine utterance. God spoke through him, and in that state of innocence the words and works of Adam are all truly the words and works of God. Eve is brought to him by God Himself. Therefore just as God's will is ready to establish marriage, so Adam is ready to receive Eve with the greatest pleasure and innocency. Thus even now the bridegroom has a surpassing affection for the bride, yet it is contaminated by that leprous lust of the flesh which was not present in righteous Adam.

But it is most worthy of wonder that when Adam looks at Eve as a building made from himself, he immediately recognizes her and says: "This now is bone from my bones and flesh from my flesh." These are words, not of a stupid or a sinful human being who has no insight into the works and creatures of God, but of a righteous and wise being, one filled with the Holy Spirit. He reveals a wisdom hitherto unknown to the world: that the effecting cause of the wife and of marriage is God, but that the final cause is for the wife to be a mundane dwelling place to her husband. This knowledge is not simply the product of intelligence and reason; it is a revelation of the Holy Spirit.

The word הַפַּעַם, "now" or "this time" or "at last," is not superfluous, as it appears to be; it expresses most beautifully the affection of a husband who feels his need for a delightful and full relationship or cohabitation in both love and holiness. It is as if he were saying: "I have seen all the animals. I have carefully considered the females which were provided for the increase and the preservation of their kind, but they are of no concern to me. But this at last is flesh of my flesh and bones of my bones. I desire to live with her and to accede to God's will by procreating descendants." This little word indicates an overwhelmingly passionate love. Today that purity and innocence is lost; there still remains the bridegroom's delight and his love for the bride, but because of sin it is impure and imperfect. Adam's love was most pure and most holy and also pleasing to God.

Impelled by this love, he says: "This now is bone from my bones, not from wood, not from stone, not from a clod of the earth. It concerns me more closely, for it is made from my bones and my flesh." And so he says:

This one will be called Woman, because she has been taken from the man.

And now, just as through the Holy Spirit Adam had an understanding of past events which he had not seen, and glorified God and praised Him for the creation of his mate, so now he prophesies regarding the future when he says that she must be called "Woman." We are altogether unable to imitate the nicety of the Hebrew language. אִישׁ denotes a man. But he says that Eve must be called אִשָּׁה, as though for "wife" you would say "she-man" from man, a heroic woman who performs manly acts.

Moreover, this designation carries with it a wonderful and pleasing description of marriage, in which, as the jurist also says, the wife shines by reason of her husband's rays. Whatever the husband has, this the wife has and possesses in its entirety. Their partnership involves not only their means but children, food, bed, and dwelling; their purposes, too, are the same. The result is that the husband differs from the wife in no other respect than in sex; otherwise the woman is altogether a man. Whatever the man has in the home and is, this the woman has and is; she differs only in sex and in something that Paul mentions 1 Tim. 2:13, namely, that she is a woman by origin, because the woman came from the man and not the man from the woman.

Also of this fellowship we observe some remnants today, although pitiable ones, if we look back to the first beginning. For if the wife is honorable, virtuous, and pious, she shares in all the cares, endeavors, duties, and functions of her husband. With this end in view she was created in the beginning; and for this reason she is called woman, or, if we were able to say so in Latin, a "she-man." Thus she differs only in sex from the head of the household, inasmuch as she was taken from the flesh of the man. Although this can be said only of Eve, who was created in this manner, nevertheless in Matt. 19:5 Christ applies it to all wives when He says that husband and wife are one flesh. In this way, although your wife has not been made from your bones, nevertheless, because she is your wife, she is the mistress of the house just as you are its master, except that the wife was made subject to the man by the Law which was given after sin. This punishment is similar to the others which dulled those glorious conditions of Paradise of which this text informs us. Moses is not speaking of the wretched life which married people now live but of the innocence in Paradise. There the management would have been equally divided, just as Adam prophesies here that Eve must be called "she-man," or "virago" because she performs similar activities in the home. Now the sweat of the face is imposed upon man, and woman is given the command that she should be under her husband. Yet there remain remnants, like dregs, of the dominion, so that even now the wife can be called "virago" because she has a share in the property.

24. *Therefore a man will leave father and mother and will cling to his wife.*

Christ (Matt. 19:5) and Paul (Eph. 5:31) apply this statement as a general rule also to our marriages after innocence has been lost. Accordingly, if Adam had continued in his innocence, the children that were born would have married. Then, after leaving the table and dwelling place of their parents, they would have had their own trees under which they would have lived separately from their parents. At times they would have come to their father Adam to sing a hymn and praise God, and then they would have returned to their own homes. Although sin has now brought about changes in other respects, there still remains this close bond between spouses, so that a man leaves father and mother rather than his wife. But where something different happens, as when married people mutually forsake each other, this is not only against this command; it is also an indication of the awful depravity which has come into human beings through sin and gets support from Satan, the father of all dissensions.

Moreover, the pagans, too, realized that there was nothing more proper and more advantageous than this close relationship of married people. Hence they declare that according to natural law a wife is necessary and should maintain her inseparable association until death. Christ, too, states that divorce was granted by Moses because of the hardness of the hearts of the Jews, but that it had not been so from the beginning (Matt. 19:8). These troubles arose later on through sin, just as the instances of adultery, poisoning, and the like, which sometimes occur among married people. Thus scarcely a thousandth part of that first institution remains; and yet, because of their offspring, husband and wife have their own little nest even now, in accordance with the statement by which this kind of life receives glorious and splendid support from our first parent, yes, from God Himself, as Christ declares.

This forsaking is not to be understood as though the married children would not have visited their parents at all. The reference is only to living together, namely, that the married children would dwell in their own little nest. Among the troubles caused by sin there is also this, that children are compelled to support their parents who have become feeble from age and are in need. But in Paradise our way of life would have been different and better, and yet then, too, this practice would have been kept: that because of his love for his mate the husband would choose his own little nest and give up living with his parents, just as the little birds are accustomed to do.

This statement is also in the nature of a prophecy. There were no fathers and mothers yet, and no children; nevertheless, through the Holy Spirit, Adam prophesies this way about the life of married people, about their own dwelling place, about the division of dominion over the entire world, so that individual families might live in their own little nest.

25. *But both were naked, the man and his wife, and they were not ashamed.*

It seems that this little statement, which tells of something that is not altogether necessary, could have been omitted. For of what importance is it whether they moved about in Paradise naked or clothed? Yet it is an important and necessary little statement; it uses a rather insignificant fact, as appears to us, to show how much evil this nature has acquired through original sin. All nations, particularly those who live farther toward the north, detest nakedness. Therefore the more modest and more serious people not only criticize the short and military uppergarments worn by young people but also avoid the public baths, although the private parts are carefully covered both by women and by men. This is now a matter of wisdom and a praiseworthy practice, for what father could uncover himself before his son without committing a crime? But Adam and Eve, says Moses, walked about naked and were not ashamed. Therefore it was not only not disgraceful to walk about naked; it was even commendable and delightful.

We have now lost this through sin. We are indeed born naked

into this world and with a hairless skin, although the rest of the animals all bring with them their fur, hair, feathers, and scales. Therefore we must have the shade of houses against the heat of the sun, and a variety of garments against rain, hail, and snow. Adam would have experienced none of these things; but just as the human eyes still have this characteristic that they are affected neither by cold nor by heat, so at that time the entire body would have been protected against cold. And, even better in many ways, Eve, our mother, would have sat among us naked; and no one would have been offended by the nakedness of her breasts and the other parts of the body, of which we must now be ashamed and which, because of sin, kindle lust.

Therefore this passage points out admirably how much evil followed after the sin of Adam. For now it would be regarded as the utmost madness if anyone walked about naked. Therefore what would have been our greatest glory at that time is now extreme shame. It would have been something glorious for man that, though all the animals needed hair, feathers, and scales to cover up their ugliness, he alone was created with such prestige and beauty of body that he could walk about with a hairless and naked skin. This glory has perished. For we must cover our bodies with greater effort and care than the rest of the animals — not only because of necessity but rather to avoid disgrace. The rest of the animals have been covered by nature.

Thus this chapter presents the work of the sixth day a little more clearly: how by a special counsel man was created; how the Garden of Eden was made, in which man would be able to live delightfully; how finally, while the tree of the knowledge of good and evil is forbidden, the outward worship of the future church is established by divine authority — the worship in which they would have borne witness of their obedience to God if they had avoided the devil's snares. And so during that night, according to the opinion of some, Adam was in Paradise with his Eve until the following Sabbath. But the following chapter will tell what happened on the Sabbath.

CHAPTER THREE

1. *But the serpent was more clever than all the animals of the earth which God had made.*

IN the preceding chapter we heard how man was created on the sixth day according to the image and similitude of God, so that his will was good and sound; moreover, his reason or intellect was sound, so that whatever God wanted or said, man also wanted, believed, and understood the same thing. The knowledge of all the other creatures necessarily followed this knowledge; for where the knowledge of God is perfect, there also the knowledge of the other things that are under God is necessarily perfect.

But these words show how horrible the fall of Adam and Eve was; for through it we have lost a most beautifully enlightened reason and a will in agreement with the Word and will of God. We have also lost the glory of our bodies, so that now it is a matter of the utmost disgrace to be seen naked, whereas at that time it was something most beautiful and the unique prerogative of the human race over all the other animals. The most serious loss consists in this, that not only were those benefits lost, but man's will turned away from God. As a result, man wants and does none of the things God wants and commands. Likewise, we have no knowledge about what God is, what grace is, what righteousness is, and finally what sin itself is. These are really terrible faults, and those who do not realize and see them are blinder than a mole. Experience, of course, gives us information about these losses. Nevertheless, we do not fully appreciate their enormity unless we look back at that image of the state of innocence — whatever its nature may have been — in which the will was upright, and the reason was sound. Furthermore, there was the greatest dignity of the human body. When, in contrast, we reflect on the deprivation or loss of these gifts, then, in some measure, we can appraise the evil of original sin.

Therefore it is a cause for great errors when some men minimize this evil and speak of our depraved nature in the manner of the philosophers, as if it were not depraved. Thus they state that the natural endowments have remained unimpaired [1] not only in the nature of man but also in the devil. But this is obviously false. What has remained, and how little, we see and experience in some measure. But those who maintain that the natural endowments have remained unimpaired surely do not see how much we have lost. For the will that is good and righteous, that pleases God, obeys God, trusts in the Creator, and makes use of the creatures with an expression of thanks has been lost to such an extent that our will makes a devil out of God and shudders at the mention of His name, especially when it is troubled by God's judgment. Tell me, does this mean that the natural endowments are unimpaired?

But consider less important matters. The marriage of man and woman was divinely ordained. But how deformed it is now after sin! How our very flesh is kindled with passion! And so now, after sin, this union does not take place in public like a work of God; but respectable married people look for solitary places far away from the eyes of men. Thus we have a body, but what a wretched one and how damaged in various ways! We also have a will and a reason, but how depraved in many ways! Just as reason is overwhelmed by many kinds of ignorance, so the will has not only been confused but has been turned away from God and is an enemy of God. It enjoys rushing to evil, when the opposite should have happened. Therefore this manifold corruption of our nature should not be minimized; it should rather be emphasized. From the image of God, from the knowledge of God, from the knowledge of all the other creatures, and from a very honorable nakedness man has fallen into blasphemies, into hatred, into contempt of God, yes, what is even more, into enmity against God. I am now saying nothing about the tyranny of Satan, to whom this wretched nature has been subjected because of sin. This should be emphasized, I say, for the reason that unless the severity of the disease is correctly recognized, the cure is also not known or desired. The more you minimize sin, the more will grace decline in value.

Moreover, to this emphasis properly pertains what Moses said above: that though Adam and Eve were naked, they were not ashamed. That hideous lust was not aroused in them, but as the one looked at the other, they acknowledged God's goodness, rejoiced in

---

[1] Cf. p. 166, note 19, and *Luther's Works*, 12, p. 308, note 3.

God, and felt safe in God's goodness, while now we not only cannot refrain from sin but are even troubled by despair and by hatred of God. This awful contrast clearly shows that our natural endowments are not unimpaired.

But how much more impudent it is when the sophists assert this very thing about the devil, in whom there is even greater enmity against God, greater hatred and fury, than in man, in spite of the fact that he was not created evil but had a will in conformity with the will of God. This will he has lost; he has also lost his very beautiful and very excellent intellect and has been turned into an awful spirit which rages against his Creator. Is this not the utmost depravity, to change from a friend of God into the bitterest and most obdurate enemy of God?

But in opposition they quote Aristotle's statement: "Reason pleads for the best"; this they try to support also by certain sacred statements and by the opinion of the philosophers that sound reason is the cause of all virtues.[2] I do not deny that these statements are true when they are applied to matters that are subject to reason: to managing cattle, building a house, and sowing a field. But in higher matters they are not true. How can a reason which hates God be called sound? How can a will which resists God's will and refuses to obey God be called good? Therefore when they say: "Reason pleads for the best," you should say: "For the best in a mundane sense, that is, in things about which reason can judge." There it directs and leads to what is honorable and useful in respect to the body or the flesh. As for the rest, since it is full of ignorance of God and detestation of the will of God, how can it be called good on this level? Moreover, it is a well-known fact that when the knowledge of God is preached and this subject is dealt with in order to restore reason, then those who are the ablest and, so to speak, are endowed with a better reason and will hate the Gospel all the more bitterly.

Therefore in theology let us maintain that reason in men is most hostile to God, and that the respectable will is most opposed to the will of God. From this source arise the hatred of the Word and the persecution of godly ministers. For this reason, as I said, let us not minimize this evil which human nature has contracted as a result of the sin of our first parents; rather let us emphasize it. Then we shall both regret deeply this state of ours and have a profound longing

[2] Aristotle, *Nicomachean Ethics*, III, chs. 4—5.

for Christ, our Physician, who was sent by the Father to heal those evils which Satan brought upon us through sin, and to restore us to the eternal glory which we had lost.

As for the historical event of which Moses gives us an account in this present chapter, I stated my opinion before, that this temptation appears to me to have taken place on the Sabbath; thus Adam and Eve were created on the sixth day, Adam earlier and Eve toward evening. Early on the following Sabbath Adam preached to Eve concerning God's will: that the most gracious Lord had created the entire Paradise for the use and enjoyment of people; that, also as a result of His extraordinary goodness, He had created the tree of life, through the use of which the powers of the body would be refreshed and perpetual youth would be maintained; that one tree — the tree of the knowledge of good and evil, from which it was not permitted to eat — was forbidden; and that in this respect they should obey so gracious a Creator. Perhaps he led Eve about in Paradise and showed her the forbidden tree when he said this.

In this way Adam and Eve, resplendent with innocence and original righteousness, and abounding in peace of mind because of their trust in God, who was so kind, walked about naked while they discoursed on the Word and command of God and praised God, just as should be done on the Sabbath. But then, alas, Satan interfered and within a few hours ruined all this, as we shall hear.

Now here, too, a sea of questions arises. Inquisitive people ask why God permitted Satan to tempt Eve. Furthermore, why Satan waylaid Eve through the serpent rather than through a different animal. But who can supply the reason for the things that he sees the Divine Majesty has permitted to happen? Why do we not rather learn with Job that God cannot be called to account and cannot be compelled to give us the reason for everything He does or permits to happen? Why do we not likewise register a complaint with God because the earth does not produce plants and because the trees are not green throughout the year? I am fully convinced that in Paradise there would have been perpetual spring without any winter, without snow and frosts, such as we have today after sin. But these are all things under the divine power and will. To know this is enough. Besides, it is wicked curiosity to investigate these problems in greater detail. Therefore let us, who are clay in His hands, cease to discuss such questions. Let us not sit in judgment on our God; let us rather be judged by Him.

Hence the answer to all such inquiries must be only this: It pleased the Lord that Adam should be tempted and should test his powers. So it still is today. When we have been baptized and brought into the kingdom of Christ, God does not want us to be idle; He wants us to use His Word and gifts. For this reason He allows us weak beings to be sifted by Satan (Luke 22:31). Thus we see the church, which has been cleansed by the Word, still exposed to continual danger. The Sacramentarians rise up; so do the Anabaptists and other fanatical teachers, who greatly trouble the church with their various temptations. In addition, there are internal troubles. These God allows to happen this way, not because He has decided either to abandon the church or to want it to perish; but, as Wisdom says (Wisd. 10:12), those conflicts befall the church and the godly that the church and the godly may prevail and learn by experience itself that wisdom is more powerful than everything else.

Here there is another question. Perhaps it can be discussed with less danger but with greater profit. It is: "Why does Scripture make this account so obscure? Why does it not rather state directly that the angel who had fallen entered the serpent, was speaking through the serpent, and deceived Eve?" But I answer: "This account is so obscure in order that all things might be held over for Christ and for His Spirit, who was to shed light throughout the entire world like the midday sun and to open all the mysteries of Scripture." Because this Spirit of Christ was in the prophets (1 Peter 1:11), the holy prophets understood such mysteries of Scripture.

But we said above that as animals have their different endowments, the serpent excelled in the gift of cleverness. For this reason it was more suited for this game of Satan. A sufficiently clear proof of this is this text of Moses, which declares that there was extraordinary cleverness in the serpent, more than in the other animals. We marvel today at the cleverness which foxes display in lying in wait, then also at their wonderful skill in escaping from danger. Sometimes, after it is worn out by running, it throws its tail before the pursuing dogs. When the dogs fall upon it with great vehemence and stop their running, it gains some distance by its wonderful speed and so escapes. There are also some other animals whose extraordinary skill and industry we admire. But this quality in the serpent was extraordinary. Therefore it appeared to Satan to be a convenient tool through which to tempt Eve.

Who said to the woman: Did God really command you not to eat from every tree of Paradise?

The sophists also discuss the nature of this temptation, namely, of what sort it was. Was their sin idolatry, pride, unconcern, or just the simple eating of the fruit? But if, as is proper, we consider these matters a little more carefully, we shall find that this was the greatest and severest of all temptations; for the serpent directs its attack at God's good will and makes it its business to prove from the prohibition of the tree that God's will toward man is not good. Therefore it launches its attack against the very image of God and the most excellent powers in the uncorrupted nature. The highest form of worship itself, which God had ordained, it tries to destroy. It is, therefore, vain for us to discuss this or that sin. Eve is simply urged on to all sins, since she is being urged on against the Word and the good will of God.

Accordingly, Moses expresses himself very carefully and says: "The serpent said," that is, with a word it attacks the Word. The Word which the Lord had spoken to Adam was: "Do not eat from the tree of the knowledge of good and evil." For Adam this Word was Gospel and Law; it was his worship; it was his service and the obedience he could offer God in this state of innocence. These Satan attacks and tries to destroy. Nor is it only his intention, as those who lack knowledge think, to point out the tree and issue an invitation to pick its fruit. He points it out indeed; but then he adds another and a new statement, as he still does in the church.[3]

For when the Gospel is preached in its purity, men have a sure guide for their faith and are able to avoid idolatry. But then Satan makes various efforts and trials in an effort either to draw men away from the Word or to corrupt it. Thus even at the time of the apostles various heresies arose in the Greek Church.[4] One denied that Christ was the Son of God; another denied that He was the Son of Mary, just as the Anabaptists today wickedly deny that Christ took anything from Mary's flesh.[5] At the time of Basil some made a special effort to deny that the Holy Spirit is God.[6]

[3] Luther makes this observation at greater length in his sermon of 1526 on the temptation story in Matt. 4:6 (Weimar, XX, 276—278).

[4] This is probably a reference to the heretic Cerinthus (cf. *Luther's Works,* 22, p. 7, note 2).

[5] Cf. *Luther's Works,* 22, p. 21, note 19.

[6] Basil, *De Spiritu Sancto,* Ch. IX, *Patrologia, Series Graeca,* XXXII, 107 to 110.

Our age, too, has instances like these before its eyes, when, after the purer doctrine of the Gospel came to light, several kinds of assailers of the works and the Word of God arose. Of course, the other temptations do not cease; Satan still incites to fornication, adultery, and similar infamous deeds. But this temptation — when Satan attacks the Word and the works of God — is far more serious and more dangerous, and it is peculiar to the church and the saints.

Therefore Satan here attacks Adam and Eve in this way to deprive them of the Word and to make them believe his lie after they have lost the Word and their trust in God. Is it a wonder that when this happens, man later on becomes proud, that he is a scorner of God and of men, that he becomes an adulterer or a murderer? Truly, therefore, this temptation is the sum of all temptations; it brings with it the overthrow or the violation of the entire Decalog. Unbelief is the source of all sins; when Satan brought about this unbelief by driving out or corrupting the Word, the rest was easy for him.

Thus when Eve had permitted herself to be driven away from the Word by a lie, it was very easy to approach the tree and pick fruit from it. Therefore it is stupid to think, as the sophists and the monks think about this temptation, that when Eve had looked at the tree, she gradually became inflamed with a desire to pick the fruit, until at last, overcome by her desire, she brought the fruit to her mouth. For the chief temptation was to listen to another word and to depart from the one which God had previously spoken: that they would die if they ate from it. But let us consider Moses' words in their order.

In the first place, Satan imitates God. Just as God had preached to Adam, so he himself also preaches to Eve. What the proverb says is true: "Every evil begins in the name of the Lord." Therefore just as from the true Word of God salvation results, so also from the corrupt Word of God damnation results. By "corrupt word" however, I do not mean only the ministry of the spoken Word but also the inner conviction or opinions that are in disagreement with the Word.

Moreover, Moses indicates this by the word: "It said." Satan spoke in order to lead them away from what God had said; and after he had taken away the Word, he made corrupt the perfect will which man had previously had, so that he became a rebel. He corrupted the intellect also, so that it doubted the will of God. The eventual result is a rebellious hand, extended against the will of God, to pick the fruit. Next the mouth and the teeth become rebellious. In short, all evils result from unbelief or doubt of the Word and of God. For what can be worse than to disobey God and to obey Satan?

This slyness and villainy of Satan is imitated by all the heretics. Under the appearance of something good they rob men of God and of His Word before their very eyes; and they fabricate for them another, new god, who exists nowhere. If you look at their words, there is nothing holier, nothing more devout. They call upon God as a witness that with all their heart they are seeking the welfare of the church; they call down curses upon those who, they claim, are teaching the ungodliest doctrines; and they avow that it is their desire to spread the name and the glory of God with great zeal. What need is there of many words? They do not want it to appear that they are teachers of the devil or that they are heretics; yet they busy themselves with this one task of trying to suppress the true doctrine and to obscure the knowledge of God.

And so later on the fall is an easy matter. People who are not wary allow themselves to be drawn away from the Word into dangerous discussions. Because they are not satisfied with the Word, they ask: "Why and wherefore do these things happen thus?" Just as Eve was lost when she heard the devil casting doubt upon the command of God, so, when we doubt whether God wanted us who are hard pressed by death and sin to be saved through Christ, how easily we are deceived and allow a monk's cowl to be put on us in order to receive the crown on account of our perfect works!

Thus a new god is invented by Satan for men without their even being aware of it. For he also sets a word before them, but not the kind which has been put before us by God, namely, that repentance and remission of sin should be preached in the name of Christ (Luke 24:47). When the Word of God is changed or perverted in this way, then, as Moses says in his song (Deut. 32:17), "come new and recent gods, whom our fathers did not worship."

It is useful to know these snares. If Satan were to teach that people ought to kill, commit fornication, and disobey their parents, who would not realize that he is suggesting something that is forbidden by the Lord? Therefore it would be easy to be on one's guard against him. But here, when he propounds another word, when he discourses about the will of God, when he uses the names "God," "the church," and "the people of God" as a pretext, then people cannot so readily be on guard against him. But we need the keenest judgment of the spirit to distinguish between the true God and the new god, as Christ distinguished when Satan tried to persuade Him to demand that the stones become bread and to hurl Himself from the pinnacle of the temple (Matt. 4:3-7). Satan wanted to persuade Christ to attempt something without the Word. But he could not deceive Christ as he deceived Eve, for He held to the Word and did not allow Himself to be led away from the true God to the false, new god.

The source of all sin truly is unbelief and doubt and abandonment of the Word. Because the world is full of these, it remains in idolatry, denies the truth of God, and invents a new god.

A monk is an idolater. He imagines that if he lives according to the rule of Francis or of Dominic, this is the way to the kingdom of God. But this is equivalent to inventing a new god and becoming an idolater, because the true God declares that the way to the kingdom of heaven is by believing in Christ. Therefore when faith has been lost, there follow unbelief and idolatry, which transfer the glory of God to works. Thus the Anabaptists, the Sacramentarians, and the papists are all idolaters — not because they worship stones and pieces of wood, but because they give up the Word and worship their own thoughts.

And so this passage helps us to learn that this temptation of the devil was the beginning of original sin, when he led Eve away from the Word of God to idolatry, contrary to the First, the Second, and the Third Commandments.

Here properly belong these words: "Did God actually command you?" This is an instance of the awful boldness of the devil, as he invents a new god and denies the former true and eternal God with such unconcern and assurance. It is as if he were to say: "Surely you are silly if you believe that God has given such a command, for it is not God's nature to be so deeply concerned whether you eat or not. Inasmuch as it is the tree of the knowledge of good and evil, how can such ill will come upon Him that He does not want you to be wise?"

Furthermore this unspeakable villainy is sufficient proof that Satan was the contriver of this affair, although Moses makes mention of the serpent only and not also of Satan. Although these statements are ever so veiled, nevertheless, through the enlightenment of the Holy Spirit, the holy fathers and prophets readily saw that this was not an affair of the serpent, but that in the serpent there was that spirit, the enemy of innocent nature, of whom Christ declares clearly in the

Gospel that he did not stand in the truth and that he is a murderer
and liar (John 8:44). It remained for the Gospel to present all this
with greater clarity and to point out this enemy of God and men.

Moreover, the fathers realized this very thing on the basis of the
following reasoning: It is certain that at that time all creatures were in
perfect obedience, according to the statement (Gen. 1:31): "And God
saw all that He made, and it was very good." But here, in the case of
the serpent, a spirit betrays itself who is the enemy of God and who
corrupts the Word of God in order by this means to lead the innocent
human being into sin and death.

It is clear, therefore, that in the serpent there was something
worse, something that could properly be called the adversary of
God, a lying and murderous spirit, in whom there is the utmost and
most awful smugness. He is not afraid to distort the command of God
and to urge man on to idolatry, which he knew would result in the
destruction of the entire human race. All this is truly horrible when
we appraise it properly; and even now, among the papists and other
sects, we see instances of a similar smugness, with which they distort
the Word of God and lead people astray.

At first Eve resists the tempter admirably. For she is still being
led by that Spirit who was lighting her path, just as we showed above
that man was created perfect and according to the likeness of God.
But in the end she allows herself to be persuaded.

It is uncertain on what day the fall of the angels occurred, whether
on the second or on the third. Only this much can be shown from the
Gospel, that Satan fell from heaven, inasmuch as Christ declares that
He saw him fall from heaven (Luke 10:18). We do not know whether
the heavens at that time were finished or still crude and unfinished.

But this discussion is not pertinent to this passage. What is pertinent is that we perceive the utmost villainy, combined with an awful
smugness, which makes this spirit unafraid to cast doubt on the command of the Divine Majesty, especially when he knows what great
misfortune will follow for the whole human race.

Secondly, consideration must be given also to his extraordinary
cleverness, which becomes evident immediately, when Satan assails
the greatest strength of man and battles against the very likeness of
God, namely, the will that was properly disposed toward God. The
serpent's cleverness, says the text, was greater than that of all the
animals on earth.

But this cleverness is superior to the natural cleverness of the serpent because it discusses with man the Word and the will of God. This the serpent could not do in its natural state, since it had been placed under the rule of man. However, the spirit who is speaking in the serpent is so cunning that he outwits man and persuades him to eat the fruit of the forbidden tree. Therefore the one who speaks here is not a creature of God which is good; he is the bitterest enemy of God and of men. He, too, is a creature of God, but he was not created evil by God. "For he did not stand in the truth," as Christ says in John 8:44. These clear conclusions follow from the Gospel and from this text.

Satan's cleverness is perceived also in this, that he attacks the weak part of the human nature, Eve the woman, not Adam the man. Although both were created equally righteous, nevertheless Adam had some advantage over Eve. Just as in all the rest of nature the strength of the male surpasses that of the other sex, so also in the perfect nature the male somewhat excelled the female. Because Satan sees that Adam is the more excellent, he does not dare assail him; for he fears that his attempt may turn out to be useless. And I, too, believe that if he had tempted Adam first, the victory would have been Adam's. He would have crushed the serpent with his foot and would have said: "Shut up! The Lord's command was different." Satan, therefore, directs his attack on Eve as the weaker part and puts her valor to the test, for he sees that she is so dependent on her husband that she thinks she cannot sin.

Here, too, we are reminded of the divine permission, namely, that the devil was permitted to enter beasts, as he here entered the serpent. For there is no doubt that it was a real serpent in which Satan was and in which he conversed with Eve.

Some carry on laughable discussions about whether the serpent had a human face.[7] It was a most beautiful little animal; otherwise Eve would not have conversed with it so calmly. However, after sin it was not only the beauty of the serpent that was changed — for God threatens that it will creep on the earth, while previously it walked erect, like a rooster, and that it will eat earth, while previously it lived on the better fruits (Gen. 3:14) — but also that freedom from fear has been lost, for we flee from serpents just as the serpents, in turn, flee from us. These wounds of nature were inflicted on account of sin, just as we have lost our nakedness, our upright will, and our sound

---

[7] The source of this is probably Lyra's commentary on Gen. 3:1.

intellect. And I believe too that the serpent has also lost most of its cleverness, which Moses mentions here as an extraordinary gift of the Creator. Just as today the serpent is the evil one among the animals, so I hold that it was then a beautiful, good, blessed, and lovely creature, with which not only man but also the rest of the animals enjoyed living. Therefore it was also best suited for Satan's plan to speak through it and to incite Eve to sin.

This is my idea about the natural serpent, which Satan wanted to misuse and which at that time was a most beautiful little beast, without the poisonous tail and without those ugly scales; for these were added after sin. Similarly, we find in Moses a command that animals which have caused a death should be killed (Ex. 21:28), for no other reason than that Satan sinned through them by bringing death to a human being. Thus the serpent has been punished, in proof of this fall and devilish villainy.

But so far as grammar is concerned, the Latin translation renders the little expression אַף כִּי with "why." [8] Although this may not be quite right, it does not clash too much with the sense; for the first and foremost temptation occurs when God's counsel is discussed: "Why did God do this or that?" According to my opinion, however, the emphasis is not placed on that little word "why" or on the question but rather on the name אֱלֹהִים "God." For this lends greater force to the temptation.

It is as if Satan were saying: "Surely you are very silly if you think that God did not want you to eat from this tree, you whom He appointed lords over all the trees of Paradise. In fact, He created the trees on your account. How can He, who favored you with all these things, be so envious as to withhold from you the fruits of this one single tree, which are so delightful and lovely?" Satan is seeking to deprive them of the Word and knowledge of God that they may reach the conclusion: "This is not the will of God; God does not command this." The words which follow also support this opinion when he says: "You will not die." Satan has staked everything on this one effort to draw them away from the Word and faith, that is, from the true God to a false god.

All the fanatical spirits follow this procedure of Satan. Thus Arius raises the question: "Do you believe that Christ is God, inasmuch as He clearly states (John 14:28): 'The Father is greater than I'?" Like-

---

[8] Thus the Douay Version has: "Why hath God commanded you that you should not eat of every tree of paradise?"

wise the Sacramentarians: "Do you believe that the bread is the body of Christ, and the wine the blood of Christ? Surely Christ did not even think of such silly ideas!" When men give room to these thoughts, they gradually depart from the Word and fall into error.

Therefore since the main point of the temptation is to bring about doubt whether God said this, the emphasis is more properly placed on the noun "God." The little word "why" makes for a rather weak meaning. Hence I rather favor the translation: "Did God say: 'You will not eat from every tree of the garden'?" Satan is not really concerned with inquiring about the reason why God said this. He is rather concerned with this: in order for him to deprive Eve of the Word, she should reach the conclusion that God simply did not say this. He sees that reason can easily be deceived in this way, when, under the pretense of God's name and Word, God and Word are lost.

Again he shows his cunning by speaking in general and including all the trees together. It is as if he were saying: "You have the universal rule over all the beasts. Should not God, who gave you this universal rule over all the beasts, also give you all the trees? What you ought to think is: 'Just as God has put the whole earth and all the animals under us, so He has also permitted the use of all the things that spring from the earth.'"

This is surely a great temptation. With it Satan tries to induce Eve's mind to reach the conclusion that God is not inconsistent. Accordingly, if He turned over all the other creatures, He also turned over all the trees. Therefore it follows that the command about not eating of the tree is not God's command, or at least is not to be understood as though He did not want anyone to eat from this tree.

Thus a twofold temptation is put before Eve, by which, however, Satan has the same end in view. The first is: "God did not say this; therefore you may eat from this tree." The second is: "God has given you everything; therefore you have everything in your possession; therefore this one single tree is not forbidden you." However, each aims at the same end: that Eve be drawn away from the Word and from faith. This command about not eating from the tree, which was given them by God, is a convincing proof that even if his nature had remained perfect, Adam, together with his descendants, would have lived in faith until he would have been translated from this physical life to the spiritual life. Where the Word is, there necessarily faith also is. Here is the Word that he should not eat of this tree; otherwise he would die. Therefore Adam and Eve ought to have believed that this tree was detrimental to their welfare. Thus faith is included in this very commandment.

We who are being brought out of sin into righteousness and from our mortal body to the immortal body also live in faith. But we have a different Word, which Adam did not have when his nature was perfect, since he would have been directly translated from the physical life to the spiritual. For this reason I said above that this tree in the middle of the garden would have been like a temple in which this Word would be preached: that all the other trees were wholesome, but that this one was destructive.[9] Therefore they should have learned to obey God and to render Him the service of refraining from eating of it, since God had forbidden it.

In this way uncorrupted nature, which had the true knowledge of God, nevertheless had a Word or command which was beyond Adam's understanding and had to be believed. Moreover, this command was given to Adam's innocent nature that he might have a directive or form for worshiping God, for giving thanks to God, and for instructing his children. Since the devil sees this and knows that this command is beyond the understanding of the human being, he tempts Eve so that she herself may proceed to ponder whether this is God's command and will or not. This is the beginning and the main part of every temptation, when reason tries to reach a decision about the Word and God on its own without the Word.

It was God's intention that this command should provide man with an opportunity for obedience and outward worship, and that this tree should be a sort of sign by which man would give evidence that he was obeying God. But by getting a discussion under way as to whether God had commanded this, Satan is trying to lead man away from this obedience to sin. In this situation the only salvation would have been if Eve had laid emphasis on God's command and had not allowed herself to be drawn away to other discussions about whether God had commanded this, or whether, since God had created everything for the sake of man, this one tree had been created for the ruin of man. It seems a matter of wisdom to investigate these questions rather carefully; but the moment the mind engages in discussions of this kind, it is done for. Now let us hear what Eve's reply was.

2. *To this the woman answered: Of the fruit of the trees which are in Paradise we eat;*

[9] Cf. p. 95.

3. *but of the fruit of the tree which is in the midst of Paradise God commanded us not to eat or to touch it, lest perchance we die.*

The beginning is rather favorable: she makes a distinction between the remaining trees and this one, and she quotes God's command. But she begins to waver when she comes to the mention of the punishment. She does not mention the punishment as God had stated it. He had simply stated (Gen. 2:17): "On whatever day you will eat from it, you will surely die." Out of this absolute statement she herself makes one that is not absolute when she adds: "Lest perchance we shall die."

This is a striking flaw, and one that must not be overlooked; for it shows that she has turned from faith to unbelief. For just as a promise demands faith, so a threat also demands faith. Eve should have maintained: "If I eat, I shall surely die." On this faith Satan makes such inroads with his crafty speech that Eve adds the little word "perchance." She had been persuaded by the devil that God was not so cruel as to kill them for eating the fruit. To this extent Eve's heart was now poisoned with Satan's venom.

For this reason our text here, too, has been poorly translated. It reads as though Eve were quoting her own words; actually, she is quoting God's words, and on her own she is adding to God's Word the little word "perchance." And so the deceit of the lying spirit met with success. What he sought to achieve above all — to lead Eve away from the Word and faith — this he has now achieved to the extent that Eve distorts the Word of God; that is, to use Paul's language, he has turned her away from the divine will, so that she goes after Satan (1 Tim. 5:15). But it is the beginning of one's ruin to turn away from God and to turn to Satan, that is, not to remain constant in the Word and in faith. When Satan sees these beginnings, he now exerts himself with his utmost power, as though against a leaning wall, in order to overwhelm her altogether.

4. *And the serpent said to the woman: You will in no wise die;*

5. *but God knows that on that day on which you will eat from the tree your eyes will be opened, and you will be like God, knowing good and evil.*

This is Satanic oratory, with which he completely overpowers the pitiable woman when he sees that she has turned away from God and is ready to listen to another teacher. When he said above: "God did not give you this command, did He?" he did not openly deny the Word; but through the nature of his question he tried to raise a doubt in Eve. Now, after he sees that he has achieved this, he begins with utmost boldness to deny the Word of God directly and to charge God with lying and with cruelty. It is not enough for him that Eve added the little word "perhaps"; but out of the little word "perchance" he now makes a negative and says: "You will not die."

Therefore we see here what an awful thing it is when the devil begins to tempt a man. One lapse involves another lapse, and an apparently slight wrong brings about a prodigious lapse. It was something serious to turn away from God and from His Word and to lend her ears to Satan. But what is something far more serious now happens: that Eve agrees with Satan when he charges God with lying, and, as it were, strikes God in the face with his fists. Therefore Eve no longer shows any aversion as in the first temptation; but she joins with Satan in despising God and denying the Word of God, and she believes the father of lies rather than the Word of God.

Let these events be a warning for us that we may learn what man is. For if this happened when nature was still perfect, what do we think will happen to us now? And we have examples before our eyes. For many of those who originally thanked God with us for His revealed Word have not only fallen away but have become our adversaries.[10]

Thus after the Arians had begun to fall away from faith in the divinity of the Son, they were soon carried away to such madness that they became the enemies of the church and persecuted it with the utmost cruelty.

We see examples of the same madness in the Anabaptists. When they were misled by Satan in the beginning to accept the little word "perchance," they all, later on, turned "perchance" into a negative: "not." From deserters of God they also become persecutors of God. They imitate their father Satan. After he had fallen from heaven through sin, he became the bitterest enemy of Christ and of the church.

Nor is there any lack of similar examples today. We do not have any bitterer enemies than those who have fallen away from our doctrine. From this sin follows that well-known unhappy dictum (Ps. 14:1): "The fool said in his heart: 'There is no God.'" It is not enough for those who have fallen away to turn away from God; they also attack God and His Word.

---

10 Perhaps Luther is thinking here of Carlstadt; cf. p. 211, note 56.

Therefore there is special need of this rule, which we ought to regard throughout our life as a holy anchor: that after it has been established that what we have and profess is the Word of God, we give it our assent in simple faith and do not engage in inquisitive discussions. For every inquisitive discussion brings with it a most certain lapse.

We have Christ's clear word about the Lord's Supper, where He says concerning the bread: "This is My body which is given for you," and concerning the cup: "This is the cup of the New Testament in My blood." Therefore when the fanatics depart from faith in these words and discuss how these things can be so, they gradually get to the point where they simply deny this word of Christ and attack it, just as happened to Eve in this passage.

Thus when Arius speculates that God is the simplest unity, he begins by postulating this thesis: "Perhaps Christ is not God." Then for some time he comes up with preposterous deductions, until he maintains in so many words and declares as certain that Christ is not God. It does not bother him that John clearly declares (John 1:1): "The Word was God." It does not bother him that Christ commands Baptism in the name of the Father and of the Son and of the Holy Spirit (Matt. 28:19); or that we have the command to believe in Christ, to worship Him, and pray to Him. But what is more preposterous than that we undertake to sit in judgment on God and His Word, we who ought to be judged by God? Therefore we must simply maintain that when we hear God saying something, we are to believe it and not to debate about it but rather take our intellect captive in the obedience of Christ (2 Cor. 10:5).

The statement of Is. 7:9 is properly quoted here: "Unless you believe, you will not endure." For even if we should be torn to pieces, we shall nevertheless never understand how the eye sees, how the ear hears, or what the soul is. And yet these things are in us, and we make use of them daily and at every moment in all our activities. How, then, shall we understand those things which are beyond all our senses, in the Word alone? Thus it is in the Word alone that the bread is the body of Christ, that the wine is the blood of Christ. This must be believed; it must not and cannot be understood.

Thus so far as the passage before us in Moses is concerned, the words were most simple: "From the tree in the midst of Paradise you shall not eat." But reason did not understand the purpose of these words, why God wanted it to be so. Therefore Eve perishes while she investigates too inquisitively and refuses to be satisfied with what she had heard the Lord command. Thus this temptation is a true pattern of all temptations with which Satan assails the Word and faith. Before the desire to eat of the fruit arose in Eve, she lost the Word which God spoke to Adam. If she had adhered to this Word, she would have continued in the fear and faith of God. Where the opposite happens and the Word is lost, there is contempt of God and obedience to the devil.

All this is useful, that we may learn, as Peter says (1 Peter 5:9), to stand undaunted in temptation and to resist the tempter while holding on to the Word with a firm faith and closing our ears so as not to grant admittance to what is foreign to the Word. For truly, these afflictions of Eve and Adam are lessons for us, in order that we may not have the same experiences by being drawn away from the Word and from faith.[11]

What follows in the text: "God knows that your eyes will be opened" has a double meaning. On the one hand, it can be understood to mean that Satan said this to stir up resentment against God for not wanting man to eat so useful a fruit, that in this way Eve might begin to hate God as though He bore them too little good will. Or, on the other hand — and this is how I understand it — he praises God that he might the more easily involve Eve in his treachery. It is as if he said: "Surely God is not such a one that He wants you to live in darkness, as it were, without any knowledge of good and evil. He is good. He does not begrudge you anything that is useful and helpful to you in any way. He will take it calmly that you are like Him."

When Satan praises God in this way, then, in truth, he has a dagger in his hand to cut man's throat. The Fall becomes very easy when the pretense of the Word and the will of God are added to what desire suggests. This is the reason why I incline to the understanding that this was said by Satan in order to persuade Eve rather than to stir up resentment against God. Yet I leave it to you to adopt what you please. The gist certainly is that he is trying to lead Eve away from the Word and to persuade her to do what had been forbidden by the Word. He is a very bitter enemy of the Word of God because he knows that our salvation rests on obedience to the Word.

Here a question which is not at all senseless is raised: how it

---

[11] This is a play on the Greek words παθήματα and μαθήματα.

happens that Eve is not yet aware of her sin. Although she has not yet eaten the fruit, she has already sinned against the Word and faith; for she has turned away from the Word to a lie, from faith to unbelief, from God to Satan, and from the worship of God to idolatry. Since this was the main feature of her sin (for picking the fruit was not the main feature), how does it happen that death does not follow immediately? How does it happen that she does not realize her sin? Nay more, how does it come that after she herself has eaten the fruit, she does not experience death before she has also persuaded Adam to eat?

The schools have sundry discussions about the upper and the lower part of reason: namely, that Adam is the upper part of reason, Eve the lower.[12] But let us pass over these unlearned and scholastic arguments, and let us look for the true meaning, which is this:

In the first place, God is long-suffering; therefore He does not punish sin immediately. Otherwise it would happen that we would immediately perish in our sins. This long-suffering of God Satan abuses, since it is advantageous for his purpose that man should not immediately become aware of his sin. And so it happens that because the punishment is delayed, Satan fills the heart with smugness, and man not only does not become aware that he has committed sin, but is even glad over it and rejoices in his sins.

We observe this in the case of the popes. If they could behold with their eyes and minds the torture of consciences, nay, even the destruction of people — to which they bring them by their wicked doctrine — they would undoubtedly improve their doctrine. But now Satan makes their eyes dull, as it were, so that they cannot see the wrath of God and His judgment. And so they live in the utmost smugness and with joy and gladness in their most serious sins, and they celebrate their triumphs as if they had achieved something good.

The very same thing happens to Eve here. Through her unbelief she had fallen from the Word into a lie. Therefore before God's eyes she was already dead. Because Satan restrains her mind and eyes, however, she not only does not see death or become aware of it, but gradually she is also more inflamed by her desire for the fruit and delights in this idolatry and sin. If, then, she had not drawn away from the Word, looking at the fruit and desiring to eat of it

---

[12] On this distinction between the lower and the higher parts of the reason cf. Thomas Aquinas, *Summa theologica*, I, Q. 79, Art. 9.

would have been something horrible for her. Now she turns this sin over in her mind with pleasure. Where formerly she would have fled if she had seen someone else stretching out his hand toward that tree, she is now impatient of delay, since sin has taken over her lower limbs and has burst forth from her heart.[13] Thus this delight and desire to eat the fruit is like a disease born of sin, upon which death later follows. Meantime, while Eve is sinning, she does not feel it, as the sequel shows.

6. *And so the woman saw that the tree was good for eating and beautiful for the eyes and delightful, because it made wise. She took of its fruit and ate, and she gave to her husband, and he ate.*

See how sin is gradually spread to all the senses. After Eve has believed Satan, contrary to God's Word, that she will not die, but rather that her eyes will be opened, and she will know evil and good, what does she neglect to do that is needed to make her sin greater? Her eyes cannot be satisfied by the appearance. It is not enough for her that she has the knowledge of God and a sound reason; she wants the knowledge of evil to be added. But this is Satan's very own poison, that she wants to have insight beyond what was commanded. This wisdom is death, and it is hostile to the wisdom of God which was given her in the command; it has the effect that she regards as righteousness what is sin; and what is the utmost folly she imagines to be the highest wisdom.

The emphasis, therefore, lies on what the Latin text nevertheless has omitted, namely, that the tree appeared delightful because it would make people wise.[14] This is what the devil is wont to bring about in all his temptations, that the farther man draws away from the Word, the more learned and the wiser he appears to himself.

Thus they consider it great wisdom to say that the bread is bread and that the wine is wine, not the body and blood of Christ. Arius thinks that he has won a prize because, on the basis of some badly distorted passages, he declares that the Logos was in existence before the creatures, but that it was created. To the Anabaptists it appears to be great wisdom when they come with their big talk and rant that water cannot touch the spirit or the soul, but only the naked skin,

[13] Perhaps the "lower limbs" *(inferiora membra)* spoken of here are the legs, which now refused to flee.

[14] The words are likewise missing in the Douay Version.

and that for this reason Baptism contributes nothing to the remission of sins. And we know that fanatical spirits somewhere baptized without water and yet boasted that they had never been in disagreement with us.[15] This is indeed wisdom; but it is a devilish wisdom, contrary to the Word and wisdom of God. Such a temptation is characteristic of the devil, that thus he would make us wise against and above the Word of God, just as he himself was in heaven. But the temptation involving wisdom is far more effective than those cruder ones involving lust, greed, pride, etc.

The verb הִשְׂכִּיל denotes "to be prudent," from which is derived מַשְׂכִּיל, "wise," "prudent," as in Ps. 14:2: "God looked down from the heaven upon the children of men, whether anyone was understanding and sought God." Also Is. 52:13: "My servant יַשְׂכִּיל, will deal prudently." [16] In the strict sense it denotes that wisdom by which God is known. But Eve had that light, or sun, in her heart before, because she had the Word; then also she had the knowledge of all the creatures. But when that wisdom is not satisfied, it wants to rise higher and know God in a way different from His revelation of Himself in His Word. Here is the Fall, that, after losing the true wisdom, she plunges into utter blindness.

Moreover, as Satan acted then, so he does now. It is God's command that we should believe the Gospel about His Son and thus be saved. This is the true wisdom, as Christ also says (John 17:3): "This is eternal life, that they know Thee, the true God, and Him, whom Thou hast sent, Jesus Christ." This wisdom the monk disregards and turns to other things. He puts on his cowl, girds himself with a rope, assumes the vow of celibacy, etc.; and he imagines that in this way he will please God and be saved. This high and mighty wisdom, which makes an effort at the veneration and worship of God, was planted by Satan and by original sin into this wretched nature, so that after men have disregarded the Word which God set before them for their salvation, they might turn to their own thoughts. In this way Eve, created as the wisest of women, longs for a different wisdom, a wisdom apart from the Word; and because of this wisdom she sins in so many ways with all her senses — by seeing, by thinking, by desiring, and by doing.

---

[15] Cf. also *Luther's Works,* 22, p. 308.

[16] The original has "Is. 53."

Therefore one should not listen to those who maintain that it is cruel for this nature to be so pitiably corrupted and plunged into death and the rest of the disasters simply on account of a bite of fruit. When the Epicureans hear this, they laugh at it as a fairy tale. But to the careful reader it readily becomes clear that the bite of the apple is not the reason. The reason is sin, through which Eve sinned against both tables of the Law and against God Himself and His Word; moreover, she sins in this way that she casts aside the Word of God and offers her whole self to Satan as his pupil.

These actions dare not be regarded lightly; for they are, as the saying is, causes pregnant with the punishments which we endure, such an awful condition of sin and such an awful antipathy to God. We ought to look at and think about these, instead of confining ourselves to the fruit that was plucked and swallowed. Those who look only at the action and not at the sin from which this action followed cannot do otherwise than charge God with cruelty that because of so small a sin He has inflicted such great punishment on the entire human race. Therefore they hate God and despair; or, like the Epicureans, they laugh at this as a fairy tale.

Thus we must pay attention to the Word. Moreover, this is God's Word. And so, just as important as the Word is, so important also is the sin which is committed against the Word. To this sin our entire nature has succumbed. How could it overcome this sin, since its magnitude is inexhaustible? To overcome this sin, we need Him who brings with Him inexhaustible righteousness, that is, the Son of God.

And this also reveals Satan's cunning. He does not immediately try to allure Eve by means of the loveliness of the fruit. He first attacks man's greatest strength, faith in the Word. Therefore the root and source of sin is unbelief and turning away from God, just as, on the other hand, the source and root of righteousness is faith. Satan first draws away from faith to unbelief. When he achieved this — that Eve did not believe the command which God had given — it was easy to bring this about also, that she rushed to the tree, plucked the fruit, and ate it. The outward act of disobedience follows sin, which through unbelief has fully developed in the heart. Thus the nature of sin must be considered in accordance with its true immensity, in which we have all perished. Now follows the disclosure of the sin together with its punishments.

7. *Then the eyes of both were opened; and when they realized that they were naked, they sewed together leaves of the fig tree and made themselves girdles.*

I said above that the pattern of all the temptations of Satan is the same, namely, that he first puts faith to trial and draws away from the Word. Then follow the sins against the Second Table. From our own experience we perceive that this is his procedure. The events which now follow deal with the description of sin: what its nature is when it is active, and what it is later on when it lies in the past. For while it is active, it is not felt; otherwise we would be warned by the ill effects which sin brings on, and we would draw back. But because these lie hidden, we proceed smugly to the deed itself after we have forsaken our uprightness and faith. Eve trespassed similarly in the instance of the fruit after she had been persuaded, contrary to the Word of God, that she would not die, but that her eyes would be opened and she would become wiser. This poison of Satan she drank with her ears; she stretched out her hand to the forbidden fruit; and she ate it with her mouth. And so she sins through all her senses of soul and body, and yet she is not aware of her sin. She eats the fruit with pleasure, and she urges her husband also to do the same.

These experiences are alike in all temptations and sins, whether of lust or of anger or of greed. While sin is active, it is not felt. It does not frighten, and it does not bite; but it flatters and delights. And inasmuch as these things happened when nature was still perfect, it is not surprising that they happen likewise to us, who are infected with the poison of original sin from the soles of our feet to the crowns of our heads. And so we see in the instance of godless men and also of fanatical spirits, who either had no faith or are fallen from the faith, how unconcerned they are, how vehement and obstinate in defending their errors, so that they do not even shrink from death.[17] It is the nature of sin that it is not felt for some time. But when later on sin is revealed through the Law, then it weighs too heavily on man.

But before this revelation, while sin is being committed, Eve's eyes are not open; otherwise she would have died rather than touch the fruit. But because her eyes are not yet open and unbelief remains, there remain both the delight in the forbidden fruit and the eagerness and the desire to acquire a wisdom which was also forbidden. Poor

---

[17] Cf. *Luther's Works*, 22, p. 22, note 20.

Eve is so engrossed in unbelief both in spirit and in body that she does not realize that she is doing evil.

Church history reveals similar instances of unconcern. Arius thinks himself blessed when he finds a way to scoff at the statements about the divinity of the Son. But this smugness is not lasting. As soon as the eyes of Eve are opened, she remembers the Law which she had previously forgotten and which commanded them not to eat from the forbidden tree. Before the knowledge of this Law she was without sin, just as Paul says in Rom. 7:9: "I was living some time without the Law," not because the Law was not in existence but because he did not feel the threats and punishments of the Law. To himself, therefore, he seemed to be without sin. "For through the Law is knowledge of sin" (Rom. 3:20). Therefore when the Law becomes alive again, sin also becomes alive at the same time.

This Moses points out in the account about our first parents when he says: "Their eyes were opened." It is as if he were saying: "Satan had closed not only the eyes but also the heart of Eve through the unbelief and disobedience of all her members within and without. But after sin was allowed to enter and was committed, he blithely allows their eyes to be opened that they may see what they had done." Here Satan seeks to make another gain, namely, that those who have sinned should perish in despair.

And so this story is like an explanation of Paul's statement when he says (Rom. 3:20): "Through the Law is knowledge of sin." For the Law does nothing else than reveal sin or make it alive; before the Law was known, this sin lay there as though dead or sleeping, just as is stated below to Cain (Gen. 4:7): "If you do evil, your sin will lie still until it is revealed." It lies still while it is active; but when the Law comes, then the eyes are opened, and man becomes aware of what God has commanded and what punishment He has established for the transgressors. When the Law thus gains control in the conscience, then there is the true knowledge of sin, knowledge which human hearts cannot bear unless comfort comes from God.

But what Moses adds — that after eating the fruit they saw that they were naked — is not without a purpose. If it is carefully considered, it contains a beautiful description of original righteousness.

The scholastics argue that original righteousness was not a part of man's nature but, like some adornment, was added to man as a gift, as when someone places a wreath on a pretty girl.[18] The wreath is certainly not a part of the virgin's nature; it is something apart from her nature. It came from outside and can be removed again without any injury to her nature. Therefore they maintain about man and about demons that although they have lost their original righteousness, their natural endowments have nevertheless remained pure, just as they were created in the beginning. But this idea must be shunned like poison, for it minimizes original sin.

Let us rather maintain that righteousness was not a gift which came from without, separate from man's nature, but that it was truly part of his nature, so that it was Adam's nature to love God, to believe God, to know God, etc. These things were just as natural for Adam as it is natural for the eyes to receive light. But because you may correctly say that nature has been damaged if you render an eye defective by inflicting a wound, so, after man has fallen from right-eousness into sin, it is correct and truthful to say that our natural endowments are not perfect but are corrupted by sin. For just as it is the nature of the eye to see, so it was the nature of reason and will in Adam to know God, to trust God, and to fear God. Since it is a fact that this has now been lost, who is so foolish as to say that our natural endowments are still perfect? And yet nothing was more common and received more general acceptance in the schools than this thesis. But how much more foolish it is to make this assertion about the demons, about whom Christ says that they did not stand in the truth (John 8:44) and whom we know to be the bitterest enemies of Christ and of the church!

Therefore the perfect natural endowments in man were the knowledge of God, faith, fear, etc. These Satan has corrupted through sin; just as leprosy poisons the flesh, so the will and reason have become depraved through sin, and man not only does not love God any longer but flees from Him, hates Him, and desires to be and live without Him.

Therefore this is an excellent description of the corruption which has taken the place of original righteousness and glory. It was glory for man not to realize that he was naked. Moreover, what can be a greater depravity than that the nakedness which formerly was a glory is now turned into the greatest disgrace? No one blushes

[18] See p. 142, note 1.

because of healthy and sound eyes. Distorted or weak eyes are regarded as less becoming and bring on shame. So in the state of innocence it was most honorable to go about naked. Now, after sin, when Adam and Eve see that they are naked, they are made ashamed, and they look for girdles with which to cover their disgrace. Yet how much greater disgrace is there in this, that the will is impaired, the intellect depraved, and the reason entirely corrupt and altogether changed! Is this what they mean when they say that our natural endowments are perfect?

But see what follows if you maintain that original righteousness was not a part of nature but a sort of superfluous or superadded gift. When you declare that righteousness was not a part of the essence of man, does it not also follow that sin, which took its place, is not part of the essence of man either? [19] Then there was no purpose in sending Christ, the Redeemer, if the original righteousness, like something foreign to our nature, has been taken away and the natural endowments remain perfect. What can be said that is more unworthy of a theologian?

Therefore let us shun those ravings like real pests and a perversion of the Holy Scriptures, and let us rather follow experience, which shows that we are born from unclean seed and that from the very nature of the seed we acquire ignorance of God, smugness, unbelief, hatred against God, disobedience, impatience, and similar grave faults. These are so deeply implanted in our flesh, and this poison has been so widely spread through flesh, body, mind, muscles, and blood, through the bones and the very marrow, in the will, in the intellect, and in reason, that they not only cannot be fully removed but are not even recognized as sin.

There is a familiar saying of the comic poet: "No infamy attaches to a young man if he commits fornication." [20] The pagan must be forgiven, but it is most shameful for Christians and those who are familiar with the Holy Scriptures to incline to the opinion that simple fornication is not a sin.[21] The colleges of the canons unanimously

[19] In the years after Luther's death there was a bitter theological controversy over the question whether original sin had become part of the essence of man, and in Art. I of the Formula of Concord it was set down that it had not; that controversy may be reflected in the editing of this passage.

[20] Cf. also *Luther's Works*, 21, pp. 84 ff.

[21] The question had been raised a few years before at table by a Hussite at Wittenberg, Ignatius Perknovsky (Weimar, *Tischreden*, II, No. 1647).

approve this same opinion by their life and habits! When this happens in the case of an outward sin, what conclusion shall we reach about the uncleanness of the heart and the inner emotions which ungodly men do not realize to be sins?

Similarly, man does not realize that the glory of nakedness was lost through sin. The fact that Adam and Eve walked about naked was their greatest adornment before God and all the creatures. Now, after sin, we not only shun the glance of men when we are naked; but we are also bashful in our own presence, just as Moses states here about Adam and Eve. This shame is a witness that our heart has lost the trust in God which they who were naked had before sin. Therefore even if Adam had been blind, he still would have been afraid to show himself naked to the eyes of God and of men, because through his disobedience his confidence in God was lost.

Moreover, all this proves that original righteousness was part of man's nature; but when it was lost through sin, it is clear that the natural endowments did not remain perfect, as the scholastics rave. Just as it was part of man's nature to walk about naked, full of trust and assurance toward God, and to be pleasing to God and man this way, so now, after sin, man is convinced that this nakedness of the innocent nature is offensive to God, to himself, and to all the creatures; and he provides girdles to cover his body. Is this not a change of nature? The nature indeed remains; but it is corrupted in many respects, inasmuch as confidence toward God has been lost and the heart is full of distrust, fear, and shame. Thus the parts of our body remain the same. But those which, when they were naked, were looked upon with glory are now covered up as shameful and dishonorable, as a result of the inner revolt; for through sin nature has lost its confidence in God. If we believed, we would not be ashamed.

Out of this corruption which followed because of sin there followed another evil. Adam and Eve not only were ashamed because of their nakedness, which previously was most honorable and the unique adornment of man, but they also made girdles for themselves for the purpose of covering, as though it were something most shameful, that part of the body which by its nature was most honorable and noble. What in all nature is nobler than the work of procreation? This work was assigned by God neither to the eyes nor to the mouth, which we regard as the more honorable parts of the body, but to that part which sin has taught us to call the pudendum and to cover, lest it be seen. Moreover, although in the innocent nature the entire work of procreation would have been most holy and most pure, after sin the leprosy of lust has made its way into this part of the body. Hence those who live outside the married state burn most shamefully. And unless those who live in the married state restrain their passions and carefully guard their relations with each other, they encounter all sorts of temptations.

Are we not, then, going to realize at last what a hideous and awful thing sin is, inasmuch as lust alone can be cured by no remedy, not even by marriage, which was ordained by God as a remedy for our weak nature? Most of those who are married live in adultery and sing the familiar little verse about their wives: "I can live neither with you nor without you." [22] This awful disgrace has its source in the most honorable and most excellent part of our body. Most excellent I call it because of the work of procreation, which is a most excellent one inasmuch as it preserves the species. And so through sin the most useful members have become the most shameful.

Assuredly this would not have been the case in the instances of Adam and Eve. They were full of faith toward God. And so, as often as they would have wanted to beget children, they would have come together, not urged on by that passion which is now in our leprous flesh but admiring God's dispensation and obeying Him with the utmost restraint, just as we now come together to hear the Word of God and to worship Him. All these things we have lost through sin to such an extent that we can conceive of them only in a negative and not in a positive way. From the evil which we have with us we are forced to infer how great the good is that we have lost. However, we owe thanks to God that we still have remnants of the work of procreation, be they ever so corrupted, which the church and state both need.

It is surprising that among the writers in all languages there cannot be found a trace which would indicate that nakedness became disgraceful through sin when previously it had been honorable. So we have Moses as the one and only teacher of this knowledge. With his very brief words he points out that after falling away from faith, man was brought to ruin, and that the glory of the genitals was turned into the utmost disgrace, so that man was compelled to cover them with a girdle.

[22] A proverbial saying that goes back at least to Ovid.

The word חֲגוֹרָה, which occurs here in the plural, strictly denotes a girdle. From this you will understand that the fig leaves covered every part of the thigh, so that the part which was most honorable before sin was covered as though most disgraceful and unworthy of the eyes of men. Oh, what an awful fall into sin! The eyes of man are opened in such a way that what was most honorable he now looks upon as most disgraceful.

And so it still is. Only after the Law has come, does it become clear what we have done. But when sin has been brought to light, it appears to carry with it such great disgrace that the minds cannot bear having it looked at. Therefore it tries to cover it. No one wants to appear as what he is, even though he is a thief, an adulterer, or a murderer. The heretics, too, refuse to acknowledge their error but defend it most obstinately and wish to appear as true Catholics.[23] In order to attain this they sew together very wide leaves of the fig tree; that is, they try every device they can find to gloss over and mitigate their error.

This characteristic of sin is also observable in children. When they have been caught in the very act, they still go to great lengths to persuade their parents otherwise and to excuse themselves. Such is simply the habit of people. Even when they have been caught and are being held, they nevertheless try to get off, so that they may not be dismayed but may appear good and righteous. This poison, too, has been infused into our nature through sin, as the passage before us proves.

8. *And when they had heard the voice of the Lord God, who was walking in Paradise at the breeze of the day, Adam and his wife hid among the trees of Paradise from the face of the Lord.*

This now is the third evil of original sin [24] which proves that original righteousness has been lost. By the way, here again the opinions of the rabbis confuse Lyra.[25] Some explain "at the breeze of the day" as referring to a place or a direction between south and west. Others explain it as a reference to the time, namely, that this

[23] Luther's use of this word here indicates his continued usage, despite his revision of the text of the creeds.

[24] The first evil was their shame at being naked; the second was their girdles; the third, their concealment.

[25] Lyra on Gen. 3:8, sec. "s."

happened at evening, when the heat subsides and the winds begin to blow.

My own opinion is that we should understand "spirit" simply in the sense of wind,[26] and that after their conscience had been convicted by the Law, Adam and Eve were terrified by the rustling of a leaf (Lev. 26:36). We see it to be just so in the case of frightened human beings. When they hear the creaking of a beam, they are afraid that the entire house may collapse; when they hear a mouse, they are afraid that Satan is there and wants to kill them. By nature we have become so thoroughly frightened that we fear even the things that are safe.

Therefore after their conscience has been convicted by the Law and they feel their disgrace before God and themselves, Adam and Eve lose their confidence in God and are so filled with fear and terror that when they hear a breath or a wind, they immediately think God is approaching to punish them; and they hide. I, too, think that by the voice of the Lord, who was walking about, Moses means the wind or the sound of the wind, which preceded the appearance of the Lord. Similarly, in the Gospel Christ says of the wind (John 3:8): "You hear its sound." When they heard the leaves rustling as if they were being moved by the wind, they thought: "Behold, now the Lord is coming to demand punishment from us."

Therefore when Moses later adds: "Toward the wind of the day," it seems to me that he is explaining himself, as if he were saying: "There was a sound like that of the wind of the day," so that emphasis lies on the word "day." He does not refer to the wind in the night, because he wants to lay greater emphasis on the prodigious fear which followed sin, as if he were saying: "They were so fearful that even in the bright light of day they were afraid of the rustling of a leaf." What would have happened if God had come in the dark and during the night? For then the terror is far greater. Just as light makes men courageous, so darkness increases their fear. This fear, which overtook Adam and Eve in the very light of day after their sin, is a clear indication that they had fallen completely from the faith.

This I believe to be the true sense of this passage; it also agrees with the threat in Lev. 26:36, where Moses is speaking of the punishments that will follow sin, namely, that sinners will become frightened

26 Cf. the discussion of the Hebrew and Greek terms in *Luther's Works,* 22, pp. 298—301.

by the sound of a falling leaf and will take to flight as though from a sword. When the conscience is truly and thoroughly frightened, man is so overcome that he not only cannot act but is unable even to do any thinking. They say that such a thing happens in battle when soldiers who are overcome by fear cannot move a hand but permit themselves to be slain by the enemy. Such a terrible punishment follows sin that at the rustling of a leaf conscience is full of fear, nay, that it cannot even bear that most beautiful creature, the very light of day, which is by nature so refreshing to us.

Here again you see the immensity of original sin, with which we are born and which has been planted in us through the sin of our first parents. Moreover, this detriment also helps us to gain an insight into original righteousness on the basis of what we have lost, or by way of contrast. For in man there was the most admirable confidence in God, and man could not have been afraid even if he had seen the heavens collapse.

With what great unconcern Eve listens to the serpent! We do not talk so intimately with a puppy that has been raised in the home and has been made accustomed to it — or with a chick. So, then, before sin they did not look for hiding places; but because they had understanding, they stood upright and praised God with uplifted face. But now they are terrified by the rustling of a leaf. Oh, what a grievous downfall, to plunge from the utmost sense of security, from confidence and delight in God into such awful terror that man shrinks from the sight of God more than from the sight and presence of the devil! Adam and Eve were not avoiding the devil; it was God, their Creator, whom they were avoiding! Him they judged to be more troublesome and more dreadful than Satan. But Satan they consider better than God, for they do not avoid Satan. And so this fear is really an avoidance and hatred of God.

Moreover, it is worthwhile to note how sin gradually grows until it becomes exceedingly sinful sin, as Paul is wont to call it (Rom. 7:13). First man falls from faith into unbelief and disobedience. Then fear, hatred, and avoidance of God follow unbelief, and these bring with them despair and impenitence. For where should the heart in its fright flee from the presence of God? To the devil? This is neither an advantageous nor an advisable thing to do, and yet it turns out this way. And so this account shows that God created man and made him lord of all, and yet man avoids Him and considers nothing either more hateful or more unbearable than God. Otherwise he would not have turned away from God; he would not have avoided Him; and he would not have trembled at the voice of God when He was coming, not at night, not with lightning and thunder, as at Sinai, but in the clear light of day, while a light and delightful breeze was blowing and the leaves of the trees were gently stirring. Thus there is nothing more grievous, nothing more wretched, than a conscience frightened by the Law of God and by the sight of its sins.

This brings about what is worst: that Adam and Eve avoid their Creator and God and take refuge under the protection of the fig trees, both to cover themselves and to hide in the midst of the trees. What can be termed more horrible than to flee from God and to desire to be hidden from Him?

Here again it becomes evident how righteous our will and intellect is after sin! Their very action shows that their will has become depraved, because they have a desire for what was forbidden by God; they aspire to become disobedient to God but obedient to the devil. Nor can we have any doubt that their intellect was depraved when we look at the stratagem by which Adam and Eve think they are safe. Or is it not the height of stupidity, in the first place, to attempt the impossible, to try to avoid God, whom they cannot avoid? In the second place, to attempt to avoid Him in so stupid a way, that they believe themselves safe among the trees, when iron walls and huge masses of mountains could not save them? When confidence in God has been lost in this way, there follows an awful fright in the will; and when the superb gifts of wisdom and understanding have been lost, there follows the utmost stupidity, so that they attempt the impossible by the most stupid means. To such an extent original sin is an inexhaustible evil. And yet these instances are, as it were, preludes. For the verdict, which is ghastly and terrible, had not yet been reached.

9. *And the Lord God called Adam and said to him: Where are you?*

This is the description of the trial. After Adam has become terrified through the awareness of his sin, he avoids the sight of God and realizes that not only Paradise but the entire world is too narrow to be a safe hiding place. And now, in that mental agony, he reveals his stupidity by seeking relief from sin through flight from God. But he had already fled too far from God. Sin itself is the real withdrawal from God, and it would not have been necessary to add any further flight. Thus it happens — and this is the nature of sin — that the farther man withdraws from God, the farther he still desires to withdraw; and he who has once fled and apostatized keeps on fleeing forever. And so some also maintain concerning the punishments of hell that this will be the most terrible thing: that the ungodly will desire to flee and yet will realize that they cannot escape.[27] So it was with Adam here; although he was caught, nevertheless he does not stop fleeing.

Accordingly, when Moses says: "He called him," this must be understood to mean that He called Adam to judgment. Here some raise a question about the person through whom Adam was called. It is not unreasonable to answer that God did all this through the ministrations of the angels and that an angel acted in God's stead and, as God's representative, spoke these words to Adam. Similarly, when officers of the state either do or say something, they are not acting and speaking for their own persons but in God's stead. For this reason Scripture gives the name of God's judgment to the judgments administered or transacted through the agency of human beings. Accordingly, I have nothing against the idea that Adam was called by an angel and was shown that flight was impossible.

But it should be noted particularly that Moses specifically says that Adam was called, namely, that he was the only person to whom on the sixth day the Word of the Lord regarding the fruit of the forbidden tree was addressed. Therefore just as he alone heard the commandment, so he alone is first called to trial. But because Eve also sinned and fell away from God, she hears the verdict at the same time and shares in the punishment.

The words "Where are you?" are words of the Law. God directs them to the conscience. Although all things are plain and known before God (Heb. 4:13), He is speaking according to our way of thinking; for He sees us considering how we may withdraw from His sight. Therefore when He says: "Where are you?" it is the same as if He were saying: "Do you think I do not see you?" He wants to show Adam that though he had hidden, he was not hidden from God, and that when he avoided God, he did not escape God. It happens naturally in the case of every sin that we stupidly try to escape God's

[27] See *Luther's Works*, 13, p. 93.

wrath and yet cannot escape it. It is the utmost stupidity for us to imagine that our cure lies in flight from God rather than in our return to God, and yet our sinful nature cannot return to God. In what frame of mind, therefore, shall we suppose Adam to have been when he heard this voice? He had stupidly hoped to be able to hide; and, behold, he stands before God's judgment seat and is now called in for his punishment.

10. *And he said: I heard Thy voice in Paradise, and I was afraid because I was naked; and I concealed myself.*

Just as Adam stupidly began to flee, so he answers most stupidly; so thoroughly had sin deprived him of all discernment and good sense. He wants to inform God that he is naked — God, who created him naked. By this action he confuses himself, betrays and condemns himself with his own mouth. He says that he heard God's voice and was afraid. But had he not heard the voice of the Lord before, when He forbade him to eat of the forbidden tree? Why was he not afraid then? Why did he not hide then? Why did he stand glad and upright when he saw and heard God before him? But now he is terrified by the rustling of a leaf (Lev. 26:36). It follows, therefore, that Adam is no longer the same that he was, but that he has undergone a change and has become a different person, one who is looking for a fictitious reason as his excuse. How can it be true that the reason for his fear is the voice, when previously he did not fear the voice but heard God with delight?

Let us learn, then, that this perversion and stupidity always accompany sin and that sinners accuse themselves by their excuses and betray themselves by their defense, especially before God. It is in just this way that Adam here wants to cover his offense and deck himself out. He says that the reason for his flight was not that he had sinned, but that he had heard the voice of the Lord and was frightened by it and became ashamed because he was naked. The poor fellow does not reflect that he did not have this fear previously and that he had not been ashamed because of his nakedness. Since it was something that God had created, why is he afraid on account of that which God made? Naked he had previously walked about in the sight of God and of all the creatures in Paradise, assured of God's goodwill and delighting in God. Now he is ashamed because he is naked; he flees from God and conceals himself. All these facts are sure proofs by which Adam condemns himself and betrays his sin.

In the same way the ungodly will condemn themselves at the Last Judgment, when the dark recesses of human hearts will be revealed and, as though in open books, the evil deeds of every single being will be read. God indeed knows that Adam sinned and that he is guilty of death. However, He questions him so that by his own witness he himself may prove himself guilty of having committed sin; for he is fleeing from God, something which in itself is a sin, just as it is a good deed to take one's refuge in God. Although Adam hopes to be able to cover his sin with a lie, he brings this witness against himself when he says that the reason for his flight was the voice of the Lord and his own nakedness.

Let us learn, therefore, that this is the nature of sin: unless God immediately provides a cure and calls the sinner back, he flees endlessly from God and, by excusing his sin with lies, heaps sin upon sin until he arrives at blasphemy and despair. Thus sin by its own gravitation always draws with it another sin and brings on eternal destruction, till finally the sinful person would rather accuse God than acknowledge his own sin. Adam should have said: "Lord, I have sinned." But he does not do this. He accuses God of sin and says in reality: "Thou, Lord, hast sinned. For I would have remained holy in Paradise after eating of the fruit if Thou hadst kept quiet." This is in reality the meaning of his words when he says: "I would not have fled if Thy voice had not frightened me."

Thus when man has been accused of sin by God, he does not acknowledge his sin but rather accuses God and transfers his guilt from himself to the Creator. The outcome is that in this way sin grows endlessly unless God through His mercy grants His help. This wickedness and utmost stupidity Adam regards as supreme wisdom. He has become so confused by his fright that he does not realize what he is saying or what he is doing, and by excusing himself he brings the most serious charges against himself and increases his sin to huge proportions.

However, we must not think that this happened to Adam alone. We, each one of us, do the same thing; our nature does not permit us to act otherwise after we have become guilty of sin. We all prefer to accuse God rather than to acknowledge it before God. Adam does the same thing when he declares that God's voice is the reason for his fleeing. Therefore he maintains that God is the author of his flight. This sin now follows the other. For how would he, who shows no consideration to God, his Creator, show consideration to what God has created? He blames God for his nakedness as if He were the Creator of something shameful. Through sin he has become so crazed that he turns the glory of nakedness into a disgrace of the Creator.

11. *The Lord said to him: But who told you that you were naked? Have you not eaten from the tree about which I had commanded you that you should not eat?*

Here Adam's conscience is roused by the real sting of the Law. It is as if God said: "You know that you are naked, and for this reason you hid. But your nakedness is My creation. You are not condemning it as something shameful, are you? Therefore it was not the nakedness that perplexed you, it was not My voice that frightened you; but your conscience convicted you of sin because you ate the fruit from the forbidden tree." Here Adam, hard pressed in this manner, was in the midst of death and in the midst of hell. He was compelled to confess that nakedness was not evil, for it had been created by God. On the other hand, he realized that the evil was this: that now he had a bad conscience because of the nakedness in which he had previously gloried as in a unique adornment, and that he was now terrified by God's voice, which previously he had heard with the utmost pleasure.

To this thought, which the Lord observes in Adam, His words refer. It is as if He were saying: "Since you are aware of your guilt and are terrified, you surely have eaten from the forbidden tree. You did not receive a command about not killing, about not committing adultery, but about not eating the fruit of this tree. Therefore because you are terrified, you prove that you have sinned against this command." Thus Adam hears from the Lord his very thoughts. He was thinking: "I have eaten the fruit, but I shall not say that I am fleeing for this reason; I shall keep still about the sin and say that I am afraid because I am naked and that I am frightened by His voice." But while he is reflecting on these thoughts, he is forced to accuse himself, and within him he hears his conscience convicting him of a lie and charging him with sin. In addition, the Lord Himself now charges him with sin directly and in plain words. But not even in this way is He able to bring the naive Adam to an acknowledgment of his sin. For he says:

12. *The woman whom Thou gavest me as a companion gave me from the tree, and I ate.*

See how superbly the vicious nature of sin is pictured here. Adam can in no wise be forced into a confession of his sin, but he denies his sin or excuses it as long as he sees that he has any hope or any kind of an excuse left. It is not amazing that in the beginning he hoped to be able to cover his sin and that he accuses God rather than acknowledge that he has sinned. But this is amazing, that he still persists in his excuse after his conscience has convicted him and he himself has also heard his sin from God. He does not say: "Lord, I have sinned; forgive me my debt; be merciful"; but he passes on the guilt to the woman. It is the nature of sin not to permit the soul to flee back to God but rather to force it into a flight away from God.

There is a well-known teaching in the schools of the rhetoricians that if one has been charged with a crime, he should either deny it or defend it as having been committed legally.[28] Adam does both. In the first place, he denies his offense and says that he is frightened by the voice of the Lord, not by his sin. But when he is convicted, so that he cannot deny the deed, he tries to defend himself with the claim that his action is lawful. "If," he says, "Thou hadst not joined this woman to me, I would not have eaten." Thus he again traces the sin he himself had committed back to God and accuses God of his own sin. There just is no end to sinning once one has turned away from the Word. He had sinned through disobedience and unbelief; now he doubles his great disgrace and blasphemy when he says: "I did not listen to the serpent; I felt no pleasure in looking at that tree; I did not stretch out my hand to pluck the forbidden fruit. All this the woman did whom Thou didst give to me." In short, Adam does not want to acknowledge his sin; he wants to be regarded as pure and innocent.

And so this little section, too, deals with the description or the nature of sin. When there is no promise of forgiveness of sins and no faith, the sinner cannot act otherwise. If God had said: "Adam, you have sinned; but I shall forgive you your sin," then with the utmost loathing Adam would have humbly and frankly acknowledged his sin. But because the hope for the forgiveness of his sins is not yet available, he feels and sees nothing except death itself because of his transgression of the command. However, because nature is

[28] Cf., for example, Aristotle, *Rhetoric*, I, ch. 15.

unable to avoid death, Adam cannot be brought to a confession of his sin. He tries every possible device to clear himself of his guilt. In the same way every sinner hates his punishment. Moreover, because he hates his punishment, at the same time he hates God's justice and God Himself; and he tries with all his might to persuade God and everybody else that he is suffering innocently.

Thus here Adam is minimizing his sin by saying that he did not listen to the serpent and that he did not pluck the fruit. "The woman whom Thou didst give to me," he says, "gave me from this tree." Not much different from this feeling is that of despairing people who, when they come to a knowledge of their sin, either hang themselves or curse God. Familiar are Job's statements (Job 3:3, 11): "Cursed is the day on which I was born. Why was not my mother made my grave?" They pass on to God the guilt of their sin; they murmur against God that they were created for destruction and damnation. Man cannot do otherwise when no hope of forgiveness and promise of grace is available. Because death is unbearable for human nature, it begets despair and blasphemy.

Therefore the statement "The woman whom Thou didst give to me" is full of resentment and anger against God, as if Adam were saying: "Thou hast burdened me with this trouble. If Thou hadst given the woman some garden of her own and hadst not burdened me by making me live with her, I would have remained without sin. Therefore the guilt for my having sinned is Thine, since Thou didst give me a wife." Here Adam is presented as a typical instance of all sinners and of such as despair because of their sin. They cannot do otherwise than accuse God and excuse themselves, inasmuch as they see that God is omnipotent and could have prevented those sins. Such an awful evil is sin when hearts are not given encouragement in time through the promise of the forgiveness of sins. And such is the working of the Law that, when the Law stands alone without the Gospel and the knowledge of grace, it leads to despair and ultimate impenitence.

13. *And the Lord God said to the woman: Why did you do this? And she answered: The serpent deceived me, and I ate.*

Now Eve, too, is put before us as an example; and when she is corrupted by sin, she is not one whit better than Adam. Adam wanted to appear innocent; he passed on his guilt from himself to God, who had given him his wife. Eve also tries to excuse herself and accuses the serpent, which was also a creature of God. Indeed, she confesses that she ate the fruit. "But the serpent," says she, "which Thou hast created and which Thou hast permitted to move about in Paradise, deceived me." Is not this accusing the Creator and pushing off one's guilt from oneself? So we see that sin is and acts the same everywhere. It does not want to be sin; it does not want to be punished because of sin. It wants to be righteousness. When it cannot achieve this, it puts the guilt on God, so that it accuses God of a lie when He accuses sin. Thus out of a human sin comes a sin that is clearly demonic; unbelief turns into blasphemy, disobedience into contempt of the Creator.

But I call this a demonic sin and not a human one, because the devil everlastingly hates, accuses, and damns God but exonerates himself; and it is not possible for him to say from his heart: "Lord, I have sinned, forgive me." Otherwise, as we read in the account about Martin, he would not have to despair of pardon.[29] This pardon is impossible as long as he does not acknowledge his sin and blasphemes God for capriciously displaying undeserved cruelty toward His creatures.

Thus we see Adam and Eve so fallen and sunk in sin that they cannot sink deeper. After unbelief follows the disobedience of all of man's powers and parts. After this disobedience follows later on the excuse and defense of sin; and after the defense, the accusation and condemnation of God. This is the last step of sin, to insult God and to charge Him with being the originator of sin. Unless hearts are given courage through trust in mercy, this nature cannot be urged on beyond this point if there are successive steps of sin.

This is why the state of the church was terrible under the pope. Then nothing was seen or heard which could encourage a heart in such distress, except that each year the story of the Passion was taught, though quite indifferently. This faintly indicated where pardon was to be sought. Everything else led away from the promise of the forgiveness of sins toward one's own righteousness. And so in many monasteries we saw stricken and despairing people passing the entire time of their lives and in the end wearing themselves out in the conflict by their worries and griefs. Because this doctrine was unknown, the rest of the brothers did nothing more than stand near by and try to obtain the protection of the saints with their idolatrous

[29] Sulpicius Severus, *De vita beati Martini*, ch. 22, *Patrologia, Series Latina*, XX, 172—173.

prayers. Thus these wretched people wasted away in their extreme grief of soul without hope, without counsel, and without help! This is a situation filled with terror.[30]

Therefore if the papacy and all the monasteries could be overthrown with one finger, it ought to be done because of this most wretched murdering of consciences. Nothing is more terrible than to be in sin and yet to be remote from, or ignorant of, the forgiveness of sins or the promise of grace. But the pope was responsible for the concealment of the forgiveness of sins, because sound doctrine and true forms of worship were not maintained in the church. If some were saved, it was the bare reading of the Passion of Christ accepted in faith which saved them, against the will and opposition of the pope. In their last perils people were led to seek the intercessions of Mary and of the saints. They kept repeating these well-known figments: that Mother Mary showed her breasts to her Son, the Son showed His wounds to the Father, and that thus man was saved through the intercession, not of the Son but of His mother.[31]

Therefore I urge you with all diligence to consider the teaching of the Gospel a matter of the utmost importance. For we see from this passage what happens in the case of Adam and Eve when sin is present and this knowledge of the promise and of grace is lacking. The condemnation of Satan also points to the same result; for just as he lacks the promise of grace, so he cannot put an end to his transgressions, blasphemies, and hatred of God. For this reason Adam's situation is better. He is called to account that he might acknowledge his sin and, after he is thoroughly frightened by his sin, be given courage through the promise of the remission of sins. About this a most beautiful text now follows, in which the preaching about Christ is included.

However, just as the end of this affair shows the very great kindness and mercy of God toward man (inasmuch as He calls him back for the remission of his sins and for eternal life through the Seed who was to come), so also the beginnings of this affair, if we evaluate them properly, are more lenient than what Adam deserved. There is not that terrible sight as on Mt. Sinai, where trumpet blasts were mingled with flashes of lightning and peals of thunder. But God comes in a very soft breeze to indicate that the reprimand will be fatherly.

[30] This is undoubtedly autobiographical; cf. *Luther's Works*, 13, p. 86, note 20.

[31] Cf. *Luther's Works*, 13, p. 326, note 74.

He does not drive Adam away from Himself because of his sin, but He calls him and calls him back from his sin. Yet Adam does not understand or see this fatherly concern, since he is overwhelmed by his sin and terror. He does not notice that God deals far differently with the serpent. He does not call the serpent. Nor — in order in this way to call it to repentance — does he ask the serpent about the sin that has been committed. But He condemns it immediately.

This shows that even then Christ, our Deliverer, had placed Himself between God and man as a Mediator. It is a very great measure of grace that after Adam's sin God does not remain silent but speaks, and in many words indeed, in order to show signs of His fatherly disposition. With the serpent everything is done differently. And so, although the promise concerning Christ is not yet there, it is already noticeable in the thought and counsel of God.

So far, then, Moses has described for us the trial which God held after the fall of our first parents, when He questions and hears those who had been summoned to His judgment seat. Indeed, the pitiable beings desire to escape this trial, but they cannot; nay rather, when they attempt to excuse themselves, they accuse and betray themselves doubly. The woman admits the deed. Adam tries to conceal it, even though, as is the nature of sin, he does not wish to have it regarded as sin. Unless grace comes, it is impossible for a man to act otherwise than to excuse his sin and to want it considered as righteousness. Therefore God is compelled to be at continual odds with us about this in order to force out of us a confession of sin and to justify Him, as Ps. 51:4 calls the confession. But as long as the Law alone rules and stings us, the frightened conscience cannot produce this confession, as the example of Adam and Eve proves.

From this passage the holy prophets, who read this book with far greater diligence and faith than we do, drew many of their statements. Among these are: "The wicked flees when no one pursues him" (Prov. 28:1); "The wicked rages like the sea" (Is. 57:20); "There is no peace for the wicked" (Is. 48:22); "He who believes will not be ashamed" (Is. 49:23); "The righteous will be bold as a lion" (Prov. 28:1); and "The just will live by his faith" (Hab. 2:4). From this passage Christ took His striking statement which appears in John (3:20): "He who does evil hates the light." It is the nature of sin that it desires to remain hidden and not to be brought into the light, just as Adam covered himself with a girdle and fled to the trees.

But here we must give consideration to Paul's statement in 1 Tim. 2:13-14: "Adam was first formed, then Eve. And Adam was not seduced; but the woman, since she had been seduced, was in the transgression." Almost everybody understands this statement to mean that Adam was not seduced but sinned knowingly. For he did not yield to the persuasion of the devil as Eve did; but he was unwilling to cause sadness for his delight, that is, for his wife, and so he preferred his wife's love to God.[32] They try to make this interpretation likely by saying that the serpent was afraid of the male, as the master, and approached the woman; for although she herself was also holy, nevertheless, as the weaker creature, she was more likely to yield to persuasion. And thus Eve was seduced by the serpent, but Adam was not. He was seduced either by himself or by the woman: by the woman, because she handed him the apple; by himself, because, since he had seen that Eve did not die immediately after eating the fruit, he did not believe that the punishment which the Lord had threatened would follow. When a thief sees that his thefts have succeeded several times, he steals with unconcern; but if he had the magistrate and the gallows before his eyes, he would not steal.

I do not disapprove of this opinion. It indicates that both statements are true: that Adam was deceived, and that he was not deceived. He was not deceived by the serpent, as Eve was. Nevertheless, he was deceived by his wife and by himself when he persuaded himself that his deed would not result in the punishment concerning which the Lord had said that it would follow.

14. *And the Lord God said to the serpent: Because you did this, you are cursed among all the living things and beasts of the earth: on your belly you will walk, and dust you will eat all the days of your life.*

After the trial and the inquiry into the case has been carefully carried out, there now follows the execution of the sentence, as they say, by which there is rendered to each according to his deed, and yet not exactly alike, as we shall hear. Moreover, careful consideration should be given to this passage for two reasons. In the first place, nowhere else in Moses does God, in person, speak as extensively as He does here; in the second place, it does not contain any Law about what either the serpent or man should do but is

---

[32] Luther had studied this problem for his own exegesis of 1 Tim. 2:13 in 1528 (Weimar, XXVI, 47—48).

devoted entirely to promising and threatening what good and what evil will happen to both.

This, too, should be carefully noted: that after sin no Law was put upon Adam, although the perfect nature had its Law. But this happened because God sees that nature, which is now corrupt, not only can receive no support from a Law but has gone through such a complete convulsion and disturbance that it cannot bear even a syllable of the Law. Therefore He does not further burden sin-burdened nature with the Law. But He heals sin, like a wound, with a health-giving plaster, that is, with the promise concerning Christ, while He also applies the harsh cautery which the devil had brought on. Just as health-giving plasters also damage the flesh while they effect their cure, so the curative promise is put to Adam in such a way that at the same time it includes a threat, to serve as a cure for the lust of the flesh. But by "lust" I mean not only the hideous prurience of the flesh but also that filthiness of the spirit, as Paul calls it (2 Cor. 7:1), that by nature we are inclined to idolatry, unbelief, smugness, and other horrible sins against the First and the Second Table. There was need of this harsh cautery to keep this depravity of our nature in check.

It would be my wish, moreover, that I could treat this text in accordance with its importance; for it contains whatever is excellent in all Scripture. And the first part of the text is entirely in figurative language; God is speaking with the serpent, and yet it is certain that the serpent does not understand these words. These are not words of creation, as were those words above when He said to the animals: "Increase and multiply," and when He said to the earth: "Let the earth bring forth herbs and trees of every kind"; but they are words that threaten and promise. God is not speaking to an irrational nature but to an intelligent nature.

And so He mentions the serpent by name, but He is dealing primarily with Satan, who is in control of the serpent and through it is deceiving the human beings. But on account of the sin of man, who is the lord of the creatures, the animals and trees also perished in the Flood, just as subjects often suffer punishment because of the errors of their rulers. Thus it also happened to the serpent that it was punished because of the sin of the devil, who had misused the serpent for such a great evil; and yet, in a figurative sense, Satan's punishment is meant by the punishment of the serpent.

Perhaps this uncertainty of meaning was the reason why the text, which should be very well known to everybody, was not expounded by anyone carefully and accurately, so far as I know. I often wonder what the fathers and bishops did, who were engaged in ruling churches and in warding off heretics and yet did not devote themselves with greater zeal to the elucidation of passages of this kind. About the bishops in our own day I am not saying anything. They have nothing except the name "bishop" and can more truthfully be called destroyers of the churches than watchmen or supervisors. But I am speaking of the ancient ones, who are held in esteem because of their saintly life and their teaching. Among these there is no one who adequately expounded this passage. Perhaps the affairs of office which usually fall to the lot of administrators involved them too deeply.

The villainy of the more recent ones is familiar. They even falsified this passage and changed the pronoun "He" to the feminine "she," and with obvious malice they twisted this passage into a reference to the Blessed Virgin. I am excusing Lyra, who appears to have been a good man but yields too much to the authority of the fathers. And so he allows himself to become involved through St. Augustine in a most absurd allegory, which Gregory also adopts in his *Moralia*.[33] The woman must be taken to mean the lower reason; her seed, to mean its good working; the seed of the devil, his corrupt prompting. Moreover, the words of the Lord, "I shall put enmity between you and her seed," must be understood of that conflict which occurs when the devil, by means of his evil prompting, assails the lower reason, which is the woman. If she should yield to her lusts, then through her Satan hopes also to topple the man, that is, the higher reason. Furthermore, this is said to be the meaning of the statement that the serpent is lying in wait for the heel; for Satan does not make his attacks except from below, by setting before the senses the things that delight them.

I ask you, dear reader, what need is there of those obscure and most foolish allegories when this light is so very clear? For all I care, let us concede the division of reason into two parts: the higher and the lower. It would be much more correct to use the term "lower" for that which has the ability to administer the affairs of the household and of the state, and not for that brutish lust; but call that the

[33] Lyra on Gen. 3:15, sec. "k." Cf. p. 191, note 38.

"higher" by which we look upon or observe the things beyond state and home, the knowledge of God pointed out in the Word, where we effect nothing by our endeavor but merely learn and observe. But even though we were to make these statements, what have they to do with this passage? Do they not utterly smother the true meaning and replace it with an idea which is not merely useless but disastrous? For what ability or insight has reason in religious matters?

Then there is also something absurd in making Eve the lower part of reason, although it is sure that in no part, that is, neither in body nor in soul, was Eve inferior to her husband Adam. This ridiculous interpretation is the source of the familiar secular discussions about free will and about reason's striving toward the supreme good, which finally turn the whole of theology into philosophy and into specious prattle.

Therefore we shall disregard such destructive and foolish absurdities and proceed by a new route, unconcerned if the footprints of our predecessors lead elsewhere. For we have the Holy Spirit as our Guide. Through Moses He does not give us foolish allegories; but He teaches us about most important events, which involve God, sinful man, and Satan, the originator of sin.

Let us, therefore, establish in the first place that the serpent is a real serpent, but one that has been entered and taken over by Satan, who is speaking through the serpent. In the second place, let us also establish this: that what God is saying to the serpent, the serpent, being an irrational animal, did not understand; but Satan did, and he was the one whom God had especially in mind. Thus I adhere simply to the historical and literal meaning, which is in harmony with the text. In accordance with this meaning, the serpent remains a serpent, but one dominated by Satan; the woman remains a woman; Adam remains Adam, just as the following events prove. For it is not the lower and the higher reason that beget Cain and Abel, but Adam and Eve, that is, the first human beings, who had fallen into death through their sin and had been put under the rule of Satan.

Now what God says to the serpent: "You are cursed among all the animals and beasts of the earth, upon your breast you shall go" does not have the meaning which Augustine and others after him adopt, namely, that by "breast" is meant pride.[34] But because Satan

[34] Augustine, *De Genesi contra Manichaeos libri duo*, II, 16, *Patrologia, Series Latina*, XXXIV, 210.

misused the serpent for sin, the serpent is compelled to bear a part of the punishment and is cursed by becoming the most hated among all the beasts. It was not so originally; but now, through the curse, something is added to the nature of the serpent. Although before the curse it was a very pretty little beast, it is now more frightful and more hated than all the other animals. We know from experience that by nature we have a fear of serpents and that by their nature serpents also flee from us. Thus the serpent is compelled to bear a part of the curse and of the punishment. But these words are not addressed to the serpent alone. God is dealing with Satan, who is hidden within the serpent; the verdict of the Last Judgment is here announced to him, and he is actually made to stand before the judgment seat of God.

His way of speaking with the serpent is far different from His way of speaking with Adam and Eve, whom He affectionately calls back. "Where are you? Who told you that you are naked?" These words reveal God's love toward the whole human race; even after sin the human being is sought and called, and God converses with him and hears him. This is a sure indication of His mercy. Although these are words which deal with Law and judgment, they nevertheless indicate a clear hope that Adam and Eve were not to be condemned eternally.

With the serpent and Satan He deals more harshly. He does not call him, and He does not say: "Why did you do this?" But He simply announces the verdict of the court in very harsh words: "Because," says He, "you did this." It is as if He were saying: "You, Satan, have already committed sin previously, and you were condemned when you fell from heaven. To this sin you have now added another, in order to bring man into sin through your misuse of the serpent. For this reason the serpent will bear this punishment, that now it alone will lie under the curse, when previously it shared in the blessing which all the other beasts had."

From this some obvious conclusions follow: that before sin the serpent was a most beautiful little animal and most pleasing to man, as little mules, sheep, and puppies are today; moreover, that it walked upright. And so it is due to the curse and not to its nature that it now creeps on the ground, just as it is due to the curse that a woman conceives with shame, gives birth with pain, and brings up her offspring with toil. But if the work of procreation were without the curse, it would be something most honorable; birth would be very easy, and bringing up the offspring would be the greatest joy. Therefore sin has not merely deformed nature most shamefully, but has perverted it in the worst possible manner.

Nevertheless, our sophists still have the audacity to maintain that the natural endowments have remained unimpaired after sin, even in the demons.[35] The serpent, which Satan misused for sin, bears this burden because of sin: although it had previously been most beautiful, now suddenly, before Adam's eyes, it takes on a snakelike tail, creeps on the ground, and becomes an object of fear for him. If this is so, why shall we have any doubt about man, who himself sinned and drank the poison of sin which was poured into him by Satan? Therefore, just as the Egyptians were vexed to see that the rod which Moses threw down was turned into a serpent (Ex. 7:10-12), so also in Paradise, immediately after this word of the curse had been uttered, the serpent was changed from a most beautiful form into a most shameful and disgusting one.

To this curse also belongs the statement: "And the dust of the earth you will eat." The allegorists explain this to mean that by deceiving such people as love earthly things Satan will make them part of himself.[36] But I have stated that God is speaking with the serpent and that He is cursing the serpent. There are other beasts which also eat earth, but the serpent eats earth in this way; although previously it was superior as regards its cleverness, its beauty, and also its diet, which it shared with man, it now bears the punishment that the nature of its diet is changed.

It is a glory that sheep, cows, and other beasts live on herbs, also on the fruits of trees, and then produce from themselves products which are useful to people as food; such as butter, milk, meat, etc. This glory the serpent had in common with the others. Now, because of sin, it has been cast out from that company and, as it were, from this table and dinner party. It is not permitted to eat even the lowliest herbs. It dares not eat apples, pears, and nuts, on which even the mice feed; but it consumes the raw earth. These are not my words but those of Moses; they teach that the nature of the serpent was entirely changed and made different.

But although I said — and it is also true — that God is speaking with the serpent in a way that is especially aimed at Satan, as the

[35] Cf. p. 142, note 1.

[36] At least part of the information about this came from Lyra's exposition.

following events show more clearly, yet I do not agree that, like Augustine, whom Lyra follows, we should allegorically apply to Satan those statements which fit well with the nature of the serpent. For the serpent and Satan are linked together in their sinning; although Satan is the one who does the acting, the serpent is, as it were, his instrument. For the same reason they are also linked together in their punishment. But the serpent bears only its bodily punishment, while for Satan, as the originator and perpetrator, another judgment has been prepared, of which Christ says in John (16:11): "The prince of this world has already been judged." This judgment will follow later.

Some maintain that, like the serpent, the devil no longer walks upright and has lost his earlier form and stature. Although this is correct, it is out of place here and has no bearing on the explanation of the text before us. Moreover, when I say that before the curse the serpent walked upright, this is not to be understood as though it walked about upright as man does, but as a deer or a peacock does. So much for the judgment of the serpent.

What follows pertains properly to the devil. It depicts his judgment far better than those foolish and unsuited allegories. It also gives this sound comfort, that now the devil is no longer in a position to rage and do harm as freely as he would like and as he would do if there were no woman's Seed.

15. *I shall put enmity between you and the woman and your seed and her seed.*

These words deal specifically with the judgment of Satan, and in them sound comfort is given to the godly. The preceding statements, as I said, are historical and deal with the serpent; because Satan had misused it for sin, it bears the punishment of being expelled from the society and, so to speak, from the community life of the remaining animals, and of being forced to eat different food instead of enjoying what is their common fare.

These words can, of course, also be interpreted allegorically; but then they are both less pertinent and too weak in a debate. As a matter of fact, Satan has been hurled from heaven and has been condemned because of his sin. He no longer walks about like an ox or a deer; he creeps, that is, he no longer attacks the godly with open force but makes use of his wiles. And yet when the godly keep the

Word in mind, they perceive these wiles; they see how ugly his appearance is, and they shrink from him. His way of moving, namely, that he creeps in this fashion and does not walk erect, surely shows that his tyranny has been broken and that he cannot hurt the church as much as he would like.

These ideas may be arrived at by way of allegory. But they do not bring out Moses' meaning, and for this reason they are not pertinent. Therefore when we must make statements about Satan, let us fall back on other Scripture proofs that are pertinent, sure, and strong. Of this sort are John 8:44: "The devil is a murderer and the father of lies," and "He did not abide in the truth"; 1 Peter 5:8: "He goes about like a roaring lion, seeking whom he may devour"; and John 16:11: "The prince of the world is judged."

Finally, who does not realize that the statement before us deals specifically with Satan, whom the Son of God resists in such a way that he cannot undertake anything with open force as though he had no antagonist? Under this protection the church is safe; Satan not only cannot attack the church with open force, but also in other respects his tyranny and his malevolence have been broken. Otherwise he would not permit a single tree to reach maturity. He would hinder, nay, even choke everything that is brought forth by the earth. In one single moment he would put an end not only to the birth of human beings but also to the preservation of the rest of the animals. Such great eagerness to do harm proves adequately that he is unable to rage with open force, but that whatever he does, he does with trickery and deceit.

Moreover, this, too, ought to be noted here: that these words are not spoken by God for the devil's sake. God does not regard him worthy of His condemnation, but it is enough that his own conscience condemns Satan. These words are spoken for the sake of Adam and Eve that they may hear this judgment and be comforted by the realization that God is the enemy of that being which inflicted so severe a wound on man. Here grace and mercy begin to shine forth from the midst of the wrath which sin and disobedience aroused. Here in the midst of most serious threats the Father reveals His heart; this is not a father who is so angry that he would turn out his son because of his sin, but one who points to a deliverance, indeed one who promises victory against the enemy that deceived and conquered human nature.

It was through Satan that man fell into sin; and so now the judgment of Satan and that of man are not the same. God does not link them together in the punishment, as He had a right to do, but separates them to the utmost. Although He is also angry with man for obeying the enemy of God against God, yet His anger against Satan is far greater. He simply condemns and convicts him before the eyes of Adam and Eve, so that through the condemnation of their enemy Adam and Eve may regain their composure to some extent and realize that their situation is better. So the first part of the comfort lies in this, that because of Adam and Eve the serpent is accused and cursed, and Satan together with the serpent.

Thus the sun of comfort, previously enveloped by black clouds, rises above the clouds and with its most welcome light shines on their frightened hearts. For Adam and Eve not only do not hear themselves cursed like the serpent; but they even hear themselves drawn up, as it were, in battle line against their condemned enemy, and this with the hope of help from the Son of God, the Seed of the woman. Forgiveness of sins and full reception into grace are here pointed out to Adam and Eve. Their guilt has been forgiven; they have been won back from death and have already been set free from hell and from those fears by which they were all but slain when God appeared.

This comfort springs from the fact that God does not curse Adam and Eve as He curses the serpent. Only this happens: that Adam and Eve are set into conflict with this enemy to keep them busy. Therefore even this situation turns out for man's good. Moreover, the main point of the comfort is this: Although this enemy fights with cunning and treacheries, the Seed will be born who will crush the head of the serpent. These words point to the ultimate destruction of Satan's tyranny, although it will not pass away without a most bitter conflict being fought for man.

But see how uneven the outcome of the battle is. The human being's heel is in danger, but his head is uninjured and undefeated. On the other hand, it is not the tail and not the belly of the serpent but the head itself, that is to be crushed and trodden underfoot by the Seed of the woman. But this victory will also be given to us a gift, as Christ clearly states (Luke 11:22): "The spoils are divided after the defeat of the mighty one." By faith the Christian is made the victor over sin, over the Law, and over death, so that not even the gates of hell can prevail against him (Matt. 16:18).

This first comfort, this source of all mercy and fountainhead of all promises, our first parents and their descendants learned with the utmost care. They saw that without this promise procreation would indeed continue to go on among people as well as among the other living beings, but that it would be nothing else than a procreation to death. And so that gift which was given by God to our nature is here made greater, nay, even made sacred; for there is hope of a procreation through which the head of Satan would be crushed, not only to break his tyranny but also to gain eternal life for our nature, which was surrendered to death because of sin. For here Moses is no longer dealing with a natural serpent; he is speaking of the devil, whose head is death and sin. And so Christ says in John 8:44 that the devil is a murderer and the father of lies. Therefore when his power has been crushed, that is, when sin and death have been destroyed by Christ, what is there to prevent us children of God from being saved?

In this manner Adam and Eve understood this text. Their consolation against sin and despair was their hope for this crushing, which was to be brought about in the future through Christ. And through the hope based on this promise they will also rise up to eternal life on the Last Day.

And It will crush your head, and you will crush Its heel.

How amazing, how damnable, that through the agency of foolish exegetes Satan has managed to apply this passage, which in fullest measure abounds in the comfort of the Son of God, to the Virgin Mary! For in all the Latin Bibles the pronoun appears in the feminine gender: "And *she* will crush." [37] Even Lyra, who was not unfamiliar with the Hebrew language, is carried away by this error as by a swollen and raging torrent. So he is brought to the wicked position, despite the text, that he understands this passage of the Blessed Virgin, through whom, by the mediation of her Son, the power of Satan has been broken.[38] He applies to her the statement in Canticles (Song of Sol. 6:4): "Thou art terrible as an army set in array." Although he offers this opinion as one which he has received from others, his great sin consists in not refuting it. All the recent inter-

[37] Cf. p. 184, note 33.

[38] Since at this point Luther's own notes are available, Peter Meinhold (cf. Introduction, p. xi) compared them with Lyra and with Dietrich's elaboration. He came to the conclusion that although Luther did consult Lyra here, Dietrich added much from Lyra that Luther had not used.

preters have followed along and misused this most sacred statement for the purpose of idolatry, without anyone objecting to it or preventing it.

This happened through either ignorance of negligence on the part of the rulers in the church. Because they offered no resistance to idolatry, sound teaching gradually disappeared. Now that we have restored it by the grace of God, these shameful and gluttonous beasts show clearly that they do not care about the worship of God but only about their ecclesiastical revenues. Because idolatry seems to afford protection to these revenues, they are provoked when men are taught the truth. In their blindness they do not see that those who accept the teaching of the Gospel lose nothing except their sins and eternal death, but gain freedom from all idolatry and from the rule of Satan.

Therefore let us thank God that now we have also this passage unimpaired and restored. We do not want to take away from Mary any honor which is her due; [39] but we want to remove the idolatry contained in the statement that by giving birth to Christ, Mary has destroyed all the power of Satan. If this is a true statement, does not the same honor belong to all the other women who preceded Mary in the same line? In fact, a portion of this glory will belong also to their husbands and to all the ancestors of Mary. For if she had not had these, she herself would not have existed either, since she was born in wedlock according to the usual order of nature. If, therefore, she has destroyed Satan by giving birth to Christ, her ancestors must be given a position of honor on the same level.

But Scripture teaches us otherwise and declares (Rom. 4:25): "Christ died for our sins and rose again for our justification"; likewise (John 1:29): "Behold the Lamb of God, which bears the sins of the world." Therefore let the Blessed Virgin keep her place of honor. Among all the women of the world she has this privilege from God, that as a virgin she gave birth to the Son of God. But this must not be permitted to deprive her Son of the glory of our redemption and deliverance.

Then we must be careful to preserve the real meaning of the Holy Scriptures and their truly wonderful light. When we are given instruction in this passage concerning the enmity between the serpent and the woman — such an enmity that the Seed of the woman will

---

[39] Cf. *Luther's Works,* 21, p. 326, note 26; and 22, p. 215, note 2.

crush the serpent with all his powers — this is a revelation of the depths of God's goodness. Satan understood this threat well; therefore he has continued to rage against human nature with such great hatred. Adam and Eve were encouraged by this promise. Wholeheartedly they grasped the hope of their restoration; and, full of faith, they saw that God cared about their salvation, since He clearly declares that the male Seed of the woman would prostrate this enemy. The order of words in this sentence is very forceful.

He says "her Seed." It is as if He were saying: "Through the woman you, Satan, set upon and seduced the man, so that through sin you might be their head and master. But I, in turn, shall lie in wait for you by means of the same instrument. I shall snatch away the woman, and from her I shall produce a Seed, and that Seed will crush your head. You have corrupted the flesh through sin and have made it subject to death, but from that very flesh I shall bring forth a Man who will crush and prostrate you and all your powers."

Thus this promise and this threat are very clear, and yet they are also very indefinite. They leave the devil in such a state that he suspects all mothers of giving birth to this Seed, although only one woman was to be the mother of this blessed Seed. Thus because God is threatening in general when He says "her Seed," He is mocking Satan and making him afraid of all women.

In the same way the faith of all people was strengthened; from the hour in which the promise was made they waited for the Seed and derived comfort from It against Satan. When Eve had given birth to her first-born son, she hoped that she already had that Crusher.[40] Although she was deceived in this hope, she saw that eventually this Seed would be born from among her descendants, whenever it might be that He would be born. Also so far as human beings were concerned, therefore, this promise was very clear and at the same time very obscure.

Isaiah (7:14) threw some light on this when he said that a virgin would give birth, for at that time it was already sure that this Seed would not be born as the result of the union of a man and a woman. But he adds certain other statements which, so to speak, he wraps around his prophecy. So it was that this very clear promise remained dark until Mary had given birth; the angels were witnesses of this

---

[40] This reflects the interpretation of Gen. 4:1 which Luther had adopted in his translation of the Old Testament: "I have gotten a man [who is] the Lord." But see p. 242.

birth, and after the angels the shepherds and the Magi, until this birth was revealed to the entire world through the apostles.

This obscurity increased Satan's care and worry. Since it is stated: "I shall put enmity between you and the woman," he was hostile and suspicious toward all those who gave birth from that time on until Christ was revealed. In man, on the other hand, this obscurity increased and intensified faith. Although individual women realized that they were not the ones who would give birth to this Seed, they were hopeful and certain that It would be born by another. And so it is particularly to mock and irritate Satan, to comfort the godly, and stir them up to faith that God speaks so individually, if I may express myself in this way. Women gave birth up to the Flood and later until the time of Mary; but their seed could not in truth be called the Seed of the woman, but rather the seed of a man. But what is born from Mary was conceived by the Holy Spirit and is the true Seed of Mary, just as the other promises given to Abraham and David testify, according to which Christ is called the Son of Abraham and the Son of David.

This meaning Isaiah is the first to point out when he says that a virgin will give birth (7:14). Then, in the New Testament, it is more clearly explained by the angel (Luke 1:35). Therefore I have no doubt that this mystery was not understood even by many saints; although they expected that Christ would have to be born into this world by a woman and that He would deliver the human race, they did not know the manner of His birth. With this general knowledge they were satisfied, and they were saved even though they did not know how He would have to be conceived and born. This had to be reserved for the New Testament as a clearer light and had to be announced to the first world rather obscurely because of Satan, whom God wanted to mock and irritate in this fashion so that he would be ill at ease and would fear everything.

After the promise had been formulated in so general a way, it was limited a little. Through Abraham it was first linked to a certain race, thereafter through the patriarch Jacob to the specific tribe of Judah. Now the devil was unconcerned about other nations and tribes; and with amazing cruelty and treachery he pursued this one single line of descendants until at about the time of Christ it had been reduced to the utmost poverty, like a hopeless stump from which no one ever hopes for either leaves or fruit. For this reason Scripture also calls it the root of Jesse (Is. 11:1), a decayed and hopeless stump.

This hatred and wrath of Satan the Lord predicts in this passage when He makes mention of the enmity that has been established. With his malicious hatred Satan first sought the woman's Seed among all the nations and peoples of the entire world. Then, when the promise was conveyed to the descendants of Abraham, we see how he tried in devious ways to obstruct it. And the tribe of Judah, to which the Lord finally conveyed it, was visited and troubled by countless horrible misfortunes, until it finally appeared to be entirely destroyed and uprooted. At about the time Christ was to be born poor Mary was living far from Jerusalem in the insignificant little town of Nazareth, while in Jerusalem wicked men were the rulers. Therefore this tribe is correctly compared to a dead trunk. Nevertheless, because God cannot lie, that hopeless root brought forth a shoot.

And still Satan does not leave off from his cruelty, hatred, and hostility against the Seed of the woman. When He has been placed into His cradle, Satan makes a search for Him through Herod, so that Christ has to live among the Gentiles in Egypt. Later on he tries everything, and also tempts Him, until, when He had been seized in the garden, he delivers Him up to the Jews and attaches Him to the cross. But not even by His death can Satan's inexhaustible hatred be satisfied. He fears Him after He has been buried. So bitter is his enmity against the Son of God! Now when he sees Him sitting at the right hand of God and being what is called "out of range," [41] he rages with every kind of fury against the poor members of His church. There are prophecies here of all these dangers; nevertheless, we ought to sojourn among them with good courage and with confidence in the Son of God, who is crushing Satan.

But I return to the text. This very clear promise is at the same time also very obscure, because God speaks in general of "the Seed of the woman." Thus at the same time He makes all women suspect to Satan and worries him with endless concern and care. It is, therefore, an amazing instance of synecdoche.[42] "The woman's Seed," He says. This means all individuals in general; and yet He is speaking of only one individual, of the Seed of Mary, who is a mother without union with a male. Thus the first little expression, "I shall put enmity between you and the woman," seems to denote all women in general. God wanted to make all women suspect to Satan; on the other hand,

---

[41] The Greek phrase ἔξω βελῶν is used here.

[42] A figure of speech by which, in this case, the species is used for the genus.

He wanted to leave the godly with a very certain hope, so that they might expect this salvation from all who gave birth, until the real one came. In the same way this "her Seed" is spoken most individually, if I may use this expression, concerning the Seed which was born only to Mary of the tribe of Judah, who was espoused to Joseph.

This, therefore, is the text that made Adam and Eve alive and brought them back from death into the life which they had lost through sin. Nevertheless, the life is one hoped for rather than one already possessed. Similarly, Paul also often says (1 Cor. 15:31): "Daily we die." Although we do not wish to call the life we live here a death, nevertheless it surely is nothing else than a continuous journey toward death. Just as a person infected with a plague has already started to die when the infection has begun, so — because of sin, and death, the punishment for sin — this life can no longer properly be called life after it has been infected by sin. Right from our mother's womb we begin to die.

Through Baptism we are restored to a life of hope, or rather to a hope of life. This is the true life, which is lived before God. Before we come to it, we are in the midst of death.[43] We die and decay in the earth, just as other dead bodies do, as though there were no other life anywhere. Yet we who believe in Christ have the hope that on the Last Day we shall be revived for eternal life. Thus Adam was also revived by this address of the Lord — not perfectly indeed, for the life which he lost he did not yet recover; but he got the hope of that life when he heard that Satan's tyranny was to be crushed.

Therefore this statement includes the redemption from the Law, from sin, and from death; and it points out the clear hope of a certain resurrection and of renewal in the other life after this life. If the serpent's head is to be crushed, death certainly must be done away with. If death is done away with, that, too, which deserved death is done away with, that is, sin. If sin is abolished, then also the Law. And not only this, but at the same time the obedience which was lost is renewed. Because all these benefits are promised through this Seed, it is very clear that after the Fall our human nature could not, by its own strength, remove sin, escape the punishments of sin and death, or recover the lost obedience. These actions call for greater power and greater strength than human beings possess.

43 Cf. p. 80, note 7.

And so the Son of God had to become a sacrifice to achieve these things for us, to take away sin, to swallow up death, and to restore the lost obedience. These treasures we possess in Christ, but in hope. In this way Adam, Eve, and all who believe until the Last Day live and conquer by that hope. Death is indeed an awful and undefeated tyrant; but God's power makes nothing out of that which is everything, just as it makes all things out of that which is nothing. Look at Adam and Eve. They are full of sin and death. And yet, because they hear the promise concerning the Seed who will crush the serpent's head, they have the same hope we have, namely, that death will be taken away, that sin will be abolished, and that righteousness, life, peace, etc., will be restored. In this hope our first parents live and die, and because of this hope they are truly holy and righteous.

Thus we also live in the same hope. And, because of Christ, when we die, we keep this hope, which the Word sets before us by directing us to put our trust in the merits of Christ. It is vain to long for such perfection in this life that we become wholly righteous, that we love God perfectly, and that we love our neighbor as we love ourselves. We make some progress; but sin, which wars in our members (Rom. 7:23) and is present everywhere, either corrupts or altogether obstructs this obedience.

Therefore just as our very life can be called a death because of the death which lies ahead of us, so also our righteousness is completely buried by sins. By hope we hold fast to both life and righteousness, things which are hidden from our eyes and our understanding, but will be made manifest in due time. Meanwhile our life is a life in the midst of death. And yet, even in the midst of death, the hope of life is kept, since the Word so teaches, directs, and promises. Thus Ps. 68:20 offers the exceedingly beautiful comfort: "Our God is the God of salvation, the Lord of the issue of death." Let us give this title to God, not only because He grants aid in this temporal life — the devil also does this for those who worship him, as the examples of the heathen show — but because He is the Lord of the issue of death; that is, He frees those who are overwhelmed by death, and transports them into eternal life. This He does, as Moses teaches here, by crushing the head of the serpent.

Accordingly, we now find Adam and Eve restored, not indeed to the life which they had lost but to the hope of that life. Through this hope they escaped, not the first fruits of death, but its tithes; [44] that is, although their flesh must die for the time being, nevertheless, because of the promised Son of God, who would crush the head of the devil, they hope for the resurrection of the flesh and eternal life after the temporal death of the flesh, just as we do.

Now follows the second part of this sermon, in which God threatens bodily punishments, first for the woman, then also for the man.

16. *But to the woman He said: I will greatly multiply your sorrow when you are pregnant. In pain you will bear children, and you will be under your husband's power; and he will rule over you.*

This punishment is inflicted on the woman, but it is a happy and joyful punishment, because it is not out of harmony with the earlier verdict which was pronounced upon Satan. If this stands, that the head of the serpent must be crushed, the hope for resurrection from the dead is sure. Then whatever is inflicted on the human race is bearable, provided this hope remains unshaken.

Moreover, this is also why Holy Scripture is so careful not to say anything in connection with the punishment meted out to the woman that is opposed to the verdict earlier pronounced upon Satan. It inflicts punishment on the woman, and yet it leaves the hope of resurrection and of eternal life. But it assigns death, which she had deserved through her sin, to the other and less noble part of the human being, namely, to the flesh, so that because of faith the spirit may live in righteousness.

Therefore the woman is subject to death so far as the flesh is concerned; but so far as hope is concerned, she is free from death. The verdict remains sure; God threatens that the devil's head will be crushed. The physical body has its cross and death here, as St. Paul also says (1 Cor. 15:44): "The natural body dies, but the spiritual one will rise." Thus in this natural life marriages continue, and the woman experiences the punishments which the Lord here inflicts because of sin. From the time of conception, during birth, and during all the rest of her life, while she devotes herself to her children, she will encounter various dangers. But all these things pertain only to the natural life or to the flesh itself, and meanwhile the hope of a spiritual and eternal life after this life endures.

[44] An application to death of Luther's common distinction; cf. *Luther's Works*, 13, p. 90, note 24.

Therefore truly happy and joyful is this punishment if we correctly appraise the matter. Although these burdens are troublesome for the flesh, yet the hope for a better life is strengthened together with those very burdens or punishments, because Eve hears that she is not being repudiated by God. Furthermore, she also hears that in this punishment she is not being deprived of the blessing of procreation, which was promised and granted before sin. She sees that she is keeping her sex and that she remains a woman. She sees that she is not being separated from Adam to remain alone and apart from her husband. She sees that she may keep the glory of motherhood, if I may use the phrase. All these things are in addition to the eternal hope, and without a doubt they greatly encouraged Eve. Above all, there remains also a greater and more genuine glory. Not only does she keep the blessing of fruitfulness and remain united with her husband, but she has the sure promise that from her will come the Seed who will crush the head of Satan.

Without a doubt, therefore, Eve had a heart full of joy even in an apparently sad situation. Perhaps she gave comfort to Adam by saying: "I have sinned. But see what a merciful God we have. How many privileges, both temporal and spiritual, He is leaving for us sinners! Therefore we women should bear the hardship and wretchedness of conceiving, of giving birth, and of obeying you husbands. His is a fatherly anger, because this stands: that the head of our enemy will be crushed, and that after the death of our flesh we shall be raised to a new and eternal life through our Redeemer. These abundant good things and endless kindnesses far surpass whatever curse and punishments our Father has inflicted on us." These and similar conversations Adam and Eve undoubtedly carried on often in order to mitigate their temporal adversities.

Similarly we also ought to reflect often on the inexpressible treasures of the future life and by such thoughts make light the hardships of the flesh. We see Paul doing this in 2 Cor. 4:17. "Our affliction," he says, "is for a moment and light; for it works in us an eternal weight of glory if we look not at those things which are seen but at those which are not seen. For the things that are seen are temporal, but those which are not seen are eternal."

But if you take hold of the future glory and believe the promises of God, and if you also consider His physical blessings — that the Lord has granted us this world to enjoy; that He has given us wife, home, and children; that He preserves all these and increases them by His blessing — tell me, will you not endure with a calm mind whatever physical hardships may come, and say that this is a fatherly anger and not that of a judge or a tyrant? By contrast, however, the wrath of a judge appears in the instance of the serpent, who not only has no promise of deliverance but is told that he will be crushed. Satan felt this wrath and still feels it. This is why until the Last Day he will rage with such great fury against the church and the Son of God.

Therefore this is indeed a threat in which the Lord threatens Eve with definite punishments. But in those very punishments there shines forth His inexpressible mercy, which encourages Eve and gladdens her heart in the midst of her misfortunes. Moreover, we ourselves feel how necessary these punishments are for keeping our flesh in subjection. How could we stay humble unless this nature were held down by the burdens of such punishments? And so it is that in her calling and station Eve and any other wife will experience these sure adversities; her afflictions will be increased, and she will both conceive and give birth with pain.

Moreover, the word רב appears here; it denotes a quantity which is both extensive and varied. This means that Eve's sorrows, which she would not have had if she had not fallen into sin, are to be great, numerous, and also of various kinds. The threat is directed particularly at birth and conception. But conception designates the entire time during which the fetus, after being conceived, is carried in the womb, a time beset with severe and sundry ailments. From the beginning of that time a woman suffers very painful headaches, dizziness, nausea, an amazing loathing of food and drink, frequent and difficult vomiting, toothache, and a stomach disorder which produces a craving, called pica, for such foods from which nature normally shrinks. Moreover, when the fetus has matured and birth is imminent, there follows the most awful distress, because only with utmost peril and almost at the cost of her life does she give birth to her offspring.

When the heathen, who have no knowledge of God and of His works, see this, it displeases them. Because of these discomforts, they maintain that a prudent man should not marry. The female sex has been greatly humbled and afflicted, and it bears a far severer and harsher punishment than the men. For what is there of such things that a man suffers on his own body? But because through marriage the husband transfers, as it were, a part of those punishments upon himself (for he cannot without grief see those things in his wife), it has come about that wicked men prefer fornication to marriage.

Over against this wicked attitude of the ungodly, the pious must comfort themselves with true wisdom by contrasting these disadvantages with the sure and greater advantages. Pindar, too, in addressing Hiero, blames stupid people for their inability to offset their misfortunes with the good fortunes they experience, since God is wont to distribute His blessings in such a way that there is always some misfortune mixed in with them.[45] But the good and wise deck out their good fortunes and use them to bury the misfortunes that bother them, while they place their good fortunes in a well-lighted place to be seen.

The same thing should be done here. It must be granted that wives have indeed been subjected to great punishments because of sin. But is it not something greater and mightier than those punishments that in those very misfortunes they have the sure hope of immortality and of eternal life?

In the second place, those very misfortunes are not without fruit. They tend to humble and hold down our nature, which could not be held in check without a cross.

In the third place, even among those physical misfortunes there still remains that outstanding glory of motherhood and the blessing of the womb which the wiser among the heathen have also wondered at and gloriously extolled. There still remain the other gifts: that we are all nourished, kept warm, and carried in the womb of our mothers; that we nurse at their breasts and are protected by their effort and care. This is the meaning of "turning to the outside what is beautiful." [46] It means not merely looking at what is evil but delighting in God's gifts and blessings and also burying the punishments, annoyances, pains, griefs, and other things.

But this only the godly know and do. To their wives, as the weaker vessels, they grant their honor, inasmuch as they see that they are partakers of immortality and sharers in the inheritance in heaven (1 Peter 3:7). They see too that their wives are adorned with the blessing and glory of motherhood, namely, that we are all conceived, born, and nurtured by them.

[45] "These trials foolish men cannot bear with a good grace; but the noble can, by ever turning the fairer side to the front." Pindar, *Pythian Odes*, III, lines 146—148 (translated by John Sandys).

[46] A repetition in Greek of the quotation from Pindar in note 45.

To me it is often a source of great pleasure and wonderment to see that the entire female body was created for the purpose of nurturing children. How prettily even little girls carry babies on their bosom! As for the mothers themselves, how deftly they move whenever the whimpering baby either has to be quieted or is to be placed into its cradle! Get a man to do the same things, and you will say that a camel is dancing, so clumsily will he do the simplest tasks around the baby! [47] I say nothing about the other duties which mothers alone can perform.

Whoever appraises the situation correctly will take all these facts as sure signs of the Lord's blessing, signs by which God assures the female sex that although it has been punished severely because of sin, it is still an object of concern to Him and is dear to Him. Let this be enough about the first part of the curse.

The second part of the curse has to do with cohabitation. If Eve had not sinned, she would not only have given birth without pain, but her union with her husband would have been just as honorable as it is honorable today to eat or converse with one's wife at the table. Rearing children would also have been very easy and would have abounded in joy. These benefits have been lost through sin, and there have followed those familiar evils of pain and work which are connected with gestation, birth, and nurturing. Just as a pretty girl, without any inconvenience, nay, even with great pleasure and some pride, wears on her head a beautiful wreath woven from flowers, so, if she had not sinned, Eve would have carried her child in her womb without any inconvenience and with great joy. Now there is also added to those sorrows of gestation and birth that Eve has been placed under the power of her husband, she who previously was very free and, as the sharer of all the gifts of God, was in no respect inferior to her husband.

This punishment, too, springs from original sin; and the woman bears it just as unwillingly as she bears those pains and inconveniences that have been placed upon her flesh. The rule remains with the husband, and the wife is compelled to obey him by God's command. He rules the home and the state, wages wars, defends his possessions, tills the soil, builds, plants, etc. The woman, on the other hand, is like a nail driven into the wall. She sits at home, and for this reason

---

[47] Apparently another personal reference. Luther was, after all, one of the few theologians in the history of the Western Church until that time who could speak of such matters from his own experience.

Paul, in Titus 2:5, calls her an οἰκουργός. The pagans have depicted Venus as standing on a seashell; for just as the snail carries its house with it, so the wife should stay at home and look after the affairs of the household, as one who has been deprived of the ability of administering those affairs that are outside and that concern the state. She does not go beyond her most personal duties.

If Eve had persisted in the truth, she would not only not have been subjected to the rule of her husband, but she herself would also have been a partner in the rule which is now entirely the concern of males. Women are generally disinclined to put up with this burden, and they naturally seek to gain what they have lost through sin. If they are unable to do more, they at least indicate their impatience by grumbling. However, they cannot perform the functions of men, teach, rule, etc. In procreation and in feeding and nurturing their offspring they are masters. In this way Eve is punished; but, as I said in the beginning, it is a gladsome punishment if you consider the hope of eternal life and the honor of motherhood which have been left her.

17. *But to Adam He said: Because you listened to the voice of your wife and ate from the tree concerning which I had given you a command saying: You will not eat from it, the earth is cursed on your account. In hardship you will eat from it all the days of your life;*

18. *thorns and thistles it will sprout for you and you will eat the herbs of the ground.*

19. *In the sweat of your face you will eat your bread until you return to earth from which you were taken, because you are dust, and to dust you will return.*

Because the husband sinned last, the punishment is also inflicted on him last. But here the Lord's threats do not concern procreation or pains in procreation. The husband has a raging lust kindled by the poison of Satan in his body, without pain. But his position is burdened with a definite punishment, since it is the husband's duty to support his family, to rule, to direct, and to instruct; and these things cannot be done without extraordinary trouble and very great effort. On the woman obedience to her husband was imposed, but how difficult it is to bring this very condition about! I say nothing about the rule over others, who do not belong to the household.

The philosophers have wondered about the source of this perverseness in nature, that human beings can more easily rule wild beasts than other human beings. Thus Xenophon states that it is easier to rule over all the other living things than over human beings.[48] These are indeed extraordinary duties: to be a husband; to till the soil or do some other work by which children and wife are supported; to rule the home, the family, cities, kingdoms; to instruct and bring up both the people of the household and others with a view to godliness and good manners. But these very important duties have their own punishment added to them, namely, that they cannot be carried on without the utmost difficulties, as is shown by examples all around us.

The earth is cursed because of Adam. Where the Latin translation has "in your work" the Hebrew is בַּעֲבוּרֶךָ, "on your account." And so the similarity of the letters made the translator go wrong, for he read עָבַד בַּעֲבֹדֶךָ. עָבַד denotes "to till the earth." [49]

Moreover, it appears here what a great misfortune followed sin, because the earth, which is innocent and committed no sin, is nevertheless compelled to endure a curse and, as St. Paul says Rom. 8:20, "has been subjected to vanity." But it will be freed from this on the Last Day, for which it is waiting. Pliny calls the earth a kind, gentle, and forbearing mother; likewise, the perpetual servant of the need of mortals.[50] But, as Paul points out, the earth itself feels its curse. In the first place, it does not bring forth the good things it would have produced if man had not fallen. In the second place, it produces many harmful plants, which it would not have produced, such as darnel, wild oats, weeds, nettles, thorns, thistles. Add to these the poisons, the injurious vermin, and whatever else there is of this kind. All these were brought in through sin.

I have no doubt that before sin the air was purer and more healthful, and the water more prolific; yes, even the sun's light was more beautiful and clearer. Now the entire creation in all its parts reminds us of the curse that was inflicted because of sin. Nevertheless, there have remained some remnants of the former blessing, namely, that the earth is, as it were, forced to work hard to yield those things that

[48] Xenophon, *Cyropaedia*, I, i, 3. According to Meinhold, this was supplied by the editors.

[49] An illustration of Luther's interest in conjectural emendation of the text.

[50] Pliny, *Natural History*, II, 154—159.

are necessary for our use, although they are marred by thorns and thistles, that is, by useless and even harmful trees, fruits, and herbs, which the wrath of God sows.

This curse was made more severe through the Flood, by which the good trees were all ruined and destroyed, the sands were heaped up, and harmful herbs and animals were increased. Accordingly, where, before sin, Adam walked about among most fertile trees, in lovely meadows, and among flowers and roses, there now spring up nettles, thorns, and other troublesome sprouts in such abundance that the good plants are almost overwhelmed.

Consider a field that has been plowed and prepared for planting. The moment it has been sown, weeds and darnel come up more quickly than the crops that are useful for life. Unless they are destroyed with diligent care by the farmer every day, those pernicious plants gradually take possession of the field, and the good seed is choked. The earth indeed is innocent and would gladly produce the best products, but it is prevented by the curse which was placed upon man because of sin.

And so both the man and the woman bear the penalty of sin. The woman bears hers on her own body when she suffers distress in her function as childbearer, although the penalty is bearable; and the husband bears his penalty in the management of the household, when with difficulty and hard work he exercises authority in the home and supports his family. On his account the ground was cursed, although before sin no part of the earth was barren and inferior, but all of it was amazingly fertile and productive. Now the earth is not only barren in many places; but even the fertile areas are defaced by darnel, weeds, thorns, and thistles. This is a great misfortune, which might well lead Adam and all of us to self-destruction; but it is mitigated by the promise of the Seed, who will remove the penalty of eternal death, which is infinitely greater.

What is added — "in sorrow you will eat from it all the days of your life" — is readily understood. Who does not know what a hard life it is to be a farmer? It is not enough to ready the earth for planting, something which calls for work that is hard and varied. But also when the crop is developing, almost each individual day requires its definite tasks. I am saying nothing about the almost endless troubles from the sky, the harmful animals, and similar things, all of which increase this sorrow or hardship. Before sin there were not only no such troubles; but if Adam had not sinned, the earth would have produced all things, "unsown and uncultivated," [51] more quickly than one could have hoped.

Furthermore, this misfortune which sin brought on was lighter and more bearable in many respects than that which followed the Flood. Here mention is made only of thorns, thistles, and hard work. But now we learn from experience that countless others have been added. How many kinds of damage and how many diseases affect the crops, the plants and the trees, and finally everything that the earth produces! How much harm is done to the vegetables by harmful insects! Furthermore, frosts, lightning bolts, injurious dews, storms, overflowing rivers, settling of the ground, earthquakes — all do damage. Of all these things no mention is made in the words before us. Therefore I am fully of the opinion that because of the increase of sins the punishments were also increased and that these troubles were added to the curse of the earth.

But if it seems to someone that Moses includes all these when he says that the earth was cursed, I shall surely not argue with him. Yet no one will deny that as the sins increased, so also the troubles. Thus today we experience more frequent disasters to crops than in former times. The world is deteriorating from day to day.

There are clear indications that these misfortunes were brought upon Adam as a warning to the first world to maintain stricter order. But gradually, at the time of Noah, this maintenance of order weakened; people began to live more disorderly, until finally the earth was filled with violence, unrighteousness, and oppression. Then, just as more serious diseases in the body demand more powerful cures, so also other more severe or more frequent penalties had to be inflicted.

Accordingly, when the entire earth had been laid waste by the Deluge, and every living thing on earth, with the exception of a few human beings, had been destroyed, the age which followed the time of Noah undoubtedly lived in the fear of God. But as the years advanced, they, too, were corrupted and depraved by Satan. Therefore a more stringent example was necessary, such as the destruction of Sodom and its surrounding cities. Similarly, Scripture says that the iniquities of the Amorites had to become full (Gen. 15:16). And finally the entire synagog was destroyed when it had turned to paganism and manifest ungodliness. Rome also made great advances

[51] The Greek words used here are a direct quotation from Homer's *Odyssey*, IX, 123.

while the ancient maintenance of order was in effect; but when vices made their inroads, it also became necessary for punishments to draw closer.

The period when the Gospel first became known among us was rather respectable. Now there is almost no fear of God, our short-comings grow daily, and false prophets are even making their appearance. What else can we hope for except that when our iniquities have become full, either everything will be destroyed, or Germany will pay the penalties for its sins in some other way? Thus it is a general truth that as sins increase, the penalties also increase.

I spoke earlier about the damages suffered by the products of the earth. I am also convinced that the human body was healthier then than it is now. Proof of this lies in the length of life among people before the Flood, which seems incredible to us. For the Lord does not threaten Adam with apoplexy, leprosy, epilepsy, and other pernicious evils.

When I was a boy, syphilis was unknown in Germany.[52] It first became known when I was about fifteen years old. Now even children in the cradle are stricken with this evil. In those days everyone was terrified by this disease, but now so little is thought of it that even friends who are bantering among themselves wish each other a case of syphilis.

Until my adult years the sweating sickness was an endemic disease, as the physicians call it.[53] Just as individual areas have their particular advantages, so, after they misuse them against God, they are also troubled and stricken with particular hardships. But this disease became common also in parts of inland Germany, far distant from the ocean. It is awful to hear that some have snakes in their bellies and worms in their brains. In my opinion these sicknesses were unknown to the ancient physicians, although they counted almost four hundred kinds of diseases.[54]

But if all these sicknesses had existed in the first world, how

[52] In his chronology, "Computation of the Years of the World," first published in 1541, Luther speaks of "a new disease, the French disease, otherwise known as the Spanish disease, which was brought to Europe, so it is said, from the newly discovered islands in the East. One of the great signs before the Last Day!" (Weimar, LIII, 169.) This is one of his only references to the discovery of the Americas.

[53] This "sweating sickness" had broken out in Wittenberg in 1529.

[54] Pliny, *Natural History*, Books XX—XXVII, gives a detailed enumeration of these.

could Adam and others before Noah have attained such a great length of life? Therefore Moses is speaking only about the barrenness of the earth and the difficulty of providing food.

Anyone who desires to become wordy and wants to appear as an orator should count up all the evils of the human race. He will find such an abundant crop of misfortunes of every kind that he will have only one request to make of God: that He do not permit him to live a single hour among such great dangers.

Why are we speaking only about sicknesses? All creatures are against us, and they are all equipped for our destruction. How many people are there whom fire and water destroy? How great is the danger from wild or poisonous beasts? And they harm not only our bodies but also the foods which have been produced to support us. I am saying nothing about the fact that we ourselves are plunging into mutual slaughter as if there were no other plagues lying in wait for us.[55]

And so if you look at human endeavors, what else is this life than daily conflict, treachery, robbery, and slaughter, in addition to the troubles which are brought upon us by foreigners? I do not think that before the Flood all these were either as numerous or as severe as they are now. But because sins grew, the penalties were also increased.

Hence the misfortunes which were placed upon Adam were insignificant in comparison with ours. The more closely the world approaches its end, the more it is overwhelmed by penalties and catastrophes. But, to make it worse, the more the world is smitten, the more hardened and unconscious of its own evils it becomes. It is just as Prov. 23:35 says: "He drew me, but I felt it not; he beat me, but I felt no pain." This blindness is worse than all those misfortunes of the body.

Is it not an amazing and wretched thing? Our body bears the traces of God's wrath, which our sin has deserved. God's wrath also appears on the earth and in all the creatures. And yet we look at all these things with a smug and unconcerned attitude! And what of thorns, thistles, water, fire, caterpillars, flies, fleas, and bedbugs? Collectively and individually, are not all of them messengers who preach to us concerning sin and God's wrath, since they did not exist before sin or at least were not harmful and troublesome?

Despite what we know and see, therefore, we live in a darkness

55 A reflection of the transition from medieval to modern patterns in warfare.

worse than that which covered Egypt (Ex. 10:21-23). Although everything on all sides warns us of God's wrath and all but forces it into our very eyes, we still ignore it and embrace this life as our only delight. Just as the sins increase, therefore, the smugness grows, too, and people become insensible and hardened toward their misfortunes.

Thus the evils are increased, not only in this life but also in the future life. I am speaking of the ungodly. For if a person in hell were to endure his punishments and tortures only with his feelings and did not realize that he had deserved the punishments he was enduring, his tortures would be more bearable. Similarly, we are unwilling to acknowledge our evils and, so to speak, "grieve them out." But this insensibility, which now prevents us from realizing our wretched state, will be removed in the future life. All our senses will be opened; not only will our body realize the punishment, but our very mind will realize the wrath of God and admit that we have deserved that wrath by our vileness. This will sharpen the tortures of the wicked and increase them in countless ways.

"Thorns and thistles it will bring forth for you." Here again we are reminded that the earth does not produce anything of this kind on its own, but because of Adam's sin, as He said above in so many words, "on your account." Therefore whenever we see thorns and thistles, weeds and other plants of that kind in a field and in the garden, we are reminded of sin and of the wrath of God as though by special signs. Not only in the churches, therefore, do we hear ourselves charged with sin. All the fields, yes, almost the entire creation is full of such sermons, reminding us of our sin and of God's wrath, which has been aroused by our sin.

Therefore we should ask the Lord to take away this amazing insensibility from our eyes, our senses, and our hearts, so that, after being admonished so many times about our sin, we may rid ourselves of our smugness and walk in the fear of God. For it is for this purpose that we are cast down and overwhelmed in various ways by the curses, as Moses now explains at greater length.

You will eat the herbs of the field.

This is a new misfortune. Earlier the Lord had given man the most beautiful and delightful gifts, namely, that he was to live on all the trees of Paradise except two. He gave him the rule over the fish and over all the fruits and animals on the entire earth. Now all these are taken away from him because he ate the fruit, and nothing is left to him except the herbs. This passage seems to me to give sufficiently strong proof that Adam did not live on butter, milk, eggs, cheese, meat, apples, and pears, but on vegetables and seeds, such as peas, beans, fennel seeds, millet, rice, spelt, and the like. What a glorious feast to spread before his guests as he gave away a daughter, or at the wedding of his children, when the only food he could provide was herbs!

Such was the frugality of this early period: the most ordinary and simple food with water. Now an awful gluttony has come over the world. Now it is not enough to prepare all kinds of meat for one's pleasure; but they mix meats with fish, add spices, and attempt the unnatural perversion of using condiments to sour those foods that are sweet by nature, and to sweeten those that are sour.

What great variety there is also in the matter of drink! Who would not feel insulted if he saw water placed before him by his host. We are not satisfied with the beer that is brewed among us and with the native wine, but we desire those from beyond the sea. If our father Adam were to return now, he would be amazed at this insane gluttony among his sons! The things we eat and drink with delight he would shun like poison, and he would prefer to all our delicacies either beets or barley groats with cold water.

And so, moderation in food is commended to us in this passage when we are told concerning our first parents that they were deprived of all other foods and had left only the food consisting of herbs. This plainness of their food made their bodies healthy, not subject to those sicknesses which more luxurious food and gluttony bring on.

These words should suggest to us not only moderation but also patience, when we see others having an abundance of every kind of delicacies while we hardly have bread and salt with water. We must consider that this punishment was placed upon Adam: although in Paradise he could have lived on every kind of fruit in conformity with God's will, command, and gift, and could have been the lord of the entire earth, because of his disobedience he, together with his descendants, is now forced to live on plain vegetables.

19. *In the sweat of your face you will eat your bread.*

In what various ways God increases the hardship of the husband's labor, so that he is engrossed by the worrisome task of supporting, defending, and ruling over his own! Moreover, because of the perversity of people, these tasks are far more difficult in our age than they were in the beginning. Even where there is a sure prospect of food, we see how hard it is to hold the household to their duties. Nor was Adam unacquainted with this evil. Although he presided over his household in the most saintly manner, nevertheless he lived to see the murder which Cain committed, to say nothing about the other griefs which a long life compelled him to see and bear among his descendants. Thus the husband is forced to perform a task which is not very pleasant or very successful. There ought to be no one who does not feel this sweat. The life of the papists is very dangerous because for their own pleasures and idleness they all misuse the wealth produced by the labor of others.

But here the question arises whether we all ought to be farmers or at least work with our hands, as some foolishly maintained when the Gospel was first proclaimed.[56] They misused this passage, as well as others which command the work of the hands, to make young men give up their studies and follow occupations requiring manual labor. Thus their leader Carlstadt gave up his position, bought a country place, and dug and tended it himself. But surely, if it were right to abandon one's calling, it would be far easier and more pleasant for me to be in the garden, to dig with a hoe, and to turn the ground with a spade than it is to carry on the work which I am now doing. For work on the farm does not compare with this strenuous exertion of ours.

Therefore we must utterly reject the opinion of those who maintain that only manual labor may be called work. Christ's statement is clear; He commands that those who teach should have the benefit of the labor of others. "When you enter a house," says He (Luke 10:5-7), "first say: 'Peace be to this house,' eating and drinking what they have; for the laborer is worthy of his hire." Here the Lord takes the bread from the table of those who hear the Word of God and gives it to the teachers. Likewise, Paul also says (1 Cor. 9:14): "He who teaches the Gospel should also live by the Gospel." And in support of this statement he also quotes the command of the Law (Deut. 25:4): "You shall not muzzle the mouth of the ox that treads out the corn." Moreover, why was the command about paying tithes

[56] Andreas Rudolph Bodenstein Carlstadt (d. 1541) had moved from Wittenberg into the country in 1523. Like Tolstoy, he dressed as a peasant, had his neighbors address him as "Neighbor Andrew," and sought to escape the sophistication of the town and the university.

given to the husbandman who works and tends his field if the ministers of the Word ought to gain their living by their own labor?

These and similar passages show clearly that the sweat of the face is of many kinds: the first is that of the farmers or householders; the second is that of the officers of the state; and the third is that of the teachers in the church. Among these classes the best-situated are the farmers, as the poet also says: "Exceedingly happy if they realized their blessings!" [57] Although they are plagued with hard labor, that labor is seasoned with matchless pleasure, as daily the new and wonderful sight of the creatures impresses itself upon their eyes. In both state and church, on the other hand, there are daily dangers and countless burdens, if you desire to perform your duty faithfully. We are not speaking here of idle people who do not acknowledge the punishments of sin but are only bent on satisfying their lust. Let these voluptuaries be left to their evil spirit! We are speaking of those who earnestly perform their duty. In one single day these people work and sweat more than a farmer does in an entire month, if you consider the vastness of their work and its various dangers.

This is also the reason why taxes, revenues, and other payments of this kind are paid to a king or a ruler by his subjects. Moreover, who does not see that if he does his duty carefully, the thanks or compensation he gets in return for such a great task is very small? But if some are careless, this is no reason to give up the lawful appointment of officials.

I have heard that Emperor Maximilian was so occupied with the affairs of state that he never had enough leisure for taking food. And so at times he was compelled to get away from his tasks and to hide in the forests, where he went hunting. At times he used to change his clothes and mix with the crowds of common people, in order to have the benefit of their freer conversations. Although his interest in the hunt has been charged against him as a fault, those who had a knowledge of his work and of his private life were of the opinion that he adopted it because of necessity rather than for pleasure.[58]

Now what plowing or digging or other farm labors will you liken to the labor which the governing of such a large empire calls for? Therefore they are called kings and princes as a mark of their dignity, when in truth kings and princes are the most wretched of all servants.

[57] Vergil, *Georgics*, II, 458.

[58] Cf. p. 70, note 108.

Thus the monks and the whole crew of the pope are the only ones who lead a royal life, inasmuch as they leave the labors, transactions, and dangers to others. They themselves enjoy their comforts in idleness.

We say the same thing about the worry of a pastor, which must be considered so much the greater because the duties he performs are the more important. Or shall we suppose that Augustine lived in idleness and indulged in his pleasures when daily he had to be in conflict against so many opponents, lest the Pelagians, the Donatists, the Manichaeans, and similar disturbers of the churches completely overthrow the teaching of Christ? By the grace of God we also conduct our affairs in such a way that I hope no one will envy us for such busy leisure. It is, therefore, the utmost stupidity for the enthusiasts to insist on manual labor, which is useful for strengthening the body, when, by contrast, these very great labors in the state and church wear out the body and drain off all vitality, as it were, from its innermost centers.

We should, therefore, differentiate between degrees of hard work. The hard work in connection with a household is great; greater is that connected with the state; and greatest is that in connection with the church. Look at Paul, and you will readily understand how much hard work he did. Moreover, because the church in all ages is beset by devils and harassed by heresies, offenses, sins, unjust oppression of tyrants, and by evils of every sort, shall we say that there are no strenuous exertions in it, no hard work? Or shall we say that those who are at the head of the church do not earn their keep?

But we may say this about the pope, the cardinals, and the whole pack of wicked men who use up great wealth, although they do no work and are concerned only with their bellies and their leisure. They are the ones to whom that familiar statement of Paul's applies (2 Thess. 3:10): "He who does not work should not eat." But to work in the church means to preach, administer the Sacraments, contend with the enthusiasts, remove offenses, edify the godly, etc. Of those who do this Christ says (Luke 10:7): "The laborer is worthy of his hire."

And again, the situation of Adam, as the initiator of sin, was worse than ours, if we appraise it correctly. Where we work hard, each one in his own station, Adam was compelled to exert himself in the hard work of the household, of the state, and of the church all by himself. As long as he lived, he alone held all these positions among his descendants. He supported his family, ruled it, and trained it in godliness; he was father, king, and priest. And experience teaches how each one of these positions abounds in grief and dangers.

Therefore we must comfort ourselves in the face of such troubles and teach our hearts to be patient; for we see that these misfortunes are placed even upon the elect, who have the hope of resurrection and eternal life. Furthermore, since this hope remains for these very wretched people, we ought to have courage and overcome these evils through hope; for we shall not remain here forever. When those who journey abroad encounter a niggardly innkeeper, they comfort themselves with the thought that the inconvenience is a matter of one night, whether they have to fast or must sleep in a hard bed. We, too, should take a similar attitude in the midst of these misfortunes. For when compared with eternity, what are the two or three years we spend in sleep almost without being aware of them?

Therefore let misfortunes come as the Lord passes them out to each, whether in the household or in the state and church. We shall not allow ourselves to be driven to impatience. We shall not let them divert us from our concern for the state, the household, or the church. Such softness is not becoming to brave soldiers, to throw down their weapons and run away at the first attack of the enemy, as if we were intended for pleasures and idleness, not for work and activity. "Do not yield to evils, but encounter them more boldly," says the poet.[59]

But this we shall be able to do if we compare the troubles of the present time with the hope of resurrection and eternal life. Just as no one would be willing to lose this hope, so each individual must be convinced that he should not abandon the position into which God has placed him. He who has been called to teach the churches, let him do this with courage; let him not be influenced either by his own dangers or by the indolence of the popes. When they ought to help the churches by preaching the Gospel, by ruling the churches, by hearing cases involving sacred matters, and by deciding disputes concerning doctrine, they turn over these most important tasks to silly monks, while they themselves are concerned with gathering money and providing pleasures. Therefore since they flee the hard work, they will also be without the comfort; since they do not suffer with Him, they will also not reign with Him (2 Tim. 2:12).

---

[59] Vergil, *Aeneid*, VI, 96. Luther also quotes this in his *Commentary on Galatians* (Weimar, XL-2, 28). Meinhold maintains that in both cases the passage came from the hand of the editors.

By contrast, let us, who carry on this hard work, each in his own situation, keep in mind that even if we must endure something painful, these hardships will have their end. Therefore Moses now adds this comfort in every evil, however great it may be.

Until you return to the earth, because from it you have been taken. Since you are dust, you will also return to dust.

Godless people endure endless hardships in the hope of getting a little pleasure. How many dangers the merchant encounters on land and sea for the sake of his profit! How cheaply the soldier sells his life! The prostitute in the brothel must endure far more evil than any wife in her home. In consequence, a German proverb calls such people "the devil's martyrs" as of their own accord rush into dangers which they could avoid if they were willing to live a godly life.[60] How many troubles drunkards bring upon themselves through their revels! They would not have these if they drank with greater moderation.

Therefore one may properly doubt how it would be possible to give counsel to the human race, which is so hardened by Satan that it does not even perceive its evils but eagerly strives for them and does not give them up. For if it perceived them, I ask you, would it not flee from them? Now there is such great stupor in their hearts that you see men being delighted by their evils. Most people are so perverse that for the sake of a foolish and slight pleasure they involve themselves in sure evils. But it is amazing that the godly do not interpret it properly and say: "Although here we must live in sundry misfortunes, there will be an end to them, and they must be replaced by a better life."

The statement we have before us points out this comfort. It promises that all those misfortunes will surely come to an end, and that this will happen after the head of the serpent has first been crushed and bruised. "Until," He says, "you return אֶל־הָאֲדָמָה – to the earth." The word in general denotes earth; in this way it is used below: "And Cain became a tiller of the earth." The word עָפָר properly denotes earth that has just been dug up, or a clod, while our translation has "dust," to suggest the idea of loose earth. Now Adam was made out of a clod into a living human being. And so, says the Lord,

---

[60] The proverb is: "It requires more perspiration and toil to get into hell than into heaven," *Luther's Works,* 13, p. 123.

when that combination is dissolved, he will again turn into a clod or dust.

But here we are reminded again how through the gradual increase of sins punishments also increase. The method of committing corpses to the earth to disintegrate into earth was rather gentle and appropriate for a human being. Later on, however, it became the custom of almost all nations to cremate corpses. And how often it happens that living people are devoured by wild beasts and have animals as their tomb, just as in the prophets the teeth of beasts and the ragings of serpents and of other poisonous animals appear among the four punishments.[61] The more insensible we become toward our punishments, the severer are those which God inflicts in order to crush us and to break our hardness of heart, just as Lev. 26:18-19 states: "But if, even for all this, you will not obey Me, I shall punish you seven times more for your sins, and I shall break the pride of your hardheartedness."

Thus the fall of Adam was from life into death, from health into sickness. And yet it was, thus far, truly a golden age, if you consider ours. Gradually everything deteriorated, as the image described in the Book of Daniel shows (Dan. 2:32). The closer the world is to its end, the worse human beings become. For this reason it also happens that harsher punishments are exacted from us. How stubbornly the papists today attack the truth! What great cruelty they inflict on those who confess the truth! Not to mention their truly devilish greed, lusts, treacheries, and endless wrongs. And so the punishments cannot be too far off, can they?

Thus far Moses has told about the punishments that were inflicted on Adam and his descendants on account of sin; and although these are massive, they were less severe in the beginning than they are now. At that time they were punishments in the positive degree, so to speak; now because of sin, all of them have been increased to the superlative degree.

But before we proceed with what follows, some discussion is needed of the passage on which we touched above, where the woman is told: "I shall multiply your sorrow and your conception, or your pregnancy." The Hebrew has הרנך, which interpreters generally understand to refer to all those inconveniences and anguishes by which women are troubled from the time of conception until birth.

---

[61] Although the word "prophets" is used here, the passage being referred to seems to be Deut. 32:24.

Since a wife becomes pregnant and gives birth only once in a year, the question is raised: Is it also a punishment to become pregnant only once? Likewise, why does God say here that He wants to multiply her conception? Now so far as the latter is concerned, I think the correct explanation is: "I shall multiply conception, that is, the pains and inconveniences which follow conception. The punishment is that though no more than one child is conceived in a year, she is burdened with countless inconveniences." If the human race had continued to remain in innocence, the fertility of the women would have been far greater. We see some traces of this when in one birth twins, often triplets, and sometimes even quadruplets, are brought into the world.

And of this fertility there are examples among the rest of the beasts. The fertility of birds and fish is great. Dogs, cats, and pigs also give birth to a large number of young. Although some larger animals give birth to only one at a time, I nevertheless have no doubt that if there were no sin, women would have given birth to a much more numerous offspring. Now those who are most fertile give birth at most to one child in a single year, and that shameful and heinous lust has been added to it. All this reminds us of the enormity of sin.

Here there arises a trivial Jewish objection about the serpent: that if the Seed of the woman is to be understood of a natural seed which is born from her womb, as we have explained, it appears to be a logical conclusion that also the seed of the serpent is that which is born from the belly of the serpent.[62] Otherwise there will not be a contrast, to which Moses points when he says: "I shall put enmity between your seed and her Seed."

From this trivial objection many consequences will follow. In the first place, God would be speaking with the natural serpent only, and punishing it; in the second place, Christ would be nothing, and nothing could be proved about Christ by means of this passage. This trivial objection has some appearance of validity, but it actually amounts to nothing.

My first answer is (Rev. 22:11): "He who does not know, let him not know; and he who is filthy, let him be filthy still." When someone does not believe the revealed and plain Gospel, it serves him right if he does not understand these darker statements of Scripture and does not believe them. Nor is it our intention to confirm the Gospel

62 The source of this is Lyra on Gen. 3:15.

or to throw light on it by means of this passage. But we make use of the Gospel as the clear light to illumine this darkness.[63] Therefore why should it be amazing if those who refuse to believe the clear Gospel do not believe the darker statements of the prophets either, and propose new and silly ideas? The promise of the Gospel has been divinely revealed; furthermore, it has been preserved among so many tyrants and awful tortures. Because the Jews obstinately oppose it and do not want to believe, they must be left to their own devices. But we shall now concern ourselves with those who believe and who obey the Gospel.

Christ says in John 8:44 that Satan is the father of lying and a murderer, and that he did not stand in the truth. This is that light of the Gospel by which the darkness of the Old Testament is made clear. For if Satan was a murderer from the beginning, tell me, whom did he kill? Was it not Adam and Eve — through sin? Where did he kill? Was it not in Paradise? When did he kill? Was it not when he weakened the authority of the divine command and promised that they would be like gods if they ate from the forbidden tree? Therefore both conclusions are true: that in Paradise there was a natural serpent; and that through that serpent the old serpent, the devil, deceived man and killed him.

This, therefore, is the chief meaning of this passage, so that you may understand that the devil was the originator of this catastrophe. Similarly, when someone commits a murder, it is correct to say of the murderer's dagger: "The dagger killed him." Surely, it was not the dagger alone or by itself, but the human being who used the dagger. But it is a common synecdoche that by the instrument we understand the actor himself.[64] Therefore we utterly reject this trivial objection of the Jews.

In the second place, this, too, is true: that contraries need not be opposite in every way.[65] For there is a manifold relationship of opposites, as the dialecticians teach. Some are in opposition relatively, others privatively, and still others contrarily. Our natural father by whom we were begotten and the father of lies are opposites. Even though we should accede to the Jewish understanding that Moses is speaking about a natural serpent, the text nevertheless clearly sug-

---

[63] Cf. p. 223, note 68, for another illustration of this principle of interpretation.

[64] Cf. p. 195, note 42.

[65] The basis of this seems to be Aristotle, *Categories*, ch. 5.

gests a synecdoche if we compare it with the words of Christ. It says: "God said to the serpent: 'Because you did this, you will be cursed.'" What did it do? Obviously this, that it deceived Eve and so killed her.

Apply to these words the light of the Gospel (John 8:44): "The devil was a murderer from the beginning." Does it not clearly appear that God is speaking with the natural serpent in such a way that He means the devil hidden in the natural serpent, the devil who had cast mankind into sin, death, and the wrath of God? Therefore the seed must not be understood as the natural seed of the natural serpent but as the seed of the devil, just as Christ also calls him in the Gospel (Matt. 13:25): "The enemy came and oversowed evil seed." This seed is the contrary of the spiritual seed, just as flesh and spirit are contraries.

It is unnecessary for contraries to be opposite to each other throughout, just as likes do not correspond to each other throughout. Adam is a figure of Christ. The similarity consists in this, that just as through Adam sin came to all, so also Christ's righteousness comes to all who believe in Him. So much fits; everything beyond this does not fit. Therefore let the Jews have their error. As the result of Christ's interpretation, we who believe know that this serpent is the devil.

20. *And Adam called the name of his wife Eve, because she was the mother of all the living.*

We heard above that the punishment of being under her husband's power was inflicted on the woman. An indication of that power is given here. It is not God who gives her a name; it is Adam, as the lord of Eve, just as he had previously given names to the animals as creatures put under him. No animal thought out a name for itself; all were assigned their names and received the prestige and honor of a name from their lord Adam. Similarly even today, when a woman marries a man, she loses the name of her family and is called by the name of her husband. It would be unnatural if a husband wanted to be called by his wife's name. This is an indication and a confirmation of the punishment or subjection which the woman incurred through her sin. Likewise, if the husband changes his place of residence, the woman is compelled to follow him as her lord. So manifold are the traces in nature which remind us of sin and of our misfortune.

The name which Adam gives his wife is a very pleasing and delightful name. For what is more precious, better, or more delightful

than life? Familiar is the popular little verse: "That you may pur-
chase back your life"; [66] for neither gold nor jewels nor the wealth
and glory of the whole world can be compared to life, just as Christ
also says in Matt. 16:26. The Jews commonly give their children
names derived from roses, flowers, and jewels; the name Eve, however,
was not taken from valuable objects but from life itself, which surpasses all other objects.

Moreover, Adam adds the reason: "Because she is the mother of
all living." It is clear from this passage that after Adam had received
the Holy Spirit, he had become marvelously enlightened, and that
he believed and also understood the saying concerning the woman's
Seed who would crush the head of the serpent. Moreover, he wanted
to give an outward indication of this faith of his and lend distinction
to it by means of his wife's name. He gave it to no other creature.
By this designation of his wife he gave support to the hope in the
future Seed, strengthened his own faith, and comforted himself with
the thought that he believed in life even when all nature had already
been made subject to death.

If Adam had not been aware of the future life, he would not have
been able to cheer his heart; nor would he have assigned so pleasing
a name to his wife. But by assigning this name to his wife he gives
clear indication that the Holy Spirit had cheered his heart through
his trust in the forgiveness of sins by the Seed of Eve. He calls her
Eve to remind himself of the promise through which he himself also
received new life, and to pass on the hope of eternal life to his
descendants. This hope and faith he writes on his wife's forehead
by means of this name as with colors, just as those who are freed
from their enemies set up trophies and other marks of their joy.

But you will ask: "Why does he call her 'mother' when she was
still a virgin and had not yet given birth?" He does this, too, to bear
witness to his faith in the promise; for he believes that the human
race is not to be cast away or to be destroyed, but is to be preserved.
And so this name expresses a prophecy of the future grace and points
to the comfort which is necessary against the temptations of Satan in
the continual misfortunes of this life. Moreover, it is possible that
this delightful assignment of the name, which is a superb witness
of Adam's faith and of his cheerful spirit, prompted the holy fathers
later on to regard as more festive and joyful the day on which an

[66] Apparently a reference to a folk song of the time.

infant was circumcised and named than the one on which it was born. In this way the assignment of this first name to Eve was celebrated. In contrast to this reminder there now follows another reminder, one of sorrow.

21. *And the Lord God made for Adam and his wife garments of skins and clothed them.*

This is not at all as pleasing and delightful as was the assignment of the name. Even though the Lord had said: "On whatever day you eat from this tree, you will surely die," Adam had used his wife's name as a means of finding comfort in the life which was to be restored through the promised Seed, who would crush the serpent's head and would slay the slayer himself.

Here Adam and Eve are dressed in garments by the Lord God Himself. Whenever they looked at their garments, these were to serve as a reminder to them to give thought to their wretched fall from supreme happiness into the utmost misfortune and trouble. Thus they were to be constantly afraid of sinning, to repent continually, and to sigh for the forgiveness of sins through the promised Seed. This is also why He clothed them, not in foliage or in cotton but in the skins of slain animals, for a sign that they are mortal and that they are living in certain death.

Therefore just as the name Eve is a joyous omen of life, so these skins are a reminder not only of past and future sin, but also of their present misfortunes, which their sins deserve.

Human nature has need of such reminders and, as it were, signs; for we very readily forget the things that are gone by, both good and bad. Thus Peter also says (2 Peter 1:9): "He who lacks these is blind, having forgotten his cleansing from his former sins." "But for this reason," says he (2 Peter 1:12), "I shall not be negligent to put you continually in remembrance of these things, although you know them and are established in the present truth." It is in truth an awful statement of the apostle that some are forgetting the forgiveness of their sins. Although they began to believe quite nicely, they are departing from the faith and are not adorning themselves with the beautiful chain of Christian virtues but are indulging in greed, pride, envy, lust, etc. We who have experienced those mischievous burdens under the papacy are very much in need of this exhortation to prevent us from being ungrateful to so merciful a God, as, alas, the greater part of the world is.

To counteract this forgetfulness, Adam and Eve were given a pelt as a reminder, or as a kind of sign, by which they, together with all their descendants, would be put in mind of their pitiful fall. But later on the world began to go crazy about this sign of our misfortune. Who can tell how much effort and expense men go to in their dress! And so it should no longer be called a pleasure or an excess, but rather a madness, that people, like donkeys raised for carrying gold, are more intent on loading themselves down than on adorning themselves. More decent dress is certainly commendable, especially in persons of standing. But the crudity which is now in style cannot help being an offense to the eyes of respectable people. Therefore, if Adam came back to life now and saw this madness among all classes, I surely believe that he would be petrified with amazement. A pelt was his daily garb as a daily reminder of his lost bliss. But we clothe ourselves flashily and go to extremes in order to prove to everyone that we have forgotten not only the evils out of which we were snatched but also the good things we have received. Now the Lord uses a word to point out what had been symbolized by their clothing.

22. *And the Lord God said: Behold, man has become as one of Us, so that he knows good and evil. And now, lest perchance he stretch out his hand and take also from the tree of life and eat and live forever —*

This is sarcasm and very bitter derision. Therefore the question is asked: Why does God deal so harshly with wretched Adam? Why, after being deprived of all his glory and falling into sin and death, is he further vexed by his Creator with such bitter scorn? And is the visible sign not enough to remind him of his present misfortune and of his lost glory? Why must He also add the audible Word?

My answer is: Adam had the promise of mercy; with this he ought to have lived content. But to make him fear future sin and beware of it, this harsh reminder is given him. God sees what sort of people his descendants will be. He puts this Word into Adam's mouth for Adam to make it known to his descendants and thus to teach them that when he wanted to become like God, he became like the devil. So they themselves are to be on their guard lest they add their own sin to that of their parents and thus withdraw still farther from God.

As in the case of the pelt, so here, by His very Word, God calls attention to both past and future evils. It is not as though He were pleased by so sad a fall, for then He would not warn Adam in this way but would keep silence. What He wants is that man should long for the lost image of God and begin to hate sin as the cause of this great evil, and that Adam should warn his descendants about what followed after sin, namely, that when he was deprived of his mind by Satan and believed that he would be like God, he became like Satan himself.

At this passage another question is raised: Why is God, who is one, speaking in the plural number? There are not several gods, are there? Nicholas of Lyra and others think that these words were spoken in the name of an angel or to angels: "He has become one of Us," that is, he has become an angel.[67] But this is altogether too insipid. For God does not call Himself an angel; nor is the stress placed on the word "one" but rather on the pronoun "Us." Therefore we reject this insipid comment. If this is spoken in the name of an angel, it is certain that God did not say it. But the text says: "And the Lord God said."

Therefore we must take into account the light of the Gospel, just as I said above;[68] it makes clear the dark statements of the Old Testament. But if you interpret these words as dealing with angels, your interpretation will not agree with the previous passages. Satan had said (Gen. 3:5): "And you will be like gods, knowing good and evil." Therefore Adam and Eve actually attempted to become like God. And the passage before us must not be understood otherwise than as referring to equality with God.

The Jewish error which Lyra adopts here should, therefore, be entirely rejected, and it should be established as a literal statement that in God there is a plurality, just as He also said above (Gen. 1:26): "Let Us make man according to Our image." All these passages clearly indicate the unity of the divine essence. For there is always prefixed: "And God said." Furthermore, they also clearly indicate the plurality of Persons or, as it is called, the Trinity. But these mysteries are more definitely unfolded in the New Testament, as when Christ commands Baptism in the name of the Father and of the Son and of the Holy Spirit (Matt. 28:19). And so in this way

[67] Lyra on Gen. 3:22, sec. "a."
[68] Cf. p. 218.

the three Persons of the Godhead were pointed to immediately at the beginning of the world; later on they were understood by the prophets; and finally they were fully revealed through the Gospel.

Hence the opinion stands that Adam and Eve made the attempt to become the image of God. But the image of the invisible God is the Son, through whom all things hold together (Col. 1:15, 17). Therefore through his sin Adam struck against the Person of Christ, who is the true image of God. All this is only briefly and dimly suggested here, but Adam undoubtedly based countless sermons on these words. Similarly, it is plain that the prophets referred to these mysteries in various ways and marvelously veiled what later on the Gospel pointed out clearly.

Our opinion is also supported by the name of God in this passage, יְהֹוָה, which cannot denote any creature but is given exclusively to the Creator Himself. But what is the Creator saying? Obviously, "Adam has become one of Us." Surely, here our religion and faith does not permit us to understand these words as being spoken to the angels. For who will say that God is one of the angels? Or an angel one of God? God is above the angels and over all creatures. How, therefore, could He put Himself on the same level with the angels?

Let us, therefore, accept this passage as a sure proof of our doctrine of the Trinity: that there is one God and three Persons. Moreover, the text here vaguely points out concerning Adam's sin that he wanted to be, not like the angels but like God. Furthermore, if Adam had sinned only against the angels, he would not have been sentenced to death. But because his sin was directed against the majesty of the Creator, whom he wanted to resemble and even to imitate, for this reason it was followed by such an awful punishment.

When someone escapes the gallows, everybody reminds him of his danger and urges him henceforth to be on his guard. So after Adam has been comforted again with the hope of life through the divine promise, God reminds him by this bitter scorn not to forget this awful fall, not to strive again after the godlikeness he had so unsuccessfully attempted to gain, but to humble himself before God's majesty and henceforth, together with his descendants, to beware of such a sin. For these words are not spoken only to Adam; they also concern us, who, after being baptized and renewed by grace, must make every effort to guard against falling back into our former ungodliness.

In the same way there is scorn and the bitterest ridicule in what

God says about the tree of life, as though He were not able by a single nod to prevent and forestall Adam's touching it. Then God adds these fear-inspiring words:

23. *And the Lord God sent him away from the Garden of Eden to till the ground from which he was taken,*

24. *and He drove man out, and He stationed to the east of the Garden of Eden the cherubim and the flame of the turning sword for the purpose of guarding the way to the tree of life.*

These words are also intended for our correction and warning, as St. Paul says in Rom. 15:4, that whatever has been written, was written for our sakes. There is a great danger that if we forget our former sins, we shall be overcome by them again. Christ also issues a similar warning in John 5:14, when He says: "Behold, you have been healed. Sin no more, lest something worse befall you." And Peter, in 2 Peter 2:22, speaks of the sow that was washed and of the dog that returned to his vomit. Likewise, 2 Peter 1:9 mentions "those who forget their former sins."

These and other passages of Scripture are warnings to guard against sin in the future, because, as in the case of sicknesses, a relapse is more difficult to cure than the first disease. So in this passage Adam and all his descendants are warned in various ways; after receiving the hope of life through the promise of the Seed, they should be on their guard lest they sin and lose it again. The familiar parable (Matt. 12:43-45) tells about the house which has been swept after Satan was cast out, but which he takes over again with the assistance of seven spirits worse than he.

This is why the Lord makes use of such harshness, as if He were saying: "Previously I forbade Adam and Eve to touch the tree of death, but such was their arrogance that they did not even refrain from what was harmful to them. Surely, now the effort must be made to keep them from approaching the tree of life too; for probably they will not be able to stay away from it either. Therefore I shall guard against this by prohibiting the use of all the trees of Paradise. Therefore go outside, and eat the herbs of the field and whatever else the earth produces. Henceforth you will be forbidden to eat not only from the tree of life but also from the rest of the trees in Paradise."

This passage also shows that the trees of Paradise were in no wise similar to those which the rest of the earth produced. Now, therefore, the food which Adam and Eve eat also reminds them of their sin and of the most wretched state into which they were placed by their sin. Our misfortunes have been painted in such various ways that not only our lack of spiritual endowments but even our clothing and our food remind us of them.

Here the question arises whether, if God had permitted Adam to eat of the tree of life, Adam would have overcome death by means of this food, as he became subject to death after he had eaten of the tree of death. There seems to have been a parallel between them: the tree of death kills, and it does this through the Word "on whatever day you eat of this tree you will die"; therefore by the power of the Word the tree of life makes alive and delivers from death.

Lyra and others answer to this question that the tree of life would indeed have had the power of preserving life so far as the length of life was concerned, but not forever; therefore it would not have restored the life which had been lost through sin.[69] Adam was not created to remain forever in this physical life, but from this physical life and from the physical eating he was to pass over into the spiritual life. Just as when a private citizen is elected burgomaster, no death intervenes on that occasion, but his honor and prestige is simply increased, so Adam, without any intervening death, would have exchanged his mortal life for the immortal one. But this tree of life, says Lyra, served only the physical life. Therefore he explains the text "lest he live forever" to mean "for a long time." So much for Lyra.

I myself am of a different opinion, however. I believe that if Adam had been permitted to go to the tree of life, he would have been restored to the life he had lost, so that thereafter he would not have died but simply would have been transferred from the physical life into the spiritual. The text states both most clearly: that on this account he was forbidden the tree of life; and that eating from it he would live לְעֹלָם, that is, forever. I reject Lyra's opinion because he assigns the power of making alive directly to the nature of the tree, although it is certain that the tree did not have this power by its nature but only through the efficacy of the Word. In the same way also the tree of the knowledge of good and evil did not kill because its fruits were poisonous and destructive, but because a word

---

[69] Lyra on Gen. 3:22, sec. "b."

or kind of label had been attached to it with the warning written on it: "On whatever day you eat from this tree, you will surely die."

In the first place, therefore, there hangs on the tree of death the spiritual death, namely, disobedience. And so, after Adam and Eve had transgressed this commandment through their sin, which was active in them even then, they thought: "Behold, God has forbidden us to eat, but what do we care?" This disdain of the command was the poisoned barb by which Adam and Eve were killed after it had been driven into their throats. Because of the added threat their eating brought about death through their disobedience. The tree was not poisonous; but, as we said above at great length,[70] it was a tree of divine worship, for man to bear witness through his obedience that he knew, honored, and feared his God. For God saw that everything He had made was very good (Gen. 1:31). The situation with the tree of life I believe to have been wholly the same; not by its inherent character but through the efficacy of the Word was the tree life-giving. And so, because the Word was still attached to that tree, Adam would have been restored to his former life if he had eaten from it.

Thus the serpent which Moses raised up in the desert (Num. 21:9) did not make alive through its inherent character (for it was made of bronze, just as we could form a serpent from bronze now); but the Word which was added to that brazen serpent was life-giving because God commanded the serpent to be set up, and added the Word (Num. 21:8): "Whoever looks at it will be healed." This Word you do not have if you form a serpent from bronze today. Moreover, the reason for the healing lay not in looking at it but in the command from God that they should look at the serpent and in the promise of deliverance. But because the rabbis do not pay attention to the Word, they blunder miserably and come out in favor of the opinion that the inherent character of those trees was either death-dealing or life-giving. They do not realize that all these things happen because God either promises or threatens.

Similarly, the sophists also talk nonsense when they discuss how Baptism makes righteous. Thomas and Bonaventura think that some power for bringing this about has been given by God to the water when the child is baptized, with the result that the baptismal water

[70] Cf. p. 96.

brings about justification by its own power.[71] In contrast, we say
that the water is water, in no wise better in quality than that which
a cow drinks. But we maintain that to the simple water the Word
of promise has been added (Mark 16:16): "He that believes and is
baptized will be saved"; likewise (John 3:5): "Man must be born
again of water and the Spirit." If someone should want to call this
Word or this promise a power that has been given to the water of
Baptism, I shall not object. But the idea of the sophists was something different. They do not attribute this power to the Word, but
concerning the element they state that it has a special power given
to it. Scotus speaks more correctly when he defines Baptism as
a divine covenant standing by the element.[72]

Therefore the Word must always be taken into consideration and
honored as that by which God takes hold of and, as it were, clothes
the creatures; and a difference must be made between the creature
and the Word. In the Sacrament of the Altar there are bread and
wine; in Baptism there is water. These are creatures, but creatures
apprehended by the Word. As long as the creature is apprehended by
the Word, so long it is and does what the Word promises.

Nevertheless, this is not to be understood as though we were
now joining cause with the Sacramentarians when we link Baptism
with the Lord's Supper.[73] Baptism has the promise that it, together
with the Holy Spirit, brings about the new birth. In the Lord's Supper there is also the promise of the forgiveness of sins, as well as
this, that together with the bread and wine the body and the blood
of Christ are truly offered, just as Christ says: "This is My body,
which is given for you"; "This cup is the New Testament in My
blood." In this way it can also be said that the human nature in
Christ does not redeem us, but that because the human nature is
physically apprehended by His divinity, and Christ, God and man,

---

[71] Thomas Aquinas, *Summa theologica*, III, Q. 66; Bonaventura, *Commen-
taria in quattuor libros sententiarum Magistri Petri Lombardi*, IV, Dist. III,
Part II, Art. I, Q. 2 in *Doctoris seraphici S. Bonaventurae opera omnia*, IV
(Quaracchi, 1889), pp. 78—81.

[72] The designation of Baptism as a covenant is not common in Luther, but
it does occur, as in a sermon from 1519 or 1520 (Weimar, IV, 704).

[73] This seems to mean that Luther and his supporters usually preferred to
treat Baptism and the Lord's Supper as distinct theological issues rather than
to discuss them on the basis of a general theory of the sacraments, as their
opponents on both the Roman Catholic and the Protestant sides did.

is one Person, therefore the redemption is effective. Therefore the Son of Man is called and is the Savior.

The pope invented holy water, extreme unction, and many similar things to which he has ascribed forgiveness of sins. Always consider here whether God has added His command and promise. If there is no promise and command of God, decide at once that it is idolatry and a desecration of the name of God. Yet they say: "Pious prayers are being added. We are also imitating the examples of the saints in this." But do not concern yourself with prayers, with examples, or even with the intention. Consider only whether there is a promise and a command; for this is what imparts to the creatures a new power beyond that power which they have through their nature.

Thus the tree of the knowledge of good and evil was indeed good by its nature; but because of the Word which had been added, it was poison for man, for his spirit, and not only for his body. In contrast, the tree of life had the power of preserving life because of the Word; it would have preserved life also for Adam. But God, being angry, was unwilling to permit him to return to that tree after his fall, not only in order to remind him of the sin he had committed but also because Adam already had a better promise, namely, that the Seed of the woman would crush the seed of the serpent. Therefore though he had been made subject to physical death, he still remained in possession of the hope of immortality through the Son of God. Thus an angry father may stop short of depriving his son of his right of inheritance, but he may punish him by throwing him out of the house.

Therefore the Lord God wants man to be satisfied with the promise of a life better than that in which Adam was created. Even if Adam had eaten from the tree of life and had been restored to his former life, he still would not have been safe from Satan. Satan could still deprive him of it through temptation. Therefore God provided man with a condition in which we may be sure that, because of the blessed Seed, we shall never die an eternal death, even though this physical life is troubled in manifold ways. Thus all these words are words of derision and anger from God to Adam after he has already been made righteous, to make him more cautious in future instances and to prevent him from losing the remembrance of bygone events.

Then, too, Moses neatly changes the words to the contrary so as to remind the human being of what he had previously said. Previously he said: "He placed man in the Garden of Eden to work and guard it." Here he says: "God sent man out of the Garden of Eden to till the earth." He wants man to reflect that he was formed from a clod and was put in a very excellent place, but that sin caused him to be put back on the earth out of which he was created. This striking change to the contrary reminds Adam and his descendants that they should not only guard against future sins but should also keep in mind those of the past. And so Adam, for whom previously a special fare had been provided in Paradise at a place apart from the rest of the animals, now shares a place with the animals and almost shares their food.

Nor is Adam merely driven out of Paradise; but a guard is assigned to the place to make any approach to it impossible, just as watches are stationed in the vicinity of fortresses and armies. By going into such detail in this passage Moses indicates that this expulsion was of the utmost necessity for our salvation, namely, in order that we may avoid sin and live in the fear of God while remaining on our guard against Satan, who inflicted such great harm on nature through sin.

About the word מִקֶּדֶם we said above that it denotes "toward the east" or "toward the eastern region." [74] Moreover, Moses implies that Paradise had a road or a gate toward the east through which there was an access to this garden. Likewise, in connection with the temple structure in Ezekiel (40:6) mention is made of the gate of the sanctuary which faced toward the east, obviously to have us realize that the temple was a figure of Paradise; for if nature had remained perfect, Paradise would have been the temple of the entire world. And so, on the road toward the east, which alone led to Paradise, cherubim or angels were placed, to guard that way so that neither Adam nor any of his descendants could enter Paradise. The Lord did this according to human fashion in order to inspire fear and provide a conspicuous reminder of their terrible fall.

Moreover, those cherubim on the way did not have a metal sword to ward off such as would approach, but the לַהַט of a movable sword, that is, a flash or a flame, such as of lightning, which is unsteady and blinds the eyes. This flame or lightning had the form of a sword that is in continuous motion or moves to and fro. Similarly in Acts 2:3 it is related that the tongues of the apostles appeared to be divided, like fire; such is also the appearance of the flying dragons. These

[74] Cf. p. 89.

angels continually sent out flames in such a way that they were driven
in all directions, making it impossible for anyone to approach.

Origen's pratings we reject. Nor do we approve of Lyra's absurd
ideas.[75] He maintains that the flaming sword signifies that because
of a mortal sin a sinner ceases to be part of the church militant
according to merit, but not according to number; moreover, that it is
designated as "turning" because if true repentance should follow,
man is called back into the church according to merit. Just as we
took the position that Paradise was a true and visible garden in
a certain place of the earth,[76] so here we explain this sword historically
to be a visible flame or fire in the form of a sword, with which the
cherubim, or angels, frightened and drove away Adam and his
descendants so that they would not dare come too close to the garden.

The angels maintained watch over Paradise up to the time of the
Flood to serve as a reminder of the wretched and disastrous fall. The
lake of Sodom and the pillar of salt performed a similar function
for later generations. Our indifference and disregard stand in need of
such memorials. But after the Flood Paradise disappeared, together
with the angels and the sword. The generation then arising needed
new examples, closer at hand, to make an impression on smug people,
although not even this achieves anything in the case of the ungodly.

In the course of these three chapters we have the story of the
creation of all creatures. We have heard how heaven and earth were
created, the sea and everything in them; how Paradise was established
by God to be a palace for man, the lord of creation; how in Paradise
God founded for man a temple intended for divine worship, namely,
the tree of the knowledge of good and evil, in which he was to give
evidence of his obedience to God. We have also heard of man's
activity in Paradise, how he fell wretchedly and sinned against God,
thereby losing all the glory of his innocence and immortality.

According to our ability, we have treated all these facts in their
historical meaning, which is their real and true one. In the interpretation of Holy Scripture the main task must be to derive from it some
sure and plain meaning, especially because there is such a variety
of interpreters — Latin, Greek, and Hebrew too. Almost all of these
not only do not concern themselves with the story but bury it and
confuse it with their nonsensical allegories.

[75] Lyra on Gen. 3:24, sec. "d."
[76] Cf. p. 89.

The ridiculous procedure which Origen and Jerome follow in these chapters is well known. Everywhere they depart from the historical account, which they call "the letter that kills" and "the flesh"; and they bestow lofty praise on the "spiritual meaning," of which they have no actual knowledge. In fact, Jerome followed Origen as his teacher. The same thing happens in our time; those who are influential, either through their native ability or through their eloquence, strive with all their power to persuade their hearers that the historical accounts are dead matter and useless for building the churches. Thus it came about that with common zeal we rashly strove for allegories. When I was a young man, my own attempts at allegory met with fair success.[77] It was even permissible to come up with foolish ideas, since these great teachers of the churches, such as Jerome and Origen, had at times given wide range to their imagination. And so anyone who was somewhat more skilled in contriving allegories was also regarded as a rather learned theologian. Augustine, too, was led astray by this conviction; and, especially in the instance of the Psalms, he disregards the historical sense and has recourse to allegories.[78] They were all convinced that, especially in the historical accounts of the Old Testament, the allegories represented the spiritual meaning; but the historical account itself, or the literal sense, represented the carnal meaning.

But, I ask you, is this not a desecration of the sacred writings? Origen makes heaven out of Paradise and angels out of the trees.[79] If this is correct, what will be left of the doctrine of creation? Particularly for beginning students of the Sacred Scriptures it is, therefore, necessary that when they approach the reading of the ancient teachers, they read them with discretion, or rather with the definite intention to disapprove of those statements for which there is less support. Otherwise they will be led astray by the authority of the name of the fathers and teachers of the church, just as I was led astray and as all the schools of the theologians were. Ever since I began to adhere to the historical meaning, I myself have always had a strong dislike for allegories and did not make use of them unless the text itself

[77] As Luther says here, his early exegesis was filled with allegorical interpretation, of which his commentary on Judges of 1516 (Weimar, IV, 529—586) is a good illustration; there are some scholars who attribute it to John Agricola rather than to Luther.

[78] For an instance of Luther's use of Augustine's works on the Psalms cf. *Luther's Works*, 13, p. 95, note 32.

[79] Cf. p. 90, note 16.

indicated them or the interpretations could be drawn from the New Testament.[80]

But it was very difficult for me to break away from my habitual zeal for allegory; and yet I was aware that allegories were empty speculations and the froth, as it were, of the Holy Scriptures. It is the historical sense alone which supplies the true and sound doctrine. After this has been treated and correctly understood, then one may also employ allegories as an adornment and flowers to embellish or illuminate the account. The bare allegories, which stand in no relation to the account and do not illuminate it, should simply be disapproved as empty dreams. This is the kind which Origen and those who followed him employ. Where can it be proved from Scripture that Paradise denotes heaven, and that the trees of Paradise refer to the angels? These ideas have been thought up as something most absurd and altogether useless.

Therefore let those who want to make use of allegories base them on the historical account itself. The historical account is like logic in that it teaches what is certainly true; the allegory, on the other hand, is like rhetoric in that it ought to illustrate the historical account but has no value at all for giving proof. In these circumstances an allegory has value, as when we say that heaven denotes the church, but that earth denotes the governments and the political order.[81] Christ Himself calls the church the kingdom of heaven and the kingdom of God; but the earth is called the land of the living, where kings and princes rule.

Similar is the allegory which Paul employs: that Adam and Eve, or marriage itself, is a type of Christ and the church (Eph. 5:32). This allegory is ingenious and full of comfort, for what more delightful statement can be made than that the church is the bride and Christ the Bridegroom? It expresses that most happy association and bestowal of all the gifts which the Bridegroom possesses, as well as the obliteration of the sins and all the misfortunes with which the poor bride is burdened. Therefore it is a most delightful saying when St. Paul states (2 Cor. 11:2): "I have espoused you to one husband that I may present you to Christ as a chaste virgin."

[80] Luther's break with allegorical interpretation was part of his rediscovery of the meaning of the Scriptures, but the commentaries even of his maturer years suggest that the break was not as sharp as the text seems to make it here.

[81] The most famous application of this allegory to church and state was in the bull *Unam sanctam* of Boniface VIII (November 18, 1302).

Likewise, in Rom. 5:14 he states: "Adam was the first figure of Him that was to come." How? "For just as through Adam many have died, much more has the grace of God and the gift by grace, which is of one Man, Jesus Christ, abounded unto many." See how well this allegory ties in with the historical account as its basis.

Similarly, in Gal. 4:24 Paul makes two testaments out of Sara and Hagar. Let those who want to devise allegories follow this lead and look for their basis in the historical account itself.

Earlier we heard the statements about the Seed of the woman and that of the serpent. On this historical account Christ bases His parable about the enemy who sows evil seed, that is, wicked doctrine and evil ideas (Matt. 13:24-30). Who does not realize that these allegories are more appropriate, more enlightening, more profitable, and better than those which Augustine, Lyra, and others devised about the relationship of the higher and the lower mind? [82]

Dealt with in this manner, what else can the closed Paradise and the cherubim with their swords, stationed to guard Paradise, signify than that without faith in Christ man can endure neither the Law nor the Gospel? Paul speaks this way when he says that the Jews were unable to look at Moses' shining face and that Moses was compelled to place a veil before his face (2 Cor. 3:7).

The tree of death is the Law, and the tree of life is the Gospel, or Christ. Those who do not believe in Christ cannot draw near to these trees. They are prevented by the sword of the angel, who cannot put up with hypocrisy and corrupt righteousness. But for him who acknowledges his sin and believes in Christ, Paradise remains open. He brings with him not his own righteousness but Christ's, which the Gospel announces to all so that we all may place our reliance on it and be saved.

There is no need at all for dwelling at greater length on this matter of allegory. Let this reminder suffice: that those who wish to make use of allegories, make use of those which the apostles point out and which have a sure basis in the words themselves or in the historical account. Otherwise it will happen that we build chaff and stubble on the foundation, and not gold (1 Cor. 3:12).

As for the cherubim, it should be stated that frequent mention is made of them here and there in the Holy Scriptures. About them there is nothing in the Latin theologians except the statement that

[82] On this distinction cf. p. 159, note 12; p. 184, note 33.

the term denotes fullness of knowledge.[83] Among the Greek theologians there is Dionysius.[84] They boast that he was a disciple of Paul, but there is no truth to this. He is full of the silliest prattle when he discusses the hierarchy of heaven and that of the church. He invents nine choirs, just like the spheres, assigning the seraphim to the highest rank, then, in order, the cherubim, the thrones, the dominions, the virtues, and the principalities; thereafter, in the lower hierarchy, the powers, the archangels, and the angels. Who does not realize that these are nothing but idle and useless human ideas?

Then Dionysius maintains that in the ecclesiastical hierarchy there are bishops, deacons, subdeacons, lectors, exorcists, etc. Such prattle comes from one who is supposed to have been the disciple of the chief of the apostles and teacher of the Gentiles! Nevertheless, his authority is vaunted so highly that the puffed-up hypocrites claim all his statements were derived from divine oracles, although nowhere does he have a single word about faith or any useful instruction from the Holy Scriptures. Who told him that there were nine choirs? Why did the Franciscans later on add a tenth as a palace for the Holy Mother to live in?[85] In short, these are trifles worthy for the papists to learn and admire after assailing the sound doctrine so stubbornly.

So, then, I shall express my opinion about the term "cherub" so far as I have been able to form it as a result of my reading. It seems to me that "cherub" denotes the ruddy face which girls and boys have at an early age. Thus painters also depict the angels in the likeness of infants. By cherubim, therefore, you may understand angels who appear with a face that is not wrinkled or sad, but with a happy and friendly expression, with a chubby and well-rounded face, whether this be a human face or some other. And so "cherub" is a general term, which does not represent a particular name among the ranks of the angels, as Dionysius dreams, but refers to their appearance, because they show themselves to men with ruddy appearance and youthful face.

This is also the opinion of the Hebrews, who say that כְּרוּב is an Aramaic word: כ is a servile letter, and רוּב denotes a handsome young man with a chubby and florid face; therefore the angels are called

[83] Peter Lombard, *Sententiae*, II, Dist. IX, col. 669—672.

[84] Cf. *Luther's Works*, 13, p. 110, note 55.

[85] During the later Middle Ages various Franciscan theologians had speculated about the role of Mary in the universe, and the cosmology being discussed here is a reflection of such speculation.

כְּרוּבִים because they have a florid face and are happy and charming, just as they are also generally depicted.[86]

Likewise, "seraphim," from fire or brilliance, is also a general term for angels because of the nature of their appearance, as the passage in Num. 21:6 shows: "God sent among the people הַנְּחָשִׁים הַשְּׂרָפִים, seraphim serpents," that is, burning or fiery ones. Therefore one may conclude that the seraphim are angels who not only are handsome and have a chubby face, like the cherubim, but are also endowed with brilliance. In this way they are described in the Gospel as seated by the tomb of the Lord: "His appearance," says the text in Matt. 28:3, "was like lightning." Ps. 104:4 [87] refers to the same thing: "Who makes His angels spirits and His ministers a flaming fire," that is, a brilliant fire. Thus it is stated in Luke 2:9 that when the angel came to the shepherds, the brightness of the Lord shone round about them. Such was also Christ's countenance on Mt. Tabor (Matt. 17:2). Such will be our countenances when on the Last Day we are raised for the glory which Christ has gained for us.

Moreover, what appears in the Books of Kings (1 Kings 6:29) about the curtains with cherubs also denotes the chubby and cheerful faces of angels with wings — not because the angels actually have wings, but because they cannot be depicted otherwise. Thus in Is. 6:6 the name cherub is given to the angel who comes flying with a glad and handsome face, the way they are depicted on tapestries.[88] But if luster is added to express myself thus — the way the face of Stephen is said to have been glad and joyful, from whose eyes shone pure joy (Acts 6:15) — then they are called "seraphim." We can say in German that the faces "blow and glow." [89]

So we, too, shall be. Our faces will shine like the sun at noon; no longer will there be those familiar wrinkles, the contracted brow, and the watery eyes. But, as it is stated in Rev. 21:4: "The Lord will wipe away all tears from our eyes, so that no death, no sorrow, no laments, or any hardships remain." Let us hold fast to this hope, and let us live in the fear of God until, set free from this life fraught with misery, we shall live that angelic and eternal life. Amen, Amen.

86 Like much of the Hebrew etymology in this commentary, this may have come from Santes Pagninus; cf. p. 297, note 55.

87 The original has "Ps. 103" because of the difference in the numbering of the psalms; cf. *Luther's Works*, 13, Introduction, pp. ix—x.

88 Actually, the angel in Is. 6:6 is called a seraph, not a cherub.

89 The German phrase is *blühen und glühen*.

CHAPTER FOUR

At last we have passed over that expanse of text on which all expositors have toiled exceedingly — to some degree also we ourselves, although its entire content was rather clear to us because we did not concern ourselves with allegories but adhered to the historical and strict meaning. Since the majority of the interpreters did not concern themselves with this but attached greater importance to Origen, Dionysius, and others than to Moses himself, it is no wonder that they went astray. The chapters which now follow are less subject to debate and are clearer. Moreover, they support our conviction; for nobody can fail to see that Moses does not intend to present allegories but simply to write the history of the primitive world.

1. *And Adam knew his wife, and she conceived and bore Cain.*

Although Adam had fallen because of his sin, he had the promise, as we heard above, that from his flesh, which had become subject to death, there should be born for him a shoot of life. And so he understood that he was to produce offspring, especially since the blessing, "Increase and multiply" (Gen. 1:28), had not been withdrawn, but had been reaffirmed in the promise of the Seed who would crush the serpent's head (Gen. 3:15). Accordingly, in our judgment Adam did not know his Eve simply as a result of the passion of his flesh; but the need of achieving salvation through the blessed Seed impelled him too.

Therefore no one should take offense at the mention of the fact that Adam knew his Eve. Although original sin has made this work of procreation, which owes its origin to God, something shameful, at which we see pure ears taking offense, nevertheless spiritually minded men should make a distinction between original sin and the product of creation. The work of procreation is something good and holy that God has created; for it comes from God, who bestows His blessing on it. Moreover, if man had not fallen, it would have been a very pure and very honorable work. Just as no one has misgivings

[237]

about conversing, eating, or drinking with his wife — for all these are honorable actions — so also the act of begetting would have been something most highly regarded.

So, then, procreation remained in nature when it had become depraved; but there was added to it that poison of the devil, namely, the prurience of the flesh and the execrable lust which is also the cause of sundry adversities and sins, all of which nature in its unimpaired state would have been spared. We know from experience the excessive desire of the flesh, and for many not even marriage is an adequate remedy. If it were, there would not be the occurrences of adultery and fornication which, alas, are only too frequent. Even among married people themselves, how manifold are the ways in which the weakness of the flesh displays itself! All this stems, not from what was created or from the blessing, which is from God, but from sin and the curse, which is the outgrowth of sin. Therefore they must be kept separate from God's creation, which is good; and we see that the Holy Spirit has no misgivings about speaking of it.

Not only is there no disgrace in what Moses is saying here about God's creation and His blessing, but it was also necessary for him to impart this teaching and to write it down because of future heresies, such as those of the Nicolaitans, Tatian, etc., but especially because of the papacy.[1] We see that the papists are in no way impressed by what is written above (Gen. 1:27): "The Lord created them male and female." The way they live and the way they bind and obligate themselves by vows, it seems that they regard themselves as neither male nor female. It makes no impression on them that it is written above (Gen. 2:22-23): "The Lord brought Eve to Adam, and Adam said: 'This is bone from my bones.'" The promise and the blessing make no impression (Gen. 1:28): "Grow and multiply." The Ten Commandments make no impression on them (Ex. 20:12): "Honor father and mother." Their own origin makes no impression on them, namely, that they were born as the result of the union of a man and a woman. Passing over, disregarding, and casting aside all these considerations, they force their priests, monks, and nuns into perpetual celibacy, as if the life of married people, of which Moses is speaking here, were detestable and reprehensible.

But the Holy Spirit has a purer mouth and purer eyes than the pope. For this reason He has no misgivings about referring to the

---

[1] The Nicolaitans were a Gnostic sect; Tatian, who lived in the second century, founded the Encratites, who regarded marriage as adultery.

copulation or sexual union of husband and wife, which those saints condemn as execrable and unclean. Nor does the Holy Spirit do this in only one passage. All Scripture is full of such accounts, so that on this score, too, some have restrained young monks and nuns from reading the holy books. What need is there of saying more? Such was the devil's raging against holy matrimony, God's creation, that the papists compelled men to forswear married life; they established orders with their celibate life; and they declared the life of married people detestable in comparison with their celibacy. This wickedness has not been without its punishments; for there are manifest examples of what fruits have come from the impure celibacy, and even in their books there exist traces of awful crimes.

St. Ulrich, Bishop of Augsburg, bears witness to the following account: [2] Pope Gregory wanted celibacy established and had prohibited the marital relation even for those who were already married prior to the decree concerning celibacy. By chance he wanted to have some fishing done in a pond he had in Rome, and in it more than 6,000 heads of infants were found. Moreover, the same Ulrich writes that in his intense dismay at the sight Gregory set aside his wicked directive. But the successors of Gregory readily suppressed both this hideous incident and the pious annulment of the decree concerning celibacy, since they judged that celibacy helped not only to provide them with wealth but also to gain prestige for them.

A similar example happened in our time.[3] The nuns in the Austrian village of Closter Neumberg were compelled to move to another place because of their disgraceful life, and the monastery was turned over to the Franciscans for occupancy. When the monks made alterations for their convenience in some of the buildings, twelve jars were discovered in the new cellars. Each jar contained the corpse of an infant.

Countless incidents of this kind have happened here and there. And so Gregory, as Bishop Ulrich relates, correctly made a neat change in Paul's statement: "Paul says: 'It is better to marry than to burn' (1 Cor. 7:9); but I add: 'It is better to marry than to provide an occasion for death.'"

[2] This apocryphal document is reprinted in Edmund Martene and Ursinus Durand (eds.), *Veterum scriptorum et monumentorum historicorum, dogmaticorum, moralium amplissima collectio*, I (Paris, 1724), col. 449—454.

[3] Luther recounts this story at greater length in his *Table Talk* (Weimar, *Tischreden*, VI, No. 6941).

In Rome monasteries were built because of the large number of exposed children whose father is said to be the pope, and they do walk closest before him in the public processions. I pass over in silence countless other facts which my mind shrinks from relating.

One should, therefore, guard against those doctrines of demons (1 Tim. 4:1) and learn to hold matrimony in honor and to speak with respect of this way of life. For we see that God instituted it, and we hear it praised in the Ten Commandments, where it is stated (Ex. 20:12): "Honor your father and your mother." And to this is added the blessing (Gen. 1:28): "Grow and multiply." About this we hear the Holy Spirit speaking here, and His mouth is chaste. But the vices and the ignominy, which through sin became attached to what God had created, we should not ridicule or laugh at; but we should cover them, just as we see God cover naked Adam and Eve with garments after their sin. Marriage should be treated with honor; from it we all originate, because it is a nursery not only for the state but also for the church and the kingdom of Christ until the end of the world.[4]

The heathen and other godless men do not understand this glory of marriage. They merely compile the weaknesses which exist both in the life of married people and in the female sex. They separate the unclean from the clean in such a manner that they retain the unclean, but what is clean they do not see. In this manner also some godless jurists pass a wicked judgment on this very book of Genesis and say that it contains nothing but the lewd activities of the Jews. If, in addition to this, there is a contempt of marriage and an impure celibacy, are not these men worthy of being exposed to the crimes and punishments of the people of Sodom? But let us disregard these men, and let us hear Moses.

It is not enough for the Holy Spirit to state: "Adam knew Eve"; but He also adds "his wife." For He does not approve of dissolute licentiousness and promiscuous cohabitation. He wants each one to live content with his own wife. Although the intimate relationship of married people is in no respect as pure as it would have been in the state of innocence, nevertheless, in the midst of that weakness brought on by lust and of all the rest of our misery, God's blessing persists. This is written here, not because of Adam and Eve (for they had long since been reduced to ashes when these words were written by Moses), but because of ourselves, so that those who cannot contain

---

[4] Cf. also *Luther's Works*, 21, p. 91, note 66.

themselves might live content with their own Eve and might not touch other women.

The expression "He knew his wife" is unique to Hebrew, for Latin and Greek do not express themselves in this way. However, it is a very apt expression, not only because of its chasteness and modesty but also because of its specific meaning; for the verb יָדַע has a wider scope than "to know" has among us. It denotes not only abstract knowledge but, so to speak, feeling and experience. For example, when Job says of the ungodly: "They will know what it is to act contrary to God," he wants to say: "They will experience and feel it." [5] So also Ps. 51:3: "For I know my sin," that is, "I feel and experience it." Likewise Gen. 22:12: "Now I know that you fear the Lord," that is: "I have learned the fact and have experienced it." So also Luke 1:34: "For I know no man." [6] Mary indeed knew many men, but she had experienced and felt no man. In this manner Adam, in this passage, knew Eve, his wife — not objectively or speculatively, but he actually experienced his Eve as a woman.

The addition, "And Eve conceived and bore Cain," is a sure indication of a better physical condition than there is today. For at that time there were not so many ineffective cohabitations as there are in this declining world; but when Eve was known only once by Adam, she immediately became pregnant.

Here the question arises why Moses says: "She bore Cain" and not rather, as below, "She bore her son Seth." Yet Cain and Abel were also sons. Why, then, are they not called sons? The answer is that this happens on account of their descendants. Abel, who was slain by his brother, perished physically; but Cain perished spiritually through his sin, and he did not propagate that nursery of the church and of the kingdom of Christ. All his posterity perished in the Flood. Therefore neither blessed Abel nor cursed Cain has the name of son; but it was Seth from whose descendants Christ, the promised Seed, would be born. And so Seth was the first who received the name of son.

And Eve said: I have gotten the man of the Lord.

From this statement another reason may be gathered why Eve did not call Cain a son, namely, that because of her excessive joy and reverence she was unwilling to call him son but had something

---

[5] Apparently either Job 9:5 or Job 19:29 is meant here.

[6] The original has "Luke 2."

greater in mind about him, as though Cain would be the man who would crush the head of the serpent. For this reason she does not simply call him a man, but "the man of the Lord," of whom the Lord God had promised (Gen. 3:15): "Your Seed will crush the head of the serpent." Although this was a false hope, it nevertheless is clear that Eve was a saintly woman and that she believed the promise concerning the future salvation through the blessed Seed. And because she believes, she is so happy about her son and speaks of him in such grand terms: "I have gotten the man of God who will conduct himself more properly and with greater good fortune than my Adam and I conducted ourselves in Paradise. For this reason I do not call him my son, but he is the man of God who was promised and provided by God." This also could have been the reason why she did not call Cain a son.

Eve does right in holding fast this way to the divine promise and to her faith in the deliverance through her son. Through this faith in the future Seed all the saints were justified and sanctified. But she is mistaken in the person; she believes that it will be Cain who will put an end to the misfortunes into which Satan had hurled mankind through sin, but she believes this on the strength of some opinion of her own, without a definite sign and without a definite Word. The promise indeed was definite and sure; but nothing had been indicated about the person, that either Cain or Abel would be that Victor over the serpent.

Therefore when Eve reaches a decision about the person, she errs, and vainly assigns so lofty and joyful a name to her son. The text points out that he was called Cain from the verb קָנָה, which denotes "to possess" or "to acquire," so that she might comfort herself by means of this name in the evils that they had met with and might set the winning of life and salvation through the Seed against the loss of life and salvation through sin and Satan. It is as if she were saying: "I remember what we have lost through sin. But now let our hope and speech be of nothing else except winning this back and keeping possession of it. For I have gotten the man of God who will obtain that lost glory for us again." Her extreme trust in the promise causes Eve to reach a hasty conclusion, and she believes that her first son is the one about whom the Lord had given His promise.

But the poor woman deceives herself. She does not yet fully realize her misfortune: that from the flesh nothing but flesh can be born (John 3:6), and that sin and death cannot be overcome by

flesh and blood. Then, too, she does not know the point in time when
the blessed Seed, conceived by the Holy Spirit, is to be born into the
world by a virgin. The patriarchs had no knowledge of this point of
time either, although the promise was made clearer and clearer
through the revelation of the Holy Spirit. Similarly, we know today
that there will be a Last Judgment; but the day and the hour we
do not know, as Christ also tells His apostles in Acts 1:7.

2. *And she gave birth again — to his brother Abel.*

It is impossible to know for sure whether Cain and Abel were
twins or not, although it is rather likely that they were twins. Whatever the case may be, diverse thoughts arose in our first parents after
the birth of these two sons, and they believed that their redemption
was very close at hand. Moreover, without a doubt Cain was very
highly regarded and considered the favorite; but Abel was not so
acceptable, nor was so great a hope attached to him, as the very
names show. Cain is called Cain as if he were the one who would
restore everything; by contrast, Abel means vanity and something
that is worthless or cast aside. Some have rendered it in our Bibles
by "sorrow," but the word for sorrow is אֵבֶל, not הֶבֶל. Moreover,
הֶבֶל is of very common occurrence in the Holy Scriptures; for how
often is it repeated in Ecclesiastes: "Vanity of vanities, and all is
vanity"! And in Ps. 78:33 we read: "Their days wasted away in
vanity," that is, they did not obtain the promise of the land of Canaan.

Thus he to whom no hope attached, or only a futile one, is called
Abel; but he from whom everything is hoped is called Cain. So the
very names reveal clearly enough the thoughts and sentiments of
the parents. Since the promise concerned a seed, Adam and Eve
thought that it was to be fulfilled through Cain. But they supposed
that after his brother had brought his entire undertaking to a happy
conclusion, Abel would accomplish nothing; and so they call him הֶבֶל.

Moreover, this hope was undoubtedly the reason why these
brothers were not brought up with the same care and diligence. Abel
was given charge of the cattle, but Cain was directed to his father's
tasks in the cultivation of the soil as the better occupation. Abel is
the shepherd; Cain, as the first-born son, is king and priest, who was
born into the glorious hope of the restoration of all things (Acts 3:21).

But consider at this point God's wonderful design. From the
beginning of the world primogeniture was a matter of the utmost
importance, not only among the people where the right of primo-

geniture was established by God Himself and was given honor but
also among the heathen. And yet, particularly among the holy people,
actual experience proves that first-born sons disappointed the hope
of their parents and that those who were born later assumed their
place, rank, and prestige.

How bitterly Cain, the murderer, thus disappointed the hope of
our first parents! Abraham, too, was not the first-born son; Haran
was. Esau is the first-born son, but the blessing passes on to his
brother Jacob. David was the youngest among his brothers, and yet
he is anointed king. So it was also in the case of others. Although by
divine right the first-born enjoyed the prerogative of rule and priesthood, nevertheless they lost it, and those who were born later were
given preference over them.

How did this abnormal situation arise? It was unquestionably due
both to the fault of the parents and to the personal haughtiness of
the first-born son. The parents regarded their first-born sons as something distinguished. Then the first-born sons themselves were spoiled
in this way by the indulgence of their parents. Relying on their right,
they despised and lorded it over their brothers. But God is the God
of the humble; He gives grace to the humble and resists the proud
(1 Peter 5:5). Because they are proud, the first-born sons are deprived
of their right, not because they did not have the right of primogeniture
but because they begin to be proud of their gifts and become conceited. This God cannot bear.

Similarly, when the angels in heaven who were endowed above
others with the best and most beautiful gifts began to be proud and
despised the humility of the Son of God, they were hurled into hell
and became most hideous devils.[7] For God cannot bear pride; He
wants His majesty to be respected and unimpaired everywhere, just
as He declares in the prophets (Is. 48:11): "My glory I shall not give
to another."

The nation of Israel was God's possession, and the holy city of
Jerusalem was God's dwelling place. But when the people had given
up their fear of God and, relying on their gifts, were becoming proud,
the nation was destroyed, and their city was laid waste by the heathen.
This is the universal bane of our nature, that we are not satisfied
with God's gifts but abuse them and thus mock their Donor and
Creator. Now God bestows empires and kingdoms, peace and other

---

[7] Cf. p. 23, note 37.

gifts in order that kings and princes might acknowledge Him, worship Him, and give thanks to Him. But kings and princes abuse these gifts as though He had given them in order that they might despise their Creator and generous Giver.

The same thing happens in the family. The purpose for which God gives us good health, wife, children, and property is not that we might offend Him by means of these gifts, but that we might recognize His mercy and give thanks to Him. For this reason He has granted us the enjoyment and, as it were, the rule of almost all the creatures. But how few there are who do this! Do not almost all of us live in the most shocking abuse of the gifts of God? He is, therefore, compelled to employ the same remedy that Vespasian employed.[8] Vespasian calmly allowed his citizens and courtiers to become rich; for he used to say that rich men are like a sponge which, after being filled with water, gives it off in abundance when vigorously squeezed. In the same way God again reduces those whom He has enriched with His gifts when they are unthankful and misuse His kindness. As the Blessed Virgin says (Luke 1:53): "The rich He has sent empty away."

This, then, is the reason why God does not spare Cain, the first-born. He did not give primogeniture to Cain that he might become proud because of it and despise God. He had given him this adornment that he might worship and fear God. When Cain does not do this, God casts him aside.

The sin of the parents, too, plays a part; they give their support to this pride, as the names clearly indicate. Adam and Eve place their hope in their first-born son alone; him they call their treasure. But Abel, they feel, is nothing and will never amount to anything. Cain they adorn like a king, for they regard him as the blessed Seed. Therefore they promise themselves grand achievements from him, and he himself on his part acts proudly. Abel they disregard as a worthless person.

But God reverses all this: Cain He casts aside, and Abel He makes an angel and the first among all the saints. When Abel is slain by his brother, he becomes the first to be freed from sin and from the misfortunes of this world; and throughout the entire later church he shines like a brilliant star through the distinguished testimony concerning righteousness which God and all Scripture gives him.

---

[8] Suetonius, *Lives of the Caesars*, VIII, 16 (Vespasian).

Thus Abel — whom Adam, Eve, and Cain despise as a worthless person — is given a position before God as lord of heaven and earth. After his death he is in a better state than if he possessed a thousand worlds with all their goods.

This is the end of pride and arrogance over against God. Cain put his trust in his primogeniture; he despised his brother, and he did not believe the promise concerning Christ. Abel, on the contrary, by faith took hold of the promise given to Adam concerning the Seed; and this faith is also the reason why he offered a better sacrifice than Cain, as the Epistle to the Hebrews states (Heb. 11:4).

And Abel was a shepherd, but Cain was a husbandman.

Just as the names do, so the occupation to which each is directed by his parents reveals the parents' glorious hope concerning Cain. Although each pursuit is honorable, nevertheless Abel's is concerned with the home only; but Cain's has to do with the government. Because Adam was a husbandman, he trains Cain, for whom he has the greater love, for his father's occupation. To Abel meanwhile is assigned the chore of tending the flock, so that it might appear that the latter is regarded by his parents as a servant, the former as a lord.

3. *And it happened at the end of days that Cain brought an offering of the fruit of the earth to the Lord.*

"At the end of days," that is, after some years have passed. In the first place, we are reminded here that Adam and Eve, as pious parents, preached often and much to their children about the will and worship of God, inasmuch as both bring an offering to God. But you will ask: "What, or about what subject, did they preach?" Assuredly they had the most excellent themes for sacred discourses. They made mention of their first state and of Paradise, and without a doubt they often showed their children the place which was being guarded by the angels. Moreover, they urged them to guard against sin, through which they had been stripped and robbed of so many good things. On the other hand, they admonished them to live in the fear of God, so that they might find comfort in His kindness; then it would happen that after this life they would receive a better one. Moreover, who could count up all the benefits of their earlier life? To this they added the second part of their instruction, namely, that which dealt with the promise of the Seed and the future deliverance out of these misfortunes. Perhaps the pious parents delivered these discourses before their children in a definite place and particularly on the Sabbath. By these sermons, accordingly, the children were prompted to bring sacrifices and to worship God.

And here is the first passage of Scripture where mention is made of מִנְחָה, or an offering. From this it appears that the custom of offering and of sacrificing sacrificial animals was not something new but existed from the beginning of the world. It is, therefore, nothing remarkable that the procedure at the sacrifices, which was continued from Adam onward to the time of Moses and was passed on, as it were, from hand to hand, was later on separated by Moses into its various kinds and put into some definite order after he had removed and discarded many features the empty superstition of men had added. Thus there appear also in Homer and Vergil examples of pagan sacrifices, which, without a doubt, the pagans had taken over from their fathers and imitated, adding to them through their superstition.[9]

But in connection with this passage let the reader ponder the following, above all: Adam and Eve are not only parents, nor do they merely provide for their children and educate them for this present life; but they also perform the office of priests. Inasmuch as they are filled with the Holy Spirit and are enlightened by the knowledge of Christ, who is to come, they set before their children this very hope of a future deliverance and exhort them to show their gratitude to so merciful a God. It is evident that the sacrifices which were handed down had no other purpose.

Consider, I beg you, what sort of pupils such pious and excellent teaching gains. Here there are two kinds of hearers. Cain, the first-born, who appears to be saintly and believes that he is a lord, is wicked and does not believe the divine promise. Abel, on the other hand, who has no prestige and is thrust aside to tend cattle, is godly and believes. Nevertheless, the wicked Cain covers up his wickedness both by listening to the instruction of his parents as if he took a profound interest in the Word and by bringing an offering just as the other, godly brother does. This is an example of the twofold church, the true and the hypocritical one, as we shall show at greater length in another place.[10] Moreover, although in this passage mention

[9] Cf. p. 4, note 5.
[10] See pp. 252—255.

is made only of the sacrifice and not of the preaching, it must nevertheless be maintained that they did not offer a sacrifice without the
preaching of the Word. For God is not worshiped by means of
a speechless work; the work must be accompanied by the Word which
rings in the hearts of men and in the ears of God. Thus calling upon
the name of God also accompanied this sacrifice.

But at this point the question is raised whether they had a word
or command to sacrifice. I answer yes. For all the sacred accounts
give proof that by His superabundant grace our merciful God always
placed some outward and visible sign of His grace alongside the
Word, so that men, reminded by the outward sign and work or
Sacrament, would believe with greater assurance that God is kind
and merciful. Thus after the Flood the rainbow appeared in order
to serve as a convincing proof that in the future God would not give
vent to His wrath against the world by a similar punishment. To Abraham, as we shall hear, circumcision was given, so that he might firmly
believe that God would be his God and that He would give him
the Seed in whom all the nations would be blessed. To us in the
New Testament, Baptism and the Eucharist have been given as the
visible signs of grace, so that we might firmly believe that our sins
have been forgiven through Christ's suffering and that we have been
redeemed by His death. Thus the church has never been deprived
to such an extent of outward signs that it became impossible to
know where God could surely be found.

Moreover, even though the world in general follows Cain's
example and misuses the signs of grace for hypocrisy, nevertheless
God's mercy in revealing Himself to us by such various ways is surely
inexpressible, just as Prov. 8:30 also bestows glorious praise on this
very gift: "I was delighted every day, playing before Him, playing
in the world, and My delight was with the children of men." But
the Hebrew verb שׂחק is incorrectly reproduced by the word "play."
What Wisdom is saying is that Its concern was for men and that It
revealed Itself to them. It is as if It were to say: "I have always displayed Myself to the eyes and ears of men in such a way that they
could become aware of My presence in the sacrifices, in circumcision,
in burning incense, in the cloud, in the Red Sea, in the manna, in
the brazen serpent, in the tabernacle of Moses, in the temple of
Solomon, and in the cloud. And it was My delight to display and
reveal Myself in this manner to the children of men."

It was a great comfort for Adam that, after he had lost Paradise, the tree of life, and the other privileges which were signs of grace, there was given to him another sign of grace, namely, the sacrifices, by which he could perceive that he had not been cast off by God but was still the object of God's concern and regard. This is what God was indicating when He kindled and consumed the sacrifices and offerings with fire from heaven, as we read about the sacrifice of Moses (Lev. 9:24) and of Elijah (1 Kings 18:38). These were true manifestations of the divine mercy which the wretched people needed in order not to be without some light of the grace of God.

In the same way the very Word, Baptism, and the Eucharist are our lightbearers today, toward which we look as dependable tokens of the sun of grace. We can state with certainty that where the Eucharist, Baptism, and the Word are, there are Christ, forgiveness of sins, and eternal life. Contrariwise, where these signs of grace are not present, or where they are despised by men, there is not only no grace, but execrable errors follow, and men set up for themselves other forms of worship and other signs. Thus the Greeks worshiped Apollo, and others worshiped other demons; the Egyptians worshiped Anubis, Serapis, crocodiles, garlic, and the onion; the Romans worshiped Jupiter, Quirinus, and those execrable images, Priapus, Venus, etc.[11]

The same thing happened in the papacy. After those genuine signs of grace began to be regarded with indifference and were despised, superstition could not remain inactive but sought other signs: vows, orders, pilgrimages, intercessions by the saints, and other things. All these devices are full of errors and are linked with wickedness, and yet poor human beings embrace them as genuine signs of divine grace. In these matters you hear no bishop and no school loudly disavowing these blasphemies and teaching things that are sounder. When the light of the Word and these signs of grace which have been given by God have been lost, men run, of necessity, after the desires of their hearts. Thus after despising the tabernacle and the temple, the Jews brought their sacrifices under trees and in groves, until in the end inhuman parents sacrificed their own children.

These varied and dissolute practices of idolatry prove how great a gift it is to have the Word and those signs of grace which God has pointed out and commanded. But if the heathen had been willing

---

[11] Cf. also *Luther's Works*; 22, p. 25.

to walk in the footsteps of the Jews, they would never have sunk to those monstrous practices. Nor would the Jews ever have had anything to do with those blasphemous rites if they had given heed to the Word. If we ourselves had appreciated Baptism and the holy Eucharist as we should, we would not have become monks, and nothing would have been taught in the church about purgatory, about the sacrifice of the Mass, and about other wicked things. But after the light of the Word had been put out by wicked popes, it was easy to force these abominations upon men.

Therefore this gift is something inexpressible: that God not only deigns to speak to men through the Word but adds to the Word visible signs of grace, such as Baptism, the Eucharist, and absolution are in the New Testament. Those who despise these, or treat them with contempt, are worthy of purchasing, adoring, and praising the pope's excrement as balsam. Why do they despise the goodness of the Divine Majesty? They could have the most reliable sign of grace in their own house without expense and without any exertion. But since they despise it, they go to Rome, Compostella, etc.; [12] they use up their money, torture their bodies, and at last deservedly lose their souls. Eternal thanks be to God, who today through His Word has called us back from these uncurbed errors and idolatrous practices and has so richly given us the signs of His grace that we can have them before our doors, yes, even in our houses and in our beds.

In order to reinforce the promise of our salvation, God had this in mind from the very beginning of the world: Men were to have signs by means of which they might comfort themselves in their sins and gain courage through their reliance on divine grace. It is not the worth of the work itself that is of value in the sacrifice; it is the mercy and power of the divine promise, because God prescribes this form of worship and promises that it will be pleasing to Him. Therefore what Baptism and the Lord's Supper are for us, sacrifice and offering was for Adam after the promise. God revealed His grace in the sacrifices and gave His approval of them by kindling and consuming them with fire.

Moreover, the father gave instructions to his sons concerning these forms of worship so that in this manner they might thank God, praise God, and gain a sure hope of God's mercy. But the wicked Cain, puffed up by his prestige of primogeniture, despises these most excel-

12 Cf. *Luther's Works*, 22, p. 250, note 37.

lent discourses of his father. In accordance with his father's command, he indeed brings an offering. But since he is puffed up because of the delusion of his saintliness, he is convinced that God will give His approval to the work itself because of the prestige of the person. But Abel, who in accordance with his name, is nothing in his own eyes, also brings an offering; but he does so in the faith of the promise, as the Epistle to the Hebrews states (Heb. 11:4).

4. *But Abel, too, brought of the firstlings of his flock and of their fat.*

If you look at the work itself, you cannot prefer Abel to Cain. The Jews, in their folly, have a silly idea when they dream that Cain did not offer selected grain but chaff, and that for this reason he was rejected by God.[13] From them this is to be expected, for they act as judges and pay attention only to works. But the verdict of the Epistle to the Hebrews is different; it declares that because of his faith Abel brought the more excellent offering (Heb. 11:4). And so the fault lay not in the materials which were offered but in the person of him who brought the offering. The faith of the individual was the weight which added value to Abel's offering, but Cain spoiled his offering. Abel believes that God is good and merciful. For this reason his sacrifice is pleasing to God. Cain, on the contrary, puts his trust in the prestige of his primogeniture; but he despises his brother as an insignificant and worthless being. What, then, is God's decision? He gives to the first-born the position of one born later, and to the one born later He gives the position of the first-born. He looks toward Abel's offering and shows that the sacrifice of this priest pleases Him, but that Cain does not please Him and is not a true priest.

The word "he looked," שָׁעָה, has a wide meaning, and I carefully explained this in my writing against Latomus.[14] It occurs in Isaiah (17:7-8): "In that day a man will look to his Maker, and he will not look to the altars which are the work of his hands." Likewise in 66:12: "Upon their knees they will fondle you." Here it refers to the fact that when a mother has her child on her lap, she shows it a cheerful and sweet face. Such a showing or display is what this verb denotes. And so it has a wider meaning than the verb "to look." For when a mother looks at her child, at the same time she also smiles at it and

13 The source of this is Lyra on Gen. 4:3.

14 Luther had treated this in his *Refutation of Latomus* of 1521 (Weimar, VIII, 86).

by her facial expression conveys a special indication of her love. Our native language has no word by which this can be fully expressed; nor, so far as I know, is there one in the Latin language.

Somewhat similar in meaning is Moses' statement (Ex. 33:15): "Unless Thy face goes before us, we shall go nowhere"; that is: "Let us always have Thy signs among us by which Thou dost appear and indicate Thy presence and good will." Such signs, as I said above, were the pillar of fire, the clouds, etc. Although in this passage Moses does not explicitly state by what sort of sign God showed that Abel's offerings were pleasing to Him, it is nevertheless likely that it was fire sent from heaven which encompassed and consumed the sacrifice before the eyes of all. From this it appeared that God delighted in Abel's conduct. Moreover, God here makes it clear that He judges the hearts and reins. He does not look at the distinction of primogeniture in Cain; instead, He looks at the heart of despised Abel.

Moreover, here the church begins to be divided into two churches: the one which is the church in name but in reality is nothing but a hypocritical and bloodthirsty church; and the other one, which is without influence, forsaken, and exposed to suffering and the cross, and which before the world and in the sight of that hypocritical church is truly Abel, that is, vanity and nothing. For Christ also calls Abel righteous and makes him the beginning of the church of the godly, which will continue until the end (Matt. 23:35). Similarly, Cain is the beginning of the church of the wicked and of the bloodthirsty until the end of the world. Augustine treats this story in a similar way in his book *The City of God*.[15]

It is both very instructive and very comforting to trace each of the two churches from these men as the originators and to note by what a marvelous plan God has always directed their affairs. At one time the true church was the greater; at another time it was the smaller — yet always in such a manner that the hypocritical and bloodthirsty church enjoyed honor before the world and crucified the church which was the true one and was loved by God. Even then the divine promise began to work itself out, in that the serpent's seed bit the heel of the blessed Seed (Gen. 3:15), just as we experience today. Therefore this lot should not frighten us. It should rather be a source of comfort for us to learn from experience that we are being dealt with by our adversaries in the way bloodthirsty Cain dealt with righteous Abel.

[15] Augustine, *The City of God*, XV, ch. 7.

We today are not the first to whom it happens that we are deprived of the name "church," that we are called heretics, and that those who kill us pride themselves on being the true and only church and maintain their claim to this name with the sword and with every sort of cruelty. The same thing happened to righteous Abel and also to our Lord Christ, who was not a priest or a king in Jerusalem but was driven to the cross by the priests and rulers. But, as Paul says, we must be conformed to Christ (Rom. 8:29). Therefore the true church is hidden; it is banned; it is regarded as heretical; it is slain. But Cain has a glorious name; he alone has a reputation; he gives promise of great things to come. For this reason his hostile heart impels him to fall upon his brother and slay him.

These things pertain neither to the state nor to the household; they pertain primarily to the church. Abel is slain, not because of his activity in the state or in the household but because of his worship of God. For Cain it is not enough that he is the lord of the house; he also wants to be the Son of God; he wants to be the pope and the father of the church. Therefore he appropriates to himself the right to pass judgment on the sacrifices, and he condemns and slays his brother as a heretic.

Similarly, Christ also foretells that His church will be exposed to sundry dangers and that those who slay the godly will regard themselves as performing a service to God (John 16:2). Accordingly, those who want to be the most saintly are the bane and the persecutors of the church. The true church is not regarded as the church; but, in harmony with the name Abel (who is not only a figure of the true church but its beginning), it is considered so worthless that its slayers believe that God does not care about it. Cain is the lord and ruler who does everything and has the power to do everything.

But this is the offense against which we must contend. We dare not come to believe that we are not the church because our adversaries condemn us with such assurance and pursue us with every kind of cruelty; but we must gain the conviction that the cross and those verdicts are true and infallible signs of the true church, as Ps. 10:14 also indicates. Also Ps. 72:14: "Their blood will be regarded precious in His sight," and Ps. 116:15: "Precious in the sight of the Lord is the death of His saints." [16] In these passages you hear that when people are slain in this manner, this does not mean that they are of no concern to God, but that this death is precious in the sight

[16] The original has "Ps. 117."

of God. Therefore they are truly the people of God, on whom God bestows His care.

Let us, therefore, endure the cruelty of our adversaries and joyfully give thanks to God that we are not among the number of those who kill and, under the pretense of being the church, fall upon and seize the possessions of others and give vent to their cruel fury also on their bodies. For the history of every age bears witness to this: that the true church always endured hardships; but that it was the false church which carried on persecutions, while the true church was always condemned by that other hypocritical one. Therefore there is no doubt among us today that the church of the pope is the church of Cain. We, however, are the true church. Just as Abel did no harm to Cain, so we, too, not only do no harm to them but allow ourselves to be harassed, condemned, and slain by the pope's church.

Nor are these statements contrary to the truth. It is known to the entire world how often we were excommunicated, harassed by being declared outlaws, and found guilty by sundry verdicts. Nor was there in almost any region of Europe any lack of those who proved themselves passionate executors of the cruel sentences. Spain, France, England, Belgium, Bohemia, Poland, Hungary, Austria, and Bavaria were not exempt from this cruelty and unrighteous fury.[17] Yet what else did they persecute except the doctrine which is godly and in agreement with the writings of the apostles and the prophets? The verdict as to which is the true church cannot be uncertain, can it? You are not of the opinion, are you, that the church is there where no sound doctrine is to be found, where an unjust tyranny is exerted and very great power is linked with wealth? Or is the church rather to be found where there is doctrine beneficial to consciences and where, on account of this doctrine, there are the cross, contempt, poverty, shame, etc., which the small flock of the godly always endured, as history records?

It is, therefore, not only something useful but also a source of delight to have in one's possession this most convincing evidence which points out the distinction between the two churches: the one, that of the malevolent, namely, the purple-clad harlot going by the name of the true church; and the other, the one which is regarded as nothing and suffers, hungers, thirsts, and lies oppressed, just as

17 Cf. p. 288, note 45.

Christ declares in Matt. 25:35 that He Himself hungered and thirsted in this world. But there is a judgment coming between the full and the hungry, between the goats and the sheep, and between Abel and Cain. In it God will announce His approval of that suffering and hungering church, and also His condemnation of the hypocritical and bloodthirsty one. This is our comfort and, as it were, the sugar with which our present hardships must be flavored and overcome. These thoughts belong into the field of theology. Let us now return to the affairs of the world, and let us consider God's verdict.

Justifiably indeed we wonder why God allowed Adam's first son, on whom destiny bestowed primogeniture among all the human race so far as his birth was concerned, to experience so awful a fall that later on all his descendants were destroyed by the Flood. But the reason is the same as the one because of which, as we stated above,[18] Adam was mocked by God with such bitter words when He said: "Lest he become like one of Us," and when He guarded the garden with cherubim (Gen. 3:22-24). God wants to crush the arrogance and pride which has been implanted, as it were, into man's heart by sin. But we are so constituted that we can endure nothing less readily than this crushing of our pride. We observe how conceited and supercilious the clowns at court are because of the meaningless nobility of their lineage. Truly meaningless is any nobility which is not the product of valor and of outstanding service to the state.

Moreover, historians relate about the philosopher Plato that he was accustomed to thank God for three things: that he was born a human being and not an animal, that he was a Greek born at Athens and not a barbarian, and that he was born a man and not a woman.[19] Of a similar nature is the foolish idea of the Jews, who pride themselves that they were born as human beings and not as beasts, as Jews and not as Gentiles, as males and not as females. But, I ask you, what do those boasts of descent or birth amount to? What does it amount to that some ass at court who wears a necklace not only considers himself better than the common man but also displays his arrogance against God? The Greeks looked down on all the other people of the earth as barbarians in comparison with themselves, but by their glorious achievements the Romans in the end cleared themselves of

[18] We have adopted the emendation suggested by the Weimar editors, reading: *propter quam, ut supra diximus;* the reference is to p. 222.

[19] This may be a summary of the argument in Book V of Plato's *Republic.*

the censure of being barbarians. In short, the more each nation regarded itself as superior, the more overweening it became. This lies in the nature of all men because of sin.

But look at God's verdict here. Cain could properly and truthfully take pride in his very high nobility, for he was the first to be born of men. Yet the more glorious his origin was, the more terrible was his fall. Accordingly, human experience has been expressed in the proverb which declares that "the sons of outstanding men turn out badly."

Nor do these reverses affect individuals only; great empires experience them too. The nation of the Greeks was most outstanding, for they ranked high both because of their glorious history and because of their scientific pursuits. But to what disgraceful conditions did the country decline and how pitifully was it laid waste! You will observe the same disasters in the rest of the nations.

Therefore God acted properly when He permitted Cain to fall this way as an example for the entire world, so that no one might boast of the nobility of his blood, as the Jews pride themselves on their father Abraham or the Greeks on their wisdom. God wants to be feared; He wants us to be kept humble. But His desire to achieve this is almost without result; for neither the manifestations of His great wrath nor the corruption and the annihilation of the first human beings and of the first nations have an effect on us.

Accordingly, experience attests the truth of the statement of the Virgin Mary (Luke 1:52): "He has put down the mighty from their seat." The things that are first and best become the most damnable, not simply because of their intrinsic nature but because of devilish arrogance and pride. The pagans, too, were aware of this ultimate outcome, as the philosopher's saying proves. When he had been asked what God was doing, he replied: "What is humble, He exalts; and what is exalted, He humbles." [20] But they were not aware of the reason.

In the estimation of the flesh it is a great glory to be a male and not a female. But we observe that God has carefully avoided that a man should be born of a man; even Christ Himself wanted to be called the Seed of a woman, not the Seed of a man. Yet how great would the pride of the men have been if God had willed that Christ should be brought forth by a man! But this glory has been completely

[20] A parallel to Prov. 3:34.

taken from the men and assigned to the women (who nevertheless are subject to the rule of the men) so that the men should not become vainglorious but be humble. Since a woman obviously cannot bear children without a man, God has so arranged it that women give birth not only to males but also to females. Human nature is unable to apply to good advantage any glory which it has; it always misuses this glory to bring on pride, and it rebels against Him from whom it has received its gifts. The fact that Cain falls in such a distressing manner and loses his right of primogeniture serves as a warning for us. We should fear God, and, while giving thanks to Him, we should not misuse His gifts to become proud.

4. *And the Lord had regard for Abel and his offering,*

5. *but for Cain and his offering He had no regard.*

This is an outstanding passage. Therefore it must be carefully taken note of and methodically studied. It would be sufficient if the New Testament had a statement praising the trust in God's mercy over against the trust in works as clearly as it is praised here at the beginning of the world. When Moses says: "The Lord had regard for Abel and for his offering," does he not clearly indicate that God is wont to look at the individual rather than at the work, to see what sort of individual he is? If, then, the individual is good, his work also pleases Him; but if the individual is not good, his work displeases Him.

This is the essence of our teaching. We teach and confess that a person rather than his work is accepted by God and that a person does not become righteous as a result of a righteous work, but that a work becomes righteous and good as a result of a righteous and good person, just as the text here proves. Because God has regard for Abel, He has regard also for his offering; and because He has no regard for Cain, He has no regard for his offering either. The text gives clear support to this conclusion, and this cannot be denied by our opponents. Moreover, there follows from these words the very clear and very valid conclusion that Abel, rather than his work, was righteous and that the work pleases because of the person, not the person because of his work. The latter is what our adversaries maintain when they teach that a man is justified through his works and not by faith alone.

Thus the author of the Epistle to the Hebrews has looked at this passage with pure and clear eyes when he says (Heb. 11:4):

"By faith Abel offered a more excellent sacrifice than Cain, by which he obtained witness that he was righteous, God bearing witness concerning his gifts." Cain also brings an offering, and indeed first; but when he brings his offering, he is puffed up by the glory which was his by birth, and he hopes that the sacrifice will please God because it is brought by the first-born. Thus he comes without faith, without any confession of sin, without any supplication for grace, without trust in God's mercy, without any prayer for the forgiveness of his sins. He comes in the hope that he will please God by nothing else than that he is the first-born. All the work-righteous do the same thing even now. They are concerned only with their own work, and so they hope that they will please God because of it; they do not trust in God's mercy, and they do not hope that God will pardon their sins because of Christ. Cain, too, was such a person, for he could not have displeased God if he had had faith.

Abel, on the other hand, acknowledges that he is an unworthy and poor sinner. Therefore he takes refuge in God's mercy and believes that God is gracious and willing to show compassion. And so God, who looks at the heart, judges between the two brothers who are bringing their offerings at the same time. He rejects Cain, not because his sacrifice was inferior (for if he had brought the shell of a nut in faith as a sacrifice, it would have been pleasing to God), but because his person was evil, without faith, and full of pride and conceit. By contrast, He has regard for Abel's sacrifice because He is pleased with the person. Accordingly, the text distinctly adds that first He had regard for Abel and then for his sacrifice. For when a person pleases, the things he does also please, while, on the contrary, all things are displeasing if you dislike the person who does them.

Therefore this passage is an outstanding and clear proof that God does not have regard for either the size or the quantity or even for the value of the work, but simply for the faith of the individual. Similarly, by contrast, God does not despise the smallness, the lack of value, or the lowly nature of a work, but only a person's lack of faith.

Therefore of what importance is it that the Jews boast (Jer. 7:4): "The temple of the Lord, the temple of the Lord"? Of what importance is it that the papists extol their Masses, their sackcloth garments, their hardships, their toils, and the size, the quantity, and finally the value of their works? God is not interested in works, not even in those which He Himself has commanded, when they are not done in faith, as the passage of Jeremiah just quoted shows. He is even less interested in the works which have been invented by men without a Word of God; He is interested in faith alone, that is, the reliance on His mercy through Christ. Through it people begin to please God, and after that their works also please Him. Thus Cain's offering did not please because the unbelieving Cain did not please. On the other hand, Abel's offering pleased because Abel pleased; and this was so because of his faith, since it did not rely on his own worthiness, his sacrifices, or his work, but on the plain promise which had been given about the woman's Seed.

Accordingly, this text has to do with our conviction concerning justification, namely, that a human being, rather than his works, must be just, and that he is accepted by God without any works, solely through grace, which faith believes and apprehends. Nor does faith, as a work, make just; but it makes just because it apprehends the mercy which is offered in Christ. The true church walks in this trust in God's mercy, together with a humble confession of its sins and unworthiness, which hopes that God will grant His pardon through Christ.

But the works which follow are evidences, as it were, of this faith; they please God, not simply on their own account but because of faith or because of the believing person. This faith the other church, namely, that of Cain, not only does not have but even persecutes. Moreover, just like Cain, it maintains that it will please God because of its works. But God hates this pride, for He cannot bear the contempt of His grace. This passage is altogether worthy of careful consideration.

Therefore Cain became very angry, and his face fell.

Matters of language will cause us a little trouble in the words which now follow; but I hope that we shall find our way successfully out of these difficulties. We have heard that Cain was disappointed in his hope. He despised his brother in comparison with himself and concluded that because of the privilege of primogeniture he would have first place also with God, just as he had with his parents. But God's verdict is a different one from that of men; He shows that He approves of Abel but disapproves of Cain.

And so it happens that Cain becomes intensely incensed against

his brother. He cannot take it calmly that he is put out of the church
and at the same time is deprived of rule and priesthood. We observe
similarly that up to the present time kings and princes are most
intolerant of the church's censure. It is not enough for them to be
kings and princes; but they also want to be righteous and saints
before God, and they usurp the title "church." In the same way Cain,
too, is filled with resentment when he sees that he is being deprived
of the glory of righteousness and grace before God. Is this anything
else than being cast out and excommunicated from the church? This
bothers him all the more because of his high opinion of himself in
comparison with his brother. For now the thought arises: "Behold,
my brother is aiming at the lordship after he sees me despised and
disregarded by God." For this reason Moses adds the adverb "very";
it indicates that Cain is violently insulted because he is so shamefully
disgraced in public when he himself wants to appear to have the
first place.

This wrath of Cain we also observe in the Cainite church of the
pope. What irritates the pope, the cardinals, kings, and princes more
than that I, a beggar, give preference over their authority to the
authority of God and in the name of the Lord reprove what deserves
reproof? Even they themselves acknowledge that there are many
things which are in need of a thoroughgoing reformation.[21] But that
an inconspicuous human being, and one who stepped out of an inconspicuous nook into public life, should carry this out — this is something
utterly unbearable for them. Therefore they oppose us with their
authority and attempt to overwhelm us by means of it.

Indeed, no wrath in the entire world is more cruel than that of
this bloodthirsty and hypocritical church. Where the government
shows its wrath, there is still something left of human emotion.
No bandit, be he ever so brutal, is led to execution without people
being touched by some compassion. But when that false and bloodthirsty church falls upon a son of the true church, it is not enough for
it to have shed his blood; it also slanders him, curses him, declares
him damned, and rages against his poor corpse. The Jews were not
satisfied either when they had nailed Christ to the cross, from which
they were not going to release Him until He was dead; but when
He was thirsty, they gave Him vinegar and gall to drink and uttered
blasphemies against Him when He was already at the point of

---

[21] Cf. the quotations in *Luther's Works*, 13, p. 352, notes 2 and 3.

death. Such violent passion is not encountered in the wrath of the government.

Accordingly, the wrath and pharisaical fury of the false church is clearly a devilish fury. It had its beginning in Cain and continues in all the children of Cain. We can truly glory in enduring such wrath in company with the godly Abel. If the bishops and some rabid princes could kill all of us in a single moment and if, as that notorious Roman wished, all of us had one neck,[22] who has any doubt that they would wield the sword against us with the greatest pleasure? Consider the plots hatched in recent years, and you will conclude that I am speaking the truth.[23]

But Moses' added statement, "And his face fell," is a Hebrew expression. It describes not only an act but also a mind so aroused that it could not come to rest; while it was unable to inflict harm, it nevertheless displayed its anger in the countenance. Cain was not friendly, nor did he speak in a kindly manner with his parents as formerly. If he had to give an answer, it was more likely to be a growl than a word. At the first sight of his brother he turned pale, and with his threatening eyes he revealed a heart burning with a desire for vengeance.

All this is what Moses says when he states that Cain's countenance fell. He is not speaking of only one expression on Cain's face or of one part of the expression on his face, but of all the expressions on his face, that is, all the gestures and movements. Similarly, Paul also, in imitation of the Hebrew expression, says ἡ ἀγάπη οὐκ ἀσχημονεῖ (1 Cor. 13:5), that is, love does not assume a grim appearance, stellet sich nicht ungeberdig, does not contract its brow, does not cast angry looks, does not threaten with the mouth, but has a noble face, kindly eyes, is prepossessing, etc. For these expressions of the face are becoming, but the others are unbecoming and scandalous.

Therefore this bit of the text also serves to describe Cain's hypocritical anger: that he could neither see nor hear his brother Abel and could not converse, eat, or drink with him.

If you wish to observe an example of this Cainlike wrath, then associate with some papist who desires to gain in his generation an outstanding reputation either for his doctrine or for his piety; and you will become fully aware of the diabolical madness, compared with

[22] Cf. Suetonius, Lives of the Caesars, IV, 28 (Gaius Caligula).

[23] See Luther's Works, 22, p. 412.

which you will say that a judge's wrath is not wrath but the utmost clemency and the utmost fairness. In this instance there is no wrath except that of judicial authority; for it is directed at the crime, not at the person. But that wrath of the Cainites distorts the eyes, wrinkles the brow, puffs up the mouth, and supplies the hands with weapons. In short, it manifests itself in all parts of the body and in every gesture, and does so without end; for it does not abate in time as does wrath in the community or in the home.

Now follows Adam's fatherly and very stern admonition. He would gladly have brought his son to his senses and preserved him from harm. But this wrath recognizes no cure: Cain and the Cainites do not listen to father, to mother, or to God Himself.

6. *And the Lord said to Cain: Why are you so angry, and why has your countenance fallen?*

These words give adequate proof that Cain was in an agitated frame of mind, not only at the time of his sacrifice, but that from that hour he walked about restlessly, sadly, gnashing his teeth, and without looking steadfastly at either father or mother. We similarly stated about the pharisaical wrath that it is wont to change the entire expression of the face. For Cain considered it a great disgrace that at the sacred rite, in sight of his father and mother, God gave preference to Abel, whom he had always despised and whom his parents also had regarded as nothing, and declared him to be worthy of the honor of sovereignty and priesthood.

When Cain clearly showed his disaffection for his brother, his parent Adam reproved him. I believe that these words were spoken by Adam himself. Moses says that these words were spoken by the Lord, because Adam had now been accounted just and had been endowed with the Holy Spirit. What he now says in accordance with the Word of God and through the Holy Spirit is correctly declared to have been said by God. Similarly today, those who preach the Gospel are not themselves directly the preachers, but Christ speaks and preaches through them. Without a doubt these words were spoken with unusual sternness. Adam sees that his son is impatient of his disgrace and that he is grieving because of his lost prestige. He also realizes what the tempter, who had inflicted such great injury on man in the state of perfection, is now able to achieve in a depraved nature. Therefore he became deeply concerned and began his very earnest sermon. Although none of the fathers has explained this sermon adequately — perhaps because they did not have leisure from their ecclesiastical duties — still it seems to me worthwhile for us to undertake this task.

7. *If you do well, will there not be forgiveness? But if you do not do well, sin lies at the door.*

I cannot marvel enough at how Moses was able to compress such great topics into so few words. Our translation is not so accurate. Although Augustine was not altogether unfamiliar with the Hebrew language, nevertheless he did not have a thorough knowledge of it.[24] This is the way he renders this passage: "If you bring your offering properly, and you do not divide properly, you have sinned. Be calm." Those who are versed in Hebrew know what errors have been made here, although the meaning he derives from his translation is good and theologically sound. The translators of the Septuagint likewise appear not to have had adequate knowledge to cope with the vastness of the task they had undertaken.[25] Therefore, passing by both the translations and the opinions of others, we shall direct our attention to the authentic Hebrew text. This is what it has: "If you do well, there will be forgiveness, or a lifting up; and if you do not do well, sin lies at the door."

Now nature has so ordered it that, as the philosopher asserts, words should suit the events; the events should not suit the words.[26] And there is a well-known opinion of Hilary, which the Master also quotes among the *Sentences:* that words should be understood in agreement with the matter under discussion.[27] Therefore in every exposition the subject should be given consideration first; that is, it must be determined what is under consideration. After this has been done, the next step is that the words should be adapted to the matter if the character of the language so permits, not the matter to the words. Because the rabbis and those who pattern after them do not do this (for they have dispensed with the matter and adhere

[24] Augustine, *The City of God,* XV, ch. 7.

[25] The translation which Luther is criticizing comes out in the rendition of this verse by the Douay Version: "If thou do well, shalt thou not receive? But if ill, shall not sin forthwith be present at the door?"

[26] Apparently a reference to Aristotle, *Rhetoric,* III, chs. 1—2.

[27] Perhaps an allusion to Hilary, *On the Trinity,* II, ch. 5, *Patrologia, Series Latina,* X, 53—54.

only to the words), they often arrive at the most absurd opinions. Since they do not have thoughts that are worthy of the spiritual things with which Holy Scripture deals, they stray from the matter and interpret the words in such a way that they convey idle and carnal thoughts.

Moreover, since it is an assured fact that the Jews have renounced Christ, how, then, can they correctly understand what pertains either to the Gospel or to the Law? They do not know what sin is, what grace is, what righteousness is. How, then, can they properly explain passages of this kind? Somewhat like them are our sophists, for what do they have about such important subjects that is sound? And so, if the matter is not understood, it is impossible for the words to be correctly understood either. Although a knowledge of the words comes first, nevertheless a knowledge of the matter is of greater importance. When the matter changes, the words also change to another meaning, and a completely new language set-up arises.

Gerondi has an excellent knowledge of the words (just as there are many today who far surpass me in their knowledge of the Hebrew language); [28] but because he does not understand the matter, he distorts the passage with which we are dealing. This is the way he explains it: "If you do well, your offering will be more acceptable than that of your brother, because you are the first-born." You note that he understands the terms, but the matter he does not understand. God's main purpose in this passage is to show that He is unwilling to give any consideration to primogeniture. How, then, can an offering be better because of primogeniture? The author of the Epistle to the Hebrews understood the matter and, therefore, has an entirely different statement, namely, that Abel, because of faith, brought a more excellent sacrifice (Heb. 11:4). Jerome's translation is better: "If you do well, you will receive; if evil, sin [he added the pronoun 'your' of his own accord] will be present at the door." But not even by translating this way does he hit the real meaning. For I believe that no one will approve his explanation of נשא (which denotes "to lift up") by "to accept." But he gets this very idea from the Jews, who adhere to this opinion; hence their understanding is that God would have rewarded Cain if he had brought a generous offering. Therefore I shall now state simply what my own conviction about this passage is.

It is necessary at the very outset, as I have said, that we have

28 Cf. p. 297, note 55.

in mind the matter which is involved. But the matter which cannot escape notice, inasmuch as it is the basic issue, is this: that nothing is pleasing to God unless it is done in faith. This is in agreement with that well-known general statement of Paul (Rom. 14:23): "Whatsoever is not of faith is sin." And Solomon declares (Prov. 15:8): "The sacrifice of the wicked God loathes." The second basic issue is that sin is something so enormous that it cannot be blotted out by sacrifices and other works but only through God's mercy, which must be accepted by faith. In like manner, the first promise of the woman's Seed, without whom there is no salvation, points this out and confirms it. The rabbis lack this foundation. This knowledge comes only from the Spirit of Christ, who, like the noonday sun, brings light into our darkness. Therefore let us reject as wicked and false whatever is at variance with these basic facts.

Furthermore, although I do not object to understanding the word "sin" in this passage as a reference either to the past or to the future, it nevertheless appears to me to be better to explain it as referring to sin in general. The entire meaning hinges on the verb שְׂאֵת, from נָשָׂא, "to lift up." Moreover, here we have a clear example of how great a difference there is between the knowledge of a word and the knowledge of the matter. If you apply the word "lift up" to a concrete object, it meants "to raise up" or "to raise high," as in Is. 6:1: "I saw the Lord sitting upon a throne, high and lifted up." This is something far different from what we have in Ps. 32:1: "Blessed is the man whose sins are forgiven." And yet in both passages the verb is the same. One who knows merely the language understands the former statement in Isaiah, but the latter statement he does not understand, because he has no knowledge of the matter. It is one thing to elevate a throne on high; it is another thing to lift up sin, that is, to remit it, to remove it, or to take it away.

Therefore the sense is: "If you did well, or if you were good, that is, if you believed, you would have a gracious God and there would be a true lifting-up, that is, forgiveness of sins. But because I see that God had no regard for you, it assuredly follows that you are not good and are not freed from your sin; but your sin remains."

Above all, it is something elegant that through the use of the verb "to lift up" the text compares sin to a huge burden under which Cain lies oppressed so that he cannot breathe unless it is removed. The Epistle to the Hebrews points out the way in which we are rid of this burden when it says that by faith Abel offered a more excellent sacrifice (Heb. 11:4). In this way grammar, or the words, agrees with the matter, namely, that God has regard for faith and judges only those to be good who believe. But these words also contain a very stern rebuke, as if Adam were saying to Cain: "Pride has brought on your destruction. You came puffed up with the glory of your primogeniture, and you believed that you would be accepted by God because of it. But I observe that, inasmuch as God judges and reproves you, you are without faith. For God rejects only those who do not believe."

None of the rabbis explain this passage in this manner. They do not understand that Adam, doing the same thing Paul does, is impressing the familiar saying of the Gospel on his son (Mark 16:16): "He who believes will be saved"; and also (Rom. 3:28): "Faith alone justifies." What else is he saying here than that God is merciful to those who believe in the blessed Seed and discard all trust in works and all conceit about their merit? He says: "If you did this, sin would not lie so heavily on you. You would be relieved of this burden and not mutter with wrath as you are doing. For God has given His promise that He does not want to charge his sin against anyone who believes."

If you apply the text to Cain's past sin, it is also a fatherly and very stern admonition: "So far you have not believed, and for this reason you were rejected. If you continue in this way, you will be cast aside altogether. But if you do well or if you are good, that is, if you believe in the promised Seed, I am still promising you that you will be relieved of your sin, that is, as Ps. 32:2 explains, that sin will not be imputed to you."

The addition, "Your sin lies at the door," is a rhetorical description of sin, which I should like to see taken as a proverb. This is truly the nature of sin, that it lies there like a slumbering beast while it is being committed; that is, it does not bite, it does not frighten, and it does not torment, but it rather fawns. Thus when Eve first and Adam after her ate the forbidden fruit in Paradise, they did not believe that this was being observed by God; much less did they believe that the punishment would be so severe. In like manner, when the hunger of wild beasts is satisfied, they are more tractable and want to sleep. In the same way, while sin is being committed, it is pleasant, and its poison is not felt; but it lies down and keeps quiet. Who has ever seen a miser resentful when there is a great opportunity for gain? Who has ever seen an adulterer mourn when he attains his desire? If you were to beat his skin with whips or his head with a hammer, the temptation would leave him; but while sin is quiet and the punishment is not felt, the miser finds his utmost pleasure in pouncing upon his gain, and the adulterer in having another man's wife, all with the idea that there can be no limit or end to the pleasure.

Therefore in this passage Adam is not only speaking of Cain's sin, but he is describing the nature of sin in general. What happened to Cain happens to everybody. Before Cain brought his sacrifice, he was vainglorious about the prerogatives of his primogeniture, and he despised his brother; he claimed first place for himself. At that time sin was lying at the door and was keeping quiet; but it was lying at the door, that is, in a place that is not quiet. Through the door we go in and out, and the place is, therefore, poorly suited for sleep. This, too, is a part of the nature of sin, that although it is quiet for a time, it is quiet in a place where it cannot be quiet for long. It is just as Christ says in Matt. 10:26: "There is nothing covered that will not be revealed." The wicked person believes that sin is quiet and hidden. But at the door it cannot be quiet, and in the end it manifests itself and emerges into public view. For a door and sleep, or rest, do not fit together. Just as there is no darkness in light, so there is no quiet in an unquiet place; for darkness and light, quiet and noise are in conflict by nature. Thus this explanation can be given of any past sin.

If you explain it as dealing with a future sin, the meaning is the same: "If you hurt your brother and yield to the anger which has arisen in your heart, I tell you, your sin will be quiet. But it will be quiet at the door, that is, in a place which is very much devoid of quiet. Therefore it cannot avoid being roused and falling upon you like an infuriated beast." This is how it turned out. Cain was alone when he buried his brother after he had committed the murder; then his sin kept quiet. But for how long? Well, until the voice came to him: "Where is your brother Abel?" And so this description holds good of every sin: that it lies at the door. Such is the disposition of human beings that they believe their sin will remain secret so long as they escape the notice of the eyes of men. But it is disclosed and roused if they do not do what is good, that is, if they do not believe that God will pardon it for Christ's sake.

Thus this proverbial figure of speech expresses a very important thought, namely, that nothing remains hidden, but everything will be revealed, as Paul also states (1 Tim. 5:24): "Some men's sins are manifest so that a judgment can be made about them." We observe unusual judgments of God, particularly in cases which involve crimes. How many are slain in secret, and yet the perpetrators of outrageous murders are brought to light through extraordinary events! Adam, therefore, admonishes his son not to give way to sin; for it would not be secret, but there would be One who would bring it to light and punish it. And that the poets represent Cupid as naked, but also blind, seems to be in harmony with this conviction.[29] Because our sin appears to us to be hidden, we believe that it is not being noticed by others either. But in the end God reveals even those things that have been most carefully concealed.

I am convinced that this is the true and simple meaning of this passage, in which the father tells his son that he should believe in God and in the promised Seed, and that then God will be merciful to him. "But," says he, "if you follow your desires, then sin will be lying there for you, that is, it will seem secret and hidden. But it will lie at the door, that is, in that place in which it cannot remain quiet for a long time or stay hidden. What is at the door is seen by all who go in and out."

But, as I said above, let us not forget the main thought, namely, that from the beginning of the world God declared that He is the judge between the flesh and the spirit and that He does not have regard for persons. He had regard for Abel, not because He was moved by any work, but simply because He was moved by his faith, in which he also brought his offering. But for Cain He had no regard, not as though his work were less grand or splendid, but because he lacked faith; and it did not benefit Cain that he was the first-born.

This is a forceful argument against the Jews, who gloried in their descent, that they were the sons of Abraham, as is related in John 1:13.[30] If any worth attaches to the prerogative of descent, Cain surely had something to boast of. What value does it have for the Jews to boast that God spoke with them through Moses? We are not going to believe that Adam, the first teacher, was inferior to Moses, are we? In many ways he was superior to him and greater. For he did

29 The most famous poem about Cupid is in Apuleius' *Metamorphoses*.

30 Cf. *Luther's Works*, 22, pp. 90—96, on this passage.

not, like Moses, teach circumcision and the other ceremonies of the Law which the intractable nation needed to prevent superstitious practices; but he taught faith in the promised Seed who would crush the serpent's head. Yet primogeniture and other advantages availed Cain nothing, for God has regard only for faith in the promised Seed. Thus in the New Testament Paul plainly states: "They which are of faith, the same are the children of Abraham" (Gal. 3:7); and John 1:12-13 declares: "He gave them power to become the sons of God, who are not of the blood nor of the will of a man nor of the will of the flesh, but who believe in His name."

This I consider to be the real and true meaning of this passage. In the first place, it is in harmony with the basic teaching of Holy Scripture and with the subject matter. In the second place, the language is not against it but throws light on the subject matter beautifully and in various ways. But because the rabbis have no knowledge of the subject matter, they are not benefited by their knowledge of the words. How absurd it is that some have so understood the statement "and there will be a lifting up" as though it meant: "Then you will again be able to raise your face, which now is entirely changed and has fallen." Our more recent interpreters here and there take note of absurdities of this kind.[31] Nevertheless, one is indebted to them for their faithful effort to reproduce a linguistically correct text, although there is need of theology, which alone correctly determines and points out the content.

And its desire is for you, but you should rule over it.

Some have most stupidly perverted this statement to prove free will.[32] It is obvious that Adam is not simply asserting that Cain *can* do this, but he merely exhorts or directs that he *should* do this. It does not follow that we are able at once to carry out what we have been commanded to do. Adam says: "The desire of sin is for you"; that is, as Paul declares (Rom. 7:5): "Sin is in your members," and likewise (Gal. 5:17): "The flesh lusts against the spirit." "But you will not be condemned because you feel this impulse of sin. If sin entices you, rule over it through faith, and do not permit it to rule over you; otherwise you will perish." Likewise, Paul also commands that the deeds of the flesh must be put to death by the spirit (Rom. 8:13).

[31] The source of this information is Lyra on Gen. 4:7.

[32] This is a reference to Erasmus' *Diatribe,* ch. 10, discussed in Luther's *The Bondage of the Will* (Weimar, XVIII, 676).

And so this little section is intended to describe for you the life of the godly in this flesh, namely, that it is a never-ending conflict of the spirit with the flesh. Therefore those who are sound asleep do not prepare themselves for this battle and are easily vanquished. But it seems that Adam wanted to make use of this address not only to exhort his son about being on guard against sin in the future but also to give him comfort. He saw that his son was greatly agitated because of his rejection by God, and that now he was being incited to revenge. "But," says he, "rule over sin, and you will find that God is merciful and pardons sin."

In this passage the same verb, מָשַׁל, occurs that the Lord employed above when He said to the woman (Gen. 3:16): "The man will rule over you." There He wanted the wife to obey her husband and listen to him and not to assume the management of all their affairs; but if she did not do this, the man, by virtue of his authority, was to reprimand and forbid her. In the same way he says here: "Sin will urge you on and will incite you to revenge (for this is the meaning of 'Its desire is toward you'); but you must say: 'I refuse to obey' and so keep sin under your control and rule over it." Thus the exhortation is very rich in comfort; for on account of the blessed Seed we are no longer under the domination of sin. Therefore we should rule over sin. At all events, the exhortation gives expression to two doctrines, one dealing with fear and the other with faith. We should fear God because sin lies at the door; and we should trust God because He is merciful.

8. And Cain spoke to his brother Abel.

Our translation adds that Cain said: "Let us go outside." [33] But this, too, is a fabrication of the rabbis; and I pointed out above to what extent they should be believed. Lyra, whose source is Eben Ezra, mentions that Cain told his brother how severely he had been scolded by the Lord.[34] But who wants to give credence to assertions that do not have the support of Scripture? We, therefore, adhere to the opinion which Scripture suggests: that Cain, who was already rejected by God, is giving way to his wrath and now adds to his previous sin also the contempt of his parents and of the Word. More-

[33] These words are missing from the Masoretic text of Genesis, but they appear in the Samaritan text and in all the versions and thus found their way also into the Revised Standard Version.

[34] Lyra on Gen. 4:8, sec. "x."

over, he reasons: "To me, as the first-born, the promise of the woman's Seed belongs. But Abel, that worthless and despised fellow, is given preference over me by divine authority, through the fire which consumed his sacrifice. Now what shall I do? I shall disguise my wrath until an opportunity presents itself for appropriate vengeance."

Therefore I understand the words "Cain spoke to his brother Abel" to mean that Cain disguised his wrath and behaved like a brother toward Abel. He conversed with him and lived with him as though he were calmly bearing the verdict which had been rendered by God. There is a similar instance involving Saul, who feigns a kindly disposition toward David (1 Sam. 24:20): "I know," he says, "that after me you will be king." But meanwhile he thinks that this may not happen if David is slain. Cain spoke to Abel in this manner: "I see that you have been chosen by the Lord; I do not envy you this blessing." This is the way hypocrites act. They feign friendship until an opportunity to inflict harm presents itself.

Moreover, the circumstances suggest this meaning. If Adam and Eve could have had any suspicion of the murder that was going to happen, do you not think that they either would have restrained Cain or would have removed Abel and put him out of danger? But when Cain changes his behavior, and when he converses affectionately as with a brother, they believe that everything is safe and that their son has acquiesced in his father's admonition. This semblance deceived Abel, too; he would have fled if he had feared any violence from his brother, just as Jacob fled when he feared Esau's wrath. What, then, gets into Jerome's mind to cause him to believe the rabbis, who say that Cain had remonstrated with his brother? [35]

Accordingly, Cain is a figure and image of all murderers and hypocrites who, under the guise of piety, kill good men. Possessed by Satan, therefore, he conceals his wrath and waits for his chance. Meanwhile he speaks with Abel as with a beloved brother, so that he might catch him off guard and overpower him more quickly.

Thus this passage is concerned with giving us some instruction about the ways of murderers and hypocrites. For truly this is what takes place: Every Cain speaks like a brother in a brotherly manner with Abel. On the other hand, every Abel trusts Cain like a brother and so is killed; and meanwhile all godly parents are deceived too.

Today the pope and the bishops do much talking and counseling

[35] This is also from Lyra on Gen. 4:8, sec. "x."

about the peace and harmony of the church, but he is surely deceived who does not perceive that those counsels have the opposite intent. Ps. 28:3 states the truth: "The workers of iniquity speak peace with their neighbor and have evil in their heart." It is the nature of all hypocrites to appear good, to speak in a kindly manner; to feign humility, patience, love; to give alms, etc.; yet meanwhile they turn over murderous designs in their minds.

Let us, therefore, learn to recognize a Cain and then to be on strict guard against him when he is speaking in a brotherly way, just as today our adversaries, the bishops and the pope, speak with us while they feign an eagerness for harmony and strive for agreement in doctrine. If they had a favorable opportunity for pouncing upon us and raving at us, you would be hearing something far different. For truly "there is death in the pot" (2 Kings 4:40), and under their finest and most endearing words deadly poison is concealed.

And it came to pass when the two were in the field that Cain rose up against his brother Abel and killed him.

Here you have the comment on those ingratiating words. By divine authority Cain was admonished by his parent to guard against future sin and to hope for pardon of his past sin. But he disregards both admonitions and yields to sin, just as the ungodly are always accustomed to do. For Solomon's statement is true (Prov. 18:3): "When the wicked man has come into the depths of sin, he contemns; but ignominy and reproach follow him."

Today no charge can be brought against our ministry. We teach, we exhort, we adjure, we scold, and we employ every form of expression in order to recall the masses out of their smugness to the fear of God. But the world goes its way like an untamed beast and follows, not the Word but its own desires, which it nevertheless strives to cloak in an appearance of morality. The examples of the prophets and apostles are familiar to everybody, and we are also taught by our own experience. Our adversaries have been admonished and convinced so often and know that they are in error, yet they do not give up their murderous hate against us.

Therefore learn from this passage what a hypocrite is, namely, one who pretends to worship God and to be charitable and meanwhile destroys the worship of God and kills his brother. Every pretense of kindness has the aim of finding a much better opportunity to inflict harm. If Abel had foreseen that implacable wrath and truly fiendish rage, he would have preserved himself by running away. But because Cain gives no such indication, greets him affectionately, and pretends to be as kind as usual, Abel perishes before any fear of danger arises in him.

When Abel saw his brother rising up against him, he undoubtedly entreated and exhorted him not to defile himself with so great a sin. But no entreaties, no suppliant hands, can restrain a mind possessed by Satan. Just as Cain had despised his father's admonition, so he also despises his brother, who is lying before him at his feet.

These facts give us an insight into the cruel tyranny with which Satan oppresses our nature now that it has become entangled in sins. For this reason St. Paul (Eph. 2:3) calls men by nature children of wrath, and declares (2 Tim. 2:26) that they are held captive at Satan's will. If we are nothing more than human beings, that is, if we do not apprehend the blessed Seed in faith, we are like Cain and lack nothing except the opportunity to prove this. When our nature is without the Holy Spirit, it is impelled by the same evil spirit by which Cain was impelled.

But if any man ever possessed either adequate strength or a free will by which he could protect himself against the assaults of Satan, these gifts would surely have existed in Cain, who was in possession of the primogeniture and of the promise of the blessed Seed. But the state of all men is the same: If this nature is not assisted by God's Holy Spirit, it cannot stand. Why, then, do we engage in unprofitable boasting about our free will? And now follows another outstanding passage.

9. *And the Lord said to Cain: Where is your brother Abel? He answered: I do not know. For I am not the keeper of my brother, am I?*

Good God, to what depths our nature falls when it is impelled by the devil! A murder has now been committed, and perhaps murdered Abel has been lying unburied for some days. Therefore when Cain returns to his parents at the usual time, but Abel does not return, the worried parents ask Cain: "You have arrived, but where is Abel? You return home, but Abel does not return. The herd is without its shepherd. Now tell us where he is." At this point Cain gives vent to his displeasure and very disrespectfully replies: "I don't know. I am not his keeper, am I?"

The same thing happens to him that happens to all the wicked:

by excusing himself he accuses himself. In a like sense, Christ also states (Luke 19:22): "By your own words you will be judged, you wicked servant." Among the heathen, too, there is current a notable proverb: "A liar must have a good memory." [36] Of course, they had no knowledge of God's judgment and of conscience; they reached this conviction solely under the influence of what they observed in the conduct of their affairs as citizens. It is true that liars take many risks by which they can be proved guilty and wrong. For this reason the Germans say that a lie is a fertile thing. One lie gives birth to seven other lies that are needed to give support to the first lie. Yet it is impossible for conscience to avoid rashly betraying itself — if not by words, then at least by its demeanor, as endless examples prove. I shall relate only one.

In Thuringia there is the little town of Neustadt on the Orla River. A harlot there had killed the baby to which she had secretly given birth and had thrown it into a neighboring pond, but the linen cloth in which the infant was wrapped betrayed the deed. The matter was brought before the magistrate. When the simple people knew no other adequate method of investigating the crime, they summoned all girls to the town hall and questioned them individually. But both from their mien and from their speech the verdict was clear that, except for the guilty one, the rest were innocent.

But when they came to the one who had committed this great crime, she did not wait until she was questioned but loudly maintained that she was not guilty of the crime. Suspicion at once arose in the magistrate that she was not guiltless, for she disclaimed any guilt with greater ostentation than the rest. And then, after she had been put under arrest by the bailiffs, she confessed the murder at once.

Countless examples of this kind occur daily where men accuse and betray themselves by anxiously disclaiming their guilt. It is true, as we heard above, that sin reposes indeed, but at the door.

So in this passage Cain believes that he has eloquently disclaimed any guilt when he refuses to be his brother's keeper. But the moment he calls him his brother, does he not confess that he ought to be his keeper? Does he not also accuse himself of being unfriendly to his brother, and does he not at the same time raise the suspicion in his parents that the murder has been committed, since Abel nowhere puts in an appearance? In Paradise, Adam, too, disclaims any guilt and

---

[36] A proverb from Quintilian, *Institutio oratorica,* IV, ii, 91.

passes the blame on to Eve. But Cain's excuse is much more foolish; for truly when sin is disclaimed, sin is doubled, while a free confession of sin obtains mercy and overcomes wrath.

In the history of St. Martin it is related that Satan reproached him for absolving some notorious sinners and asked him why he was doing this.[37] Martin is said to have replied: "I would surely absolve you, too, if you said sincerely: 'I am sorry that I have sinned against the Son of God, and I beg for forgiveness.'" But the devil does not do this, for he perseveres in his sin and in defending it.

Cain and all hypocrites imitate the father of lies (John 8:44) by denying or excusing their sin. Therefore they cannot obtain forgiveness. In the home we see how wrath is increased when a shortcoming is defended. Whenever the wife, the children, and the servants have committed a fault but deny their fault, the head of the household becomes more incensed, while a confession gains either a pardon or a milder penalty. It is characteristic of hypocrites to extenuate their sin or to deny it, and, under the guise of religion, to kill innocent people.

But here let us recall the order in which the sins follow and grow. In the first place, Cain sins by his arrogance and unbelief when he is inflated by his privilege of primogeniture and believes that he will be approved by God because of his merit. Upon this pride and glorying in his righteousness there follow envy and hatred of his brother, who, as he sees by a clear sign, has preference over him. Upon this envy and hatred follow hypocrisy and lying when he affectionately addresses his brother, whom he wants slain, in order to make him feel more at ease. Upon hypocrisy follows a murder. Upon the murder follows a denial of the sin. The last step, with which we shall deal a little later, is despair. And this, finally, is the plunge from heaven to hell.

Although Adam and Eve in Paradise do not deny their sin, they nevertheless admit it in an altogether spiritless manner and lay the blame on another — Adam on Eve, and Eve on the serpent. Cain, however, goes farther. He not only does not confess the murder, but he also declares that the care of his brother is a matter of no concern to him. Does this not indicate clearly that he is hostile toward his brother? Therefore although Adam and Eve make their confession with indifference, they obtain forgiveness and receive a milder punish-

[37] Cf. p. 179, note 29.

ment. But Cain, who denies his guilt so insistently, is rejected and despairs.

The same judgment awaits our Cainites — the popes, the cardinals, and the bishops — who day and, night turn over murderous plans in their minds and, like their father, still go on saying: "I do not know."

There is a common proverb: "Of what concern is it to the Romans that Greeks are dying?" We suppose that only our own dangers concern us. But how does this accord with God's command that He wants all of us to live together as brothers? Therefore Cain brings a serious charge against himself by this very statement, when he declares that his brother's care was of no concern to him. If he had said to his father: "Alas, I have killed Abel. I am sorry for this deed. Inflict whatever penalty you wish," there would have been room for redress. But when he denies his guilt and, contrary to God's will, simply puts aside any concern for his brother, his sin becomes greater, and no room for mercy remains.

Moreover, Moses put down these words with extraordinary care as an evidence and as a reminder for all hypocrites. He gives a vivid description of hypocrites and points out the horrifying extent to which they are in Satan's grasp and are being incited against God, His Word, and the church. For this murderer it was not enough to have killed his brother in violation of God's command, but he adds this sin, that he becomes indignant and is offended when God inquires about his brother. But I am saying "when God inquires" because, although Adam spoke these words to his son, he nevertheless spoke by divine authority and by the Holy Spirit. In the case of so enormous a sin, are these not very gentle words: "Where is your brother Abel?" To these words, which are not at all rude, the hypocrite and murderer nevertheless gives such an insolent and proud answer that he says: "I do not know" and becomes indignant at being questioned about the matter. Cain's reply reflects a spirit that is rebellious and is enraged at God.

To this sin Cain adds another that is worse. Although he ought to be accused because of the murder which he has committed, he himself accuses God and remonstrates with Him: "I am surely not my brother's keeper, am I?" He prefixes no term of respect such as was due either God or his father. He does not say: "Lord, I do not know"; nor does he say: "My father, you did not assign me to him as his keeper, did you?" These terms would have given some indication of his respect for God or his parent. But, like a lord, he gives a haughty answer and indicates plainly that he resents being called to account by Him who has the right to call to account.

This is a true picture of all hypocrites, who are very stubborn and haughty in their manifest sins and nevertheless want to appear very saintly. They refuse to yield to God and to His Word when He scolds them; but they resist God, contend with Him, and excuse their sin. Thus Ps. 51:4 also declares that God is being judged by men, but that in the end He is justified. This stubbornness of the hypocrites is what Moses wanted to depict.

But how does Cain's effort turn out for him? In this way, that he accuses himself most vehemently while he vigorously excuses himself. Similarly, Christ also says (Luke 19:22): "I judge you from your own words, you worthless servant." That servant wanted to appear blameless, and so he said (Luke 19:21): "I knew that you are a hard man and that you reap where you have not sown; and so I hid the talent." But how could he bring a more severe charge against himself? Accordingly, Christ turns these very words against the servant himself. This is the wisdom of the Holy Spirit.

But these examples are useful for us, to keep us from contending with God. When you feel in your conscience that you are guilty, guard with your utmost effort against striving with God or with men by defending and excusing your sin. Rather do the following: Do not flee from God when He is pointing His spear at you, but flee to Him with a humble confession of your guilt and a request for forgiveness. Then God will draw back His spear and spare you. On the other hand, the farther you try to flee from God by denying and excusing your sin, the more closely and aggressively God pursues you and harasses you. Therefore there is nothing better and safer than to come with a confession of your guilt. The outcome of this is that while God triumphs, we also triumph through Him.

Cain and the hypocrites do not do this. God points His spear at them. Yet they do not humble themselves or seek forgiveness, but they also point a spear at God, just as Cain is doing here. He does not say: "Lord, I confess it. I have killed my brother. Forgive me!" But he himself, who should be accused, even accuses God: "I am surely not the keeper of my brother, am I?" What does he accomplish by this haughtiness? This, that he freely admits that this Law (Lev. 19:18), "Love your neighbor as yourself," is of no concern to him; and likewise the command (Matt. 7:12), "What you do not want done to yourself, do not do to another." This Law was not promulgated for the first time in the Decalog but is written in the hearts of all men. Cain contends against it. He gives proof that he does not concern himself with it and that he simply despises it.

In this way Cain is the picture of a man who is not simply evil but extremely so, one who is bloodthirsty and yet is a hypocrite. He wants to appear holy and wants to accuse God rather than appear to merit the accusation himself. All hypocrites act this way. They blaspheme God and crucify the Son of God. Nevertheless, they want to be righteous. After their murders, blasphemies, and all sorts of other sins they look for a way to excuse and extenuate them. But then it happens that they betray themselves and are condemned by their own verdict.

While Cain exerts himself to be excessively righteous, he befouls himself in the most loathsome manner. He thinks that "I am surely not my brother's keeper, am I?" is very neatly put; but he brings a most disgraceful charge against himself by this very utterance. Thus, according to Hilary's statement, stupidity always goes hand in hand with wickedness.[38] If Cain had been as wise as he was evil, he would have excused himself in a far different manner. But now, since God so arranges it that stupidity is always paired with wickedness, he accuses himself. And for this reason it is easy to defend the truth against its opponents. Like Cain, they give proof by their words and by their demeanor that they are not concerned about their brother but hate him; and so in various ways they themselves also betray their wickedness.

Thus this text presents the important facts from which we may learn that God does not permit hypocrites to remain undetected for long but compels them to betray themselves when they cleverly endeavor to cover up their hypocrisy and sin.

In his portrayal of events Moses does not employ the familiar profusion of language of the heathen, who embellish and give finish to a single scene, sometimes with one descriptive detail, then with another. But we know from experience that human eloquence cannot draw an adequate picture of the emotions, and oftentimes a profusion of words has the result that the emotion being described appears less intense than it actually is. Moses, therefore, proceeds differently and by means of few words suggests a great profusion of situations.

Above he said: "When the two were in the field." He indicates

[38] Hilary, *On the Trinity*, VI, ch. 15, col. 168—169.

there that Cain, the murderer, had watched for a chance when he would be alone and could fall upon Abel while he, too, was alone. The circumstances readily show that Abel was busy at that time. He was in the field, where the tasks assigned by his father had to be performed. Moses also indicates here that the parents had no fear whatever of any danger. Although they were afraid at first that Cain's anger would explode into another more serious sin, Cain's complacence and his feigned friendliness caused them to suspect no evil. If any trace of suspicion had remained, they surely would not have let Abel go alone; they would have assigned him his sisters as companions — by that time he undoubtedly had some — or the parents themselves, by their presence and authority, would have prevented such a great crime. I said above that Abel did not feel apprehensive either. If he had suspected anything evil from his brother, he would at least have saved himself by running away. But after he hears that Cain is taking God's verdict calmly and does not envy his brother this honor, he does his work in the field without anxiety.

But what rhetorician could fitly describe what Moses expresses with one verb: that Cain "rose up" against his brother? Many denunciations of cruelty appear here and there. But how can cruelty be depicted as something more shocking and detestable than it is depicted here?

"He rose up against his brother Abel," says Moses, as if to say: against him whom at that time Cain had as his only brother, with whom he had been brought up and had lived until now. He not only forgets this intimate association, but he also forgets their common parents. It does not enter his mind what great sorrow he is about to bring upon his parents by this saddening crime. He does not reflect that this is his brother, who has never offended him. He knew that Abel had received the honor of bringing the more acceptable sacrifice, not as the result of his own effort and ambition but because God Himself had bestowed it. Finally, he gave no consideration to himself; until now he had stood in highest favor with his parents, but now he would lose their favor by this crime and would incur their utmost displeasure.

Among historical accounts there is one about a painter who painted the story of Iphigenia at the moment when she was about to be sacrificed. To each of the spectators he assigned his own particular demeanor, expressive of his sorrow and grief. But the head of the father, who was present at the scene, he covered up, because he held that the depth of the father's feeling could not be expressed in a painting.[39]

I hold that Moses really did the same thing when he employed the verb קָם, "and he rose up." What highly tragic scenes of these events would Cicero or Livy have created as they depicted in lofty style the fury of the one brother and the fear, the laments, the entreaties, the tears, the suppliant hands, and other actions of the other! But even so these cannot be adequately described. Therefore the procedure of Moses is correct: he suggests by dots, as it were, situations that cannot be expressed in words. He does so in order by that brevity to stimulate the reader's feelings to pay closer attention to a situation which would be disfigured and spoiled by the meaningless adornment of words, just as happens to a beautiful physical appearance through the addition of rouge.

Thus when he adds: "And he slew him," he is not speaking of an ordinary murder, the way at times we see men start a quarrel for trivial reasons and commit murder. Murderers of this kind become appalled shortly after the murder has been committed; they grieve over their deed and recognize the delusions with which the devil blinded their minds. But Cain is not appalled; he does not grieve. He denies the deed.

To this Satanic and insatiable hatred of the hypocrites Christ directs our attention when He says (John 16:2): "They will think that they have done God a service if they kill you." Priests and kings filled Jerusalem with the blood of the prophets. Moreover, they exulted as though they had achieved something successful. They regarded it as zeal for the Law and for the house of God.

Today the popes and the bishops are just as cruel. It is not enough for them to have excommunicated us so many times and to have shed our blood; they also desire to blot out our memory from the land of the living. Ps. 137:7 describes this kind of hatred: "Raze it down to its foundations!" These are instances of hatred that is satanic and not human. Human hatred abates with time or ceases entirely — at least after we have avenged the offense against us and have obtained satisfaction. But this pharisaical hatred daily assumes larger proportions, since it is cloaked with the appearance of piety.

And so Cain is the father of all those murderers who kill the saints

---

[39] According to Meinhold, this was supplied by Veit Dietrich.

and whose wrath exceeds all bounds so long as a hair of their victims remains, just as Christ's example also proves. In Cain's instance there is no doubt that he hoped to keep his glory of primogeniture after Abel had been destroyed. Thus the ungodly believe that their cruelty will benefit them; but later on, when they realize that their hope was vain, they sink into despair.

After such an outrageous murder was reported to the parents, what sort of clamor do we think arose? What sort of laments? What sort of groanings? But I pass these over, for they are the concern of a mind able to express itself with facility and rich in ideas. It is indeed remarkable that the parents did not pass away from grief. It made the disaster so much greater that their first-born, who had given rise to such a grand hope about himself, is the perpetrator of this outrageous murder.

Therefore Adam and Eve would have been unable to bear up under this disaster in their home if they had not received divine help. This was an event without precedent. Consequently, they lacked the comfort we generally have in sudden and unexpected mishaps: that similar misfortunes befall others as well, and that we are not the only ones to whom they happen. At that time our first parents had only these two sons, although I am of the opinion that they also had daughters. Hence they lacked the examples which the masses supply, but which are available to us.

Moreover, who can have any doubt that by a new kind of temptation Satan increased the grief of our first parents? Their thoughts ran as follows: "Behold, this is our sin. In Paradise we wanted to become like God, and through our sin we became like the devil. The same thing has happened to our son. Him alone we loved, and him we regarded most highly. To us the other was righteous compared with this הֶבֶל, that is, this worthless person. We hoped that he would crush the serpent's head. And behold, he himself has been crushed by the serpent. He has even become like the serpent, inasmuch as he has become a murderer. But how did this come about? Was it not because he was born to us and because our sin has made us what we are? Therefore that disaster had its origin in our flesh and in our sin."

And so it is likely — and the chronology gives support to the idea — that the distressed parents were so shocked by this incident that for a long time they refrained from cohabitation. Cain appears to have been thirty years old, more or less, when he committed this murder. Meanwhile several daughters were born to Adam. For since it says later on that Cain married (Gen. 4:17), he no doubt married a sister. Moreover, Cain states below (Gen. 4:14): "Everyone who finds me will kill me." Furthermore (Gen. 4:15), "the Lord placed a sign on Cain so that no one would kill him." Therefore it is likely that at that time Adam had a number of children. But because of the extraordinary and noteworthy story and because Cain and Abel were the first and foremost children, only these two are mentioned. I fully believe that during the first thirty years the marriage of our first parents was very prolific. Elsewhere we find the names of daughters of Adam: Calmana and Dibora. But I do not know whether the writers deserve credence.[40] Thus because it is related that Seth was begotten a long time after this murder (Gen. 5:3), it appears likely to me that the parents were so distressed by this shocking crime in their family that for a long time they refrained from begetting children. With all these matters Moses does not deal; he merely suggests them in order to stimulate the reader to reflect on this noteworthy story, which Moses nevertheless presents in the smallest possible number of words, like a view through latticework.

But I return to the text before us. Cain is a wicked person and a rogue, and yet in the eyes of his parents he is like a divine possession and a divine gift. In accordance with his name, Abel, on the contrary, is regarded as nothing by his parents; but in God's eyes he is a truly holy human being. Thus Christ also (Matt. 23:35) honors Abel with a glorious statement when He calls him "righteous." Cain does not put up with this verdict of God. He thinks that not only will his hatred be satisfied by the murder, but that in this way he can also keep his birthright. The thought that he is sinning by this murder is far from him. He believes that he is allowed to do so by right, as it were, because he is the first-born. And so he kills Abel, not with a sword, I think (for I believe that at that time iron weapons were not in existence), but with a club or some stone.

After Cain has committed the murder, he is calm; he thinks he can conceal his deed by hiding the corpse and removing it from view. He either buried it or perhaps threw it into a river to make sure that it could not be found by his parents.

40 Cf. p. 312, note 75.

When Abel remained away from home longer than was his custom, the Holy Spirit inspired Adam with these words to make inquiry about Abel: "Where is your brother Abel?" Thus Adam's prophecy and sermon, of which we heard above, here begins to be fulfilled: that sin reposes at the door. Cain thinks that he has laid his sin to rest and that it can remain hidden. And it is true. His sin does lie quiet, but it is at the door. Who opens the door? Indeed, the Lord Himself rouses what is resting. He brings the hidden sin to light.

The same thing must needs happen to all. Unless you get ahead of your sin through repentance and confess it to God yourself, God Himself comes and makes the sin manifest. He cannot endure to have anyone disavow the sin which he has committed. To this also Ps. 32:3-4 bears witness: "When I kept silence, all my bones became old, and my moisture was turned into the drought of summer." Even though sin reposes free from anxiety, it is nevertheless a repose at the door, a repose that is neither long-lasting nor concealed.

I take Moses' statement to mean that God spoke in the same sense as above,[41] namely, that Adam spoke these words through the Holy Spirit and as God's representative, a position which he, as the father, held toward his son. And so this expression of the Holy Spirit is concerned with extolling the authority of parents. When children listen to and obey them, they are listening to and obeying God. Furthermore, I believe that by the revelation of the Holy Spirit Adam knows that Abel has been killed. He makes a statement about the murder in spite of the fact that Cain is hiding it (Gen. 4:10).

But when Eve heard these words, how do you think the poor woman felt? Her grief was truly inexpressible. Nevertheless, the calamity involves Adam himself more directly. Because he is the father, his position compels him to denounce his son and to excommunicate him for his sin. Although he does not kill him — since the law about putting murderers to death is given below in the ninth chapter (9:6), after the patriarchs saw murders increase in number — and although, prompted by the Holy Spirit, he protects Cain with a sign so that he would not be killed, nevertheless a severe punishment is inflicted on him and all his descendants. In addition to that physical disgrace, there is the fact that Cain is excommunicated and is driven out from the presence of his parents and from the companionship of

[41] Cf. p. 173.

the rest of his brothers and sisters, who stayed with their parents as though in a church.

These things Adam could not do without deep grief, and Eve could not hear of them without the same feeling. For a father is a father; a son is a son. He would gladly have spared him and gladly have kept him at home, the way we sometimes see murderers become reconciled with the brothers of the slain. But here there is no room for reconciliation; he is simply commanded to be a fugitive on the earth. Thus the grief of the parents is made twice as great, inasmuch as they see their one son killed and the other excommunicated by God's judgment and shut out from the companionship of the rest of the brothers.

Moreover, when we speak of excommunication from the church, you need not think of our vast churches which are lavishly constructed of hewn stone. Adam's temple, or church, was some tree or some small hill beneath the open sky, where they used to come together to hear the Word of God and to bring sacrifices, for which they had erected altars. As Abel's example shows, God was present with those who sacrificed in this manner and heard the Word.

Other historical accounts also prove that there were altars under the open sky and that sacrifices were brought there. Today, too, it would serve a good purpose in many ways for us to meet under the open sky, there on bent knees to pray, to preach, to give thanks, to bless one another, etc. From this temple and from this church, which was not in one definite place, Cain is cast out and so is punished in a twofold way: first, with the physical punishment that the ground is cursed and the sign of a murderer is placed upon him; secondly, with the spiritual punishment that he is cast out through excommunication from the second Paradise, as it were, namely, from the temple and church of God.

The jurists, too, have made use of this passage and have dealt with it very respectfully because, before the Lord declares guilty, He inquires into the case.[42] From this they draw the application that no one should be declared guilty until the case has been investigated and unless he has first been given a summons, has confessed, and has been found guilty. The Lord did the same thing also in Adam's case (Gen. 3:9): "And He called Adam and said: 'Where are you?'" And also in chapter 11 (v. 5): "The Lord descended to see."

[42] For us, in turn, this provides a useful insight into juridical procedures in Luther's day.

But so far as we are concerned, let us pass over teachings which concern matters of government, and let us consider the excellent theological doctrine and comfort, namely, that the Lord inquires about Abel, who was dead. This plainly indicates the resurrection of the dead, inasmuch as God declares Himself to be the God of Abel, who is dead, and inquires about Abel, who is dead. From this passage we may draw the very sound argument that if there were no one to take care of us after this life, no inquiry would have been made about the slain Abel. But God inquires about Abel, who has been removed from this life. He does not want to forget him; He keeps him in mind and asks where he is. Therefore God is the God of the dead (Matt. 22:32); that is, therefore, the dead, too, live and have a God who cares for them and preserves them in a life that is different from this physical one in which the saints are afflicted.

This passage is noteworthy, since God takes care of Abel, who is dead, and so, because of Abel, who is dead, excommunicates and destroys the first-born Cain while he is alive. This is truly an important matter. Abel, though dead, lives; and in another life he is canonized by God Himself in a better and truer manner than all whom the pope has ever canonized. But Cain, though alive, is excommunicated and dies an everlasting death. Abel's death is indeed frightful, for he suffered death with great torment and with many tears. But it is a truly salutary death, inasmuch as he now lives a better life than before. We live this physical life in sins, and it is subject to death; but that other life is eternal and without any afflictions, physical or spiritual.

God does not inquire after sheep and cattle that have been slaughtered, but He does inquire after men that have been killed. Therefore men have the hope of resurrection and a God who leads them out of bodily death to eternal life, who inquires after their blood as after something precious, just as the psalm also says (116:15): "Precious is the death of His saints in His sight."

This is the glory of the human race, which was won by the Seed when He crushed the serpent's head. This is the first example of that promise given to Adam and Eve, by which God shows that the serpent does not harm Abel even though it succeeds in having Abel killed. This is indeed why the serpent lies in wait for the heel of the woman's Seed. But while it bites, its head is crushed. Because of Abel's trust in the promised Seed, God inquired after Abel's blood when he was dead and showed that He is his God, as the following words also prove.

10. *And He said: What have you done? The voice of your brother's blood is crying to Me from the earth.*

So far Cain's sin lay quiet at the door. The preceding words show clearly the great effort Cain made to have it remain quiet. When he is asked where Abel is, he answers that he does not know. Thus he adds a lie to the murder. This answer gives adequate proof that these words were spoken by Adam himself and not by the Divine Majesty. Cain thinks that his deed was unknown to his father Adam because Adam is a human being; about the Divine Majesty he could not have this thought. Therefore if God had spoken with him, he would have given a different answer. Now, when he thinks that he is dealing with a human being only, he denies the deed and says: "I do not know." For how varied are the perils by which a person may perish! Wild beasts consume some, others drown, and still others meet with another kind of death.

And so Cain believes that his father would rather suspect anything else than that he had committed a murder. But he could not deceive the Holy Spirit in Adam. Therefore, as God's representative, he openly accuses him and says: "What have you done?" It is as if he were saying: "Why do you continue to deny your deed? You surely cannot deceive God, who has revealed it to me. You think that your brother's blood is covered with earth, but it is surely not covered and swallowed up so well that it does not cry to God from the earth." This indeed amounts to rousing the sin which reposes at the door and making it known.

Therefore this text is full of comfort against the murderers and enemies of the church. It teaches us that our afflictions, blood, and death fill heaven and earth with their cries. I, therefore, believe that at these words of Adam, "What have you done?" Cain was so stunned and perplexed that he was dumbfounded and did not know what to do or say. These were his thoughts: "If my father Adam has knowledge of the murder which I have committed, how can I have any doubt that God, the angels, heaven, and earth have the same knowledge? Now where shall I flee? Where shall I turn, wretched being that I am?"

The same thing happens today to murderers. After they have committed murder, they are so fiercely pursued by the Furies that they are indeed dumbfounded and think that heaven and earth have taken on another appearance; and they do not know where to flee.

The poets describe Orestes in similar terms when he was pursued by the Furies.[43] Such an awful thing is this outcry of the blood and of an evil conscience.

But the very same thing happens in the case of other heinous sins. And those whom sadness of spirit seizes experience similar sensations, for to them all creatures appear changed.[44] Even when they speak with people whom they know and in turn hear them, the very sound of their speech seems different, their looks appear changed, and everything becomes black and horrible wherever they turn their eyes. Such a fierce and savage beast is an evil conscience. And so, unless God comforts them, they must end their own life because of their despair, their distress, and their inability to bear their grief.

Here, too, Moses indulges in his customary conciseness; but this is superior to any elaborate language. In the first place, the personification is striking, because he ascribes to the blood a voice which fills heaven and earth with its cries. For how can that be a thin and weak voice if God hears it in heaven when it makes itself heard from the earth? And so Abel, who bore his wrongs patiently when alive and was quiet and gentle, is utterly disinclined to put up with the harm done to him now that he is dead and buried; and he who formerly did not dare mutter against his brother now cries out persistently and with his cries troubles God to come down from heaven and make the murderer known. Therefore Moses also employs a stronger term. He does not say: "Your brother's voice speaks," but "It cries," like town criers who call the people together with a loud voice for a meeting.

However, these facts are recorded, as I stated above, that we may realize that our God is merciful and loves His saints, takes care of them, and inquires after them, whereas He is angry with murderers, hates them, and is determined to punish them. This comfort is something that we need above all. When we are afflicted, we think that God has forgotten us and no longer concerns Himself about us. We think that such things would not be happening to us if He were taking care of us. Abel, too, could have thought: "God cares nothing for me. Otherwise He would not have permitted me to be killed in this way by my brother."

[43] Cf. Aeschylus, *Eumenides*, 321 ff.

[44] Apparently an autobiographical reference to Luther's *Anfechtungen*, when all the creatures joined to accuse and condemn him.

But consider what follows. Does not God bestow greater care on Abel than he could have bestowed on himself? How could Abel, when he was alive, have avenged himself on his brother in the same way God now avenges him after he is dead? How could he, while he was alive, pass so awful a judgment on his brother as God now passes on him? The fact is that Abel's blood, which, during his life, was very quiet, now cries out. Now Abel accuses his brother before God as a murderer, although while living he had disregarded all his brother's wrongs. Who betrays the fact that Cain has killed his brother? Is it not, as the text declares, Abel's blood, which now deafens the ears of God and men with its persistent cries?

These facts, I say, are full of comfort, especially for us who suffer persecution at the hands of the popes and the wicked princes because of our doctrine. They have proceeded against us with the utmost cruelty. Not in Germany only but also in other parts of Europe their rage has displayed itself against godly people. This sin, as if it were a pastime, the papacy regards as a trifling matter; nay, it even considers it a service rendered to God (John 16:2). And so until now this sin reposes at the door, but in due time it will manifest itself. The blood of the very excellent and steadfast martyr Leonhard Kayser, which was shed in Bavaria, does not remain silent. The blood of Henry von Zütphen, which was shed in Ditmarsen, does not remain silent. The blood of our Anthony of England, who was cruelly put to death by his own Englishmen without a hearing, does not keep silent.[45] I am saying nothing about a thousand others who, although their names were less renowned, nevertheless were comrades of these men both in the confession of their faith and in their martyrdom. The blood of all these will not keep silence. In due time it will compel God to come down from heaven and execute on the earth a judgment that will be unbearable for the enemies of the Gospel.

Thus we must not assume that God is disregarding our blood. We must not assume that God has no regard for our afflictions. "Our tears, too, He gathers into His bottle," as Ps. 56:8 says. And the cry of the blood of the godly penetrates the clouds and heaven until it arrives at God's throne and urges Him to avenge the blood of the righteous (Ps. 79:10).

[45] On Leonhard Kayser cf. *Luther's Works*, 13, p. 59, note 30; Henry von Zütphen died as a martyr to the Evangelical cause on December 10, 1524; since "Anthony of England" (Robert Barnes) was not executed until 1540, this is evidently an addition by Veit Dietrich.

Just as these words have been written for our comfort, so they have been written to fill our adversaries with terror. What, in your opinion, is more awe-inspiring for those tyrants to hear than that the blood of those whom they have slain cries and incessantly accuses them before God? God is indeed long-suffering, especially now near the end of the world. Therefore sin reposes for a longer time. Vengeance does not follow immediately. But it surely is true that God is most profoundly outraged by this sin and will never allow it to go unpunished.

I, too, believe that this judgment of Cain did not take place on the first day, but that there was a lapse of some time. God is by nature long-suffering because He anxiously desires sinners to return to Him. But He does not for this reason postpone punishment indefinitely. He is the righteous judge both of the living and of the dead, as we confess in our Creed. This judgment He executes immediately at the beginning of the world in the case of those two brothers: the live one He judges to be a murderer and condemns, but the dead Abel He declares just; Cain He excommunicates and drives to such anguish of heart that the whole world appears to him to be narrow.[46] Cain realizes that he is nowhere safe after he realizes that God will be the avenger of this blood. To Abel, on the other hand, He gives room with safety, not only on earth but also in heaven.

Therefore why shall we have any doubt that God in His heart considers and counts the afflictions of His children and that He measures our tears and records them on unbreakable tablets which the enemies of the church are completely unable to destroy except by repentance? Manasseh was a very great tyrant and a most terrible persecutor of the godly. Therefore his exile and captivity would not have been sufficient to atone for those sins; but when he recognizes his sin and is truly repentant, the Lord shows him mercy (2 Chron. 33:1-16).

Like Paul,[47] so also the pope and his bishops have this one way left to them, namely, that they recognize their sin and beg for forgiveness. But when they do not do this, God in His wrath will demand the blood of the godly from their hands. Let no one have any doubt about this. Abel was killed, but Cain lives. But, good God, what

---

[46] See also *Luther's Works*, 13, p. 7, note 6.

[47] The lecture notes simply have the initial P, which usually refers to Paul, but would seem from the context here to mean Peter instead.

a wretched life he lives! He could wish that he had never been born, because he hears himself being excommunicated and expects death and vengeance for his sin every single moment. In due time the lot of our adversaries and of the oppressors of the church will be similar.

11. *And now you are cursed from the earth which opened its mouth to receive your brother's blood from your hand.*

Up to this point, we have heard how Cain's sin was revealed by Abel's blood, and how he himself was convicted of his sin by his father Adam. This was God's judgment about the two brothers: the one was not only declared righteous but was also canonized and declared a saint as the first fruits of that blessed Seed; the other, however, who was the first-born, was condemned and excommunicated, as the following events show. Now Moses proceeds to relate the punishments that resulted from this murder.

At the very outset the discrimination of the Holy Spirit is worthy of special note. Above, when punishment is inflicted on Adam because of his sin, the person of Adam is not cursed, but only the earth. Even this is not done directly, but a kind of excuse for the earth is added. This is the statement (Gen. 3:17): "The earth is cursed because of you." Similarly, Paul declares also in Rom. 8:20: "The creature is subjected to vanity, not willingly." Inasmuch as it sustained the sinning human being, it is also compelled, like a tool, to bear the curse. Similarly, a sword, gold, etc., are cursed because through their instrumentality sins are committed by people. This is an instance of very fine reasoning, that the Holy Spirit in this way distinguishes between the earth and Adam: the curse He turns aside to the earth, but the person He preserves.

Here, in regard to Cain, the Holy Spirit uses a different language; for He curses the person. Why does He do this? Is it because Cain, the murderer, sinned more grievously than Adam and Eve? No, but because Adam was the root from whose flesh and loins Christ, the blessed Seed, would be born. This seed is spared, and for the sake of this blessed fruit the curse is transferred from Adam's person to the earth. Hence Adam bears the curse placed on the earth, but not a curse placed on his person. For from his descendants Christ was to be born.

Because Cain forfeited this glory through his sin, his person is cursed, and he is told: "Cursed are you," to have us understand that he has been cut off from the glory of the promised Seed and that he would not have among his descendants a seed through which the blessing would come. This amounts to his being cut off from the sublime glory of the future Seed. Abel had been killed, and so there are no descendants from him. But Adam is obliged to serve God by begetting children.[48] If we disregard Cain, the hope of the blessed Seed depends on this one person until Seth is born to him.

The words indeed are brief; but surely they deserve much careful thought when Cain is told: "You are cursed"; that is: "You are not the one from whom the blessed Seed is to be hoped for." With this statement the Holy Spirit excommunicates Cain and cuts him off as a branch from the root, so that he can no longer hope for the glory he was seeking to obtain. Cain indeed wanted this glory of the blessing to be transmitted through him; but the more he strove, the less he succeeded. The same thing happens to all wicked men. The more they exert themselves to achieve their purposes, the more they fail.

And here is the beginning of the two churches that are utterly opposed to each other: the one, the church of Adam and the godly, which has the hope and promise of the blessed Seed; the other, the church of Cain, which has lost this hope and promise through its sin and cannot regain it. In the Flood all of Cain's descendants were completely wiped out, so that no prophet, no saint, or any head of the true church has arisen from among the descendants of Cain. So completely is everything denied to Cain and taken from him by this one word when he is told: "Cursed are you."

But the words "from the earth" are added. This phrase serves to mitigate, as it were, this awful expression of wrath. If the Holy Spirit had said "from heaven," He would have deprived Cain's descendants in general of any hope of salvation. Now, because He says "from the earth," He does indeed make the threat that they have forfeited the promise of the Seed; and yet it might happen that by divine impulse [49] some individuals of Cain's progeny might join Adam and be saved. And so it also happened later on. According to Ps. 147:20, "He has not dealt so with any nation," the Jews alone had the glory and promise of this Seed. Nevertheless, the Gentiles had, so to speak, the privilege of begging; and because of God's mercy they obtained

---

[48] The Latin phrase *ad generationem* could possibly mean "by begetting children" or "for a generation."

[49] The Weimar edition has *instinctu divino;* the St. Louis edition has *aus Eingeben des Heiligen Geistes.*

the same blessing that the Jews had as a result of God's truth or promise.

In this manner any rule in the church had been absolutely denied to the Moabites and the Ammonites. And yet many individually embraced the religion of the Jews. In the same way any right in the church was absolutely taken from Cain and his descendants, but they were not prohibited from begging, as it were, for this privilege. Because of his sin he is debarred from the right of sharing the common table. Nevertheless, he still had the right to gather the crumbs with the dogs (Matt. 15:27) if he so desired. This is the meaning of the expression מִדְהָאֲדָמָה, "from the earth."

But I submit this idea for consideration because in all likelihood many of Cain's descendants joined themselves to the holy patriarchs. But they were in the church as individuals and without office, as men who had completely lost the promise that the blessed Seed would be born from their body. It is a serious matter to lose the promise; and yet this very curse is made milder in this way, that the right of begging, as it were, was granted them, and heaven was not unconditionally denied to them, provided that they joined the true church.

This, however, Cain undoubtedly tried to hinder by various means. He established new forms of worship and devised rituals in order that he himself might also appear to be a church. Those who deserted him and joined the true church were saved, although they had to despair of the glory that Christ would be born from their body. But let us return to the text.

Here we have a remarkable personification.[50] Moses is speaking of the earth as a wild beast which has opened its mouth and has drunk the innocent blood of Abel. Why does he deal so harshly with the earth when these actions took place without its being consulted? What is more, because it is a good creature of God, they were done against its will and in the face of its opposition, just as Paul states that the creature was made subject to vanity, but not willingly (Rom. 8:20).

My answer is that this is done to inspire fear in Adam and in all his descendants, to make them live in the fear of God and shun murder. Adam means to say: "Behold, the earth has opened its mouth and consumed your brother's blood. But it should have consumed you, the murderer. The earth indeed is kindly disposed toward the upright and godly, but for the ungodly it is full of chasms." In this

---

50 The technical term used here is *prosopopoeia*.

way he makes use of harsh words in order to frighten and perplex murderers. There is no doubt that after Cain had heard these words from his angry father, he was terrified and perplexed within himself, just as Judas was, so that he did not know where to turn. These are harsh words: "which drank the blood of your brother from your hand"; and they express the hideousness of this murder better than any pictures.

12. *When you till the earth, it will no longer give you its strength.*

Above God said to Adam: "Thorns and thistles the earth will bring forth for you." Here He speaks differently, as if to say: "You have watered and fertilized the earth, not with beneficial and life-giving rain but with your brother's blood. Therefore it will be less fruitful for you than for others. The blood which you have shed will be a hindrance to the fertility and productiveness of the earth."

Here we have the second part of his punishment, namely, the physical curse, that though the earth is tilled in the same way by both Adam and Cain, nevertheless it will be more fertile for Adam and will respond to his toil; but to Cain's toil it will not respond — because of the blood, which hinders the earth from fulfilling its desire to give its yield according to its fertility and productiveness.

Something else should be brought out about the language. In this passage Adam calls the earth הָאֲדָמָה, but in the statement which follows — "And you will be a wanderer on the earth" — the word is אֶרֶץ. Now according to those who have a knowledge of the language, אֲדָמָה denotes the part of the earth which is cultivated, on which there are trees and other fruits useful for food; but אֶרֶץ denotes the entire earth, whether under cultivation or not. Therefore this curse especially concerns the earth which is tilled for the sake of food; where one ear produces 300 seeds for Adam, there barely ten seeds are produced for the murderer Cain, that he may see proofs everywhere that God hates and punishes the shedding of blood.

A wanderer and fugitive you will be on the earth.

This is the third punishment, and it persists for murderers up to the present time. Unless they bring about a reconciliation, they will nowhere have a secure home and a permanent dwelling place. Two words appear here: נָע וָנָד, "a wanderer and fugitive."

I am in the habit of distinguishing between them in this way:

נוּעַ denotes the insecurity of the place where one is. Thus the Jews are wanderers because they have no secure and permanent dwelling place. From hour to hour they are in fear of being forced to emigrate. But נוּד denotes the uncertainty of the place to which one wants to get. When one has no secure place to stay, there is this additional feature that when it becomes necessary to emigrate from that insecure place, one does not know where to go. Thus a double punishment is included in the one: the inability to remain permanently in a place and, at the same time, the lack of knowledge about where to go after one's expulsion from that place. In Ps. 109:10 we read: וְנוֹעַ יָנוּעוּ בָנָיו, "Let his children wander about." The meaning of this is: "Let them never find a secure place; but if they are in Greece this year, let them be forced to wander to Italy next year, and so on."

Such is now actually the wretched state of the Jews, for they are unable to establish secure homes anywhere. In addition to this hardship, the Lord also imposes another on Cain: that when he has once been driven out, he does not know where to turn. And so, suspended, as it were, between heaven and earth, he cannot settle permanently anywhere. The result is that he has neither a secure dwelling place nor a secure place of refuge.

Thus one sin is punished by a threefold punishment. In the first place, Cain is deprived of a spiritual or ecclesiastical glory; for there is taken from him the promise of the blessed Seed, who was to be born from his descendants. In the second place, the earth is cursed, and this is a punishment that affects his domestic establishment. The third punishment — that he is to be a wanderer and is to find a permanent dwelling place nowhere — involves civil government.

Nevertheless, there is a way left for him to come into the church, but without the promise. As I have said, if any of Cain's descendants joined the true church and the holy fathers, they were saved. Similarly, there is left to him the administration of his household, but without any blessing; likewise civil government, so that he can build a city and dwell there, but without knowing how long. Therefore he is truly like a beggar in the church, in the household, and in the government.

To these punishments is linked the mitigating circumstance that he is not immediately killed because of the murder he has committed, in accordance with the Law about murderers which was given later on, but is preserved as an example for others that they might fear

God and beware of murderers. Let this be enough about Cain's sin and judgment about the punishment for his sin.

But here the objection is raised that it is the godly who experience these curses, while the wicked fare well. Thus Paul says that he is a wanderer and has no secure dwelling place (1 Cor. 4:11). We who preach to the churches are in the same situation; we are either in exile, or we expect exile at any hour. The same thing was true of Christ, the apostles, the prophets, and the patriarchs.

Of Jacob, Scripture says (Gen. 25:23): "The older will serve the younger." But is not Jacob the servant, since he goes into exile for fear of his brother? When he returns, he entreats his brother and falls down at his feet. Similarly, Isaac is a most wretched beggar. His father Abraham is an exile among the heathen and does not own even a foot of ground in the country, as Stephen says in Acts 7:5. But Ishmael is a real king! He has sons who are princes in the land of Midian before Israel enters the Land of Promise. Likewise, it will follow a little later that Cain first built the city of Enoch and that among those who sprang from him were shepherds, several kinds of workers in metal, and musicians. All this argues that it is wrong to attribute the curses to Cain and his descendants. At any rate, they rest heavily on the true church, while the wicked fare well and flourish.

This stumbling block causes offense not only to the heathen but also to the saints themselves, as the psalms bear witness in more than one passage. And the prophets, such as Jeremiah, often are indignant when they see that the wicked are untouched, as it were, by evils, while they themselves are hard pressed and afflicted in various ways.[51] Where, then, you will say, is the curse that rests on the wicked? Where is the blessing that rests on the godly? Is not the opposite true? Cain has no settled habitation and is a wanderer, and nevertheless he is the first to build a city and a secure place to live. To this reasoning we shall reply below in detail, but now we shall return to the text.

13. *And Cain said to the Lord: My iniquity is too great to be forgiven.*

Here Moses appears to have introduced a perplexing difficulty for the linguists and the rabbis, for they torture this passage in various ways. Lyra mentions the opinions of some who explain the words

[51] A reference to Old Testament chapters like Ps. 43 and Jer. 12.

as an affirmation, namely, that Cain, in his despair, said that his sin was too great to be forgiven, just as we also translate it. Augustine, too, adheres to this opinion. "Cain," says he, "you lie. For God's mercy is greater than the misery of all sinners." [52]

But the rabbis explain this as a question and in a negative sense: "My iniquity is not too great to be forgiven, is it?" But if this is the true meaning, Cain not only did not acknowledge his sin but even excused it and reproached God for inflicting a greater punishment than he deserved. In like manner, the rabbis distort the meaning of Scripture almost everywhere. Therefore I am beginning to hate them and to advise that those who read them read with careful judgment. Although they had in their possession certain facts through tradition from the patriarchs, they nevertheless corrupted these facts in various ways. Consequently, they often deceived Jerome too. The poets have not filled the world with their fabrications to the extent to which the ungodly Jews have filled Scripture with their silly opinions. Hence it causes us much work to keep our text free from their misleading comments.

The reason for their going astray is that they are indeed familiar with the language but have no knowledge of the subject matter; that is, they are not theologians. Therefore they are compelled to twaddle and to crucify both themselves and Scripture. How is it possible to judge correctly about things that are unknown? The main thought in this passage is that Cain is being accused by his conscience. But there is no one — including not only any wicked person but even the devil himself — who would be able to endure this judgment. Thus James, in chapter two, declares that even the devils tremble in the presence of God (v. 19). And Peter, in his second epistle, chapter two, says that not even the angels, although they are greater in power and might, are able to endure the judgment which the Lord will bring upon those who blaspheme (v. 11). Manasseh, in his prayer, expresses it thus: "All men tremble before His wrathful face." [53]

These facts give adequate proof that in the case of this judgment there was not enough courage in Cain to oppose God and to remonstrate with Him. God is an omnipotent contender, and He makes His first attack on the heart itself and fastens His hold on the conscience.

---

[52] This is from Lyra on Gen. 4:13, sec. "x," where he refers to "catholic theologians."

[53] This is a quotation from the apocryphal Prayer of Manasses, v. 4.

Of this truth the rabbis have no knowledge, nor do they understand it. For this reason they speak of this judgment as if it were being carried on in the presence of human beings, where a deed is either deceitfully denied or is excused. God's judgment is something different. In it, as Christ states in Matt. 12:37, you will either "be justified by your words or be condemned by them." Therefore Cain acknowledges his sin, although he does not grieve over his sin as much as he does over the punishment that has been inflicted. Therefore we are dealing with an affirmative statement which reveals his awful despair.

Additional proof of this despair is the fact that Cain adds absolutely no expression of respect. He does not use the terms "Lord" and "father," but his startled conscience is so overwhelmed by terror and despair that it is unable to give consideration to any hope of pardon. Concerning Esau the Epistle to the Hebrews, chapter twelve, makes this statement (vv. 16-17): "Esau sold his birthright for a dish of food. But you know that later on, when he desired to obtain the blessing, he was rejected. He found no room for repentance, even though he sought it with tears." Thus Cain here feels the punishment, but he grieves more about the punishment than about his guilt, just as all men do in despair.

These two words, מִנְּשׂוֹא and עֲוֹן, are linguistic cruxes. Jerome translates them: "My iniquity is greater than that I deserve forgiveness." [54] Santes Pagninus, a learned philologist and apparently also an industrious one, translates thus: "My punishment is greater than I can bear." [55] But in this way we would make a martyr out of Cain and a sinner out of Abel. However, I stated above [56] that where the word נָשָׂא is applied to sin, it means to lift sin up or take it away, just as we use a common figure and speak of "remission of sins," and of "remitting sin." Thus we read in Ps. 32:1: אַשְׁרֵי נְשׂוּי־פֶּשַׁע, which literally means "becoming blessed, having been relieved of guilt or sin." This we express by "Blessed is he whose sin has been forgiven," or "whose sin has been taken away." Similarly also in Is. 33:24: "The people who

[54] The Douay Version has: "My iniquity is greater than that I may deserve pardon."

[55] Santes Pagninus or Pagnino (1470—1541) was a contemporary of Luther's, a Dominican. His philological work on the Bible, especially on the Old Testament, was used extensively by both Protestants and Roman Catholics. It seems that most of the textual comments in the latter part of this commentary come from his books.

[56] See p. 265.

dwell in it עָוֹן וְנֹשֵׂא," that is, "is one relieved of guilt," or "a people of the remission of sins."

The other word, עָנָו, they derive from the verb עָנָה, which denotes "to be afflicted," as in Zech. 9:9: "Your king comes to you poor or afflicted." Our translation has "meek." Likewise in Ps. 132:1: "Remember, Lord, David and all his meekness"; that is, his afflictions. From this verb is derived the term for lowliness which the Virgin Mary uses in her song in Luke 1:48. This situation caused Santes to translate עָוֹן with "punishment."

But עָוֹן here denotes "iniquity," or "sin," the same as in many other passages of Scripture, as the verb "to lift up," which has been added, also indicates. Thus we see that philologists who are nothing but philologists and have no knowledge of theological matters have their perplexing difficulties with such passages and torture not only Scripture but also themselves and their hearers. First the meaning should be established in such a manner that it is everywhere in agreement, and then philology should be brought into play. But the rabbis do the opposite. For this reason I regret that our teachers and holy fathers have, for the most part, followed their lead.

14. *Behold, you are driving me out today from the face of the ground, and I shall be hidden from your face; and I shall be a wanderer and fugitive on the earth, and it will come to pass that anyone who finds me will kill me.*

From these words it is clear that the verdict was pronounced through Adam's mouth. He acknowledges that he was being driven out, in the first place, from home and community, in the second place, also from the church.

Concerning the difference in meaning between the words אֲדָמָה and אֶרֶץ we stated above that אֶרֶץ denotes the entire earth, but אֲדָמָה denotes the ground under cultivation. The meaning, therefore, is: "You now compel me to flee from the place I have tilled. Indeed, the world lies open before me, but I shall be a wanderer and a fugitive on the earth; that is, I shall never have a secure dwelling place." Similarly among us, murderers who have escaped by flight are punished with exile. Furthermore, these words indicate clearly how one must understand what Adam said above (Gen. 4:11): "You are cursed upon the earth," namely, that he has been compelled to live in exile. This punishment is, therefore, of a political nature, and it excludes him from association with his fellow men.

But the words which Cain adds — "I shall be hidden from your face" — deal with an ecclesiastical punishment and with true excommunication. Since Adam was in possession of the priesthood and of royal rule, and Cain is excommunicated by Adam because of his sin, he is at the same time deprived of the glory of the priesthood and of royal rule. But why Adam made use of this punishment we heard above: "When you till the ground, it will not give you its strength"; that is, "You are cursed and your labors are cursed. Therefore if you remained with us in the land, we would have to perish with you from hunger. You have poisoned the earth with your brother's blood. This blood you are compelled to carry about with you, and the earth itself will exact punishment from you."

A statement of almost the same nature occurs in 1 Kings 2:31-33, where Solomon issues the order to Benaiah, the son of Jehoiada: "Kill Joab, and take away the innocent blood which was shed by Joab, from me and from the house of my father; and the Lord will return his blood upon his own head. But to David and his seed and to his house and throne let there be peace forever from the Lord." The meaning is as if he said: "If Joab does not pay the penalty for his unjust murder, the entire kingdom will have to atone for it and will be ruined by wars." So in this passage Adam wants to say: "If you remained in the country, God would so punish us because of you that the earth would never produce its fruit."

Now we shall give our answer to the question submitted above.[57] Cain is told: "You will be a wanderer and a fugitive on the earth," and yet he is the first to build a city. Thereafter his descendants increased to such an extent that they led astray, oppressed, and destroyed the church of God until it was reduced to eight persons of Seth's progeny. The entire remaining multitude which perished in the Flood followed Cain, as the text clearly states (Gen. 6:4): "The sons of God took the daughters of men, and they brought forth giants who were lords on the earth." Therefore since Cain has so many descendants and is the first to build a city, how can it be true that he is a wanderer and fugitive on the earth?

We shall give a specific answer. The additional statements — made above from the New Testament about Paul, the apostles, Christ, and the prophets too — have a different purpose. When Adam says: "A wanderer and fugitive you will be on the earth," he speaks in

[57] Cf. p. 295.

these terms in order to send Cain away without any directive. He does not tell him: "Go to the east." He does not say: "Go to the south." He mentions no place where he should go. He gives no order what he should do but simply turns him out. Let Cain go where he will, and let him do whatever he wants to do; it is of no concern to Adam. He adds no promise of a protector. He does not say: "God will take care of you; God will defend you." But just as the whole sky is open for the little bird so that it is at liberty to fly where it desires but never has a safe place where it can know it is safe from the attacks of other birds, so Adam sends Cain away. Cain realizes this. Therefore he adds: "Whoever finds me will kill me."

Adam's situation had been different and better. He had sinned, and through sin he had sunk into death; but when he was expelled from Paradise, God assigned him a definite work of tilling the ground in a certain place and clothed him with a garment of skins. This, as we said above, was a sign that God would take care of him and would defend him. But the glorious promise given to the woman concerning the Seed who would crush the serpent's head surpassed everything else. Not one of these things is granted to Cain. He is simply sent away to any indefinite place and work without the addition of any promise and command, just like a bird which roams uncertainly in the open air. This is really wandering and being unsettled!

Unsettled and roaming in this way are all those who do not have a Word and command of God designating a definite place and a definite person. Such was our lot under the papacy. There was no lack of ceremonies, of works, and of religious observances. But all these were performed and undertaken without God's command. This was truly a trial such as Cain's: to be without the Word and not to know what to believe, hope, or endure, but to do and undertake everything with no certainty as to the outcome. What monk has there ever been who could vouch that he had ever done anything right? All these things were nothing but human traditions and fabrications of reason without the Word. Among these we all roamed about and drifted like Cain, uncertain what decision God would reach about us, whether we deserved His love or His hatred. Thus we were taught at that time.

Thus all the descendants of Cain were wandering and unsettled. They did not have the promise and command of God, and they were without any sure rule by which to live and to die. Therefore if any came to the knowledge of Christ and joined the true church, this happened to them not as the result of a promise but because of pure mercy.

Seth, who was born later, as well as his descendants, had a definite promise, definite places, definite ceremonies for the worship of God, whereas, in contrast, Cain was a wanderer. Although Cain founded a city, he had no assurance as to how long he would inhabit it; for he had no promise of God. But whatever we have without God's promise lacks any assurance of how long we shall have it. At any moment Satan can either make these things unstable or take them away. However, when we walk along fortified by the command and promise of God, then the devil exerts himself in vain; for God strengthens and fortifies everything with His command.

Therefore even if Cain were the lord of the whole world and had all the wealth of the world, nevertheless — because he lacks the promise of divine help, is deprived of the protection of the angels, and has nothing else to rely on than human counsels — he is truly wandering and unsettled. As he adds:

Everyone who finds me will kill me.

This is the very obvious consequence. After Cain has been deprived of the help of God and of his parents, and after he has lost his claim to the priesthood and rule, he sees that what will happen is that whoever will find him can kill him. He has been excommunicated spiritually and physically. And yet God grants this infamous murderer a twofold favor. He had lost rule and church, but he keeps his life and his descendants. God promises him protection of life and gives him a wife. These are two favors which should not be regarded lightly and which Cain could not even have hoped for when he first heard his sentence from his father. Their purpose was that he might have opportunity and time for repentance, although they are a matter of accident and not one of command.[58] For God does not add a definite promise. Similarly, under the papacy we obtained mercy only by accident, so to speak. No definite promise had been given in advance that in our lifetime the truth would be brought to light and that the Antichrist would be revealed. But these two favors happened to Cain because of the elect; for it is very plausible that many of Cain's descendants who joined the true church were saved,

[58] The accidental mercy of God is a way of speaking about what other theologians have called "common grace" or "the uncovenanted mercies of God," i. e., His mercy to those who did not or do not belong to His covenant people.

just as later on among the Jews there was also room for proselytes and Gentiles.

Thus there was a very strict Law that no one of the Moabites and the Ammonites be admitted to the services of the church (Deut. 23:3). And yet many Ammonites and Moabites who came to the kings of Judah and served them were saved. Thus Ruth, mother and ancestress of our Savior, was herself a Moabite (Ruth 1:4). This was, to express myself in this way, accidental mercy, of which no assurance had previously been given through a promise.

In this manner Naaman, the King of Nineveh, Nebuchadnezzar, Evil-Merodach, and others from among the Gentiles were saved by accidental mercy.[59] For they did not have the promise of Christ, as did the Jews. Accordingly, because of the elect who had to be saved by accidental mercy, Cain was granted both protection of his life and a wife with offspring. Although his descendants had to live under the curse, just as we stated about the Moabites, nevertheless a few patriarchs took wives from among them.

15. *And the Lord said to him: Nay, whosoever will kill Cain will be punished sevenfold.*

In his letter to Damasus, Jerome states that Cain begged the Lord that he might be killed.[60] And he adopts this opinion wholeheartedly[61] so that he has no doubt whatever that it is correct. Lyra follows him and stoutly asserts that the context supports it.[62] But the rabbis are the ones who caused them to adopt this erroneous opinion. The true meaning is that no one must kill Cain. We are dealing here with a divine judgment, and God grants the murderer a stay of execution when He presents him with life and later on gives him a wife.

Moreover, what likelihood is there that a wicked person would ask for death when God exercises judgment? Indeed, because death is the punishment for sin, he rather flees from and trembles at death as a punishment. Let us, therefore, disregard those pratings of the rabbis. Among these is also properly counted what Lyra proposes about dividing this text: that the meaning is: "Anyone who kills

---

59 Augustine, *The City of God,* XVIII, ch. 47.

60 Jerome's letter to Damasus, *Epistola* XXXVI, 2, *Patrologia, Series Latina,* XXII, 453—454.

61 The Latin phrase is *plenis velis navigat.*

62 Cf. Lyra on Gen. 4:15.

Cain, will, of course, be severely punished." The addition — "he will be punished sevenfold" — they explain to mean that he will be punished by seven apiece, that is, to the seventh generation.

Of such pratings the rabbis are capable once they have rejected the light of the New Testament. But they cause us double labor; for we are compelled to safeguard the text and to cleanse it from such distortions, and we must correct their very absurd comments. However, I am accustomed to quote them occasionally, to avoid the impression that we are treating them with haughty contempt and that we have either ignored or slighted their writings. We read and understand them; but we read them with critical judgment, and we do not permit them to obscure Christ or to distort the Word of God.

Accordingly, in this passage the Lord does not change His sentence that Cain will be cursed on the earth. Nevertheless, He shows him this accidental mercy because of the elect who were to be saved out of these remaining dregs and this accursed mass. Therefore He declares that Cain must not be killed, as he was fearing.

Consequently, there is no need here to cut up the text, as Rabbi Solomon does.[63] He places a period after the words "Whoever kills," as if it were an aposiopesis, such as appears in Vergil: "Whom I — but it is better to quiet the agitated waters." [64] Next he refers the clause "he will be punished sevenfold" to Cain, who would be killed in the seventh generation. For Cain begot Enoch, Enoch begot Irad, Irad begot Mehujael, Mehujael begot Methusael, and Methusael begot Lamech.

Moreover, they prate that the aged Lamech, when his eyes were becoming dim, was led into a woods by his son Tubal Cain to hunt and kill wild beasts, the woods where the wandering Cain kept himself concealed, and that there by mistake he killed Cain when he shot at a wild beast. These are mere Jewish fabrications and unworthy of consideration by our schools. In addition, they militate against the truth of the text. For if the time of the seventh generation was fixed in advance as the time when he would be killed, Cain would not have been unsettled and roaming on the earth, as the Lord had threatened.

Therefore we reject this silly opinion on the basis of critical judgment, because it conflicts with what the Lord said previously. But

[63] This is summarized in Lyra on Gen. 4:15.

[64] Vergil, *Aeneid*, I, 135.

God does not change His mind as man does (1 Sam. 15:29). Accordingly, throughout Scripture this must especially be watched: that a later statement is not at variance with an earlier one. Moreover, Lyra, too, rejects their claim that the Flood was Lamech's punishment; for he declares correctly that this was the common punishment of all wicked men. Let us, therefore, disregard those pratings.

Accordingly, we adhere to the true meaning: that when Cain feared that he would be killed by anyone, the Lord prevents this from happening and announces a sevenfold greater punishment.

Here, too, Lyra discusses how anyone who killed Cain would deserve a sevenfold punishment, inasmuch as Cain had killed his brother.[65] But what gain is there in carefully inquiring into the Lord's counsel in such matters, especially since it is certain that Cain is given the protection of God's irregular mercy,[66] or, as we express it, the promise and blessing of the Law?

For there are two kinds of promises — something to which we have frequently called attention. The promises of the Law have their support, so to speak, in our works, such as this one (Is. 1:19):[67] "If you do this, you will eat the good things of the earth"; likewise (Ex. 20:6): "I am God, who shows mercy to thousands of them who love Me." Of such sort was also the one given above (Gen. 4:7): "If you are good, there will be lifting up." But in most instances these promises of the Law have threats added to them.

The other kind are the promises of grace, and these do not have threats added to them. Of such kind are (Deut. 18:18): "I shall raise up a Prophet like you"; likewise (Jer. 31:33): "I shall write My Law into their hearts"; also (Gen. 3:15): "I shall put enmity between you and the Seed of the woman." These promises are not dependent on our works, but simply on the goodness and grace of God, that He Himself wants to fulfill them. Thus we have the promises of Baptism, of the Lord's Supper, of the Keys, etc., in which God sets before us His will, His mercy, and His works.

Such a promise God does not give to Cain. He makes only this one statement: "Whoever will kill you will be punished sevenfold." Adam had such a promise of grace; and Cain, too, should have received it from his parents as an inheritance because he was the

---

65 Lyra on Gen. 4:15, sec. "q."

66 Cf. p. 301, note 58.

67 This seems to be a reference to Lev. 25:18-19.

first-born. It was a rich promise and one of eternal glory, because it promised the Seed who would crush the serpent's head without any human merit or work. It had no condition attached to it: "If you sacrifice," "If you are good," etc.

If you compare with this promise what is said to Cain, it is like a morsel of bread offered to a beggar. No absolute promise of life is given to him. God merely threatens those who would kill Cain. He does not say: "No one will kill you" or: "I shall control the others in such a way that they do not kill you." If He had done this, He would have permitted Cain to return in safety into the sight of God and to his parents. He merely gives the order that men should not kill Cain. Therefore if this is a promise, it is the kind of promise that rests on the activities of men. Nevertheless, it must not be despised, because the promises of the Law deal with matters of the utmost importance.

Augustine declares that God gave the Romans their empire because of their superior virtues.[68] Similarly, even today the blessings of those nations which refrain from murder, adultery, and theft are greater than the blessings of those who do not refrain from these crimes. And yet governments, which have been established in accordance with reason in the best possible way, do not have anything more than those temporal promises.

The church, however, has promises of grace, which are eternal. Although Cain lacked these, it was still something momentous that the physical promises were left to him: that he was not immediately killed, that a wife was given to him, that children are born to him, that he founds a city, tills the ground, breeds cattle, and that he is not completely cut off from the society and companionship of all human beings. God had it in His power not only to deprive Cain of all these but also to inflict on him the plague, epilepsy, apoplexy, bladder stones, gout, and any other troubles. And yet men inquisitively discuss how God could increase the curse on Cain seven times.

Thus just as above God takes away all blessings — the spiritual, or such as pertain to the church, as well as those pertaining to the state — so here He tempers that sentence and commands that no one should kill Cain. Nevertheless, He does not make any promise that all men will obey this command. Although this physical promise is there, Cain is still a wanderer and unsettled. If he continues to be evil, it may happen that he will be killed soon. On the other hand,

---

[68] Augustine, *The City of God*, V, ch. 12.

if he conducts himself properly, he may live for a longer time. No assurance is given to him by a definite promise. Thus the physical promises, or those of the Law, even though they are important and excellent, nevertheless are uncertain and accidental.

Accordingly, I am unable to state with certainty whether Cain was killed. The Holy Scriptures supply no clear information concerning this question. This much alone can be proved from the text: Cain did not have a definite promise; but God had abandoned him to an uncertain, insecure, and roaming life and by His command and threat had merely restrained the ungodly from killing Cain, because certain punishment would follow this murder. Moreover, God did not promise that He intended to keep Cain from being killed. But we know that it is the nature of law that it is always the minority that obeys it. Therefore even though there is no written record to tell us at what time or place or by whom Cain was killed, it is likely that he was killed. But Scripture makes no mention of this, just as it makes no mention of the number of Cain's years or of the day of his birth and death. He perished with his race (as the crude proverb has it), "without cross and without light and without God," except for the few who were saved by accidental mercy.[69]

At this point it is usually asked to whom these words, "Everyone who finds me will kill me," apply. It is certain that at that time there were no human beings in existence besides Adam and Eve and some daughters. Therefore my ready answer would be that these words take note of the fact that we see the ungodly fleeing when no one pursues them, and imagining dangers for themselves even where there are none. We observe the same thing today in the case of murderers who are afraid even of what is safe and cannot remain long anywhere, for they think that death is present everywhere.

But because in God's command there follows: "Whoever slays Cain," these words must not be referred only to the fear Cain felt. Cain had sisters, and perhaps he feared that the one whom he had married would avenge her slain brother. Furthermore, Cain had vague thoughts of a longer life; he realized that more sons would be born to Adam, and he feared Adam's entire posterity. And the fact that God has left him only an uncertain mercy increases this fear. I do not think that Cain was afraid that he would be killed by wild beasts. For what meaning has it for wild beasts that God threatens a sevenfold punishment for the murderer?

[69] Cf. p. 301, note 58.

And the Lord put a sign on Cain that anyone who found him would not smite him.

What sort of sign this was is not stated in the Sacred Scriptures. For this reason some advance one idea, others another. Nevertheless, almost all agree in their conviction that there was in Cain a violent tremor of the head and of all his limbs.[70] They give as their reason that it is not likely that God either changed or mutilated any limb on his body, but that He left his body the way it had been created and merely added an outward sign that was very noticeable, namely, a tremor. This thought of the fathers is not bad, but it is one that cannot be proved from Scripture. It could have been a different sign. Similarly, we note in almost all murderers that their eyes immediately change and take on a sullen look after they have lost the charm which the eyes naturally have.

Whatever this sign may have been, it is surely a ghastly and awful punishment that Cain is compelled to carry it with him during his entire life as a punishment for his dreadful murder. Moreover, marked with this loathsome sign, he is sent into exile by his parents, is hated and detested. Although the life he had asked for is granted him, it is nevertheless a life of disgrace, which had attached to it the mark of murder, not only to remind him of the sin he had committed and to keep him appalled by it but also to deter others from committing murders. Nor could this sign be removed by any repentance; but Cain was compelled to bear this indication of God's wrath as a punishment for the murder, just like his exile, the curse, and other penalties.

However, it should be remarked here that the verb above (Gen. 4:14) is הָרַג, which means "to kill." But in this passage the verb is נָכָה, which denotes "to smite." And so God grants him security not only from death but also from the danger of death. But it is, as I said above, a security of the Law; for it merely forbids anyone to slay Cain and threatens a sevenfold punishment. But there is no promise that all men will obey this command. Nevtheless, it is better for Cain to have this promise of the Law than to be without any promise at all.

16. *And Cain went out from the presence of the Lord and dwelt in the land of Nod, to the east of Eden.*

This, too, is a strange text; and it is remarkable that the rabbis, in accordance with their habit, have not fabricated some prodigious

[70] Lyra on Gen. 4:15, sec. "r."

story in connection with it. But here Moses leaves it to the reader's discretion to picture to himself how sad and tearful this departure was. The godly parents had lost Abel. By the Lord's command their second son now goes into exile, weighed down with curses because of his sin, although his parents had hoped that he would be the sole heir of the divine promise and for this reason had loved him dearly from infancy. Nevertheless, Adam and Eve obey God's command and, on the basis of God's command, cast out their son.

Therefore their obedience to God, or their fear of Him, deserves to be given praise in this passage. They had learned from their own experience in Paradise that it is not a light sin to deviate from God's command. And so they thought: "Behold, our sin was punished by death and countless other afflictions into which we have been thrust after being expelled from Paradise. Now, when our son, too, has committed an outrageous sin, it is improper for us to oppose the will and just judgment of God, although it is most painful for us to bear it."

Familiar is the story of the woman of Tekoah, whom Joab engaged to intercede for the exiled Absalom (2 Sam. 14:5-7). She submits that after she had lost one son, it would be most unfair if she were deprived of the other too. And after Rebecca had become aware of Esau's resentment, she said to her husband Isaac (Gen. 27:45): "Why shall I be deprived of both sons?" Over this grief Adam and Eve prevailed and thus brought their fatherly and motherly affections into subjection. Besides realizing that they must obey the will of God, they were also warned by their own example. Previously they had been expelled from Paradise because of sin, and now they feared that they would be expelled from the entire earth if, contrary to God's will, they kept their son.

This is truly a noteworthy story; it bestows outstanding praise on obedience to God and incites us to the fear of God. Paul does the same thing in his First Epistle to the Corinthians (10:1-12), which was written wholly against the smugness of human hearts. God indeed is merciful, but this is no reason for sinning. For He is merciful only to those who fear Him.

Just as it was most distressing for the parents to lose their son, so also, in my opinion, this departure was most painful for Cain. He is compelled to leave not only the common home, dear parents, and the protection of parents but also his hereditary birthright, the prerogative of rule and priesthood, and the fellowship of the church.

For this reason the text says that "he went out from the face of the Lord." But we stated above what Scripture calls "the face of the Lord," namely, those things by which God shows that He is with us.[71] Thus in the Old Testament faces of the Lord were the pillar of fire, the cloud, and the mercy seat; in the New Testament, Baptism, the Lord's Supper, the ministry of the Word, and the like. By means of these God shows us, as by a visible sign, that He is with us, takes care of us, and is favorably inclined toward us.

Accordingly, from that place at which God declared Himself to be present, where Adam dwelt like a high priest and like the lord of the earth, Cain went out and came to another place. Here there was no face of God and no visible sign by which he could comfort himself that God was with him and was favorably inclined toward him — apart from those signs that are common to all beings, even to the wild beasts, namely, the enjoyment of sun, moon, day, night, water, air, etc. But these are not signs of His changeless grace; they are blessings or signs of His kindness toward all creatures.

Cain's departure was piteous and tearful because he was compelled to leave his parents. In his lonely and unsettled condition they gave him a daughter to wife, to live with him; but they did not know what the lot of their son and their daughter would be. And so their grief increases because they lose three children. What else can be considered to be the meaning of what is later added: "And Cain knew his wife"?

Where, then, did Cain dwell? Moses answers: "In the land of Nod." The land received this name from its wandering and unsettled inhabitant. Where is this land located? Beyond Paradise, toward the east. This is a notable passage. Cain came to a certain place located toward the east. But when he came there, he was neither carefree nor safe. It was the land of Nod, in which he was unable to gain a firm foothold because there was no face of God there. He had left this behind with his parents, who dwelt in such a location that they had Paradise either at their side or toward the west. But Cain, the exile, went to the east so that the Cainites were separated from the descendants of Adam by Paradise, which was located between them. Moreover, this passage proves that Paradise remained in existence after Adam had been driven out of it. In the end it was completely destroyed by the Flood.[72]

[71] Cf. p. 252.
[72] See p. 98.

This passage is also not in disagreement with the opinion of those who conclude that Adam was created in the region of Damascus and that afterwards, when he had been driven out because of his sin, he had also dwelt in Palestine. Thus the center of Paradise was where Jerusalem, Bethlehem, and Jericho were located later on, the places where Christ and John spent the greater part of their life. The fact that the present sites do not well agree with this is due to the devastation by the Flood, by which mountains, rivers, and fountainheads were changed. It is possible that later on Calvary, where Christ offered Himself for the sins of the world, was located where the tree of the knowledge of good and evil had been while Paradise was still standing. Thus so far as the place is concerned, death and destruction through Satan would be matched by life and salvation won through Christ.[73]

Daniel also purposely employs an unusual expression (9:26): "And its end will be in a flood," as if he intended to say: "The first Paradise was ruined and laid waste by the Flood; the other Paradise, in which our redemption was achieved, will be laid waste by the flood of the Romans."

With these thoughts the following also agrees. Just as Babylon brought about the destruction of the Jewish people, so this misfortune had its beginning the moment Cain and his descendants dwelt in that part of the earth where later on Babylon was founded. These are my thoughts and surmises. I have drawn them in part from the fathers. Even if they are not correct, they do have some evidence in their favor, and they contain nothing ungodly. For after the Flood Noah saw a surface of the whole earth far different from the one he saw before the Flood. Mountains were torn apart, fountains were broken up, and the courses of rivers were changed by the immeasurable force of the rushing waters.

17. *And Cain knew his wife, and she conceived and gave birth to Enoch; and when he built a city, he called the name of that city Enoch according to the name of his son.*

It causes surprise that Moses gives a description of the generation of the sons of Cain before writing about the sons of God. But this is done according to a definite plan of God. In this life the children of this world surpass the children of God in accordance with the first promise. The Seed of the woman possesses a spiritual blessing;

[73] Pseudo-Tertullian, *Adversus Marcionem carmina*, II, 196—197, is an early instance of this speculation.

but the seed of the serpent obtains for itself a physical blessing, for it bites the heel of the blessed Seed (Gen. 3:15). Accordingly, what is carnal comes first; but what is spiritual comes later.

From this fact a great dissimilarity arises later on. Even though Cain's descendants are mentioned first, nevertheless we see that the descendants of the godly were objects of greater concern to the Holy Spirit. He does not write down a bare listing of their names, but He carefully records their years and makes mention of their death. He tells not only what they themselves did, as the narrative deals with the children of Cain in this passage, but what the Lord did and spoke with them — what He promised them, how He preserved them in dangers, how He blessed them, etc.

None of these things are mentioned in connection with the wicked descendants of Cain. But when He has stated: "Cain begot his son Enoch and founded a city to which he gave the name of his son," He at once cuts the account of Cain short and virtually buries him completely with these words, so that He appears to have had no regard or concern for his life and death. He merely mentions the physical blessing, how they begot children and how they were building. Just as the gift of procreation was not taken from the murderer Cain, so the gift of ruling was not taken from him. But, as we pointed out above, he lost the rich blessing of the earth, because the earth drank the blood of his brother.[74]

But the Holy Spirit relates these things that we may realize that at the very beginning there were two kinds of churches: the one, that of the children of Satan and of the flesh, which quickly makes great increases; the other, that of the children of God, which makes slow gains and is weak. Although Scripture does not relate how they lived with each other, nevertheless, because it is stated: "I shall put enmity between you and her Seed," it is certain that Cain's church was most hostile toward the church of Adam. Our text also indicates very plainly that the children of men became so predominant in power that they destroyed almost the entire church of the sons of God. In the Flood only eight people were saved. All the rest of the race perished in the waters because of their sin.

However, this is the usual misfortune of all ages. When the true church begins to increase, she opposes Satan and the ungodly with great zeal. But the wickedness of the enemy exhausts her strength;

[74] Cf. p. 292.

and either she yields to the raging enemy after she is overcome by cross and sorrow, or she succumbs to pleasures and riches. In this way the descendants of Adam were discouraged by continuous warfare with the sons of men and succumbed, with the exception of eight persons who were preserved. Therefore, when ungodliness gains the upper hand and even the godly are giving ground, God finally comes and preserves the godly remnant. But the rest, seducers and seduced alike, He includes in the same judgment and punishes them, just as we believe and hope will be the case at the Last Judgment.

Many questions arise here. Questions are asked both about Cain's wife and about the time when the murder was committed, whether before he was married or during his marriage. The Jews declare that at each birth Eve had twins, a male and a female. Cain, they say, married his sister Calmana; Abel married Dibora.[75] Whether these claims are true I do not know. Nothing of importance to the church is endangered thereby, even if there is nothing sure about them.

This much is certain: that Cain had his sister for a wife. Although nothing certain can be stated about whether Cain was married when he committed the murder, yet the text rather favors the opinion that he was already a husband by that time. It states that the inheritance is divided between the brothers, since cattle raising is assigned by their parent to Abel, but the tilling of the ground to Cain I would, therefore, be inclined to believe that both brothers were married.

What was said above — that after the end of days Cain and Abel brought an offering (Gen. 4:3) — favors this opinion. The Jews explain this to mean that at the end of the year the newly married husbands brought offerings from the new fruits that were granted them during the first year of their marriage — Cain, the first fruits of the earth; Abel, the firstlings of the sheep.[76] The time of the year was fall, when the crops have already been gathered from the fields. Similarly, the Jews later on had their Feast of Atonement at this time. Moses seems to have carefully noted and collected the practices of the fathers and to have formulated them into law. Therefore, when the newly married husbands, who were about to give thanks to God for His blessing, brought their sacrifices, and Abel's sacrifice was pleasing to God, Cain's heart was filled by Satan with hatred of his brother, and then this deplorable murder followed.

[75] See p. 282, note 40.
[76] Lyra on Gen. 4:17.

This is the opinion of the Jews. I quote it because it does not seem to be at variance with the truth. As I stated above, we must read the writings of the Jews with critical judgment, so that we may keep what is likely to prove true but reject and refute what has been fabricated.

If Cain was not married at that time, it is surely a far more remarkable fact that later on he obtained a wife. Furthermore, the girl who married him must be lavishly praised. How could she be glad at the marriage of her brother, who was a murderer, accursed, and excommunicated? Moreover, she undoubtedly asked her father humbly why he was joining her, an innocent person, with the accursed man and was forcing her into exile. Cain's conduct, too, justifiably filled her with fear that he would dare to do to his sister and wife what he had dared to do to his brother.

When Adam was bringing this marriage about, he, therefore, had to be extremely eloquent in order to persuade his daughter that she should not reject her father's command, and that, although Cain was cursed and was bearing the punishment for his sin, God would nevertheless preserve her, who was innocent, and would bless her.

I have no doubt whatever that because of his wife, who married her bloodthirsty brother in holy trust in God and out of obedience to her parents, God bestowed many personal blessings on Cain through all his descendants. Just as Christ was a servant of the circumcised (Rom. 15:8) because of the truth and trustworthiness of the promise given to the Jews, but a servant of the Gentiles because of God's mercy (for they had no promise), so also that accidental mercy was extended to Cain's descendants.[77]

Thus there are two opinions about Cain's marriage, but which is the true one I do not know. If he became a husband after he had committed the murder, his wife must surely be distinguished and lauded with extraordinary praise for yielding to the authority of her parents and permitting herself to be united with the accursed murderer.

Nevertheless, it seems to me that the first opinion is more in harmony with the truth; for in the text we have clear evidence about the division of the inheritance. Furthermore, his wife was obliged to follow him. Adam was unwilling to separate them, because wife and husband are one body (Gen. 2:24). Moreover, the wife is com-

[77] Cf. p. 301, note 58.

pelled to bear part of her husband's misfortunes just as, in contrast, Cain's descendants received part of the blessings which fell to his guiltless wife. Pharaoh, king of Egypt at the time of Joseph, was saved, and the king of Nineveh was saved, even though they were not part of the people of God. In the same way, I believe, some of Cain's descendants were saved, although Cain had completely forfeited the promise concerning the blessed Seed.

THE DESCENDANTS OF CAIN

So far as the names of the descendants of Cain are concerned, I think that they, too, like those of the godly patriarchs, were not meaningless and haphazard but indicated some definite forethought and presentiment. Adam means human being, Eve means mother of the living, Cain means possession, and Abel means vanity. Meanings of this kind are often attached to many names of the Gentiles, for true presentiments are sometimes connected with names.

Thus Enoch is a name with an omen and is expressive of a future hope of comfort for Cain, or rather for his wife, who called him Enoch from חָנַךְ, "he dedicated" or "he initiated." It is, moreover, a verb that occurs in Moses' writings, as when he says (Deut. 20:5): "If anyone has built a house and has not yet dedicated it, let him not go out to war." But "dedicate" in this passage means to have possession of, to enjoy. Whenever people do this first, they always do it with a happy omen and with a prayer that predicts happiness. Thus when Cain's wife gave birth, she said to Cain: "Enoch, dedicate, initiate"; for it is a verb in the imperative, as though he were saying: "May this be a happy and auspicious beginning! For my father Adam cursed me because of my sin; I was driven out from his presence. Now I dwell alone. The earth does not yield me her wealth. It would yield more abundantly if I had not sinned. Nevertheless, God now shows me accidental mercy. This is a fine and happy beginning. Let it continue happily." [78]

Just as here, in the family of Cain, Enoch is the beginning of a physical blessing, so later on, in the family of the godly, there is Enoch, under whom the worship of God and spiritual blessing again begin to flourish.

The additional statement about the founding of the city deals with history. I said above that when Cain had been separated from the true church and had been driven into exile, he hated the true

[78] Here Luther breaks into German: *Es gehe wol an.*

church. And so this, too, that he is the first to build a city, has to do
with his purpose to show that he not only despises the true church
but also intends to suppress it. These were his thoughts: "Behold,
I have been driven into exile by my father and am accursed; but
my marriage does not happen to be barren, and so there is hope of
a numerous posterity. What do I care that I was driven out by my
father? I shall build a city in which I can gather my own church.
Away with my father and his church!"

Thus Cain did not build the city on account of fear and for his
defense but because of his sure hope of success and his pride and
lust for ruling. There was no need to fear his father and mother, who
had already driven him away into a strange land. He could not have
been afraid of his children either. But he is puffed up by the accidental mercy and, as the world is accustomed to do, seeks an occasion
to become prominent. Meanwhile, the children of God are concerned
with the other city, which has solid foundations and has been built
by God Himself, as the Epistle to the Hebrews says (11:10).

18. *Furthermore, to Enoch was born Irad.*

I do not know what to make of this name. Its origin is rather
unclear. And yet I think that it, too, is in the nature of an omen and
not haphazard. In the Book of Joshua appears the city Ai, and the
same word is used as an appellative. But the word עַי denotes
"a heap," such as of destroyed buildings. If you establish a connection
between the noun and this name, the word עִירָד denotes "a heap that
comes down." And so Enoch called his son Irad that the latter might
be prosperous and might come down with a great heap, so that Cain's
posterity would not perish altogether but would be preserved and
increased, although it was like a ruin heap because of Cain's excommunication. If someone else has a better suggestion, I shall not be
against it; for where the meaning is uncertain, one has to make a guess.

Irad begot Mehujael.

This name is compounded of מָחָה, which denotes "to destroy,"
and of אָל, "he began" or "he dared." Thus the meaning is that Cain's
posterity has now gained such an increase that it has dared oppose
itself to the true church and despise and pursue it, inasmuch as Cain's
descendants were superior in means, wisdom, glory, and numbers.
This is generally the way the true church is overcome by the world
and the false church.

Mehujael begot Methusael.

מוּת denotes "death," and שָׁאַל means "to ask for," "to demand." From this verb comes the name Saul, that is, "one asked for." This is a more arrogant name than all the others. My understanding of it is that they are threatening to avenge their dead parents, whom the other church had punished with excommunication and exile.

Methusael, however, begot Lamech.

Thus far the Cainites seem to have troubled the true church with impunity and to have prevailed. But the word לֶמֶךְ denotes that God had punished them at the time when Lamech was born. It is derived from the verb מָכַךְ, which means "to humble," "to diminish," or "to suppress." Or it can be taken in the active sense, that then the descendants of Cain had increased to such an extent that the true church had been almost completely suppressed by them.

These are the descendants of Cain — men who no doubt were outstanding for their wisdom and prestige. I also believe that some of them were saved in accordance with the accidental mercy, as I stated above. But the greater part of them hated the true church most intensely and persecuted it. They were not disposed to be inferior to the sons of Adam. For this reason they introduced their own worship and other practices in order to suppress the church of Adam.

Moreover, because the false church had in this way become separated from the true, I believe that Cain joined his sons and daughters in marriage. At the time of Lamech the descendants of Cain began to increase very much. For this reason Moses at this point brings the list of their names to an end.

19. *And Lamech took to himself two wives; the name of the one was Ada, and the name of the other was Zilla.*

A double question arises here.[79] In the first place, the theologians discuss whether Lamech married two wives because of his lust or whether he did so for some other reason. I myself do not think that he became a polygamist solely because of his lust, but because of his desire to increase his family and because of his desire for rule, especially if, as his name indicates, the Lord at that time punished the descendants of Cain either with the plague or with some other

[79] This is from Lyra on Gen. 4:19.

disaster. It was then that Lamech thought that he ought to repair that loss by this procedure. Similarly, some foreign nations continue the practice of polygamy even now, in order to give support and permanence both to their household and to their government.

One of Lamech's wives has the name Adah, which means the same as if one called her "Adorned" or "Wearing a necklace." עֲדִי is a term for women's finery, and the verb עָדָה denotes "to adorn," "to put on." Perhaps she had this name not only because she was the handsomely adorned mistress of the home but because she was also beautiful. The other wife has the name Zilla, which means "her shadow."

20. *And Ada bore Jabal, who was the father of such as dwell in tents and of shepherds.*

Jabal comes from the verb יָבַל. It means "to bring," "to raise."

21. *But the name of his brother was Jubal; he was the father of such as play the harp and wind instruments.*

The origin of this name is the same as that of the preceding one, for it denotes "brought," "raised." Moreover, these two names include the wish that the family might be increased. For Cain's descendants aimed at surpassing the others in numbers. Over against the true church they no doubt laid great stress on that blessing as clear proof that they had not been cast off by God but were themselves also the people of God.

22. *Zilla also gave birth to Tubal Cain, who was an artisan in every kind of skillful work of bronze and iron; but the sister of Tubal Cain was Naamah.*

Tubal Cain means "produce wealth." In a similar way the Latins give the name Valerius or Augustus.[80] Naamah got her name from her pleasing person or beauty.

These descendants of Cain increased endlessly, and so Moses breaks off his account of them.

However, regarding the fact that he mentions not only the names but also what each one's attainments and occupations were, the opinion of the Jews is to be rejected.[81] They imagine that Cain's

[80] The name Valerius refers to the power, the name Augustus to the dignity, of the Roman emperor.

[81] Lyra on Gen. 4:22.

descendants were compelled to engage in other occupations because for them the earth was cursed, and that for this reason they gained their livelihood by another method. Some became shepherds; others, workers in bronze; still others devoted themselves to music, in order to obtain from the descendants of Adam grain and other products of the earth which they needed for their support. But if the Cainites had been so hard pressed by hunger, they would have forgotten their harp and the other musical instruments in their poverty. There is no room for music among people who suffer hunger and thirst.

The fact that they invented music and devoted their efforts to developing other arts is proof that they had a plentiful supply of everything needed for sustenance. They had turned to these endeavors and were not satisfied with their simple manner of life, as were the children of Adam, because they wanted to be masters and were trying to win high praise and honor as clever men. Nevertheless, I believe that there were some among them who went over to the true church and adopted Adam's faith.

Moses' description here of the generation of the ungodly, or of the false church which existed before the Flood, is still appropriate, and it will remain so until the flood of fire. "For the children of this world are in their generation wiser than the children of light" (Luke 16:8). Therefore they promote and expand their endeavors, they extol themselves and their achievements, and they acquire riches and positions of honor and power. Meanwhile, the true church lies there despised and is harassed, suppressed, excommunicated, etc.

23. *And Lamech said to his wives Ada and Zilla: Hear my voice, you wives of Lamech, hearken to my speech; for I have killed a man because of my wound, and a young man because of my bruise.*

So far Moses has told the story of the generation of the children of this world. And when he has finished with this enumeration, he buries them as though there were no promise left for them either of the future life or of the present. For they had nothing besides that accidental blessing which granted them children and a livelihood. Nevertheless, they so increased in power and numbers that they filled the entire world. In the end they also brought about the downfall of the holy generation of the children of God, who had the promise of the future life; they worked havoc among them and plunged them into such a deep hell of ungodliness that only eight persons remained spiritually alive. Although there is no doubt that some were saved both before the Flood and during the Flood, nevertheless Scripture does not state this, for the reason that we may fear God and walk according to His Word. But men's hearts are thoroughly hard if they are not touched by the example of the Flood, for no period of history has anything more dreadful to relate than this.

Now when Moses has buried the ungodly in this manner, he relates one little incident about Lamech; but he does not make clear what its nature was. And so I surmise that no other passage of Holy Scripture has been dealt with in such a variety of ways and has been mangled as badly as this one.[82] For even though a lack of knowledge is not eloquent, it at least is a fertile source of many opinions and errors. On the other hand, language which states a fact is readily understood. Nevertheless, I shall mention the prevalent opinions.

The Jews concoct a tale such as this. When Lamech was an old man and was already turning blind, he was led into the woods by a young man to hunt and kill wild animals, not for their flesh but for their skins. (These ideas are indeed preposterous and at once betray their fictitious character.) Moreover, Cain had hidden in a dense thicket, and there he not only had repented but had sought some safety. Now the boy who was in charge of Lamech's weapon suspected that a wild animal was in the thicket, and he directed Lamech to kill it. Lamech shot his arrow and, contrary to expectation, pierced Cain. But after he had become aware of the murder he had committed, he shot the boy, who died as a result of the shot. In this way, they maintain, a man and a youth were killed by Lamech.

These ideas are not worth refuting. Moses himself adequately refutes them by stating that Cain did not flee to lonely places but that he founded a city; that is, he set up a government and established for himself a kingdom, as it were. In the second place, the chronology does not fit either. It is not likely that Cain remained alive up to the time Lamech was already an old man and was becoming blind.

Another Jewish figment is this. After Lamech had killed Cain, his wives were no longer willing to live with him, for fear of the punishment which would be inflicted on him. And so Lamech, to comfort and conciliate his wives, said that he who killed Lamech would be punished seventy-seven times. The Jews also have some

82 Cf. p. 316, note 79.

foolish ideas about his sons, whom he is supposed to have taught how to make weapons for killing people. Still others declare that the sense is negative, namely: "If I had killed a man, as Cain killed his brother, then I would deserve to be reproved by you."

Now my own conclusion is this. I think that those words, "If Cain will be avenged sevenfold, etc.," are not to be regarded as God's words. That generation did not have the Word of God. Since it did not have the Word of God, how, then, could Lamech have been regarded as a prophet? Jerome also invents something like that.[83] He states that after seventy-seven generations Lamech's sin would be taken away, because, according to Luke, that many generations can be counted from Adam down to Christ. If it is legitimate to reach conclusions in this ludicrous way, it will not be difficult to invent anything whatever on the basis of Scripture. Moreover, Jerome forgets that Lamech is the seventh from Adam. Therefore these words are not to be taken in the same way as those addressed above to Cain; for those were God's words. These, however, are the words of an ungodly man and a murderer. They are not true; they are rash, fabricated after the pattern of the words Adam addressed to Cain. Why does Lamech make this announcement in his home and only in the presence of his wives, rather than before his church?

Moreover, it is possible that the good and godly wives were perturbed by the murder their husband had committed. Therefore the ungodly murderer, in order to appear to be in a similar situation with his father Cain, desires to reassure his wives, so that they might not think that he ought to be killed. This is the custom of the wicked church: it wants to utter prophecies which have their origin in its own head. But such prophecies are futile.

This one fact we can gain from the text: that the source of this address by Lamech is not the Word of God but his own head.

So far as Cain is concerned, I do not think that he was killed by Lamech, but that long before Lamech he had ceased to live. Because there was continuous enmity between the church of Cain and that of Adam (for the Cainites did not permit themselves to be regarded as excommunicated), I think that Lamech killed some prominent man and some boy of the generation of the righteous, just as his father Cain had killed Abel, and that then he wanted to protect himself after the pattern set by Cain. He was without a doubt a man

[83] Jerome's letter to Damasus, *Epistola* XXXVI, *Patrologia, Series Latina,* XXII, 452—456.

of superior ability and the mightiest in the community. He also increased his household by an innovation, inasmuch as he was the first to marry two wives. Moreover, he troubled the church of the godly in various ways, just as men who have outstanding ability and at the same time are full of malice are wont to do. Therefore he provided his people with weapons, riches, and pleasures, in order to vanquish the true church completely. It had the holy faith and the pure Word with pure forms of worship and made these its exclusive concern; to all the rest it gave rather indifferent attention.

But it is likely that at about this time Adam, the first patriarch, died. So Lamech took advantage of this opportunity to assume the entire sovereignty and to govern everything alone, just as the world is still in the habit of doing. For the church is situated in the middle, as it were. It is hard pressed on both sides by tyrants and bloodthirsty men as well as by those who are occupied with the pleasures and cares of this world. Just as the tyrants employ force and the sword, so the latter allure by means of blandishments.

It is for this reason that Moses relates with special care that the bloodthirsty seed of the Cainites devoted itself to the pleasures and the other concerns of the world. Christ also declares that much blood was shed even before the Flood, when He says in Matt. 23:35: "Upon you will come all the righteous blood which was shed upon the earth, from the blood of righteous Abel unto the blood of Zacharias." And when Moses says below (Gen. 6:11) that the earth was filled with iniquities before the Flood, he is saying this not merely about the iniquities and wrongs of thieves, adulterers, etc.; but he is referring to the tyranny of the Cainite church, which raged against the holy posterity of Adam with the sword. For this reason he calls the descendants of Cain "giants" (Gen. 6:4).

These reasons lead me to conclude that Lamech patterned himself after the conduct of his father Cain and killed some outstanding man among the holy fathers together with his son.

In the characteristic fashion of a tyrant, he does not grieve over his deed after being reproved by his wives; but even though he must fear punishment, he disregards it. "I have killed a man," says he. "What concern is this of yours? This results in my being wounded. I shall be wounded, not you. I have killed a youth. This results in my bruise; that is, I shall be beaten, not you." What more scornful statement could be made in regard to a manifest sin? These are my thoughts. The text shows that the Cainites were prosperous and pleasure-loving tyrants. Lamech's very words show that he was a proud person who did not grieve over the murder he had committed but even gloried in it as a righteous cause. The Cainite church always has an excuse for the tyranny it practices on the godly. Just as Christ says (John 16:2): "Whoever will kill you will think that he is doing God a service." And so Lamech adds:

24. If Cain will be avenged sevenfold, truly Lamech seventy-seven times.

He sets himself above his father, as though he had a more just reason for the murder he had committed. He does so to protect himself against those who would avenge the murder. These are not the words of the Lord; they are Lamech's very own. The pope does the same thing. He defends himself with force, tyranny, threats, and the ecclesiastical curse that he may be secure; for he has a conscience like Cain's and Lamech's. "Let him become aware," says he, "that whosoever acts contrary to these incurs the displeasure of SS. Peter and Paul." [84]

Lamech is a type of the world, by which Moses wishes to show what sort of a heart, will, and wisdom the world has. It is as if he were saying: "This is the way the seed of the serpent conducts itself. This is the way the children of this world conduct themselves. They amass riches; they pursue pleasures; they strive after power, and by their tyranny they misuse it against the true church, which they pursue and kill. But while they commit such great sins, they have no feeling of alarm; but they are proud and smug. They even boast (Ps. 11:3): "What can the righteous do?" or (Ps. 12:5): "Our lips are with us; who is our master?" Likewise (Ps. 10:11): "The ungodly man says in his heart: 'God has forgotten; He hides His face; He will never see it.' "

Although the text does not indicate in so many words that this is the meaning of the passage, nevertheless the subject matter proves it to be such; for the true church always has Satan as its enemy. Under the guise of saintliness he incites the Cainites against their brother, just as Christ declares in John 8:44 that the devil is a murderer from the beginning. And here and there in Scripture it is stated about the church that the ungodly shed her blood. Familiar are the statements

---

[84] This is in mock imitation of the style used by papal bulls, including the one that excommunicated Luther.

in the psalms: "Their blood is precious in His sight" (Ps. 72:14); "Precious is the death of His saints in His sight" (Ps. 116:15); "For the sake of Thy name we are killed all the day long" (Ps. 44:22). Add to these passages the Biblical accounts to the same effect.

Therefore since the church at all times has given its blood to be shed by ungodly and false brothers, in that first era, too, it suffered at the hands of its enemies, whom Scripture calls giants and of whom it declares that they filled the earth with violence (Gen. 6:4, 11). Among them was also that notorious Lamech, a person similar perhaps to Julius II or Clement VII, who wanted the appearance and the reputation of great saintliness even though they indulged in the utmost cruelty.[85] Lamech, too, wants it to appear that he had a righteous cause for the murder. For this reason he threatens a far severer punishment for anyone who intends to avenge that murder than the one which God had fixed for the killer Cain.

In this manner the church was troubled by crosses and persecutions from the beginning of the world, until God was compelled by the wickedness of men to destroy the entire world by the Flood. Similarly, when Pharaoh's malice had reached its limit, he was drowned in the sea. When the measure of the malice of the heathen was full, they were overrun and exterminated by Moses and Joshua. In the same way, later on, when the Jews persecuted the Gospel, they were destroyed to such an extent that in Jerusalem not one stone was left upon another (Matt. 24:2). Similar instances are those of the Babylonians, the Medes, the Persians, the Greeks, and the Romans.

Therefore Scripture does not tell whom Lamech killed. It merely states that he committed a murder and that Lamech, impenitent like his father Cain, tried to defend himself by establishing a law which would prove that he had a just cause for the murder he committed. But even if this interpretation turns out to be incorrect, this much is true: that the generation of the Cainites was bloodthirsty, hated the true church, and also persecuted it.

Furthermore, this, too, is true: that Lamech did not have the Word. Therefore his words are not to be understood in the same way as those addressed to Cain, which were words of truth. Lamech's words are words of pride; they reflect the reign of Satan and the hypocritical church, which is smug in its sins and boasts of them as deeds well done.

[85] On Julius II cf. Luther's *Explanation of the Ninety-Five Theses, Luther's Works*, 31, p. 171, note 57. . Clement VII was pope from 1523 to 1534.

THE GENERATION OF THE RIGHTEOUS

25. *And Adam knew his wife again, and she bore a son and called his name Seth, saying: God has appointed for me another seed in place of Abel, whom Cain killed.*

Up to this point Moses has been telling about the generation of the ungodly, whom he completely buries, as it were, by this brief listing. Now he turns to the description of the godly and of the true church. Here, in the first place, note must be taken of his expression, that it is stated about Seth: "And she called his name Seth." This statement he did not make about Cain when he was born or about the righteous Abel. Neither does he make it later on about Enoch or about any of the rest. His purpose was to indicate that Seth is the first to whom was passed on the promise given to his parents in Paradise. Eve also indicates this when she explains the meaning of this designation or name. Moreover, in this passage Eve clearly reveals her faith and piety by giving her son such a name.

But the fact that she recalls the murder perpetrated on his brother by the godless Cain is also proof that there was bitter enmity between those two churches and that Eve had both observed and suffered many indignities from the Cainites. The reason why she recalls the outrageous murder is that thereby Cain had intended to destroy the righteous seed in order that he himself alone might be lord. "But thanks be to God," says she, "who has appointed for me another seed in the place of righteous Abel!"

In his customary way Moses expresses very important facts in few words in order to stimulate the reader to give careful thought to the works of God. About the sorrow and the fitting grief of the parents we have spoken above.[86] I for my part see no reason not to believe that after that murder had been committed, no son was born to Adam until Seth. The danger they had experienced induced the godly parents to refrain from begetting children. And so I believe that they again received courage and vigor through a special promise given to them by an angel, that such a son would be born to them as would have the firm promise that, even if Cain's entire generation should perish, the generation of this son would be preserved until the promised blessed Seed would come into the world.

Evidence of this special promise seems to be that Eve attaches to his name a sort of little sermon, and Moses employs an expression

[86] Cf. p. 283.

which he uses in connection with no one else, when he says: "And she called his name Seth." Furthermore, Seth is from the verb שׁית, which denotes "He has placed," "He has made firm." Thus she indicated that he would be the foundation, as it were, on which the promise concerning Christ would rest, even if more sons should be born to his parents. In any case, she does not call him by a lordly name, like Cain; nevertheless, she indicates that Seth's descendants will not be suppressed.

Now after the Cainites have been driven out from the sight of their parents, they remain under the curse without any promise. Nor do they have any mercy to look forward to except what they have received from the generation of the godly as beggars, not as heirs of it — the mercy which we called "accidental mercy" [87] above. Moses does not mention who of Cain's descendants obtained it. It is his purpose to maintain a distinction between the two churches, the one being the righteous one, which has the promises of the future life but in this life is afflicted and poor, the other being the ungodly one, which prospers in this life and is rich.

And Eve, the mother of us all, is deservedly praised as a most holy woman, full of faith and love, because she so gloriously extols the true church in the person of Seth without paying any attention to the Cainites. She does not say: "I have another son in Cain's place." She prefers the slain Abel to Cain, although Cain was the first-born. It is, therefore, the outstanding glory not only of her faith but also of her obedience that she is not provoked at the judgment of God but herself changes her own judgment. When Abel had been born, she despised him; but Cain, as the possessor of the promise, she had regarded highly. Here she does the opposite, as if to say: "In the person of Abel everything was granted me. He was righteous, but the wicked Cain slew him. Therefore now another seed has been granted me in Abel's stead."

She does not give way to her motherly affection. She does not excuse or minimize her son's sin. But she herself also excommunicates the excommunicated Cain and sends him away with all his descendants into the jumble of nations which live without any sure mercy, except insofar as they have obtained accidental mercy as beggars, not as heirs.

Since the pope's church has invented such a vast swarm of saints, it is indeed amazing that it did not give a place in the list to Eve, who was full of faith, love, and endless crosses. But perhaps this

[87] See p. 301, note 58.

indicates that it wanted to side with the Cainite church rather than with the holy church.

I am not taking into account the silly and unseemly legend of the Jews that Lamech brought his disobedient wives to Adam as judge; and when he ordered them not to deny due benevolence to their husband, the wives reproached him by asking why he was not doing the same thing to Eve. And so Adam, who had refrained from relations with his wife since Abel's murder, again associated with her, for fear that by his example he might otherwise become the originator of perpetual continence and that the human race would not multiply.[88] These legends reveal the impure thoughts of the Jews. Of a similar nature is also their claim that when Seth had been born, Cain increased to the seventh generation within the space of a hundred years. Ungodly men invent such tales in order to discredit the Scriptures.

Similar is their opinion that Cain was begotten in Paradise when his parents still had their original righteousness. What can be the purpose of this except to do away completely with Christ? What need is there of Christ if original sin has been removed? Therefore these ideas do not deserve mention, but they are becoming to the enemies of Christ and the persecutors of grace.

Thus we have in Seth a new generation, which is born and exists as a result of the promise that the Seed of the woman should crush the serpent's head. Therefore this name befits him, and Eve is felicitating herself that this seed will abide, that it cannot be suppressed, etc. Ps. 11:3 employs the same verb: "What you have laid they have destroyed." And the Hebrew word is almost identical with the German one: Seth, *es steht.*[89]

26. *Thereafter a son was also born to Seth, and he called his name Enos.*

The verb יִּקְרָא, "he called," is masculine, to have you understand that the father gave this name to his son. Above it was feminine because Eve gave the name to her son. Therefore in each instance the expression is a different one; the Latin language is unable to indicate this difference.[90]

---

[88] See also Weimar, *Tischreden*, V, No. 5505.

[89] The original has "Ps. 10." See also p. 314, note 78.

[90] The masculine form is יִּקְרָא; the feminine is תִּקְרָא.

Furthermore, Enos denotes an afflicted and very unfortunate human being, as in Ps. 8:4: "What is a man that Thou art mindful of him?" [91] Seth, therefore, indicates that at this time there was some unusual persecution or affliction of the church. For that old serpent, which had driven mankind out of Paradise and had slain Abel, the beloved of God, was not sleeping or inactive. Therefore after comfort had been received through the birth of Seth, there follows another trial or tribulation at which the godly parents hint through the bestowal of this name. These names must not be considered haphazard, but either they are prophetic or they have some event as their background.

At that time calling upon the name of the Lord was begun.

The rabbis understand this as a reference to idolatry, that about at that time the name "lord" began to be assigned to creatures, the sun, the moon, etc.[92] But Moses is not speaking here of the generation of the Cainites; he is speaking of something the godly generation of Adam did, namely, that after Enos' birth there began the true worship, the calling upon the name of the Lord.

Here a most excellent definition is given of what it means to worship God, namely, to call upon the name of the Lord, a work or act of worship in the First Table, which contains the commandments about the true worship of God. But calling upon the name of the Lord includes the preaching of the Word, faith or trust in God, confession, etc. In like manner St. Paul aptly associates these in Rom. 10:13-15. The works of the Second Table also have to do with the worship of God, but they are not brought into direct relation to God.

Thus after the commotion occasioned by Cain in Adam's household the generation of the godly gradually increases, and a small church is formed in which Adam, as high priest, rules everything by the Word and sound doctrine. Moses states that this had its beginning at about the time of Enos' birth. Although his name indicates that at that time the church was hard pressed by some extraordinary misfortune, nevertheless through His grace and mercy God again raised her up and gave her this added spiritual blessing, that they could meet in a definite place, preach, pray, sacrifice, something which

[91] Cf. *Luther's Works,* 12, pp. 122—123.

[92] Lyra on Gen. 4:26, sec. "r."

perhaps up to that time had either been forbidden or hindered by
the Cainites. Here again we see the promised Seed at war with the
serpent and crushing his head.

Furthermore, the fact that Moses does not say "calling upon the
Lord was begun" but "upon the name of the Lord" is correctly
regarded as a reference to Christ, just as in other passages He is
called יְהֹוָה שֵׁם.[93] From this arises the excellent thought that at that
time men began to call upon the name of the Lord, that is, that Adam,
Seth, Enos, exhorted their descendants to wait for their redemption,
to believe the promise about the woman's Seed and through that
hope to overcome the treachery, the crosses, the persecutions, the
hatreds, the wrongs, etc., of the Cainites; not to despair about their
salvation but rather to thank God, who one day would deliver them
through the woman's Seed.

What better and more useful message could Adam and Seth preach
than the Savior Christ, who was promised to their descendants? This
agrees with a correct procedure which must be followed in religious
instruction. The primary concern must be for the First Table; and
when this has been understood, it is easy to comprehend the Second.
Indeed, it is easy to fulfill the Second. Where there is pure doctrine,
where men rightly believe, rightly call upon, and rightly give thanks
to, God, how can the other lesser fruits be lacking?

In this manner God at that time desired to comfort the afflicted
church of the godly so that it might not lose the hope it had for the
future. Thus we observe in all the historical accounts that solace and
affliction follow one after the other in uninterrupted sequence. Joseph
in Egypt gives relief to his parents and brothers, who were afflicted
by famine. Later on, when they were again oppressed by ungodly
kings, they are delivered from slavery by Moses. In Babylon Cyrus
sets them free when they are captives, etc. Whenever God permits
His own to be oppressed by the might and treachery of the devil
and of the world, He always in turn comforts them and gives them
prophets and godly teachers to restore the wavering church and for
some time to hold Satan's raging in check.

Furthermore, just as I pointed out above, the dialectical definition
must be maintained here. By worship of God Moses does not mean
the ceremonies devised and handed down by men, not the statues
which have been set up or other playthings of human reason, but

[93] On the "name of the Lord" see also *Luther's Works,* 13, pp. 384—385.

calling upon the name of "the Lord." Here, then, we have the highest form of worship, which is pleasing to God and later on was commanded in the First Table, and which includes the fear of God, trust in God, confession, prayer, and preaching.

The First Commandment demands faith, that you believe that God is a Helper in due time, as Ps. 9:9 declares. The Second demands confession and prayer, that we call upon the name of God in danger and give thanks to God. The Third, that we teach the truth and defend and preserve sound doctrine. These are the true and only forms of worship of God which God demands; He does not demand sacrifices, money, and other things. He demands the First Table, that you hear, meditate on, and teach the Word; that you pray, and that you fear God. Whenever this is done, there will follow spontaneously, as it were, the forms of worship or the works of the Second Table. It is impossible for him who worships in accordance with the First Table not to keep the Second Table also.

Similarly, the first psalm declares (Ps. 1:2-3): "He who meditates on the Word of God day and night is like a tree planted by rivers of water, which yields its fruit in its season and whose leaves do not fall to the ground." This is the clear and unfailing result. He who believes God and fears God, who calls upon God in troubles, who praises and thanks Him for His blessings, who gladly hears His Word, who constantly meditates on the works of God, and who teaches others to do the same, cannot harm his neighbor, can he? Or disobey his parents? Or kill? Or commit adultery?

The First Table, therefore, must be presented first; people must first be instructed about the true worship of God. This produces a good tree, from which later on good fruits result. Our adversaries follow the opposite procedure; they want fruits to exist before there is a tree.

I believe, however, that at that time some visible solemn act was added to the worship of God. Such is always God's way, that He joins some visible sign to the Word. When Abel and Cain were sacrificing, God showed by a visible sign that He had regard for Abel but not for Cain. Perhaps something similar happened here, when the church was again flourishing and the Word of God was being preached in public with great success. God added some visible sign in order that the church might gain the assurance that it pleased God.

This sign, whether it was fire from heaven or something else, God postponed until the third generation in order that men might learn to be content with the Word. After they had comforted themselves against the Cainites in all their misfortunes by the Word alone, God out of His mercy adds some visible sign. He appoints a place, persons, and also some ceremonies, around which the church might gather, practice its faith, teach, pray, etc. Where these are, namely, the Word or the First Table, and then also the visible sign appointed by God, the church is established, in which men carry on with teaching, hearing, partaking of the Sacraments, etc. Then also the works of the Second Table follow, which are an act of worship and are pleasing only in such as have and practice the First Table.

This gift Moses praises in this passage in few words when he states: "And at that time men began to call upon the name of the Lord." This was not done by the Cainites, as the Jews explain, but by the godly descendants of Adam, who alone were the true church at that time. Therefore if any of Cain's descendants were saved, it was necessary for them to join this church.

The burden of these first four chapters is that we should believe that after this life there is a resurrection of the dead and eternal life through the Seed of the woman. This is the lot of the godly and of those who believe, who in this present life endure hardships and are exposed to violence at the hands of all men. To the ungodly, on the other hand, are given the riches and the power of the world, of which they make use against the true church.

In the first chapter it is pointed out that man was created for immortality inasmuch as he was created according to the image of God (Gen. 1:27).

The command in the second chapter (Gen. 2:17), "On whatever day you eat from this tree you will surely die," points out the same fact. It follows that the first human beings would not have died if they had not eaten. Through their sin, therefore, they fell from a state of immortality into a state of mortality; and out of their bodies they beget descendants who are like themselves.

But in the third chapter immortality is restored through the promise about the Seed (Gen. 3:15).

In the fourth there is a clear example of immortality; for after Abel has been slain by his brother, he lives, after being received into the bosom of God, who bears witness that his blood is crying.

Furthermore, the fifth chapter, which now follows, is written chiefly because of Enoch, who was taken by the Lord. Even though there is a need for it because of the number of the years of the generation of the godly, nevertheless the most striking feature of it is that it relates that Enoch did not die like Adam, was not killed like Abel, and was not seized or torn to pieces by lions or bears, but that he was taken by the Lord Himself to immortality. This is to cause us to believe in the woman's Seed, Christ, our Redeemer and the Victor over the devil, and through Him to look for everlasting life after this troubled and mortal life.

The Jews do not see the harmony among these five chapters. For they lack the Sun which throws its light upon these matters and makes them clear: Christ, through whom we have forgiveness of sins and everlasting life.

CHAPTER FIVE

1. *This is the book of the generations of Adam.*

Moses has drawn up this list for two reasons. In the first place, because of the promise of the Seed that was made to Adam (Gen. 3:15). In the second place, because of Enoch. Again, below in the tenth chapter, after the Flood, Moses also records a genealogy, but for a reason far different from the one given here. In this present passage he lists the years, and for a special purpose he adds about each individual that he died.

This closing statement appears to be superfluous. Why is it necessary, after Moses has stated: "All the days of Adam while he was alive were 930 years," to add: "And he died"? When he states the number of his years, he has also stated the time of his death. If he had lived longer, those years would have been counted too.

But Moses does this with the definite design of bringing to our attention the immeasurable wrath and the unavoidable punishment which has been brought upon the entire human race because of sin. On the basis of this passage Paul states similarly in Rom. 5:12: "By one man sin entered into this world and death by sin, and so death passed upon all men for the reason that all have sinned." At all events, the inference is universal: Adam died; therefore he was a sinner. Seth died; therefore he was a sinner. Infants die; therefore infants have sinned and are sinners. This is what Moses wants to point out when he states of the entire series of patriarchs that they died even though they were sanctified and renewed through faith.

But in this series there shines forth like a star the most charming light of immortality, when Moses relates about Enoch that he was no longer among men and yet had not died but had been taken away by the Lord. Moses is indicating that the human race has indeed been condemned to death because of sin, but that there has still been left the hope of life and immortality, and that we shall not remain in death.

It was for this reason that the original world not only had to be

[332]

given the promise of life but also had to have immortality demonstrated to it by an example. Therefore it is stated about the individual patriarchs: "So many years he completed and died," that is, he bore the punishment of sin, or he was a sinner. But about Enoch Moses does not make this statement, not because he was not a sinner but because even for sinners there is left the hope of eternal life through the blessed Seed. And so also the patriarchs who died in the faith of this Seed clung to the hope of eternal life.

Thus this is the second example which proves that God intends to give us eternal life after this life. For the Lord says that Abel is alive and cries even though he was killed by his brother (Gen. 4:10), and Enoch was taken away by the Lord Himself.

Therefore we should not despair when we see that death has been transmitted from Adam to the entire human race. We must undergo this death because we are sinners, but we shall not remain in death. We have the hope concerning the divine plan and providence that God plans to do away with this death, just as He has begun to do through the promise of the blessed Seed; and the examples of Abel and Enoch point in the same direction. Thus through hope we are in possession of the first fruits of immortality, as Paul says (Rom. 8:23): "We are saved by hope," until its fullness appears on the Last Day, when we shall experience and see the life in which we believed and for which we hoped.

The flesh has no understanding of this. Its conclusion is that man dies like a beast. Therefore among the philosophers those who were the most outstanding held the opinion that through death the soul was released and freed from the body, but that after it was released from the dwelling of the body, it mingled with the assembly of the gods and was free from all physical inconveniences. This sort of immortality philosophers have envisioned, although they were unable to arrive at an adequately supported conviction and defense in regard to it. But the Holy Scriptures teach otherwise about the resurrection and eternal life, and they put that hope before our eyes in such a way that we cannot have any doubt about it.

This chapter further presents us with a likeness, as it were, and an outline of the entire primitive world. For up to the time of the Flood ten patriarchs, together with their descendants who belong to the lineage of Christ are enumerated. It is worthwhile to make a chart of the facts as Moses relates them, for the purpose of learning which patriarchs lived together with which other patriarchs, and for how long a time, something which I myself have done in my leisure time.[1] Cain, too, has his line of descendants, as Moses has shown in the previous chapter; and there is no doubt in my mind that he had a far more numerous posterity than the righteous Seth.

From these two families, as from roots, the earth was filled up to the time of the Flood by the branches that developed on both sides. The descendants of both the good and the evil were exterminated, and only eight souls remained, among whom one was evil. Therefore just as there is presented in this chapter a most excellent picture of the primitive world, so there is also the immeasurable wrath of God and the most dreadful fall as we see the entire offspring of those ten patriarchs reduced to eight souls.

But let us postpone this sad story until the proper time. Now let us deal with what Moses is discussing in this chapter. He wants us to reflect on the magnificence and superlative grandeur of that age. Adam outlived his nephew Enoch and died not long before Noah was born. For 126 years lay between. Furthermore, Seth died only fourteen years before Noah's birth. But Enos and the rest of the patriarchs except Enoch lived together with Noah. Those who compare the figures this way will see that a certain number of venerable patriarchs — one of whom lived 700 years, another 900 years — lived at the same time, taught, and governed the church of the godly.

This is the greatest glory of the primitive world, that it had so many good, wise, and holy men at the same time. We must not think that these are ordinary names of plain people; but, next to Christ and John the Baptist, they were the most outstanding heroes this world has ever produced. And on the Last Day we shall behold and admire their grandeur. Likewise, we shall also see their deeds. For then it will be made manifest what Adam, Seth, Methuselah, and the others did; what they endured from the old serpent; how they comforted and maintained themselves by means of the hope of the Seed against the outrages of the world or of the Cainites; how they experienced various kinds of treachery; how much envy, hatred, and contempt they endured on account of the glory of the blessed Seed who would

[1] A reference to the chronology on which Luther was working (cf. p. 207, note 52). Meinhold maintains that it was used by Luther's editors in compiling this commentary.

be born from their descendants. No one must think that they lived without the severest afflictions and endless crosses. These facts will be made manifest on the Last Day.

Now it is something useful and delightful to view with our mind, as though with our eyes, that most happy age when so many patriarchs were living at the same time, almost all of whom, with the exception of Noah, saw Adam, their first parent.

THE GLORY OF THE CAINITES

But the Cainites, too, had their glory: the wisest men in every field of human endeavor and the finest hypocrites, who were the instigators of very much trouble for the true church and in various ways maltreated the holiest patriarchs, so that we deservedly count these among the holiest martyrs and confessors. As Moses stated above, the Cainites immediately began to be superior in number and in activity. Although they were compelled to show respect to their father Adam, they tried in various ways to oppress the church of the godly, especially after Adam, the first patriarch, had died. Therefore the Cainites accelerated the punishment of the Flood with their wickedness.

But this power and malice of the Cainites was the reason why the holy patriarchs taught their church so much more zealously and carefully. How many important sermons do we suppose were delivered by them in that entire course of years, when Adam and Eve told about their first state and the glory of Paradise, and gave admonitions to be on guard against the serpent, who through sin became the cause of so many evils! How careful shall we suppose them to have been in explaining the promise concerning the Seed; how sensible in cheering the hearts of their people that the latter might not become discouraged by the grandeur of the Cainites or by their own afflictions!

All these details Moses passes over, both because they could not be written down on account of their profusion and because their disclosure is reserved for that day of glory and deliverance.

Thus although the Flood was a most horrible event, nevertheless Moses' description of it is very brief; for he wanted to leave it to men to ponder over events of such magnitude.

So in this passage Moses wanted to present briefly some picture of the first and original world. It was very good. Nevertheless, it had a large number of very wicked men, so that only eight souls were preserved in the Flood. What do we suppose will happen before the Last Day? For now, when the Gospel has been brought to light, so many despise it that it is to be feared that they will shortly predominate and fill the world with their errors, and the Word will be altogether suppressed.

Awe-inspiring indeed are the words of Christ when He says (Luke 18:8): "Do you think that the Son of Man will find faith when He comes?" And in Matt. 24:37 He compares the last times with the times of Noah. These are terrifying statements. But the smug and ungrateful world, the despiser of all the promises and threats of God, abounds with every kind of iniquity and daily becomes more and more corrupt. Now that the rule of the popes, who have ruled the world solely through the fear of punishment, is over, men, through their contempt of the sound doctrine, all but degenerate into brutes and beasts. The number of holy and godly preachers is on the decline. All men yield to their desires. But what will happen is that the Last Day will come upon the world like a thief (1 Thess. 5:2) and will overtake men who in their smugness give free reign to their ambitious desire, tyranny, lusts, greed, and all sorts of vices.

Furthermore, Christ Himself has foretold these developments, and so it is impossible for us to believe that He has lied. But if the first world, which had so large a number of most excellent patriarchs, became so pitiably depraved, how much more should we fear when the feebleness of our nature is so great? Therefore may the Lord grant that in faith and in the confession of His Son Jesus Christ we may as quickly as possible be gathered to those fathers and die within twenty years, so that we may not see those terrible woes and afflictions, both spiritual and physical, of the last time.[2] Amen.

This is the book of the generations of Adam.

Adam, as will be stated later on, is the common term for the entire human race; but it is applied to the one Adam on account of his prestige, because he is the fountain, as it were, of the human race. The word סֵפֶר, "book," is derived from סָפַר, which denotes "to relate," "to enumerate." "The book of the generations of Adam" means the narration, the enumeration, of the descendants of Adam.

---

2 Cf. *Luther's Works,* 22, Introduction, pp. ix—x.

*On the day on which God created man, He made him according
to the similitude of God.*

This clause has prompted the blind Jews to invent the legend that
on the same day on which Adam was created he cohabited with his
Eve in Paradise and impregnated her.[3] They have many legends of
this sort. Nothing sound and pure should be expected from them so
far as the meaning of Scripture is concerned.

But Moses desires to make this statement because he intends to
give an account of Adam's entire life and to count the days of his
life from the day on which he was created, in order to show at the
same time that before Adam there was no generation. For generation
must be distinguished from creation. Before Adam there was no
generation, but only creation. Therefore Adam and Eve were not
born; they were created, and that directly by God Himself.

But Moses adds: "In the similitude of God He made him," to have
you understand that he is counting his years from the first day of
his creation, when he afterwards states that he begot Seth.

Furthermore, we have stated above what the similitude of God
was.[4] Even though almost all interpreters take the similitude and
the image of God to mean the same thing,[5] nevertheless, so far as
I have been able to perceive through careful observation, there is
some difference between these two words. For צֶלֶם in its strict sense
denotes an image or a figure, as when Scripture says (Num. 33:52):
"Destroy the altars of your images." There the word denotes nothing
else but the figures or statues which are set up. דְמוּת, however, which
denotes likeness, refers to the accuracy of the image. For example,
when we speak of a lifeless image, like those that appear on coins,
we say: "This is the image of Brutus, of Caesar, etc."; but this image
does not at once reflect the likeness, for it does not show all the
features.

Therefore when Moses says that man was created also in the
similitude of God, he indicates that man is not only like God in this
respect that he has the ability to reason, or an intellect, and a will, but
also that he has a likeness of God, that is, a will and an intellect by
which he understands God and by which he desires what God
desires, etc.

[3] Lyra on Gen. 5:1, sec. "c."

[4] Cf. p. 62.

[5] See p. 60, note 95.

If man, created in this perfect image and similitude of God, had not fallen, he would have lived forever, happy and full of joy, and he would have had a will that was glad and ready to obey God. But through sin both the similitude and the image were lost. Nevertheless, as Paul says (Eph. 4:23), they are renewed to some extent through faith. For we are beginning to know God, and the Spirit of Christ helps us to be eager to obey God's commands.

But of these gifts we have merely the firstlings. This new creature in us merely has its beginning and is not brought to perfection as long as we are in this flesh. Our will is to some extent incited to praise, to thank, to confess God, to patience, etc., but only to the extent of first fruits. For the flesh, according to its habit, strives after the things that are its own, and it opposes the things that are God's. Thus these gifts merely begin to be renewed in us; but a very large part, or the fullness, of this similitude will become ours in the future life, after this sinful flesh has been done away with through death (Rom. 8:23).

2. *Male and female He created them, and He blessed them, and He called their name Adam on the day of their creation.*

I stated above that the general term "Adam" was given to Adam alone as a name on account of his superior qualities. But here I am passing over the foolish talk of the rabbis, who maintain that no man is an Adam or a human being unless he has a wife; likewise, that no woman is an Adam or a human being unless she has a husband.[6] These ideas may indeed have originated from the utterances of the patriarchs, but the Jews corrupt them with their absurd opinions.

Of the blessing, however, Moses makes mention in order to indicate that it has not been taken away from man on account of his sin. Similarly, there remained for Cain this gift of increase and rule, although he had killed his brother.

3. *And Adam lived a hundred and thirty years, and he begot a son in his own likeness after his image, and he called his name Seth.*

Moses makes no mention of Abel, for he passed away without any heir and has been set aside to be for us an example of the resurrection of the dead. Neither does he make mention of Cain, because by his sin Cain was removed from the lineage of Christ and was cast out of the true church.

6 Lyra on Gen. 5:2, sec. "e."

Furthermore, what Adam and Eve did during these hundred years Scripture does not relate. However, some of our writers add one hundred years, during which they say that Adam lived with Eve before Cain killed Abel; and so they assign two hundred and thirty years to Adam before he begot Seth.[7] To me, as I mentioned above,[8] it seems likely that during those hundred years the godly parents grieved over the misfortune which had overtaken their home. After his expulsion from Paradise, Adam begot sons and daughters that were like him. And perhaps that murder happened when Abel was about thirty years old. At any rate, the children do not appear to have been much younger than their parents; for their parents were not begotten but were created.

Therefore we believe that the godly parents gave way to their grief and refrained from the marital relationship, but not with the idea which the Jews fabricate. They make the absurd claim that Adam, like a monk, had vowed perpetual chastity and would have observed it if he had not been commanded by an angel to associate with his wife again.[9] But this legend should be read to the Roman pope during Lent, for he does not deserve anything better.[10] Adam was not that wicked; for this would mean taking vengeance for his grief and casting aside the gift of the blessing which God left even to fallen nature.

Moreover, this matter was not under Adam's control. As Moses indicated, the Lord had created him a male who would need a wife and who would have the urge to procreate implanted in his nature by God. Therefore if he abstained, he abstained in such a manner that he gave way for a time to his grief which he had suffered as a result of that calamity; and yet in due time he returned to his Eve.

But about the statement which Moses especially adds about Adam, "And he begot in his likeness after his image," the theologians hold various opinions.[11] The simple meaning, however, is this: Adam was created after the image and similitude of God, or the image was created by God and not begotten; for he did not have parents. He did

[7] Apparently a reference to Luther himself, who was occupied with the problems of Biblical chronology during these years; cf. p. 334, note 1.

[8] See p. 324.

[9] Lyra on Gen. 5:3.

[10] This seems to be an allusion to the Lenten lections.

[11] Lyra on Gen. 5:3.

not remain in this image but fell away from it through sin. And so
Seth, who is born later on, is not born after the image of God but
after that of his father Adam. That is, he is like Adam; he is the
image of his father Adam, not only in the shape of his face but also
in likeness. He not only has fingers, nose, eyes, bearing, voice, and
speech like his father but is also like him in the remaining qualities
both of mind and of body, in manners, character, will, etc. In respect
to these Seth does not reflect the likeness of God, which Adam had
and lost, but the likeness of his father Adam. But this is a likeness
and image which was not created by God but was begotten from
Adam.

This image includes original sin and the punishment of eternal
death, which was inflicted on Adam on account of his sin. But just
as Adam recovered the lost image through faith in the future Seed,
so Seth did also after he had grown up; for through His Word God
stamped His likeness upon him. Similarly, Paul also says in Gal. 4:19:
"I travail in birth again until Christ is formed in you."

Of the name "Seth" I spoke above. As an imperative it means
that it is the word of one who is uttering a prayer and giving a favorable omen, as if to say: "Cain not only has fallen but has also made
his brother fall. May God, therefore, grant that this son 'Seth' may
stand and may be established like a solid foundation which Satan
may not overturn." This name includes such a blessing or prayer.

5. *And all the days of Adam which he lived were nine hundred years
and thirty years, and he died.*

This, too, is a part of the blessedness of that era, that men lived to
an old age that is unbelievable today if you compare it with ours.
But the question is raised: What was the reason and cause for this
length of life? I am not averse to what some maintain: that at that
time men's constitutions were better and that everything they used
as food was more healthful. Added to this was also extreme moderation in food, which, needless to state, itself contributes a great deal
toward health.

But even though the bodies were sounder than they are now,
nevertheless the vigor and strength of all the limbs did not remain
the same as they had possessed in Paradise before sin. But this, too,
aided the blessing resting on their bodies: that after sin they were
renewed and born again through faith in the promised Seed. And so

sin, too, was made weaker through faith in the Seed. As for ourselves, then, to the extent that we have declined from that righteousness, we have also lost the vigor and the strength of our bodies.

But so far as food is concerned, who would not believe that at that time one fruit was more excellent and also provided more healthful nourishment than a thousand now? The roots, too, of which people made use had more fragrance, quality, and flavor than now. All these factors — namely, their holiness and righteousness, moderation, the excellence of the fruits, and the healthfulness of the climate too — helped people to attain a long life, until at last there came a new decree of God by which the life of men was very much shortened.

If, however, we consider carefully our present-day manner of life, we are harmed more by food and drink than we are nourished. In addition to the fact that we live most immoderately, how much has been lost of the excellence of the fruits? Our first parents lived moderately and chose only those foods that were suited for nourishing and refreshing their bodies. There is no doubt that after the Flood all foods deteriorated, just as in our age we see everything becoming inferior. And today there is less difference between Italian wines or fruits and ours than there was between the fruits before the Flood and those which after the Flood were produced from salt water and the refuse of the sea.

Some interpreters mention these and other possibilities as reasons for such long lives, and I find no fault with them. But for me it is enough that God wanted them to live in the best part of the world for so long a time. And yet we see, as Peter says, that God was not inclined to spare even the ancient world, just as He did not spare the angels in heaven (2 Peter 2:4-5). Such a horrible thing is sin. Sodom and Gomorrah were the best portion of the land; nevertheless, they perished on account of their sin. Thus the Holy Scriptures everywhere point out the enormity of sin and urge men to fear God.

So we now have the foundation, or rather the source, of the human race: Adam together with Eve. From them is born Seth, the first branch of this tree. But because Adam continued to live for eight hundred years after Seth's birth, he saw and had in that entire time a large number of descendants. This was also the time when righteousness was restored through the promise of the future Seed. Later on — when men continued to multiply, and the sons of God mingled with the daughters of men — the world began to become corrupt and to look down on the authority of those holy patriarchs.

If you take the trouble to make the calculation, it is a most entertaining sight to behold how in that age of the primitive world so many venerable patriarchs lived at the same time. If you carefully compute the years of Adam, our first parent, you will observe that he lived more than fifty years together with Lamech, Noah's father. Therefore Adam saw all his descendants down to the ninth generation, and he had an almost countless multitude of sons and daughters whom Moses does not enumerate, since he was content to enumerate the main line of descent and its closest branches down to Noah.

But also among that number there were without a doubt many outstanding saints whose history, if it were available to us, would excel all other histories of the world. In comparison with it the exodus of the Children of Israel from Egypt, the passage through the Red Sea and through the Jordan, the captivities and the returns, would all be as nothing. But just as the original world perished, so its history also perished. Therefore the history of the Flood occupies the first place among histories; and if you compare it with the others, they are scarcely even scintillas. But of the first world we have nothing but names, which themselves are nevertheless tokens of very important histories.

Perhaps Eve, too, lived until her eight hundredth year and saw this large posterity. But how great was her concern, how strenuous her toil, and how zealous her exertion in visiting, assisting, and instructing her descendants! How heavy were also her crosses, and how frequent her sighs because the generation of the Cainites opposed the true church with such great determination! Yet some of them, too, were converted by accidental mercy.[12]

Thus that age was truly a golden one. In comparison with it our age hardly deserves to be called an age of mud. Nine patriarchs lived at the same time with their descendants, in full agreement in their hope for the blessed Seed that had been promised. Of all these facts Moses takes notice, but he does not give any details; if he did, this would be the greatest history of all.

One history he did not wish to pass over, namely, that of Enoch, who was the seventh from Adam, inasmuch as it is extraordinary to

12 See p. 301, note 58.

the highest degree. Yet even in this instance he writes with extreme brevity. For the rest of the patriarchs he gives merely the names and the number of their years. But Enoch he portrays in such a manner that he seems to slight and, as it were, to discredit the remaining patriarchs, as if they had been ungodly or at least had been slighted by God. Did not Adam, Seth, Cainan, together with their descendants, walk before God? Why, then, does he state this of Enoch alone? Moreover, was Enoch translated by the Lord because the rest of the patriarchs are not with God and are not living? Indeed, they live, and we shall see them on the Last Day shining in brightest glory.

Why, then, does Moses show such preference for Enoch? Why does he not make the same statements about the others who, although they were not taken by the Lord but died, nevertheless walked with God? About Enos, too, we heard above that great events took place at his time, inasmuch as then people began to call upon the name of the Lord (Gen. 4:26); that is, the Word and worship of God began to flourish again; and so people walked with God then too. But why does Moses not state this about Enos, but only about Enoch? For these are his words:

21. *Furthermore, Enoch lived sixty-five years and begot Methusalah.*

22. *But Enoch walked with God after he had begotten Methusalah, for three hundred years, and begot sons and daughters.*

23. *And all the days of Enoch were three hundred and sixty-five years,*

24. *and he walked with God, and he was not seen, because God took him.*

The statement that Enoch walked with God must in no wise be understood after the fashion of the monks: that he kept himself in some secluded nook and there lived a monastic life. Verily, so great a patriarch ought to be set upon a candlestick or, as Christ expresses it, upon a mountain (Matt. 5:14), so that he may shine in his public ministry.

In this fashion the apostle Jude also praises him in his epistle and says (Jude 14–15): "Enoch, the seventh from Adam, prophesies concerning these things when he says: 'Behold, the Lord will come with His thousands of holy ones to execute judgment upon all and to convict all the ungodly of all their deeds of ungodliness, which they have committed in their ungodly way, and of all the harsh things which ungodly sinners have spoken against God.' "

I do not know where Jude got this. But it is likely that there persisted in the memory of men, like a tradition, the saintly sayings and deeds of the patriarchs; and perhaps they also wrote them down. Thus it is this public ministry that Moses praises, and he exalts godly Enoch like a sun above all the teachers or patriarchs of the primitive world.

From this we gather that Enoch had an unusual fullness of the Holy Spirit and outstanding courage, because he was bolder than the other patriarchs in offering resistance to Satan and the Cainite church. For, as we said above, to walk with God does not mean to flee into the desert or to hide in a nook but to go out according to one's calling and to offer resistance to the iniquity and malice of Satan and the world; moreover, to confess the Seed of the woman, to condemn the religion and the endeavors of the world, through Christ to preach another life after this life, etc.

This kind of life godly Enoch lived for three hundred years, like a chief prophet and priest who had six patriarchs as his teachers. Moses, therefore, properly praises him as a very excellent pupil who was taught and trained by several teachers, and those the best and most outstanding. Moreover, Enoch was so equipped by the Holy Spirit that he might be a prophet of prophets and a saint of saints in that first world. Thus in the first place, Enoch is outstanding because of his office and ministry.

In the second place, he is praised above others because God wanted him to be an example for the whole world, in order to give comfort and encouragement to the faith in the future life. Therefore this text should be written in letters of gold and should be impressed most deeply on the hearts.

This shows once more what it means to walk with God, namely, to preach another life than this one, to give instruction about the future Seed, about the head of the serpent that will be crushed, and about the kingdom of Satan that will be destroyed. This was what Enoch preached, who nevertheless was a husband and the head of a family, who had a wife and children, and also ruled his household and supplied their food with his labor. Do not give another thought to a monastic life which has the appearance of walking with God! And so for three hundred years after Methuselah's birth this godly man had lived in the greatest piety, faith, and patience, and under a thousand crosses, which he nevertheless overcame through faith in the future Seed. And then he was no longer seen.

Observe in this passage the words which are replete with very important sentiments. Moses does not state what he had stated about the other patriarchs: "He died." He says: "He was not seen," something which all the teachers have diligently taken note of as a sure proof of the resurrection of the dead.[13] In Hebrew the idea is presented briefly but very meaningfully, for it reads: "And Enoch walked with God ‏אֵינֶנּוּ‎, and not he." This means that, contrary to the hope and expectation of all the rest of the patriarchs, Enoch was lost or was not seen and had ceased to be among men.

Without a doubt, therefore, Enoch's father and grandfather were perturbed by the very serious loss of so distinguished a man. They knew with what great zeal he had taught the faith and how much he had suffered. Therefore when they suddenly lose this man, whose piety had the support of evidence before God and man, in what frame of mind do you suppose they were?

Therefore provide me at this point with an eloquent poet or orator to deal with this passage as it deserves and with feeling. Enos, Seth, and all the other patriarchs do not know where Enoch had been taken. And so they search for him; his son Methuselah searches; his other children and descendants search. They suspected malice on the part of the Cainites. Therefore they may have thought that he had been slain like Abel and had been buried secretly.

At last, through God's revelation by an angel, they learned that Enoch had been taken away by God Himself and had been given a place in Paradise. This, however, they did not learn on the first day or on the second, but perhaps after an interval of many months or years. Meanwhile they loudly lamented the holy man's wretched lot as though he had been slain by the hypocritical Cainites. This is the rule, that cross and affliction always precede comfort. God does not comfort any unless they are sad, just as He also does not give life to any unless they are dead and does not declare any righteous unless they are sinners. For He creates everything out of nothing.

It was, therefore, an extraordinary cross and affliction for the holy patriarchs when they saw the removal and disappearance of the man who had governed the whole world with sound doctrine and during

[13] Luther had developed this interpretation of Enoch in his sermons of 1527 on Genesis (Weimar, XXIV, 156—158).

his entire life had performed many outstanding deeds. While they are mourning and grieving over the misfortune of the holy man, behold, comfort is at hand, and it is revealed to them that the Lord has taken Enoch away. Such a Scripture statement we do not have of any other human being except Elijah (2 Kings 2:11-12). Thus even in the first world God desired to give a clear example to prove that He had prepared for His saints another life after this life. In it they would live with God.

Furthermore, the Hebrew verb לָקַח does not denote "He took away," as it almost seems to mean in our translation, but "He took to Himself." Therefore these words are words of life which, through some angel, God revealed to Enoch's father and to that entire generation of saints. Thus they would have in their possession the comfort and the promise of eternal life, not only in the form of a word but also in the form of an actual deed, just as He previously had done in the instance of Abel. How welcome this announcement was to them, when they heard that Enoch was not dead, that he had not been slain by ungodly men, and that he had not been taken away by the deceit and treachery of Satan but had been received by the living and almighty God Himself!

This is the special jewel which Moses wants to be particularly prominent in this chapter: that Almighty God takes to Himself not geese, not cows, not pieces of wood, not stones, and not the dead, but Enoch in person, in order to show that there has been prepared and set aside for men another and also a better life than this present life which is replete with so many misfortunes and evils. Granted that Enoch, too, is a sinner, nevertheless he departs this life in such a way that God grants him another life, an eternal life. Inasmuch as he is living with God, God is also taking him to Himself.

Thus Enoch walked with God; that is, in this life he was a faithful witness that after this life men would live an eternal life, thanks to the promised Seed. For this latter is the life with God; it is not that former life, which is physical and subject to corruption. And just as Enoch steadfastly preached this truth, so God fulfills and proves this message true in his person, in order that we may believe and maintain with assurance that Enoch, a human being like us, born of flesh and blood from the carnal Adam, as we are, was taken away to God and now lives the life of God, that is, the eternal life.

Before the generation of the holy fathers was aware of the facts, it was something dreadful to hear that Enoch, so holy a man, had disappeared in such a manner that no one knew where he was or how he had perished. Therefore his pious parents and ancestors were in great sorrow. But later on unbelievable joy and comfort was given to them when they heard that their son was living with God Himself and had been translated by God to the angelic life.

This comfort God reveals to Seth, who was the chief prophet and priest now that his father Adam, fifty-seven years ago, had fallen asleep in faith in the blessed Seed. At that time Seth was about eight hundred and sixty years old. Now an aged man and full of days and, therefore, because of his trust in the future blessed Seed, anxiously waiting for the deliverance of his body and desiring to be gathered to his people, Seth died with greater cheerfulness a short time later, namely, after fifty-two years. These years were a very short time for the holy aged man to draw up his testament, to visit his children and descendants, to preach to them, and to exhort them to persevere in faith in the promised Seed and to hope for the eternal life to which Enoch, his son and their father, had been translated and in which he was living with God. In this manner, with joy and in his ripe old age, the holy aged man comforted himself and his people and instructed them as he spent his days among them, bade them good-by individually, and blessed them.

If I were to die within six months, I would hardly have enough time to draw up a testament. For I would remind men of the sum and substance of my preaching; I would exhort and urge them to persevere in it; and, to the extent that I were able to foresee, I would admonisn them to be on guard against offense in doctrine. This task could not be completed in one day or in one month. Therefore the fifty years which Seth lived after Enoch had been taken away were a very short time (for spiritual men have a method of reckoning time that is far different from the way used by the children of this world), during which he instructed his people concerning the grand comfort that after this life they should hope for another life, which God revealed by taking to Himself Enoch, our flesh and blood.

"Therefore," said he, "do not follow your lusts, but despise this life and hope for a better one. For what evil there is in this present life! To how many diseases, to what great dangers, and to what awful misfortunes it is subject! Not to say anything for the time being about the things that are most important, namely, the spiritual evils which worry and torture the conscience: the Law, sin, and death itself.

"Why is it, therefore, that you desire this life so much and appear to be unable to get enough of it? We would have to terminate it voluntarily if God did not want us to live in order to praise Him, to give Him thanks, and to serve our brothers. Let us, therefore, zealously render God this service, and let us hasten with our sighs toward the true life to which Enoch, my son and your brother, was transferred by God Himself." These and similar matters the holy aged man taught after he got to know this comfort.

After they had realized that Enoch, while still alive, had been translated by the Lord to immortality, they undoubtedly wished that they, too, might be released from this wretched life in the same manner, or at least through death.

If the holy patriarchs had such an eager desire for the future life because of Abel and Enoch, of whom they knew that they were living with God, how much more this is becoming to us who have as our leader Christ, ἀρχηγὸν τῆς ζωῆς, as Peter calls Him in Acts 3:15! They believed that He would come in the future; but we believe that He has appeared, and that He has gone away to the Father to prepare dwelling places for us (John 14:2), and that He is sitting at the right hand of the Father and is interceding for us.

Should we not, therefore, long for the future things and hate these present ones? It was not, as in the case of the patriarchs, Enoch or Abel who revealed to us the hope of a better life; it was Christ Himself, the Prince and Author of life. Therefore we should courageously despise life and the world, and wholeheartedly aspire to the future glory of eternal life.

It is here that we realize how great is the weakness of the flesh, which burns with desire and love of the present things but feels no joy about the certainty of the future life. For how can that be anything but certain of which we have so many witnesses: Abel, Enoch, Elijah, nay, even the very Head and First Fruits of those who rise again, Christ (1 Cor. 15:20)? Therefore the Epicureans are most deserving of the hatred of God and of men. Also deserving of our hatred is our own flesh, which often incites us, too, to Epicureanism, when we give ourselves up wholly to temporal cares and so smugly disregard the eternal blessings.

Therefore these words must be noted and carefully impressed on our hearts: that Enoch was taken away and received, not by some patriarch, not by an angel, but by God Himself. This was the comfort which made death bearable for the holy patriarchs, so that they departed this life with joy. Even at that time, before He had been revealed, they saw that the Seed which had been promised them was waging war with Satan and had crushed his head in the instance of Enoch. They had the same hope for themselves and for all their descendants who believed; and they despised death with the utmost unconcern, as if it were not death but a sleep from which they would awake to eternal life. For death is not death for those who believe; it is a sleep. When the terror, the sting, and the power of death (1 Cor. 15:55-56) are lacking, it cannot be called death. Therefore the greater faith is, the weaker death is; but the smaller faith is, the bitterer death is.

But here, too, we are reminded of our sin. If Adam had not sinned, we would not be mortal men; but, like Enoch, we would, without fear and pain, be taken out of this physical life to another, better, and spiritual life. Now that we have lost that life, this story points out to us that we must not despair of having Paradise and life restored to us. The flesh indeed cannot be without pain; but since the conscience has been quieted, death is like a fainting spell through which we pass into rest. That pain of the flesh would have been absent in the innocent nature; for we would have been taken away as if by a sleep, and, awaking shortly, we would have been in heaven and would have lived the angelic life. But now, when the flesh has been corrupted by sin, it must first be destroyed by death. So Enoch, perhaps when he was lying in some place covered with grass and was praying, fell asleep; and as he slept, he was taken away by God without pain and without death.

Let us, therefore, take note of this passage, which Moses wants to stand out as by far the most noteworthy story of the first world. What more astonishing event could happen than that a perishable human being — a sinner, born of flesh and blood, polluted and depraved by sin, so triumphed over death that in spite of all he did not die? Christ is a human being and righteous; but our sins bring it about that He is subjected to a most bitter death, from which He is freed on the third day and raises Himself up unto eternal life. And so in Enoch's case this is unique that he does not die but, without an intervening death, is taken away to the spiritual life.

The rabbis very much deserve to be detested, for whatever Scripture has that is very excellent they pervert most execrably. Thus in connection with this passage they prate about Enoch that he was indeed good and righteous, but that he had a strong leaning toward fleshly lusts.[14] God, therefore, had mercy on him and took him by death before he would sin and be condemned.

I ask you, is this not an outstanding distortion of this text? What need is there to say of Enoch alone that he had evil leanings, as if indeed the rest of the patriarchs did not have them and did not feel them?

Furthermore, why do they not notice that Moses says twice that Enoch walked with God? This is surely a proof that Enoch did not yield to the temptations but by faith bravely overcame them. But when the Jews speak of evil leanings, they have in mind lust, greed, and similar desires. Enoch, however, undoubtedly lived among more grievous trials, and, with Paul, he felt the well-known thorn (2 Cor. 12:7). He wrestled daily with the old serpent; and finally, after he had been thoroughly plagued and worn out by every sort of trial, he was commanded by the Lord to depart this life and to pass into the other.

But what sort of life it is that he is now living we who are still flesh and blood cannot know. For us it is enough to know that he was taken away also in respect to his body. Of this fact the patriarchs undoubtedly had knowledge through revelation, and they needed this comfort when they were about to die. This much knowledge we also have. But what Enoch is doing, where he is, and how he is living, we do not know. We know that he is living, but surely not this physical life; for he is with God, as the text plainly states.

And so this story is a noteworthy one. Through it God desired to impart to the first and primeval world the hope of a better life after this life.

Later on in the second world, which had the Law, God gave the example of Elijah, who was taken away by the Lord even as his servant Elisha was looking on.

We in the New Testament are in the third world, as it were; and we have a more outstanding example — Christ Himself, our Deliverer, ascending to heaven with many other saints. In every age God wanted to have at hand proofs of the resurrection of the dead in order to draw our hearts away from this detestable and troubled life, in which, as long as it seems good to God, we nevertheless serve Him by per-

---

[14] Lyra on Gen. 5:24, sec. "1."

forming our governmental and civic duties and also, above all else, by leading others to godliness and the knowledge of God. But here we have no continuing place (Heb. 13:14). For Christ went away to the Father to prepare for us eternal dwelling places (John 14:3).

However, just as there are among us some who regard these truths as ridiculous and undeserving of belief, so there is no doubt that at that time, too, this account was held by the majority to be ridiculous. The world is always the same. Therefore these truths have been committed to writing by divine authority; and they were written down for the saints and the faithful that they might read, understand, believe, and follow them. They demonstrate the certain victory over death and sin, and concerning Enoch they point out the sure comfort that comes from the triumph over the Law, the wrath, and the judgment of God. For this reason there can be nothing more delightful or pleasing for the godly than these accounts.

But in the New Testament God's mercy is truly superabundant. Although we do not discard accounts of this kind, we nevertheless have far more important ones, namely, the Son of God Himself ascending to heaven and sitting at the right hand of God. In this event we see that the head of the serpent has been completely crushed and that the life which we lost in Paradise has been restored. This is far more than the fact that Enoch and Elijah were translated. And yet in this manner God wanted to give comfort to the first world and to the following one, which had the Law.

Therefore this is the main doctrine set forth in these five chapters: that men have died and have lived again. Through Adam all have died. However, those who have believed have lived again through the promised Seed, as the history of Abel and of Enoch proves. In the instance of Adam, Seth, and others their death is indicated; for thus it is written: "And he died." But in the instance of Abel and Enoch the resurrection of the dead and everlasting life are manifested.

The purpose of all this is to keep us from despairing in death and to give us the firm conviction that those who believe in the promised Seed will live and be taken to God, be it from water, fire, the gallows, or the tomb. Therefore we desire to live, and we must live — live in the eternal life which, through the promised Seed, comes after this life.

28. *And Lamech lived a hundred and eighty-two years, and he begot a son*

29. *and called his name Noah, saying: He will comfort us from the works and toils of our hands on the earth which the Lord has cursed.*

Moses merely touches on this account concerning the name of Noah. Nevertheless, the story deserves our rather careful examination. Lamech was living when Enoch was carried away out of this life to the other, deathless life. And so, after God had bestowed such great honor and had performed so outstanding a miracle in transporting Enoch, a human being like ourselves, from this lowly kind of life to eternal life — for he was a husband and the head of a household who had sons, daughters, servants, fields, and cattle — then the holy fathers, quickened and incited by their joy, came to believe that now that happy day of the fulfillment of the promise was near at hand. For it was a unique manifestation of divine mercy that Enoch was taken away to the Lord alive.

Therefore just as Adam and Eve, after the promise had been given to them, had come to hope — because of their excessive joy over seeing a human being like themselves — that Cain was that Seed, so, in my opinion, Lamech — because of a pious mistake — gave this name to Noah at birth and said: "He will bring us comfort and will deliver us from the hardships of this life. Now original sin and the punishment of original sin will come to an end. We shall be restored to the state of perfection; the curse which the earth has borne on Adam's account will cease; and the other sorrows inflicted on mankind on account of sin will come to an end."

Thus after Lamech has seen that his grandfather has been taken away to Paradise without pain, sickness, and death, he assumes that Paradise with all its glory will follow at once. It is his opinion that Noah is the promised Seed and that he will bring about the restoration of the world. For he plainly insists that the curse must be removed. Yet the curse, or the punishment for sin, cannot be removed unless original sin itself is first removed.

Therefore the rabbis, the pernicious perverters of the Scriptures, deserve to be detested. This is the way they pervert this passage: He will make us cease from the works and labors of our hands, that is, he will show us an easier way of tilling the earth, namely, that the earth will be turned up with a plow by means of teams of oxen and will not be dug by the hands of men, as was the practice until now.[15]

15 Lyra on Gen. 5:29, sec. "p."

I am amazed, however, that this view pleases Lyra too, and that he adopts it. He should have been familiar with that usual habit of perverting the Scriptures to which the Jews everywhere adhere, insofar as they — to have glory among men — assign a purely physical sense to those passages that have a spiritual content. What could be unworthier of the holy patriarch than that he rejoiced so greatly at the birth of his son Noah on account of this advantage, which pertains strictly to the belly?

It was a more important concern that troubled his mind, namely, the wrath of God and death, together with all the other hardships of this life. It was his hope that Noah would put an end to these. It was for this reason that he exulted, gave expression to a happy presentiment, and raised this hope in others too. His anxiety did not concern a plow, draft animals, and other matters of lesser importance which pertain to this life, as the blind Jews rave. It was his hope that his son Noah would be that future Seed who would re-establish that former state of Paradise when there was no curse. "Now, however," says he, "we experience the curse on the very labors of our hands, inasmuch as the earth, even though tilled with the utmost care, nevertheless produces thorns and thistles. But now there is arising a new and blessed age, and the curse which has been imposed on the earth on account of sin will come to an end because sin will come to an end." This is the true meaning of this passage.

But the godly father is mistaken. For that glory of bringing about a restoration was not intended for the son of a human being but for the Son of God. And so the rabbis are fools; even though the earth is not dug by hand, but use is made of draft animals, the labor of the hands nevertheless does not yet come to an end. The fact that Enoch was taken away did not indicate any physical comfort pleasing to the belly; it was an indication of the deliverance from sin and death. Therefore Lamech also hopes for the restoration of the former state through Noah. He realized that the beginning of this change had been made with his grandfather Enoch, and he was sure that their deliverance, or the restoration of all things, was imminent.

Similarly, when Eve had given birth to her first-born, she said (Gen. 4:1): "I have gotten a man from the Lord, namely, one who shall take away the punishments of sin that have been imposed and who shall restore us." However, just as Eve is mistaken, so also our good Lamech is mistaken — because of his excessive longing for the restoration of the world.

But these facts prove how passionately the holy patriarchs wished, hoped, and sighed for that restoration. Even if they erred — just as Eve errs and is mistaken in Cain — nevertheless this very desire for deliverance is from the Holy Spirit and proves their true and steadfast faith in the promised Seed. As for the fact that Eve calls her son Cain and Lamech calls his son Noah, these names are words, as Paul calls them (Rom. 8:22), of a creation that travails and groans and believes that the resurrection of the dead, the deliverance from sin, and the restoration of all things are at hand.

Therefore the simplest and the true meaning is this: Lamech, the grandson, realizes that his grandfather Enoch was removed from the miseries, afflictions, and hardships resulting from original sin; linked with this event there is a sure indication of a future life; and so, after a son is born to him, he calls him Noah, that is, rest, in the hope that through him will come about the deliverance from the curses of sin and from sin itself. This interpretation is in accordance with the faith (Rom. 12:6) and confirms the hope of resurrection and of eternal life.

Therefore at this point the awful lack of appreciation of our age becomes apparent, inasmuch as those most holy men, whose shoes we are unworthy to clean, display everywhere such a great longing for eternal life. But how great a difference there is between possessing and longing! Those patriarchs were most holy men endowed with superior gifts, being the heroes, as it were, of the entire world. In them we perceive the greatest longing for the future Seed. To this the highest value is attached among them; so greatly do they thirst, hunger, yearn, and eagerly long for the coming Christ. But as for ourselves, who have Christ present with us, revealed to us, given to us, glorified, sitting at the right hand of God, and interceding for us, we despise Him and value Him far less than we value any other creature. Oh, what a wretched situation! Oh, what a sin!

Thus we see what a difference there is in the times. The original world is very good and very holy. In it are the most precious jewels of all mankind. After the Flood there are also some outstanding and great men, patriarchs, kings, prophets, although they are not like the patriarchs before the Flood. Yet among them also there is manifest an extraordinary longing for Christ, as Christ Himself says in Luke 10:24: "Many kings and prophets have desired to see those things which you see and have not seen them." Our age, which is the age of the New Testament, to which Christ was manifested, is the hulls and dregs, as it were, of the world; for it values nothing less than it values Christ, who was most precious to the first world.

What is the cause of this most serious evil? Surely it is our sacred flesh, the world, and the devil. We loathe beyond measure the things that we have present with us. It is true what someone states: "All that's rare commands a price; but the commonplace, men despise." [16] Likewise, the well-known statement of the poet: "One's presence lowers one's fame." [17] So far as revelation is concerned, we are richer than the patriarchs; but they set a higher value even on a smaller amount of revelation and were, so to speak, lovers of the Bridegroom. But we are that servant who has grown fat, thick, and broad (Deut. 32:15), because we have an abundance of the Word and are too richly supplied with it.

Therefore just as the first world was the best and the holiest, so the last world is the worst and most iniquitous. However, since God did not spare the first and original world, and since He also overthrew the second world, destroying one monarchy after the other, one kingdom after the other, what do we suppose will happen to this last world, which in the utmost security despises Christ, that desirable One, as He is called in Hag. 2:8, when He thrusts Himself upon us to excess through the Word and the Sacraments?

32. *But when Noah was five hundred years old, he begot Shem, Ham, and Japheth.*

Here, too, there is great brevity. But Moses, according to his habit, expresses in a very few words important matters of which the lazy reader does not become aware. "Of what importance is it, then," you may say, "that Noah does not beget children until he is five hundred years old?" Either it was an unusual and very severe trial if he had a fruitless marriage for so long a time, or it was an instance of extreme chastity if he refrained from marriage for so long a time, something which seems more likely to me. At this point I am not saying anything about the detestable chastity of the papists or anything about our own chastity. Consider the prophets and apostles and also the rest of the patriarchs, who undoubtedly were chaste and holy. But what are they in comparison with this Noah, who is a man and yet lives chastely without marriage for five hundred years?

[16] Cf. p. 127, note 63.

[17] Claudian, *The Gildonic War*, 385.

In our age you hardly find one man among a thousand who refrains from relationship with women until his thirtieth year. But when Noah had lived unmarried for so many years, he finally marries and begets children. This is convincing proof that he was fit for marriage before that time, but that he had refrained from it for a definite reason.

Therefore in the first place, he must have possessed an extraordinary gift of chastity and an almost angelic nature. It seems unprecedented for a man to live five hundred years without a wife.

In the second place, this very situation indicates some particular dissatisfaction which Noah had with the world. Why shall we suppose that he refrained from marriage, unless it was because he saw all his cousins degenerating into giants or tyrants and filling the world with violence? Accordingly, he thought that he would rather do without children than have that kind. Therefore I think that he would never have married unless he had been urged and commanded either by the patriarchs or by some angel. Anyone who refrains from marriage until his five hundredth year will also refrain from it for the rest of his life!

Thus by means of brief words Moses indeed points out some very important facts and — something which an inept reader does not notice, since nothing appears to be said about chastity — praises Noah's chastity above the chastity of all others who were in the first and original world. Noah is an example of angelic chastity.

In accordance with their habit, the Jews talk foolishly and pretend that Noah refrained from marriage because he knew that God intended to destroy the world by the Flood.[18] If, then, like the rest of the patriarchs, he had married early, namely, in his hundredth year or sooner, he alone would have filled the world within about four hundred years; and then God would have been compelled to destroy him with his entire generation. Later on they add this fabrication: that Shem is called the first-born because he is the first to be circumcised.

In short, the Jews pervert everything and distort the sense to suit their carnal desires and vanity. If this was the reason why Noah refrained from marriage, why did not the rest of the patriarchs also refrain from begetting children and from marriage? Therefore their comments are preposterous and worthless. Why do they not rather insist that there was an extraordinary gift in Noah that, although he

[18] Lyra on Gen. 5:32.

was a male, he nevertheless refrained from marriage for so many years? No other example of such extreme continence occurs in all history.

It offends the papists that the book of Genesis so often mentions about the fathers that they begot sons and daughters.[19] Therefore they say that it is a book in which there is nothing except that the patriarchs were too fond of their wives, and they consider it an indecency that Moses so studiously makes mention of such matters.

But impure hearts besmirch even the greatest chastity with their aspersions. If you want to behold the most outstanding examples of chastity, read Moses, who relates about the patriarchs that they did not get married until they had advanced in age. And among them Noah shines like a bright star, for he remained continent up to his five hundredth year. No example of this kind of extreme chastity can be found in the papacy. Even though some do not sin with their bodies, nevertheless how great is the hideousness and indecency of their minds? And this is the punishment for making light of marriage, which God wanted to be a remedy for depraved nature.

There was another reason why Noah refrained from marriage. He did not condemn marriage, nor did he regard it as an unholy kind of life. He saw that the descendants of the earlier patriarchs had degenerated and become part of the godless generation of the Cainites. With such children he was unable to put up, but he awaited the end of the world in the fear of God. But that he got married later on and begot children, this he doubtless did when he was urged and commanded by a special directive of God.

But at this point arises the question about the order of the sons of Noah. This question is worthwhile asking, in order that the computation of the years of the world may be more reliable. It is the common opinion that Shem was the first-born because he is mentioned first. But Scripture requires that Japheth is the first-born, Shem the second, and Ham the last.

This is proved in the following manner. Two years after the Flood Shem begot his son Arpachshad. At that time Shem was a hundred years old (Gen. 11:20).[20] Therefore at the time of the Flood Shem was ninety-eight years old. But at Shem's birth Noah was four hundred and ninety-eight years old. But Japheth was older than

19 Cf. p. 239.
20 The original has "Gen. 10."

Shem (Gen. 10:21).[21] Therefore it follows that Ham alone, the younger brother, was born in Noah's five hundredth year.

Shem is placed ahead of Japheth, not because he was the first to be circumcised, as the Jews, who strive for carnal honors, falsely assert, but because through him Christ, the promised Seed, was to come. Thus, further on, Abraham, although he is the youngest, is placed ahead of his brothers Haran and Nahor for the same reason.

"But how," you will say, "does this agree with the text, which says that Noah, when he was five hundred years old, begot Shem, Ham, and Japheth?" There is agreement if you change the preterit to a pluperfect and say: "Noah, when he was five hundred years old, had begotten." Moses does not state in what year they were individually born; he simply puts down one year when he says that those three sons had been born to Noah. In this way Scripture is most simply harmonized.

Thus Moses brings this fifth chapter to a close with a very fine and very noteworthy example of chastity. Noah, now five hundred years old, begins to be a husband after living a holy and chaste life and refraining from marriage because he was offended by the licentiousness of the young people who were degenerating into the wickedness of the Cainites. Nevertheless, he obeys God when He urges him to marry, although he was able to live unmarried and chaste without a wife.

In this way Moses describes the first and original world in these five chapters, briefly indeed, but so that it nevertheless readily appears that in the beginning there was that most holy and, in truth, that golden age which the poets also mention, without a doubt as the result of the traditions and statements of the patriarchs.[22]

But when sins prevailed, God did not spare the first world but destroyed it with the Flood. Neither did He spare the second world, which was under the Law. On account of idolatry and ungodly worship not only one monarchy after the other was overthrown; but also the very people of God, after it had been troubled by sundry misfortunes and captivities, was completely destroyed in the end by the Romans.

Our third world, which is nevertheless the world of grace, abounds to such an extent with blasphemies and abominations that it is impos-

---

[21] This seems to be a reference to the problem posed by Gen. 10:21.

[22] Cf. p. 4, note 5.

sible either to express these in speech or to comprehend them with the mind. Therefore it cannot be punished with temporal punishments but will be punished with eternal death and with eternal fire, or, to express it this way, with a flood of fire. Indeed, the colors of the rainbow foretell this. The first is watery, because the first world was punished with the Flood for its acts of violence and its lust. The middle one is yellow, for God punished the idolatry and the ungodliness of the middle era with a variety of misfortunes. The third and topmost color is fire, which, in the end, will consume the world with all its iniquities and sins.

Therefore we must pray God to rule our hearts with His fear and to fill us with trust in His mercy that we may await with joy our deliverance and the punishment of the ungodly world. Amen, Amen.

Index

By WALTER A. HANSEN

Abel 80, 185, 243, 245, 247, 254, 257, 259, 261, 262, 264, 266, 267, 268, 270, 271, 272, 273, 274, 276, 279, 281, 282, 283, 284, 285, 286, 287, 288, 289, 290, 291, 292, 297, 308, 312, 320, 321, 324, 325, 327, 329, 330, 331, 333, 338, 339, 345, 346, 348

  brought the more excellent offering 251

  means vanity 314

  perished physically 241

  righteous 252, 253

  took hold of promise given to Adam 246

Abraham 13, 21, 89, 194, 244, 248, 256, 268, 295, 358

  children of 269

Absalom 308

Absolution 250

  God wraps Himself up in 11

Ad generationem 291 fn.

Ada 316, 317, 318

Adam 36, 38, 39, 57, 62, 63, 65, 66, 67, 68, 69, 70, 71, 72, 75, 76, 77, 80, 81, 82, 84, 86, 88, 89, 90, 91, 93, 94, 95, 96, 97, 98, 100, 101, 102, 103, 105, 106, 107, 108, 109, 110, 111, 113, 114, 116,
117, 118, 119, 120, 122, 123, 126, 127, 128, 129, 130, 131, 133, 134, 135, 136, 137, 138, 139, 140, 141, 142, 144, 145, 146, 147, 151, 153, 154, 158, 159, 165, 166, 167, 168, 169, 170, 172, 173, 176, 179, 180, 181, 182, 183, 185, 186, 187, 189, 190, 191, 193, 196, 197, 199, 203, 204, 205, 206, 207, 208, 209, 210, 211, 213, 215, 216, 218, 221, 222, 223, 224, 225, 226, 227, 229, 230, 233, 234, 237, 238, 240, 241, 242, 245, 246, 247, 249, 250, 255, 262, 266, 267, 268, 269, 270, 271, 274, 275, 276, 281, 282, 283, 284, 285, 286, 290, 293, 299, 300, 304, 306, 308, 309, 310, 313, 320, 324, 326, 327, 328, 331, 333, 334, 335, 337, 338, 339, 341, 342, 343, 346, 347, 349, 351, 352

  acknowledged God as Lord 64

  ate fruits of trees 37

  cannot be brought to confession of his sin 178

  condemns himself and
betrays his sin 174

  created in accordance with well-considered counsel 115

  denies his sin 177

  descendants of 312, 318, 330, 336

  figure of Christ 219

  first patriarch 321

  generations of 332, 336

  guilty of death 175

  made out of earth 121

  means human being 314

  not to live without food, drink, and procreation 56

  obliged to serve God by begetting children 291

  was father, king, and priest 214

Adler, Ada 87 fn.

Adultery 96, 106, 138, 147, 168, 176, 238, 305, 329

Adversus Marcionem carmina, by Pseudo-Tertullian 310 fn.

Aeneid, by Vergil 42 fn., 99 fn., 214 fn., 303 fn.

Aeschylus 287 fn.

Against Heresies, by Irenaeus 60 fn.

Agricola, John 232 fn.

Ai 315

Air, enjoyment of 309

Allegorists 187

[361]

INDEX TO SCRIPTURE PASSAGES